CONFEDERATE "TALES OF THE WAR" IN THE TRANS-MISSISSIPPI PART ONE

Area Battle Map 1861

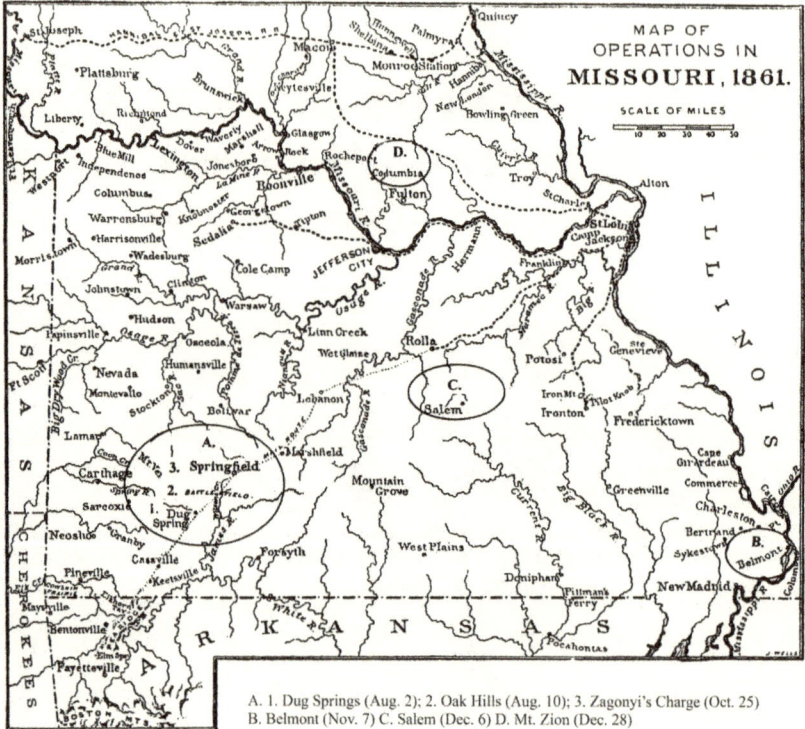

MAP OF
OPERATIONS IN
MISSOURI, 1861.

SCALE OF MILES

A. 1. Dug Springs (Aug. 2); 2. Oak Hills (Aug. 10); 3. Zagonyi's Charge (Oct. 25)
B. Belmont (Nov. 7) C. Salem (Dec. 6) D. Mt. Zion (Dec. 28)

UNWRITTEN CHAPTERS OF
THE CIVIL WAR
WEST OF THE RIVER

VOLUME VII

Confederate
"Tales of the War"
In the Trans-Mississippi
Part One: 1861

Author/Editor Michael E. Banasik

Camp Pope Bookshop
2010

Library of Congress Control Number: 2009943144

ISBN: 978-1-929919-22-2

Printed and bound in the United States of America

Press of the Camp Pope Bookshop
P.O. Box 2232
Iowa City, Iowa 52244
www.camppope.com

Series Dedication:

Dedicated to the forgotten soldiers of both North and South, who fought in the American Civil War west of the Mississippi River; their deeds of perseverance and valor shall not be lost through the ravages of time, but rather recorded for all to remember.

Volume VII, Part One Dedication:

To my son Michael and daughter Marisa; ever on my mind and in my prayers.

Acknowledgement:

I would like to thank James McGhee of Jefferson City, Missouri, who encouraged me to do this book and who has been a constant supporter of my work.

CONTENTS

Photographs and Illustrations

Maps

Series Introduction

The Civil War in the Trans-Mississippi region provides a fascinating study of Nineteenth Century warfare under the most severe conditions. Soldiers serving in the region faced an almost complete lack of a railroad net, a decrepit road system, and terrain that varied from arid deserts to rugged mountains. Battles were few, but the constant strain of living under less than ideal conditions wore heavily upon the soldiers serving west of the Mississippi River. Often the stories told by the frontier soldiers were not of great engagements, but of long marches, poor living conditions, or of simple survival. And for each story told there were always two parts, one told by a man in gray and another by one who wore the blue.

Introduction to Volume VII, Part One

This latest volume of my series comprises an extensive group of reminiscences published by the St. Louis *Missouri Republican* between 1885 and 1887. These pieces were written by the participants in the Civil War and cover the entire conflict from the firing of the first guns until the surrender of the Confederate armies in 1865. The first story appeared on July 4, 1885, and the last one, that I have discovered, on July 2, 1887. In all 94 pieces were published. Typically, in each Saturday issue, the *Republican* printed assorted reminiscences by the lowliest private to the most exulted general, all veterans of the war, covering the Civil War from every aspect, both North and South and from every front of the action, including the high-seas. In this volume of the series only those pieces dealing with the Trans-Mississippi theater, and from the Southern point of view, will be presented. Because of the extensive nature of the material, Part One of Volume VII will deal exclusively with the events of 1861, while Parts Two and Three with cover the period 1862–1865, and will follow in the coming years. The pieces from the Northern point of view will also be presented in later volumes of this series.

As to why these articles were published, the *Missouri Republican* wrote the following:

> The publication of the official orders and correspondence of the war of the rebellion made it comparatively easy for military writers to get at the exact facts of many disputed questions, and all the campaigns have been discussed by the record in recent years by competent officers of both the contending armies. Probably it is the publication of these numerous volumes, which, as much as anything else, has aroused a renewed interest in all manner of literature based on the incidents of the civil war. In response to what seems a public desire the *Republican* will hereafter publish in its Saturday edition a series of war papers, either original or selected from the best current sketches in contemporary publications.

It is not desired to make this department especially a medium for criticism of military operations. The incidents of camp life and the experiences of the private soldier will find as ready access to these columns as the history of great campaigns. What ever war reminiscences will interest the thousands of old soldiers and the greater thousands of their children, will gladly be published in the full ballet that these chronicles of personal experiences from both sides, while reviving the memories, will at the same time aid in obliterating the animosities of the great struggle.[1]

The 1861 portion of these "Tales of the War" covers the opening political strife in Missouri and many of the early engagements of the war, including Dug Springs, Wilson's Creek, Zagonyi's Charge, Belmont, Salem and Mt. Zion Church. The reader will also find interesting snippets of the soldier's life in 1861, with many of the articles focusing on the Missouri State Guard. Because of the extensive nature of this material, only those pieces which were not first published elsewhere or have not been republished in the intervening years will be included. The articles that have been published elsewhere will be listed in Appendix D, so as to provide a complete record of the series in the *Republican*. Note that the articles in this volume are arranged not chronologically as they appeared in the paper, but following the timeline of the war.

I hope you find these pieces as fascinating as I did in preparing them for you.

Michael E. Banasik

Nameplate which appeared ahead of most of the "Tales of the War" in the *Republican*.

1. Editorial Comment, *The Missouri Republican* (St. Louis, Missouri), July 4, 1885.

Chapter 1

The Opening Guns in Missouri

Item: Actions in Missouri prior to the beginning of the Civil War; Frank Blair's rise to power; C. F. Jackson elected Governor of Missouri; Captain Nathaniel Lyon at Ft. Riley and his impact on Missouri; Camp Jackson; and the meeting of Sterling Price and Jackson with Blair and Lyon; by Thomas L. Snead.[1]
Published: May 14, 1887.

The Outbreak in Missouri

Fort Sumter was surrendered to Beauregard on the 13th of April, 1861.[2] The news reached Washington City that evening. The President decided forthwith to call out the militia to the number of 75,000 men to repossess the forts and other public property which had been seized by the seceding states and to compel these states to return to their allegiance to the Union. During the next day, which was Sunday, with his own hand he wrote the proclamation, and on Monday morning it was published throughout the country.[3] It was followed the same day by the formal requisition of the Secretary of War upon the governors of all the still "loyal" states[4] for the number of militia which each was to detail for immediate service.

---

1. Thomas Lowndes Snead was born on January 10, 1828, in Virginia, attended Richmond College, where he graduated in 1846. Earning a law degree from the Virginia Law School in 1850, Snead then moved to St. Louis, where he established a law practice with Judge John Wickham. By the beginning of the Civil War, Snead had acquired the *St. Louis Bulletin*, a decidedly Southern newspaper. With the formation of the Missouri State Guard (MSG), Snead held a number of positions including aid to Governor Jackson, Chief of Ordnance and Acting Adjutant General for Sterling Price. On March 24, 1864, Snead left the army to become a member of the Confederate Congress from Missouri. After the war, he moved his family to New York City, where he again entered into the newspaper field. Snead wrote his book *The Fight For Missouri* in 1886, and he died four years later in New York. His body was returned to St. Louis where he was buried in the Bellefontaine Cemetery. William C. Winter, *The Civil War in St. Louis A Guided Tour* (St. Louis, 1994), 111, 128, hereafter cited as Winter; Richard C. Peterson, et al., *Sterling Price's Lieutenants: A Guide to the Officers and Organization of the Missouri State Guard, 1861–1864* (Jefferson City, MO, 1995), 28, hereafter cited as Peterson.
2. Snead was referring to what most historians consider the beginning of the Civil War—the siege and bombardment of Fort Sumter, South Carolina, April 12–14, 1861. Major Robert Anderson commanded the Federal garrison and General Pierre G. T. Beauregard led the Confederates. Mark Mayo Boatner III, *The Civil War Dictionary* (New York, 1959), 299, hereafter cited as Boatner.
3. On April 15, 1861, President Abraham Lincoln issued a call for 75,000 militia troops, to serve three months. The troops were to "suppress" the rebellion and "cause the laws to be duly executed." See Appendix A for a copy of the Proclamation. United States War Department, *The War of the Rebellion: A Compilation of the Official Records of the Union and Confederate Armies*, 70 vols. in 128 (Washington, DC, 1880–1901), Series 3, 1:67–68, hereafter cited as *O.R.* All citations of *O.R.* refer to Series 1 unless indicated otherwise.
4. At the time the initial call for troops was made only seven states had seceded and were considered

Missouri was called upon for four regiments of infantry.[5] To this requisition Gov. [Claiborne F.] Jackson[6] telegraphed the reply that it was in his judgement illegal, unconstitutional, revolutionary in its object, inhuman and diabolical, and would not be complied with. "Not one man," said he, "will the state of Missouri furnish to carry on such an unholy crusade." Four-fifths of the people of Missouri approved and applauded the Governor's response and thousands of men resolved to sustain him.[7]

Fortunately for the Union

there was one man in Missouri who was in every way equal to the great emergency. This man was Francis Preston Blair, Jr.[8] He instantly telegraphed to the Secretary of War[9] that he himself would furnish the four regiments within forty-

---

"disloyal"—South Carolina, Georgia, Alabama, Florida, Mississippi, Louisiana, and Texas. Ibid.

5. Missouri's portion of the call for troops was four infantry regiments with 3,123 men. Under this initial call Missouri would be credited for 10,591 men out of the 91,816 men raised, as the state provided, as Snead would later indicate, ten regiments. Frederick Phisterer, *Statistical Record of the Armies of the United States* (New York, 1907), 3, hereafter cited as Phisterer.

6. Claiborne F. Jackson was born April 4, 1807, in Kentucky, moved to Missouri in 1826, and was independently wealthy by the age of thirty. He was elected to the Missouri Legislature in 1836, and for the next several years maintained a high profile in Missouri politics. As a Democrat, Jackson supported slavery and believed in "States Rights." Elected Governor of Missouri on January 3, 1861, Jackson maintained his position throughout the Civil War, even after being driven from the state by Federal forces in late 1861. Jackson did not survive the war, dying of cancer in December 1862, at Little Rock, Arkansas. See Volume IV of this series, *Missouri In 1861: The Civil War Letters of Franc B. Wilkie Newspaper Correspondent* (Iowa City, 2001), 350–352 (hereafter cited as *Missouri in 1861*), for a complete biography of Governor Jackson. John McElroy, *The Struggle For Missouri* (Washington, DC, 1909), 20, 25, 27, hereafter cited as McElroy.

7. It is not known how Snead came up with the figure of eighty percent support for the Governor of Missouri against the call for troops; and his book *The Struggle For Missouri* does not provide an answer to the riddle. However, according to author Arthur Kirkpatrick, Governor Jackson received "almost unanimous approval of the press and of most of the population of the State" for his response to the call for troops. Thomas L. Snead, *The Fight For Missouri: From the Election of Lincoln to the Death of Lyon* (New York, 1886), 78–151, hereafter cited as Snead; Arthur Roy Kirkpatrick, "Missouri in the Early Months of the Civil War," *Missouri Historical Review* 55 (Fall 1961): 235–237.

8. Francis Preston Blair, Jr. was born on February 19, 1821, in Lexington, Kentucky, and educated at Princeton and Transylvania Universities. He later moved to St. Louis, where he practiced law, moved west for a time, and fought in the Mexican War as a private. After the war, Blair founded the Free Soil Party in Missouri, was a member of the Missouri Legislature in 1852, and was elected to the U.S. Congress in 1856. He was elected colonel of the First Missouri Infantry at the beginning of the Civil War. Blair served throughout the war, attaining the rank of major general. After the war, he returned to Missouri, was the Democratic Party vice-presidential nominee in 1868, but lost, and served in the U.S. Senate from 1871–1873. Suffering a stroke in 1873, Blair never recovered, and died on July 9, 1875. See Appendix B for complete biography. Boatner, 67; Elbert B. Smith, "Blair, Francis Preston, Jr.," in *Encyclopedia of the American Civil War: A Political, Social, and Military History* (eds. Davis S. Heidler and Jeanne T. Heidler; New York, 2000), 238–239, hereafter cited as *Encyclopedia of the Civil War*.

9. Snead was referring to Secretary of War Simon Cameron, who was appointed to the position in March 1861. Cameron would last less than a year, resigning in January 1862. Stewart Sifakis, *Who Was Who in the Civil War*, 2 vols. (New York, 1988), vol. 2: *Who Was Who in the Union: A Bibliographic Encyclopedia of More than 1500 Union Participants*, 64, hereafter cited as Sifakis, *Union*; Davis S.

eight hours, if authority to muster the men into service were forthwith sent to Capt. Nathaniel Lyon,[10] of the Second United States Infantry, who was then on duty with his company at the St. Louis Arsenal.[11] This utter contempt for the mere forms of law, this bold defiance of the state authorities, this daring offer of a slave-holder in a slave-holding state, shows what manner of man Frank Blair was. The Governor, Claiborne Fox Jackson, was no less resolute than Blair and just as brave. Though born in Kentucky, he had come to Missouri in his boyhood, and while still a young man had amassed a sufficient fortune through mercantile pursuits, farming and in other ways to retire from active business and devote his time to politics, for which he had both capacity and a great liking. From the

Governor Claiborne Fox Jackson

outset of his career he had been a pro-slavery Democrat, and soon became one of the leaders of that party, and as such was one of the most earnest opponents of "the free-soil heresies" of Missouri's great senator Col. [Thomas Hart] Benton.[12] He afterwards advocated the repeal of the Missouri Compromise and the opening of Kansas to slavery.[13] In the late presidential election he had supported

Heidler, "Cameron, Simon," *Encyclopedia of the Civil War,* 341–343.

10. General Nathaniel Lyon was born in Connecticut on July 14, 1818, attended West Point (number 11 of 52), and served in the U.S. Army until his death at Wilson's Creek, Missouri, on August 10, 1861. His actions in Missouri, during 1861 propelled Missouri into the Civil War. See *Missouri In 1861* (353–355) for a complete biography. Ezra J. Warner, *Generals in Blue: Lives of the Union Commanders* (Baton Rouge, LA, 1964), 286–287, hereafter cited as Warner, *Generals in Blue.*

11. The St. Louis Arsenal was established in 1826, with the first building constructed in 1827. Located on forty acres, three miles south of St. Louis, the arsenal housed 60,000 rifles and muskets with a large supply of ammunition, 40 cannon and equipment to manufacture arms, when the Civil War began in 1861. Guarded by a handful of soldiers, the arsenal was a prime target for either side to hold or take at the outbreak of hostilities. Winter, 38–39.

12. Thomas Hart Benton was born and educated in North Carolina in 1782, and moved to Tennessee, where he was elected as a senator to the Tennessee Legislature. A lawyer by profession, Benton moved to St. Louis in 1815, where he became the editor of the *Missouri Enquirer.* Elected as one of Missouri's first senators (1820–1850), Benton championed western causes like free navigation of the Mississippi River and a national road to New Mexico. A tacit supporter of slavery, Benton was defeated for office in 1850, won a U.S. House of Representatives seat in 1856, but died of cancer on April 10, 1858. James Neal Primm, *Lion of the Valley: St. Louis, Missouri* (Boulder, CO, 1981), 113–114, 116–117, 120, hereafter cited as Primm; James M. Volo and Dorothy Denneen Volo, *Encyclopedia of the Antebellum South* (Westport, CT, 2000), 30–31.

13. The Missouri Compromise was the first piece of legislation from the U.S. Congress to pit "Slaveholding States" against "Free States." Crafted by Henry Clay of Kentucky, this 1820 Compromise allowed Missouri to enter the Union as a slave state while Maine entered the Union as a free state. The

Douglas,[14] not because he liked him personally, not because he approved of his squatter sovereignty theories, but because to have done otherwise would have defeated his own election as governor, for in the Summer of 1860, the great majority of the people of Missouri were strongly attached to the Union and unwilling to imperil its integrity, as they thought they might do by voting for either Lincoln or Breckinridge.[15] He had been inaugurated as governor on the third of January, and from that time had used all his personal influence and all his official power to commit Missouri to the side of the South, and to get her ready to fight against the government.

Frank Blair

was a Kentuckian, too, but, his father [Frank Blair], the friend of [President Andrew] Jackson, had taken him to Washington City in his boyhood, and he had grown up there in the national atmosphere of the Federal capital and in the midst of men, who, like [Martin] Van Buren and Benton, were already assuming an attitude of hostility towards the great leaders of the southern sentiment, For Benton, who showed him much kindness, he conceived the greatest admiration and affection, and it was by his advice that, after studying a while at Princeton and reading some law, he went, in 1843 to St. Louis, where his brother Montgomery, was already at the bar. But Frank had little taste and less appetite, for the law and gladly threw away his books and went into the army when the Mexican War broke out in

---

compromise further stated that slavery would not be extended into the Louisiana Purchase area, north of the southern boundary of Missouri. However, in 1854, the Congress passed the Kansas-Nebraska Act, which nullified the Missouri Compromise and brought the nation ever closer to civil war. As written, the act formed Kansas and Nebraska into territories and allowed them to vote on whether they entered the Union as free or slave states. This voting process was better known as "popular sovereignty." The Kansas-Nebraska Act led to years of violence on the Missouri-Kansas border in what became known as the "Bleeding Kansas" years (1854–1859), and proved to be the forerunner of the Civil War. Boatner, 69, 448, 556–557.

14. Stephen A. Douglas was born in Vermont in 1813, and later moved to Illinois, where he became involved in politics. Elected to the U.S. Congress in 1842, Douglas became a U.S. Senator in 1847. He was best known for his Kansas-Nebraska Bill of 1854, and a series of debates that he had in 1858 with Abraham Lincoln. Douglas unsuccessfully ran for President as a Democrat in 1860, but died of typhoid fever on June 3, 1861, in Chicago. Ibid., 244–245; Sifakis, *Union,* 116.

15. John C. Breckinridge was born January 16, 1821, in Kentucky. He received his college degree at age seventeen, a law degree in 1841, and entered the Mexican War as a major, but saw no action. Elected to the Kentucky legislature in 1851, Breckinridge later became a representative in the U.S. Congress and the vice-president under James Buchanan in 1856. During the election of 1860, Breckinridge was the presidential candidate for the Southern Democrats. After losing to Lincoln, Breckinridge was elected to the U.S. Senate from Kentucky. He remained neutral at the beginning of the Civil War, but in November 1861, after Kentucky ended its neutrality, he accepted a commission as brigadier general in the Confederate army. By war's end, Breckinridge had been appointed a major general, served in armies in both the Western and Eastern Theaters and completed the war as the Secretary of War for the Confederacy. Following the war, he fled the country and lived for a time in Europe. He returned to the United States in 1869, where he lived out his remaining years. Breckinridge died on May 17, 1875. John C. Klotter, "Breckinridge, John Cabell," *Encyclopedia of the Civil War,* 277–279.

1847, and fought gallantly under [Zachary] Taylor[16] at Resaca de la Palma[17] and at Monterey. When, after the war, the North and the South began to contend for the possession of the territory which had been wrested from Mexico, he joined the Free Soil Party,[18] and was next to Benton, its most influential leader in Missouri. It was in the bitter personal and political contest which then took place between the Benton Free Soil Democrats and the anti-Benton pro-slavery Democrats, that there sprang up between Blair and "Major" Jackson, as the Governor was then called, that strong antagonism which was now, in 1861, reaching its culmination. A few years later Blair and Gratz Brown[19] founded the *St. Louis Democrat,*[20] which was thenceforth the exponent of his views.[21] When the struggle for Kansas

---

16. Zachary Taylor entered the military in 1808, fought in the War of 1812, the Seminole War in the 1830's and led one of the main United States armies in the Mexican War. Taylor resigned from the army as a major general on January 31, 1849, just prior to his inauguration as the twelfth President of the United States on March 4, 1849. Taylor did not survive his presidency, dying on July 9, 1850. Francis B. Heitman, *Historical Register and Dictionary of the United States Army, From its Organization, September 29, 1789, to March 2, 1903*, 2 vols. (Washington, 1903), 1:949, hereafter cited as Heitman.

17. The Battle of Resaca de la Palma, Texas, occurred on May 9, 1846. Following up the defeated Mexican Army at Palo Alto, General Zachary Taylor found them posted on a piece of ground thickly covered in chaparral, which negated the Mexican artillery advantage. Quickly surveying the situation, Taylor ordered in his dragoons, who shattered the Mexican line, capturing several pieces of artillery. The infantry followed, and a confused broken battle ensued, where the demoralized Mexicans were routed from the field, losing in the process 1,200 men to the Americans' 150. Otis A. Singletary, *The Mexican War* (Chicago, 1960), 30–31, hereafter cited as Singletary.

18. The Free Soil Party was the forerunner to the Republican Party. Organized in the late 1840's, it was mainly concerned with the extension of slavery into the newly acquired territory obtained during the Mexican War. Martin Van Buren was the party's presidential candidate in 1848. That year also marked the high point of the Free Soil Party, as it gave way to the Republican Party in 1854. Boatner, 314.

19. Benjamin Gratz Brown was born on May 28, 1826, in Lexington, Kentucky, educated at Transylvania University and Yale, graduating from the latter place in 1847. Admitted to the Kentucky bar, Brown moved to of St. Louis, where he joined the Blair law firm. Brown was a first cousin of the Blairs, an Unconditional Unionist, member of the first Republican Convention in Missouri and co-editor of the *Missouri Democrat*. In 1856, following a series of insulting exchanges between Thomas C. Reynolds (Missouri's lieutenant governor in 1860) and Brown, a duel was held in which Brown was shot, but later recovered. At the beginning of the Civil War, he commanded the Fourth U.S. Reserve Regiment from Missouri. In 1863, Brown was appointed to the U.S. Senate (1863–1866) to serve out the remainder of the term of Waldo Johnson, who had been expelled from the senate. Brown was elected to a two year term as Missouri Governor in 1870 and served as the vice-presidential nominee of the Liberal Republican-Democratic Party, with Horace Greely, in 1872. Returning to the law, Brown remained an active lawyer in St. Louis until his death in on December 13, 1885. Walter Harrington Ryle, *Missouri: Union or Secession* (Nashville, 1931), 73, 135, 196, hereafter cited as Ryle; McElroy, 65; *History of Audrain County, Missouri, Written and Compiled from the Most Authentic Official and Private Sources, Including a History of Its Townships, Towns and Villages* (St. Louis, 1884), 38, 40, hereafter cited as *History of Audrain County;* Winter, 142; Louis S. Gerteis, *Civil War St. Louis* (Topeka, 2001), 69–71, hereafter cited as Gerteis.

20. The *Weekly Missouri Democrat* was founded in 1852, and issued its first newspaper in July. It became the *Missouri Democrat* (weekly) in 1868, and merged with the *St. Louis Weekly Globe* to become the *Weekly Globe-Democrat* in 1877. The latter newspaper went out of existence in 1921 in favor of the daily *St. Louis Globe-Democrat*. Library of Congress, *Newspapers in Microform, United States, 1848–1983, Vol. I A–O* (Washington, DC: 1984), 563, 566, hereafter cited as *Newspapers in Microform.*

21. Frank Blair began a newspaper career early in life, by puttering around the offices of his family

began in 1854, he earliest opposed the repeal of the Missouri Compromise and the opening of Kansas to slavery, and running upon that issue, was elected to Congress by St. Louis in 1856, the first Free Soiler that was sent to Congress by a slave holding state. In the presidential election of that year he separated for the first time from his friend and leader Col. Benton (who continued to adhere to the Democratic Party), and in conjunction with Brown and a few others organized the Republican Party of Missouri and supported its candidate, [John C.] Frémont,[22] while spoke and voted for [James] Buchanan.[23] During the next four years Blair was the unquestioned leader of the Republicans of Missouri, it was through his exertions chiefly that they cast 17,000 votes for Lincoln in 1860.[24]

The President

hesitated to authorize Blair to furnish Missouri's quota of militia. Blair got it ready nevertheless. He had the men close at hand. Most of them were Germans, and many of them had seen service in Europe. They had been "Wide Awakes"[25]

---

newspaper, the *Globe,* in Washington, DC in the early 1830's. In 1848, he founded the *Barnburner,* a Free Soil newspaper, to support Martin Van Buren for President in 1848. After the *Barnburner* ceased in 1849, Blair wrote editorials for the *St. Louis Reporter,* which led to his founding of the *Weekly Missouri Democrat* in July 1852. Blair lasted about two years with the *Democrat,* giving up the editorial responsibilities to a Peter L. Foy in 1854. Ibid.; William E. Parrish, *Frank Blair: Lincoln's Conservative* (Columbia, MO, 1998), 4, 48, hereafter cited as Parrish; William Earnest Smith, *The Francis Preston Blair Family in Politics,* 2 vols. (New York, 1933), 1:64, 292; Boatner, 67.

22. John C. Frémont was a famous explorer, scout, Mexican War veteran, and the first Republican candidate for President in 1856. Appointed a Major General in the regular army, he assumed command of the Western Department, embracing Missouri, on July 25, 1861. Many of those who served under Frémont in Missouri had little respect for him as one veteran recalled: "If there ever was an empty, spread-eagle, show-off, horn-tooting general, it was Frémont....He had no ability of any kind." See Michael E. Banasik, *Missouri Brothers in Gray: The Reminiscences and Letters of William J. Bull and John P. Bull* (Iowa City, IA, 1998), 135, 137 for biography. *O.R.,* 3:406; E. F. Ware, *The Lyon Campaign in Missouri: Being a History of the First Iowa Infantry and of the Causes Which Led up to its Organization, and how it Earned the Thanks of Congress Which it got Together With a Birdseye View of the Conditions in Iowa Preceding the Great Civil War of 1861* (Topeka, KS, 1907; reprint ed., Iowa City, IA, 1991), 248, hereafter cited as Ware.

23. James Buchanan was the fifteenth President of the United States, serving from March 1857–March 1861. During the secession crisis of 1860, Buchanan elected to do nothing, leaving the problem to his successor, Abraham Lincoln. Boatner, 94.

24. In the Presidential Election of 1860, 165,618 votes were cast for the four candidates in Missouri; Abraham Lincoln (Republican candidate), 17,028; Stephen A. Douglas (Democratic candidate), 58,801; John Bell (Conditional Union candidate), 58,372; and John C. Breckinridge (Southern Rights Democrat—slave-holders), 31,317. Of the votes cast, 81% supported Missouri's staying in the Union, though not necessarily supporting taking up arms to put down the rebellion. Ninety percent did not support Lincoln. McElroy, 21.

25. The "St. Louis Wide Awakes" were organized in the summer of 1860, by Frank Blair, following the Republican Convention, which was held in Chicago. They were armed with lighted lamps attached to clubs to drive hecklers away from political rallies. As recalled by one witness:

At the first two meetings which the Wide Awakes thus attended, the enemy, not understanding the purpose of the club, began their usual serenade of yells and cheers, but were speedily initiated into the

during the presidential election. They were Home Guards now, and as such they had been organized into companies and drilled and disciplined and partly armed, and there were arms and equipments for the rest within easy reach arms for 60,000 men, and they all were in the custody of a soldier who was eager to put them to use for the Union. The soldier was Capt. Nathaniel Lyon of the Second United States Infantry. Born in Connecticut, of good Revolutionary stock for in his veins flowed the blood of the Knowletons, he had been educated at West Point and served honorably in Florida, had won distinction in Mexico and on the Pacific coast, and had for the last six years been doing arduous duty on the great plains. During much of these six years he was stationed in Kansas. Lyon sympathized at first with the Free State men, and then became one of their most aggressive leaders, working, writing, talking in their behalf and doing all that an officer in the army might dare to do to aid them. A story which his friend, Dr. William A Hammond,[26] tells about him throws a good deal of light upon his character.

They were all at Fort Riley,[27] and the doctor was surgeon of that post.

A Court Martial

happened to be in session there. One day[28] Capt. R. H. Anderson[29] of South Carolina gave in their honor a dinner to which all the officers at the post and their wives were invited. Among the guests were Capt. Lyon. At the first opportunity

---

mysteries of the new order; which initiation consisted in being besmeared with burning camphene, and vigorously beaten with leaded sticks.

In December 1861, the Wide Awakes disbanded, forming "Union Clubs," which took on the military aspects of drill and discipline. The clubs added muskets and rifles in February 1861, which led eventually to their becoming Union Home Guards, defending Missouri against the secessionists. James Peckham, *Gen. Nathaniel Lyon, Missouri in 1861. A Monograph of the Great Rebellion* (New York, 1866), xi–xiv, 30–31, 33–37, hereafter cited as Peckham; Ryle, 162, 187–189.

26. Doctor William A. Hammond was born in 1828, in Maryland and received a medical degree from New York College in 1848. He became an assistant surgeon in the U.S. Army in 1849, resigning in October 1860. With the beginning of the Civil War, Hammond was reinstated in May 1861, and was appointed a brigadier general surgeon in April 1862. Hammond was convicted at a court-martial in August 1864, dismissed from the service, but reinstated in March 1878 by an act of Congress. He retired as a brigadier general in 1879. He died January 5, 1900. Heitman, 1:496; Boatner, 370.

27. Fort Riley, Kansas, was established on May 17, 1853, by Captain Charles S. Lovell of the Sixth U.S. Infantry. Initially called Fort Center, because of its geographical location, the post was renamed Fort Riley on June 27, 1853, in honor of Colonel Bennett Riley, who had died on June 9. Located on the Kansas River near the junction of the Smoky Hill and Republican Rivers, the post began permanent construction in 1855, and is still in existence today. Robert W. Frazer, *Forts of the West: Military Forts and Presidios and Posts Commonly Called Forts West of the Mississippi River to 1898* (Norman, OK, 1963), 57.

28. The incident described by Dr. Hammond occurred in July 1854. Christopher Phillips, *Damned Yankee: The Life of General Nathaniel Lyon* (Columbia, MO, 1990), 85, 107, hereafter cited as Phillips.

29. Richard H. Anderson was born in 1821, in South Carolina, attended West Point where he graduated number 40 of 56 in 1842. He served in the Mexican War and on the frontier prior to the Civil War, resigning in March 1861. Unlike Lyon, Anderson survived the war, attaining the rank of lieutenant general in the Confederate Army before war's end. He died in 1879, in virtual poverty. Boatner, 14.

he plunged into a harangue against the south and its particular institutions and used all his great powers of invective against slavery and slave-holders, regardless of the fact that Capt. Anderson, and most of his guests were slave-holders. The Northern officers present were dumbfounded at the violence and virulence of Lyon's attack. The Southerners looked indigent, of course, except Capt. Anderson, who sat at the head of his table, smiling serenely at Lyon's noise, and by occasionally addressing a word or two to those that were nearest to him, trying to make the occasion pass as pleasantly as possible. The dinner ended at last and the company separated. That night the doctor and Capt. Lyon were at Maj. Merrill's[30] quarters, when Anderson, who had been looking for Lyon, entered, and approached him and said: "Capt. Lyon, you took occasion to-day, when I, from my position was helpless to repel your insults, to commit an outrage for which I am going to punish you. I am going to thrash you." Lyon, without rising from his chair, replied: "Capt. Anderson, if you come a step nearer I will kill you." Instantly the officers that were present stepped between them, and presently Capt. Anderson left the room. Within an hour he sent a challenge to Lyon, who took it straight away to the doctor. "You must accept it," said Hammond. "I will not," replied Lyon. "I have conscientious scruples against dueling, and besides, it is contrary to law, and I am a law abiding man. I shall

General Nathaniel Lyon

not accept the challenge, but if he attacks me I shall kill him like a dog." He nevertheless yielded to the doctor's advice and agreed to meet Anderson on the condition that the duel should be fought with pistols across the table. Maj. [Henry H.] Sibley,[31] who was Anderson's second, rejected these terms as being "barba-

---

30. A review of the *Historical Register of the U.S. Army*, suggests that Snead was referring to Major Hamilton W. Merrill, a 1834 graduate of West Point (No. 25). Merrill resigned in February 1857, and apparently never reentered the army. He died on July 14, 1892. Heitman, 1:704–705.

31. Henry H. Sibley was born in 1816, in Louisiana, attended West Point where he graduated in 1838 (number 31 of 45) and was assigned to the Second Dragoons. He was breveted a major in 1847 for his actions during the Mexican War. Prior to the Civil War, Sibley served in Kansas and participated in the Utah expedition in 1860. Resigning his commission in May 1861, Sibley was appointed a colonel in the Confederate Army and a brigadier general in June 1861. Sibley is most remembered for inventing the "Sibley Tent" and commanding the New Mexico Expedition in 1861–1862. After the war, Sibley journeyed to Egypt, where he joined the Egyptian Army. In 1874, he returned to the United States and lectured on his experiences in Egypt. He died in poverty on August 23, 1886. Ibid., 1:886; Boatner, 759.

rous, murderous, unusual and ungentlemanly." The matter was therefore referred to a council of officers, that decided that Lyon had been guilty of a grave offense and must apologize to Capt. Anderson in the presence of every officer at the post. As there was to be at Dr. Hammond's that evening a reception, at which all the officers were to be present with their families, it was arranged that Lyon would should present himself at 9 o'clock and tender his apology. Prompt to the minute he entered the room in full uniform, and with the doctor at his side strode its full length through the long line of officers and ladies till he got within four or five feet of Anderson, by whose side Sibley was standing. Then without a tremor in his voice, he said in his deliberate way: "Capt. Anderson, I have come to express my regret for having used language at your table which, however much I may believe it to be true, was out of place at the time and such as I, your guest, should not have spoken. Its employment under the circumstances was more injurious to me than to you." Anderson bowed, but did not say a word. Lyon bowed, then turned and strode out of the room.

At St. Louis.

On the last day of January Capt. Lyon was ordered to St. Louis with his company, where he was put in command of the troops at the arsenal.[32] He quickly gained the confidence of Blair and became his friend and military advisor; helped him to organize the Wide Awakes into Home Guards, drilled and discipline them, inspired them with his own fierce spirit and got them ready for war. The President would not authorize Lyon to muster in the four regiments which Blair had tendered to the government, but authority to do this was instead given to Lieut. John M. Schofield,[33] then on leave at St. Louis, where he was professor at Washington University. Schofield was about to muster the men in and Lyon to arm them, when Gen. [William S.] Harney,[34] who was in command of the Depart-

---

32. Lyon arrived in St. Louis on February 6, 1861, with eighty men of the Second U.S. Infantry. McElroy, 50–51.

33. John M. Schofield was born in New York in 1831, attended West Point, and graduated toward the top of his class in 1853. At the beginning of the Civil War, he was on a leave of absence, teaching school in St. Louis. Schofield became Nathaniel Lyon's Chief of Staff in mid-1861, a brigadier general on November 21, 1861, a major general on November 29, 1862, and again on May 12, 1863, after his original appointment had expired. In May 1863, he departed the Trans-Mississippi and completed his military service in the eastern theater. Schofield remained in uniform after the war, and by the time of his death on March 4, 1906, he had risen to the rank of lieutenant general and was Commander in Chief of the U.S. Army. For complete biography see *Missouri In 1861*, 360–362; Heitman, 1:865; Warner, *Generals in Blue*, 425–426.

34. William S. Harney was born in Tennessee, joined the regular army in 1818, fought Seminoles in Florida, served in the Mexican War and fought Indians on the frontier. On June 14, 1858, he received a promotion to brigadier general in the regular army. Harney assumed command of the Department of the West, in St. Louis, on November 17, 1860. By the Civil War, Harney was one of only four general officers in the U.S. Army and expected to support the South, but he never did. St. Louis Unionists did not trust Harney and successfully had him removed from command following the Camp Jackson Affair. See Appendix B for a complete biography. Frederick H. Dyer, *A Compendium of the War of*

ment of the West,[35] with headquarters at St. Louis, positively forbade the issue of arms to these men. Blair thereupon persuaded the President to order Harney to Washington City. As soon as Harney was out of the way Blair enlisted, not four regiments but ten; Schofield mustered the men into the service and Lyon armed and equipped them for the field. All of this had been accomplished before the end of the first week in May.[36]

Blair and Lyon now determined to overthrow the state government, to hang the governor

As a Traitor

if they could catch him, otherwise to drive and his adherents out of the state, and to occupy it with a sufficient force to hold it loyal to the Union. Circumstances favored their plan, for at the very time Frost's Brigade,[37] which comprised four fifths on the entire organized militia of the state, was assembled in a camp of instruction within the limits of St. Louis. Relying on the fact that this encampment was being held by the Governor's order in strict conformity to law, and without any hostile intention, [Daniel M.] Frost[38] supposed no danger. But Lyon, who

---

the Rebellion (Des Moines, 1908; reprinted Dayton, OH, 1978), 254, hereafter cited as Dyer; Warner, *Generals in Blue*, 208–209; McElroy, 30–31; Boatner, 376; Heitman, 1:502.

35. The Department of the West was in existence at the beginning of the Civil War, but was quickly discontinued on July 3, 1861. The newly created Western Department embraced the state of Illinois and all states and territories west of the Mississippi River and east of the Rocky Mountains, including New Mexico. Dyer, 254–255.

36. General Harney was temporarily removed from command on April 21, 1861, relinquished his command on April 23 and departed for Washington. On May 8, Harney was reinstated to his command and returned to St. Louis, where he arrived on May 11. Harney immediately attempted to disband the units that Blair and Lyon had raised, but Blair convinced Harney to let the units remain, thus setting the stage for Harney's eventual dismissal from command of the Department of the West. McElroy, 64–65; *O.R.*, 1:669–671; *O.R.*, 3:369–370.

37. Frost's Brigade of Missouri Militia was commanded by Daniel M. Frost and consisted of two infantry regiments. Each regiment contained ten companies, with colorful names like the Dixie Guards, the Washington Blues or the Davis Guards. Total strength was about 760 officers and men. For a complete organization of the brigade see *Missouri Brothers in Gray*, 161–163; Peckham, 132–135.

38. Daniel M. Frost was born 1823, in New York, graduated from West Point (number 4 of 25) in 1844, and served in the Mexican War. On May 31, 1853, Frost resigned from the army and moved to St. Louis. At the beginning of the Civil War, he ran a "planing mill," in St. Louis, and was a general in the Missouri State Militia. Captured at Camp Jackson (May 10, 1861), Frost was exchanged in November 1861, journeyed to Columbus, Kentucky, where he joined the Confederate war effort. He was at the Battle of Pea Ridge, Arkansas, in March 1862, and was promoted to brigadier general in October 1862. At the Battle of Prairie Grove, Arkansas, Frost commanded a Confederate division. Frost was at Little Rock in September 1863, after which he submitted his resignation and escorted his wife to Canada via Mexico. Unfortunately, Frost's resignation was never accepted and he was listed as a deserter, the only Confederate general officer so listed at the end of the war. Frost later returned to St. Louis and became a farmer. He died on October 29, 1900, and was buried in St. Louis. See *Missouri Brothers in Gray*, 138, for a complete biography. Ezra J. Warner, *Generals in Gray: Lives of the Confederate Commanders* (Baton Rouge, 1959), 94–95, hereafter cited as Warner, *Generals in Gray*; Boatner, 318; Heitman, 1:438.

looked upon Camp Jackson[39] as "a nest of traitors," cared nothing for the orders of the Governor whom he believed to be a traitor, nor for the laws which were being used to protect the enemies of the Union. So on the 10th of May he marched against the camp with 7,000 men, surrounded it, and demanded its immediate surrender. Frost, who only had 635 men, could but submit.[40] He and his offices and men were then marched off to the arsenal as prisoners of war, but were paroled the next day.[41] All their arms and equipment were held as captured property. At a single blow Lyon had disarmed the state and almost annihilated its organized militia. But this outrage on the sovereignty and dignity of their state so greatly alarmed and angered the people of Missouri that the General Assembly, in the midst of the great excitement, enacted that very day a law for raising an army and putting it into the field, and another law which conferred dictatorial powers upon the Governor.[42] Blair and Lyon would have brought this legislation to naught by marching boldly upon the capital and dispersing the state government before it could begin to enlist its forces, but Gen. Harney just at this moment returned to St. Louis, assumed command there and ordered Capt. Lyon back into the arsenal.

---

39. Camp Jackson was located on the outskirts of St. Louis in Lindell Grove, bordered by Grand Avenue on the west, Compton Avenue on the east and Lindell on the north. Winter, 46.

40. At the time of the capture of Camp Jackson, on May 10, 1861, several of the men were no longer present, including Captain Joseph Kelly's company, which was escorting an ammunition train to Jefferson City. Following the capture of the camp, General Lyon reported that he had seized 689 officers and men. However, when the exchanges took place in November 1861, only 399 enlisted men and 79 officers who were paroled, and not the 689 men that Lyon says he captured (Lyon variously reported the captures as 50, 76 or 79 officers and 590 or 639 men, depending on which part of the *Official Records* that you read). The discrepancy was not explained, except for a brief statement penned in 1862 by the Commissioner of Exchanges, Charles H. Howland, who stated that only those prisoners who "were found desirous of joining their fortunes with secession," were exchanged. *O.R.,* 3:5; *O.R., Series 2,* 1:108, 116, 123; Roster book of Camp Jackson prisoners, Camp Jackson Papers, Missouri Historical Society.

41. Despite accepting their parole, many of the men captured at Camp Jackson went on to join the MSG and later the Confederate Army. The most prominent among the captives was Captain Emmett MacDonald, who sued in Federal court and won his unconditional release. In early November 1861, the St. Louis law firm of Decker & Voorhis initiated a law suit against Frank Blair and some twenty other Unionist officers who participated in the capture of Camp Jackson. The suit sought damages of $10,000 each as "they were greatly damaged in reputation, in their business relations and in other respects...in consequence of this imprisonment and illegal and willful and malicious and wrongful detention." The results of the suit are unknown. "The Camp Jackson Affair to Be Tried In Court," *Chicago Daily Tribune* (Chicago, IL), November 7, 1861.

42. On May 3, 1861 (Snead has the date as May 2), the Missouri Legislature was called into session to place the State of Missouri into military readiness. The "Military Bill" became the point of debate, which put every "every able-bodied man into the Militia of Missouri" and provided for the organization of what would be called the Missouri State Guard. The bill was hotly contested with little progress towards passage until the early evening of May 10. Word reached the Legislature, at 4 p.m., that Camp Jackson had been taken and all the state property seized. Within fifteen minutes the Military Bill was "overwhelming passed" with only eight dissenting votes. A second bill, also quickly passed, authorized "the Governor to take such measures as he might deem necessary or proper to repel invasion or put down rebellion" in Missouri. This second bill also gave Governor Jackson $30,000 to carry out his mandate. Peckham, 167–168; McElroy, 88–90; Snead, 172–173.

The Governor

began at once to organize the State Guard. Sterling Price[43] was appointed to the chief command of the force that was to take the field. He was a native of Virginia, but had come to Missouri upon reaching his manhood, and had now resided there for thirty years. Being a man of ability, education and refinement, he soon entered upon a successful career—was speaker of the assembly in 1840 and elected to Congress in 1846. He had hardly taken his seat in that body in 1847, when he resigned it in order to raise a regiment for the Mexican War. With this regiment he marched across the plains to Santa Fe, assumed command in New Mexico fought several brilliant battles and completed the conquest of the country. He then advanced against Chihuahua, and, not knowing that a treaty of peace had been concluded, attacked Gen. [Angel] Trias [Alverez],[44] the governor of the state, and utterly defeated him and his greatly superior force. In recognition of the civic and military abilities which he displayed in this important command President [James K.] Polk appointed Col. Price a brigadier general.[45] He was Governor of Missouri from 1853–1857. In the canvas of 1860 he had zealously supported the election of Douglas, and continued to be an earnest Union man after the election of Lin-

---

43. Sterling Price was born in September 1809 in Virginia, and moved to Missouri in 1831. He served in the U.S. Congress, was governor of Missouri (1852), and became a brigadier general during the Mexican War. At the beginning of the Civil War he cast his lot with Missouri and subsequently the Confederacy. He died in St. Louis in 1867. For a complete biography see *Missouri Brothers in Gray*, 148–150; Boatner, 669.

44. Angel Trias Alverez was born in 1807, in Chihuahua City, Mexico, and educated in Europe. He campaigned against the Apaches in 1830 and was elected governor of Chihuahua Province in 1845. During the Mexican War he confronted the American invasion of his province and was defeated by Doniphan in 1847, and by Sterling Price in 1848. A liberal politician, Trias was still serving, on and off, as Governor of Chihuahua during the American Civil War. Trias was afflicted with consumption during the Civil War, and died in his home province in 1867. *O.R.*, vol. 41, pt. 3:246; Donald S. Frazier, *The United States and Mexico At War: Nineteenth-Century Expansionism and Conflict* (New York, 1998), 438–439, hereafter cited as Frazier.

45. Price returned to Missouri from Washington in June 1846, at the beginning of the Mexican War, and raised the Second Regiment of Missouri Volunteers. The unit departed for Santa Fe, New Mexico, in early August 1846, following on the heels of the Alexander Doniphan and the Stephen Kearny Southwest Expeditions. Price arrived in Santa Fe on September 28, with the remnants of his command arriving in mid-October. Kearny left for California shortly before Price's arrival and Doniphan led the First Missouri against the Navajos and then to Chihuahua before moving to Zachary Taylor's army at Moneterey, leaving Price in command of the Santa Fe area from October 26, 1846. In January 1847, Price led a successful expedition against a Mexican uprising in his district. On July 20, 1847, Price was promoted to brigadier general even as he led his Missouri troops home. Spending a short time back in Missouri, he returned to Santa Fe in January 1848. In February 1848, Price began his last campaign in the Mexican War, moving first to El Paso to fend off an attack that never materialized and then to Chihuahua. The Mexican governor and general, Angel Trias, retreated from Chihuahua to Santa Cruz de Rosales, where he awaited Price's command. Trias informed Price that the war was over, but lacking any confirmation, Price assaulted Santa Cruz on March 16 and took the town—marking it the last battle of the Mexican War. Robert E. Shalhope, *Sterling Price: Portrait of a Southerner* (Columbia, MO, 1971), 56, 58–60, 64–66, 68–73, hereafter cited as Shalhope; Frazier, 377; Heitman, 1:807; Singletary, 57–63.

coln. During the last few months he had strongly opposed the Southern policy of Governor Jackson and had done as much as any man in the state to bring about in February the election of a state convention which was unanimously opposed to withdrawing Missouri from the Union, and of this convention he was made president. In this office, which he held, he had maintained with dignity and firmness the position that Missouri would neither secede from the Union, nor consent to the invasion of the South by the Federal Government. To this position, which was, however, fast becoming untenable, he still adhered, even after the President had called out the militia. But Lyon's attack upon Camp Jackson exhausted his patience. He looked upon it as "an unparalleled wrong and insult to the state," and, hastening to Jefferson City, offered his sword to the Governor.[46]

Gen. Price.

Gen. Price was now 51 years of age a strikingly handsome man, tall, erect and stout, of a commanding presence and great dignity and courtesy of manner. His complexion was ruddy and his hair gray, his eyes were gray and somewhat small. He wore no beard at all, except a short whisker on each cheek. His hands and feet were small. In manner of dress he was scrupulously neat and careful and somewhat fond of display in manners, bearing and appearance, as well as in character and in conduct, he was every inch a gentleman. As soon as it was known that the Governor was going to resist the conquest of the state and that Gen. Price was to command her troops the people sprang to arms and volunteers began to crowd the streets of Jefferson City. War seemed to be imminent, but it was staved off for a time by a "convention"[47] between Gen. Price and Gen. Harney, whereby the neutrality and the peace of the state were to be maintained by their joint efforts. This convention gave great offense to Blair and Lyon, and Blair, whom the President had empowered to remove Harney at his discretion, now delivered the order to him. This was done on the 30th of May, and the next day Lyon, who had become a brigadier-general, assumed command of the Department of the West.

Price at once ordered the State Guard to be got in readiness for active service, but with a view to gain time—for the state was unready for war—and to cenelliate [?] the good will of those who still hoped that the neutrality of Missouri might be maintained, he and the Governor caused Gen. Lyon to be informed that they would be pleased to confer with him, in order to see whether they could not

---

46. Price was appointed a major general of the MSG on May 18, 1861. In offering his services to Governor Jackson, Price cited the "slaughter of the people of Missouri" that had occurred in St. Louis following the capture of Camp Jackson as his reason for supporting the state. McElroy, 93; Snead, 184.

47. This "convention," better known as the Price-Harney Agreement, was signed on May 21, and temporarily staved off civil war in Missouri. Under the agreement the Missouri Government would maintain order in the state while the Federal Government, represented by Harney, would not militarily interfere in Missouri. The agreement lasted three weeks, until General Lyon effectively repudiated the agreement on June 11, at the Planter's House in St. Louis, when he declared that Missouri and the Federal Government were now at war. See Appendix A for a copy of the agreement, *O.R.*, 3:374–375; Snead, 198–200; Shalhope, 160–162.

come to some agreement whereby the peace of the state might still be preserved. Lyon consented to meet them, on the condition that they would come to St. Louis and to that end sent them a safe conduct, in which he stipulated that "should Gov. Jackson and ex-Gov. Price…visit St. Louis for such interview, they shall be free from molestation or arrest…during their journey to St. Louis and their return from St. Louis to Jefferson City." Jackson was loth to go to St. Louis for the purpose of meeting Lyon, for he justly felt that the latter by insisting upon this condition meant to cast an indignity upon himself as Governor of the state, and to offensively assert his own precedence as the military representative of the Federal Government. In fact he required the utmost persuasion of Gen. Price and others to induce him to consent to this humiliation. I thought then that the general was right and that they were wrong, and I think so still. I said so to then, but the Governor consented to go. I went as aid-de-camp to the Governor. It was late on the night of the 10th of June when we reached the city.

The Barren Conference.

Early the next morning Gov. Jackson caused Gen. Lyon to be informed that Gen. Price and himself were at the Planters' House[48] and would be pleased to meet him. To this Gen. Lyon replied through his aid Maj. [Horace A.] Conant[49] that he had made preparations to confer with them at his own quarters in the arsenal and would await them there. To this deliberate impertinence the Governor made answer that he had already violated his own sense of what was due to the dignity of his office and he would not make any further concession in that direction, but, on the contrary, would meet Gen. Lyon at the Planters' House or nowhere. Lyon, who probably had some curiosity to meet the men whom he was about to engage in war and hold some argument with them before crossing swords, for he was not only fond of fighting, but of disputation, and somewhat vain of his prowess therein did not insist upon holding the interview at the arsenal, but came, instead to the Planters' House, accompanied by Col. Blair and Maj. Conant and informed the Governor that he would receive them in a room which had been set apart for the conference. Neither the Governor nor Gen. Price or I had ever met Lyon. We had known Frank Blair for years. But Price did not recognize him since the time he was Governor because of some very unbecoming language which Blair had,

---

48. The Planters House was a four and one–half story hotel, located on the west side of Fourth Street, between Pine and Chestnut streets. It began construction in 1837, and opened for business on April 3, 1841. Prior to the Civil War it was an important social center and meeting place, characterized as "'the epitome of elegance and grandeur, a place of romance and gaiety, a center of lavish entertaining and extravagant spending.'" A fire in 1887, closed the hotel. It was later refurbished, a new hotel opened in 1922, and still later it was converted to an office building. Winter, 67–68.

49. Horace Artemas Conant was secretary on General Lyon's staff and a paymaster in the First Missouri Brigade with a date of rank of May 12, 1861. He was made a captain and quartermaster on May 12, 1862, and died on October 5, 1862—cause unknown. Hans Christian Adamson, *Rebellion in Missouri: 1861 Nathaniel Lyon and the Army of the West* (Philadelphia, 1961), 99, hereafter cited as Adamson; Heitman, 1:320.

in the heat of debate, used toward him in the General Assembly. This difficulty embarrassed us somewhat on entering the room, but Blair overcame it at once by presenting the general to Lyon with great deference and by treating him otherwise with consideration. The general, who was one of the most amiable men, responded graciously to these overtures of Blair and the two men resumed the friendly relations on the very day, almost in the very hour, that they were about to take up arms against each other.

Gen. Lyon, was some 43 years of age, of medium height, thin and angular, with rough, weather beaten features, and course, reddish brown hair and beard. His deepest eyes of blue were overhung by somewhat shaggy brows, and his manner was that of a man who was too thorough in earnest to care much for any more of the conventionalities of life. Stiff, awkward and ungainly in his every movement, he took little pains to conceal the antipathy which he felt towards the opponents whom circumstances constrained him to treat with courtesy. Turning to the Governor he said slowly, "This conference will be conducted on the part of my government by Col. Blair, who enjoys the fullest confidence and is authorized to speak for it on this occasion." The discussion, thus opened, had been carried on by Blair and the Governor only a few minutes, when Lyon himself began to take part in it, for he was too thoroughly informed in the matters in dispute, too much in earnest, too fond of argument and too impatient of "the quibbling of politicians" to remain silent when the fate of the Union was at stake. He soon had the discussion pretty much all to himself, and conducted it with spirit and

With Masterly Ability.

The conference had lasted several hours, when at last the Governor said that he would disband the State Guard and break it up entirely; disarm every company that had been armed by the state; repel all attempts on the part of the Confederacy to invade Missouri, and maintain her strict neutrality in the impending war if Lyon would on his part, agree to disarm the Union Home Guards, whom he had armed, and pledge himself not to occupy any part of the state which he did not then hold. To this Lyon replied that Missouri was part of the Union, and would not be permitted to remain neutral in a contest which involved the very existence of the nation, but must furnish troops and do whatever else the government might require it to do for its preservation, and that he intended to make her do it. "I will not disarm the Home Guard. I will not stipulate not to occupy the state with my troops. On the contrary, I intend to this and to reduce her, if need be, to the exact condition of Maryland.[50] You men must learn, if you do not already know it, that the authority

---

50. Following the firing on Fort Sumter, Maryland attempted to remain neutral in the forthcoming Civil War, but to no avail. Federal troops were fired on as they passed through Baltimore on April 19, 1861. Eight days later President Lincoln suspended the writ of habeas corpus in Maryland and on May 13 Baltimore became an occupied city; martial law was declared, pro-secession newspapers were closed, arrests made, and citizens who supported the South were banished from the state. As the war progressed a hasty election was held in November 1861, "presided over by the military," ensuring

of the United States is paramount to Missouri and must be respected. Rather than to concede to the state for one single instant to dictate to my government in any matter, however unimportant, I would (rising as he said this and pointing in turn to everyone in the room) see you, and you and you, and you, and myself and every man, woman and child in the state dead and buried." Then turning to the Governor he continued: "This means war. In an hour one of my officers will call for you and escort you out of my lines." All of this was said slowly, deliberately, coldly and with a peculiar information to show that he meant every word that he uttered. Having said it and returned his watch to his pocket he wheeled upon his heels and without speaking another word to the Governor or Gen. Price, without bending his head toward either of them, without even looking toward them, he strode out of the room and went his way followed by Maj. Conant. Frank Blair lingered enough to say a few friendly words of farewell to us, whom he had known for years, and then we were left alone with our friends, who crowded around us with eager interest to learn the fateful result of the conference.

At the end of the hour that Lyon had given us we were conducted out of his lines. Before that hour had expired he was issuing orders for the movement of troops in pursuit of the Governor and others to cut off his escape southward. The latter reached Jefferson City two hours past midnight and at once called the State Guard into active service and ordered Gen. Price to take the field. And thus the war was begun in Missouri.

Thomas L. Snead

* * * * * *

---

that a pro-Union Governor was elected. Gary L. Browne, "Maryland," *Encyclopedia of the Civil War,* 1258–1261.

Item: Missouri enters the war; the fall of Jefferson City to General Lyon, and Grant takes command of the city, by C. J. Corwin,[51] resident of Jefferson City, Missouri, and delegate and observer at the South Carolina Secession Convention.
Published: November 28, 1885.

Early War Days in Missouri

St. Louis, Nov. 24
Editor, *Republican*

Your "Tales of the War" are bringing out facts which will be of immense benefit to the future historian. I had special opportunities as a seceding delegate from Missouri to judge the animus of the Southern leaders during the conventions at Charleston and Baltimore in 1860,[52] and I am quite certain that they premeditated no such contingency as would lead to secession. And here in Missouri it is quite certain that neither Gov. Jackson nor Gen. Sterling Price would have taken the field had they been satisfactorily assured that they were not to be arrested and held in durance by authority purporting to come from President Lincoln. The last evening of the late Gen. [John S.] Bowen's[53] stay in Jefferson City we passed

---

51. C. J. or J. C. Corwin, the owner and editor of the *Jefferson City Examiner* was a Democrat and supporter of John C. Breckinridge for President in 1860. A supporter of secession, Corwin, remained near Jefferson City, renting a plantation, throughout the war and in 1864, was a supposed Confederate mail carrier, though never imprisoned or charged with a crime. *O.R.*, vol. 41, pt. 2:941; *O.R.*, Series 2, 1:274–275; Ryle, 150, 208.

52. On April 23, 1860, members of the Democratic Party gathered at Charleston, South Carolina, to pick their nominee for President. Stephen Douglas of Illinois was the front runner for the nomination and espoused the position of "Popular Sovereignty." Southern Democrats wanted a platform that reaffirmed the rights of slave owners in any U.S. jurisdiction. After arguing the points without success, the convention voted and adopted Douglas's approach to slavery. The Southern Democrats left the convention, without nominating a candidate for President, causing the party to reschedule the convention for Baltimore in June 1860. On June 18, the party met in Baltimore, and failing to meet any agreements, the Southern Rights delegates bolted from the party. On June 23, the Southerners held their own convention in Baltimore, where they nominated John C. Breckinridge for President. Meanwhile, the Northern Democrats nominated Stephen Douglas for President. Mark A. Lause, "Election of 1860," *Encyclopedia of the Civil War,* 636–637.

53. John S. Bowen was born at Bowen Creek, near Savannah, Georgia on October 30, 1830. He was appointed to West Point in 1848, graduated in 1853 (number 13 of 51) and served three years before resigning. He moved to St. Louis in 1857, where he was an architect and joined the Missouri Militia, being elected a colonel in 1861. Captured at Camp Jackson and paroled, Bowen went to Memphis where he organized the First Missouri Infantry Regiment. At the Battle of Shiloh, Bowen commanded a brigade as a brigadier general, and was wounded, but recovered. At Corinth, in October 1862, Bowen again commanded a brigade. During the Vicksburg Campaign, Bowen successfully delayed Grant's army at the Battle of Port Gibson (May 1, 1863), earning a promotion to major general for his efforts. During the siege of Vicksburg, Bowen contacted dysentery and died on July 13, 1863, nine days after the surrender of the city. For complete biography see *Missouri Brothers in Gray*, 135–136; Clement A. Evans, gen. ed., *Confederate Military History,* 13 vols. (Atlanta, 1899; reprint ed. Secaucas, NJ, 1974), vol. 9: *Missouri*, by John C. Moore, 205–206, hereafter cited as Moore, *Missouri, Confederate Military History;* Warner, *Generals in Gray,* 29–30.

together. He was there especially to ascertain Gov. Jackson's intentions, and Gen. Bowen said to me: "Gov. Jackson will do nothing. He says the state has decided for the Union and tied my hands." After the Boonville skirmish[54] Gen. Lyon deputed three gentlemen—one of them the late judge Geo. W. Miller[55]—to hurry after Gov. Jackson, then on the retreat to Arkansas, and assuring him that he should not be molested if he would return to the peaceful discharge of his duties at the Missouri capital. The committees hurried after Jackson as far as Warsaw, and then gave up the chase.

Gov. Jackson and Gen. Sterling Price supported Douglas for president. But when secession commenced the idea of all Southern men in Missouri was that chaos had come and that every state was bound to stand on its own bottom until there was a reorganization. Gov. Jackson and his advisors so expressed themselves, and it was on this idea that Camp Jackson and Camp Liberty[56] were ordered.

Seldom was such consternation seen at Jefferson City when the telegram was received from George R. Taylor[57] that Gen. Lyon and Frank Blair were on the way,

---

54. Boonville is located in Cooper County, Missouri, on the south side of the Missouri River. It was the point to which Governor Claiborne F. Jackson fled from Jefferson City to avoid the advancing Federal troops under Lyon. On June 17, 1861, Lyon engaged the MSG at Boonville and easily dispersed them after a only a few minutes. During the engagement, Lyon lost 2 killed, 9 wounded (2 mortally) and 1 missing out of 1,700 men engaged. Lyon reported capturing 60 rebels, 500 arms, and 2 brass cannon. *O.R.*, 3:11–14, 809; Phillips, 217–220.

55. George W. Miller was a Democrat and a long-time resident of Jefferson City, being elected a circuit judge well before the war. Following the war, Miller lost his bid for reelection because of his political affiliation, but won again on the following election cycle. Miller married, had four daughters, and was regarded as the "best politician" in the Jefferson City area. Miller was considered a good Union man during the war, but Southern men saw him as a supporter of their rights following the war. He died while still serving on the bench. A newspaper of the day ranked "him for all times to come as one of the foremost judicial minds of the state." *O.R.*, Series 1, 1:780–781; R. E. Young, *Pioneers of High, Water and Main: Reflections of Jefferson City* (Jefferson City, MO, 1997), 146–148, hereafter cited as Young.

56. Camp Liberty is a reference to the capture of the Liberty, Missouri, Arsenal on April 20, 1861. The night before the attack, the Missourians camped near the arsenal at two different locations, possibly called "Camp Liberty," though there is no official or unofficial comments on the camp names. Captain Henry L. Route (attorney by profession) of the Missouri Militia, led a 200-man force against the arsenal, easily taking the facility from the three men who manned the place. In all, the Missourians captured 1,180 muskets, 243 rifles, 121 carbines, 923 pistols, 3 brass cannons and 13 iron guns with a large supply of ammunition. The arsenal was built in 1839 (Eakin and Hale say it was built in 1832) and was composed of a main fortress building encompassed by a fence that surrounded two acres of land; the entire arsenal occupied ten acres. Federal authorities abandoned the arsenal and in 1863 sold it at public auction. Snead, 152; Adamson, 6; Joanne C. Eakin and Donald R. Hale, *Branded as Rebels: A List of Bushwhackers, Guerrillas, Partisan Rangers, Confederates and Southern Sympathizers from Missouri During the War Years* (Independence, MO, 1993), 321, hereafter cited as *Branded as Rebels*; Peterson, 158; Gary G. Fuenfhausen, *A Guide to Historic Clay County Architectural Resources and Other Historic Sites of the Civil War* (Kansas City, MO, 1996), 83–85.

57. A Virginian by birth, George R. Taylor was a resident and business man of St. Louis. During his time in St. Louis, Taylor was also a real estate developer and at the beginning of the Civil War was the president of the Pacific Railroad, a position he held from 1860–1868. Taylor survived the war, dying in 1880. Primm, 200, 225, 227–28.

with 3,000 armed men.[58] The state convention, with Sterling Price, an avowed Union man, as president, was in secession. The legislature, also; and prominent men from all over the state were there—among others, Senator Trusten Polk;[59] and Capt. Joe Kelly,[60] with his St. Louis company,[61] was holding the fair grounds where the state powder was stored. It was a dark and stormy night with deep mud under foot, constant peals of the thunder overhead and fearful flashes of lightening. A night secession of the legislature was called, and senators and representatives bade their boarding house friends a sad good-bye and hurried off to

58. Toward midnight, on May 10, the church bells began ringing throughout the capital. Governor Jackson had received a telegram that told of General Lyon's advance on Jefferson City, with 2,000 men; Lyon was attempting to capture the Governor and the Legislature. The message proved to be in error. Still, the Governor reacted, ordering the immediate assembly of the Legislature, which passed some additional war measures. The Governor also ordered men to the two main railroad bridges, over the Osage and Gasconade Rivers that led to Jefferson City. The troops were to block the Unionists advance, and in the "excitement of the hour the detachment which was sent to guard the Osage Bridge set it on fire and partially destroyed it." Snead, 173; Dino A. Brugioni, *The Civil War In Missouri As Seen From The Capital City* (Jefferson City, 1997), 26, hereafter cited as Brugioni.

59. Trusten Polk was born in Bridgeville, Delaware, on May 29, 1811, educated at Cambridge and Yale, graduating from the latter in 1831. Polk moved to St. Louis in 1835, and established a law practice. He was elected Governor of Missouri in 1856, but resigned to become a U.S. Senator, replacing Thomas H. Benton. Polk, a proslavery Democrat, was expelled from the U.S. Senate in 1862, and joined the Confederate army. He became presiding judge for T. H. Holmes's Confederate Corps on December 20, 1862, and later an aide to General Price with the rank of colonel. Polk was captured in 1863, imprisoned at Johnson's Island, transferred to Sandusky, Ohio, on November 23, 1863, and later exchanged. In 1864, Polk, now a member of Sterling Price's staff, accompanied the army in Price's 1864 Missouri Raid. Polk returned to St. Louis following the war, and began the practice of law in 1867. Appointed a vice-president of the Southern Historical Society, in 1869, Polk represented Missouri. He died on April 16, 1876, and was buried in St. Louis. *O.R.*, vol. 34, pt. 4:696; *O.R.*, vol. 41, pt. 1:318; *O.R.*, Series 2, 6:709; *O.R.*, Series 4, 2:248; McElroy, 28; Donald R. Hale, *Branded as Rebels, Volume 2* (Independence, MO, 2003), 254, hereafter cited as Hale; R. A. Brock, ed. *Southern Historical Society Papers*, 52 vols. (Richmond, VA, 1876–1892; reprint ed, Wilmington, NC, 1990–1992), 18:352; Carolyn Bartels, *Trans-Mississippi Men at War: Volume I, Missouri C.S.A.* (Independence, MO 1998), 1, hereafter cited as Bartels, *Trans-Mississippi Men*; Winter, 127–128; Gerteis, 60, 334.

60. Joseph M. Kelly was a solider in the British army before coming to America. Prior to the Civil War, Kelly commanded the Washington Blues, St. Louis Volunteer Militia Company. At Wilson's Creek, Kelly, then colonel of his regiment, commanded 142 men and was wounded in the hand. Mosby M. Parsons appointed Kelly commander of the Sixth Division MSG on April 9, 1862. Later, Kelly joined the staff of General Parsons, being appointed Adjutant General of the brigade and later the division. During the war one veteran recalled that Kelly "was a good officer and a man of deep religious sentiment, but he had a habit of swearing with almost every sentence." *Missouri In 1861,* 380; Joseph A. Mudd, "What I Saw At Wilson's Creek," *Missouri Historical Review* 7 (October, 1912–July, 1913): 98, hereafter cited as Mudd, "What I Saw at Wilson's Creek"; National Archives, Record Group 109, Confederate Records, Chapter 7, vol. 394, Parsons's staff; Peterson, 172, 181; *O.R.*, 8:815.

61. Kelly's all Irish Washington Blues was ordered to Camp Jackson with the other St. Louis militia units in May 1861. It was sent to Jefferson City, escorting some munitions, just prior to General Lyon taking the camp on May 10, 1861. Kelly's company joined the First Rifle Regiment, Sixth Division, MSG on May 23, 1861, and was present at the Battle of Wilson's Creek on August 10, 1861. Peterson, 291; J. Thomas Scharf, *History of Saint Louis City and County, From the Earliest Periods to the Present Day: Including Biographical Sketches of Representative Men* (2 vols., Philadelphia, 1883), 2:1860–1861; John G. Westover, "The Evolution of the Missouri Militia 1804–1919," Doctoral Thesis submitted to the University of Missouri, Columbia, 1948, 104.

the statehouse. All the old muskets and pistols were brought into requisition, and all teams for hauling the powder away. And Senator Trusten Polk rushed off to Treasurer Alfred Morrison's[62] to warn him against the capture of the state money by Lyon and Blair. About 12 p.m. I made the tour of the corners. Everything was dark except the saloons; but on all corners and in the saloons were the gravest men of Missouri, many of them with old muskets and pistols, discussing the terrible situation. I rode out to the fair grounds to see how my negro and team, which had been requisitioned, were getting along. I overtook Capt. Kelly on the way. I found my wagon at the head of a procession of half a dozen, all well loaded with kegs of powder, waiting for someone to tell them where to haul it. I felt bound to tell my own darky what to do, and I knew better than Capt. Kelly the people of the surrounding country, and so I said: "Take it out to Christy Watson's." Poor Christy, one of nature's noblemen, now gone, had a fine plantation three miles away, out on the Moreau, with a large cave on it, and there this lot of powder was hauled. It rained fearfully and the lightening flashed horribly, and except for the lightening it was as dark as Erebus.

But Blair and Lyon did not come for some time after. In the interim, as I recollect, that famous interview between Gov. Jackson and Gen. Price on the part of the state, and Blair and Lyon, on the part of the government, was held here in St. Louis. Under the excitement, however, of the Taylor dispatch these famous measures organizing the State Guard, diverting the school money, etc., were passed.[63]

On the day Blair and Lyon did arrive I was returning from the country and was met by numerous fleeing citizens. They said lots of people had been killed. I found that Blair and Lyon troops were still on the steamers at the penitentiary landing. They finally formed on the penitentiary hill and marched up to town with banners flying and lively music, and Blair, arm-in-arm with United States Judge [R. W.]

---

62. Alfred W. Morrison, a Democrat and supporter of Claiborne F. Jackson, was a resident of Cole County in 1856, and was living in Howard County by 1860. Elected the Treasurer of Missouri in 1851, and subsequent years thereafter through 1860, Morrison was captured by Federal troops at Hermann, Missouri, on June 18, 1861, and returned to Jefferson City. Morrison turned over the state books to Colonel Henry Boernstein, commanding Jefferson City, and was later released. Ryle, 96, 142, 242–243; Hale, 227; *History of Audrain County*, 39.

63. The "Military Bill," organizing the Missouri military force, was passed following the Camp Jackson Affair and was signed by Governor Jackson on May 14, 1861. The bill organized Missouri into eight military districts or divisions and provided the guidelines for the establishment of the MSG. Other measures were quickly passed, providing money to support the military effort; these other bills "perverted the funds for the State charitable institutions into the military chest, seized the school fund for the same purpose and authorized a loan from the banks of $1,000,000 and another $1,000,000 of State bonds, to provide funds by which to carry out the program." Overall the most far reaching act by the legislature gave Governor Jackson authority "'to take what ever measures as in his judgement he may deem necessary or proper to repel such invasion or put down such rebellion.'" This final act essentially gave the governor dictatorial powers to do as he saw fit under the current circumstances. Shalhope, 158; Snead, 173, 184; McElroy, 89; Peterson, 5, 22–23; *State of Missouri, An Act to Provide For the Organization, Government, and Support of the Military Forces State of Missouri Passed at the Called Session of the Twenty-first General Assembly* (Jefferson City, MO, 1861; reprint ed, Independence, MO, n.d.), 77.

Wells,[64] in the rear. It was a gay sight and made a good impression.[65]

After the war was well under way Col. [James] Mulligan[66] was placed in command of the Capital District and he took me under surveillance. I was required to report every morning at his headquarters. There was always an imposing lot of bayonets at the front door and of shoulder straps in the state-room, and about the long table in the rear room, at the head of which the colonel, a most gentlemanly man, sat and dispensed justice. Finally one day he told me that he had been superseded and I would have to report the next morning to the new commander. I was there on time, and a most modest place it looked in comparison with the glittering scene it had previously been. No soldiers at the front door; no brass buttons or shoulder straps anywhere. Only a plain man in citizens' clothes seated at the long table and very busy writing. "A new clerk," I said to myself, "whose uniform the tailor has not yet had time to make." He simply said, "Good morning," as I entered. I paced the room for a quarter of an hour, when a party entered who wanted a pass. "Are you a Union man?" was the query. "By my faith, ye never knew a better," answered the Irishman; and forthwith a pass was written out and handed to him. The gentleman at the table was smoking a cigar and wearing a well-worn slouch hat. I walked up to him, feeling that here was a Federal officer that I could talk freely to. "You are Gen. [Ulysses S.] Grant[67] I suppose?" I said. He dropped his pen and rose to his feet. "Yes," he replied, "I am Gen. Grant from Illinois.

---

64. Robert W. Wells (Young has it as R. A. Wells) was born in Virginia and moved to Missouri. He was appointed Attorney General of Missouri in 1826, and served until 1836, when Andrew Jackson appointed him the judge for the District of Missouri. Holding court in both St. Louis and Jefferson City, Wells was at first a Whig and later a Democrat. Wells was, according to one man, a "slave owner but cast his lot with the Unionist...He was a brave man, upright judge, good neighbor, and sincere friend," though not popular with the public in general. Wells was married, with six children, from two marriages. His most famous case occurred in 1854, when Wells heard the Dred Scott case in St. Louis. Young, 48–50, 129; Gerteis, 28–29.

65. On June 15, 1861, General Lyon disembarked from the Steamer *Iatan* at Penitentiary Hill, to a waiting crowd of Union supporters. With flags flying, Lyon marched into Jefferson City and took possession of the capital. Brugioni, 34.

66. James Mulligan was born in Utica, New York, in 1830. He commanded the Twenty-third Illinois Infantry Regiment, and by virtue of seniority assumed command of the Lexington, Missouri, garrison in September 1861. Captured at Lexington, Mulligan was exchanged in October 1861, for General Daniel M. Frost, and served the rest of the Civil War years on the east side of the Mississippi River. On July 24, 1864, Mulligan was wounded at Kernstown, Virginia and captured; he died shortly thereafter. McElroy, 206; *O.R.*, vol. 37, pt. 2:601; *O.R.*, Series 2, 1:554.

67. Ulysses S. Grant was born on April 22, 1822, in Ohio, graduated from West Point (number 21 of 39) in 1843, and fought in the Mexican War where he was breveted a captain. Resigning on July 31, 1854, Grant tried farming, real estate, and clerking in his brothers' Galena, Illinois, leather shop. Grant was appointed colonel of the Twenty-first Illinois Infantry on June 17, 1861, and was sent briefly to Missouri. He commanded in Jefferson City, as a newly appointed brigadier general, for a week in August 1861, after which he was transferred to southeast Missouri. On November 7, 1861, he fought the Battle of Belmont, Missouri, his only engagement in the Trans-Mississippi area. Grant completed his Civil War service in the East, rising to the rank of Commander of the United States Army. Elected President of the United States in 1868, Grant served two terms, after which he traveled and entered into some unfavorable business adventures. Grant died on July 23, 1885 in New York City. Warner, *Generals in Blue*, 183–186; Boatner, 352–352; Heitman, 1:470.

I arrived last night[68] and superseded Col. Mulligan. What can I do for you?" I could only reply that I was required to report daily, but without any reason being assigned. He replied in substance that non-combatants were being too much annoyed; that there were plenty of fighting men to look after; that only to the extent that his orders required should he interfere with anybody. He walked and talked for about half an hour. He said he was a Democrat and had worked, talked and voted for Douglas for president. Finally he dismissed me saying that I need report no more; if he needed me he would send for me. He left within a week to report to Frémont here in St. Louis. I met him again before he left, however, riding out to examine the few defenses of Jefferson City.[69] It was remarkable the ease with which he sat his high mettled horse—how lightly he held the reins and the air of deep-thinking self-possession which characterized him.[70]

C. J. Corwin

* * * * * * *

---

68. Grant arrived in Jefferson City on August 21, 1861, and was assigned by General John C. Frémont to fortify the city. A week later, on August 28, Grant was reassigned to Cape Girardeau and on August 30, 1861, he assumed command of the District of Southeast Missouri. Sifakis, *Union,* 161; Brugioni, 50, 55.

69. Though sent by General Frémont to fortify Jefferson City, Grant did nothing, instead informing General Frémont that the picket guards were sufficient to protect and provide warning for the area. Brugioni, 50, 52.

70. During his time at West Point, Grant earned no honors, except one, being considered an excellent horseman. Upon graduation Grant wanted to enter a cavalry regiment, but as there were no positions "for the best horseman at West Point," Grant joined the infantry. Warner, *Generals in Blue,* 184.

Item: The Battle of Dug Springs, August 2, 1861, by A. V. Rieff, Captain, Independent Company of Arkansas Cavalry.[71]
Published: September 25, 1886.

Dug Springs.[72]

Waveland, Yell County, Ark., Sept. 20

Editor, *Republican*

In answer to Dr. [J. F.] Snyder's[73] request for light on this fight I will give the particulars as I remembered them after a lapse of a quarter of a century. I was in the advance guard of Gen. McCulloch's command[74] August 1, 1861, commanding about 100 cavalry Arkansas troops from Fayetteville; also fifteen or twenty men

---

71. Captain A. V. Rieff commanded an independent company of Arkansas cavalry, that was raised in Fayetteville, Arkansas. The company was the bodyguard of General Ben McCulloch. Rieff would later rise to the grade of lieutenant colonel in Monroe's Arkansas Cavalry Regiment and played a prominent role in several of the engagements in the Trans-Mississippi including: Wilson's Creek (August 10, 1861), Cane Hill (December 6, 1862), Prairie Grove (December 7, 1862), Camden Expedition (May–April 1864), and Price's 1864 Missouri Raid (September–November 1864). In the latter expedition he became the brigade commander of Cabell's Brigade after General William Cabell was captured on October 25, 1864. Michael E. Banasik, *Embattled Arkansas: The Prairie Grove Campaign of 1862* (Wilmington, NC, 1996), 284, hereafter cited as Banasik, *Embattled Arkansas*; William Garrett Piston and Richard W. Hatcher III, *Wilson's Creek: The Second Battle of the Civil War and the Men Who Fought It* (Chapel Hill, NC, 2000), 157, 170, 335, hereafter cited as Piston; *O.R.,* vol. 22, pt. 1:607; *O.R.,* vol. 34, pt. 1:792, 794; *O.R.,* vol. 34, pt. 1:646–647.
72. Dug Spring is located about a mile southwest of Clever, Missouri. It consisted of a fresh spring of water and "two or three houses in the ravine." Elmo Ingenthron, *Borderland Rebellion A History of the Civil War on the Missouri-Arkansas Border* (Branson, MO, 1980), 78, hereafter cited as Ingenthron; *Missouri In 1861,* 132.
73. Dr. John F. Snyder was born in St. Louis in 1830, lived in Bolivar, Polk County, Missouri and was editor of the *Bolivar Courier* newspaper. He wore a variety of hats in the Eighth Division, MSG, including Inspector-General, Chief of Transportation, Chief of Ordnance, Division Chaplain, Provost Marshal-General and Assistant Division Surgeon. In making his comment about Dr. Snyder, the writer was referring to a previous article that Snyder wrote (See second article following this one). Peterson, 28, 211; Carolyn M. Bartels, *The Forgotten Men: The Missouri State Guard* (Shawnee Mission, KS, 1995), 336, hereafter cited as Bartels *Forgotten Men;* Ryle, 151.
74. On July 29–30, McCulloch's Command consisted of three divisions and an advance element:

Advance Element—Six mounted companies of Rains's Missouri Cavalry; Harbin's Battalion of Missouri Cavalry; Campbell's Missouri Cavalry Company.
First Division—3rd Louisiana Infantry; Reid's Arkansas Battery; McRae's Arkansas Infantry Battalion; 3rd Arkansas Infantry; Weightman's Missouri Brigade.
Second Division—Price's Missouri Infantry, including McBride's Command, Parsons' Command, Clark's Command, Slack's Command, and Steen's Command; 4th Arkansas Infantry; 5th Arkansas Infantry; and Woodruff's Arkansas Battery.
Third Division—1st Arkansas Cavalry; Carroll's Arkansas Cavalry; 2nd Arkansas Mounted Rifles; Price's cavalry not in advance.

O.R., 3:102–103; *O.R.,* 53:719; James E. McGhee, *Letter and Order Book Missouri State Guard, 1861–1862* (Independence, MO, 2001), unnumbered pages 18–19 (entries pages 35–37), hereafter cited as McGhee, *Letter and Order Book;* Peterson, 263, 265.

of Capt. Campbell's Company[75] of Springfield, Mo. who were temporarily with me. Edley Boyd[76] was one of the party, brother of Poney Boyd,[77] ex-member of congress, who if living, will corroborate all I may say. Should this meet his eye I would be glad to hear from him, and wish to add that no more gallant boy ever fired a gun in a lost cause. On the night of August 1 Gen. McCulloch[78] camped on Crane Creek, Gen. Price in the rear, my company about three miles in advance and two or three miles south of Dug Springs, on outpost, scouting and picket duty.

My first lieutenant, Reagor, with fifteen or twenty men, was in picket about one mile north of Dug Spring, which was a bold, running spring ten or twelve feet under ground and about midway along a narrow hollow east of the road.

The Muddy Spring

is about one mile in the rear and west of the road. My company was engaged on foot east of the road and near Dug Springs, while Gen. [James S.] Rains[79] and his Missouri troops were entirely on the west side. As there seems to be considerable controversy about the bloody little fight, I will go into details that may not interest

---

75. Leonidas St. Clair Campbell, known as "Dick" Campbell, organized Company E, First Cavalry Battalion, Seventh Division, MSG, of men from Greene County, Missouri in May 1861. Upon organization the unit contained 126 men. Campbell would later become the lieutenant colonel of the Third Missouri Cavalry. He was wounded at the Battle of Elkhorn Tavern, but survived. Peterson, 200; *History of Greene County, Missouri, Written and Compiled From the Most Authentic Official and Private Sources, Including a History of Its Townships, Towns and Villages* (St. Louis, 1883), 403, hereafter cited as *History of Greene County.*

76. Edley H. Boyd was a surgeon in a Texas cavalry regiment—unit unknown. *Pictorial and Genealogical Record of Greene County, Missouri Together With Biographies of Prominent Men of Other Portions of the State, Both Living and Dead* (Chicago, 1893), 215.

77. Sempronius H. "Poney" Boyd was born on May 28, 1828, in Williamson County, Tennessee, and moved to Greene County, Missouri in 1840. At age twenty-one Boyd went to California in search of gold and returned to Missouri in 1855, where he took up residence in Springfield and studied law. Boyd was admitted to the Missouri bar in 1861. At the beginning of the Civil War he served as the major in the Greene and Christian County Home Guard Regiment and later commanded the Twenty-fourth Missouri Infantry. In 1862, and again in 1868, Boyd was elected to the U.S. Congress. During his lifetime, Boyd also served as mayor of Springfield (two terms) and Consul General to Siam (modern-day Thailand). Ibid., 215–216; *History of Audrain County,* 41; Jeff Patrick, *Nine Months in the Infantry Service: The Civil War Journal of R. P. Matthews and Roster the Phelps Regiment Missouri Volunteers* (Springfield, MO, 1999), 67, 119, hereafter cited as Patrick, *Nine Months.*

78. Born in Tennessee in 1811, Ben McCulloch fought at the Battle of San Jacinto, searched for gold in California in 1849, and was a U. S. Marshall in Texas. He received the surrender of the Federal forces in San Antonio in February 1861, and was commissioned a brigadier general on May 11, 1861. McCulloch commanded the District of the Indian Territory, which embraced the territory south of Kansas and west of Arkansas in the early part of the war. He was killed at the Battle of Pea Ridge on March 7, 1862. *O.R.,* 3:575; Warner, *Generals in Gray,* 200–202; Banasik, *Missouri In 1861,* 356–357.

79. James Spencer Rains was born on October 2, 1817, in Tennessee, later moved to southwest Missouri, settling near Sarcoxie. He served in the militia in pre-Civil War days, and was a state senator (1854–1861) when the war began in April 1861. Appointed a brigadier general in the MSG, Rains served throughout the war. After the war, Rains settled in Texas, where he died on May 19, 1880. See Appendix B for biography. Bruce S. Allardice, *More Generals In Gray* (Baton Rouge, LA, 1995), 190–192, hereafter cited as Allardice.

the general reader, but some old veterans would like to know the facts. Early on the morning of August 2, I heard Lieut. Reagor's guns, and while moving rapidly forward to reinforce him, heard the loud boom, boom of the first cannon, the lieutenant holding his position until they opened on him with their "big guns." Forming on line with him on the hill, we could plainly see the enemy's infantry forming where the road enters the valley north.[80]

While watching their maneuvers Maj. W. D. Reagan of Fayetteville delivered us a patriotic address. We then moved forward about 500 yards to the right of the road and into some scattering brush. About fifteen sharpshooters (the balance being shotguns) were dismounted, thrown forward and were soon engaged with Gen. Lyon's skirmishers.[81] Soon we heard the song of our first minnie balls. It would have been quite interesting, viewed from a safe place, to have

Seen the Boys Dodge

and their faces blanch. This soon passed off and they were eager to become engaged. I sent three well-mounted men to pass in rear of the enemy and ascertain definitely what force was in our front. They returned in a short time and reported the road for three miles full of infantry and artillery, with two or three brass bands playing, and as they came dashing back ran into the enemy's left, half a mile in my front. I sent a dispatch to Gen. McCulloch, stating that Gen. Lyon's whole force was before us and later told him in person, and don't think he doubted it, and was prepared for battle when I reached his camp late that evening.[82]

About this time Gen. Rains with 300 or 400 cavalry came up and formed west of the road in open ground half a mile away and in plain view of the enemy. He sent his aid Jesse Cravens, asking that I make an attack on the right while he would interest the enemy on the left. I dismounted all but number four and moved

---

80. By most accounts the skirmish at Dug Springs began at 9 a.m. on August 2, 1861. According to Franc Wilkie, a newspaper correspondent, traveling with the advance of the Union army, a rebel instigated the skirmish with a long range shot that fell well short of his intended target. With rebel cavalry in their front Captain Frederick Steele, commanding the Union advance, deployed his battalion of the Second U.S. Infantry; two companies on each side of the road, with Captain James Totten's Battery in support. Totten's command responded to the sentry's shot, scattering the rebels in the distance with a couple of rounds from a six-pound gun. Banasik, *Missouri In 1861*, 132; *O.R.*, 3:49, 50.

81. Following the initial contact with the rebel pickets, Steele's Federal troops advanced cautiously forward trying to develop the position and strength of the enemy. Supporting Steele's regulars was a troop of cavalry under Captain D. S. Stanley. Meanwhile, General Lyon with the remainder of the army pulled back about a mile and a half to encamp near water. As the day progressed both sides continued to pop away at each other with no appreciable results. *O.R.*, 3:49.

82. Despite Rieff's assertions that McCulloch believed the reports of the pending engagement with Lyon's entire force; such was not true. McCulloch little believed or trusted reports received from his advance on August 2 and sent only 150 men under Captain James McIntosh to investigate the reported Federal concentration. McIntosh at first saw nothing, but later, upon closer examination, saw what appeared to be a train or encampment—nothing to be alarmed about, "not more than 150" Federals were in the area. This second phase of the skirmish lasted until about 5:00 p.m. Ibid., 3:50–52.

forward in a close skirmish line.[83] We soon found the enemy occupying a ridge with a small hollow intervening and being armed with shotguns and pistols we sank in the tall grass and received a galling fire 200 yards distant. Giving orders to go into close range we charged with a shout. Edley Boyd, Jas. Mitchell, Frank Smiley and myself on the right and in advance. The enemy's fire was so hot the men could not resist the impulse to return it and fired at eighty or 100 yards distance, halting there, while we four halted

About Half Way

between the two lines, not having fired. The enemy gave way. Just at this time part of Co. C, old United States Dragoons, came dashing over the ridge with drawn sabers.[84] They passed twenty yards to my left in splendid order, and I will say that it was the most gallant act I saw during the war. They dashed through my company cutting and slashing on every side, some halting, one especially having a private combat with a reb who was dodging around a sapling and warding off the saber blows with his gun. They passed to the rear toward our horses, my company following on the run.[85] When we four started to follow the company ten or twelve of the dragoons on their return discovered us, cut off and came charging down upon us. Sergt. Devlin[86] in advance in a very commanding voice called out, "Surrender,

---

83. With arrival of Rains's men, the rebels pushed forward, with Colonel Jesse Cravens leading 150 men into the fight. The move unhinged the Unionists, who retreated a bit to the safety of their artillery and their reserve units. General Rains reported driving the Feds "back in utmost confusion," but such was not the case—as the Union skirmishers did what they were supposed to do when confronted with a superior force; retreat to their main body. Ibid., 3:49–51.

84. The unit was a platoon of Company C, First U.S. Dragoons, commanded by Lieutenant Michael J. Kelly, and numbered about twenty men. Kelly had only been commissioned on May 8, 1861, and this was his first engagement. According to William Wherry, an aid to General Lyon, Kelly's command had been goaded into action to protect the Federal skirmishers who were falling back. A Sergeant Sullivan moved the men forward, against orders, and was quickly led by the impetuous Kelly, who took over from Sullivan. Captain Stanley, commander of Kelly's unit, ordered recall sounded, but Kelly ignored the bugle and made his attack anyway. After the battle Stanley disciplined the young Kelly, but Lyon commended him for the action and further recommended Kelly for promotion. Heitman, 1:590; Banasik, *Missouri In 1861,* 133; William H. Wherry, "General Nathaniel Lyon and His Campaign in Missouri in 1861," *Sketches of War History 1861–1865. Papers Prepared for the Commandery of the State of Ohio, Military Order of the Loyal Legion of the United States* (Cincinnati, 1896; 70 vols., reprint ed, Wilmington, NC, 1991), 4:81–82 (hereafter cited as MOLLUS), hereafter cited as Wherry, "General Nathaniel Lyon."

85. When Kelly made his charge he did so to thwart a Confederate move around the Union left, which was pushing back the Union infantry. Rains in his official report admits that he tried to flank the enemy at this time, but Totten's artillery opened upon Rains's flanking column, "a portion of whom, became panic stricken and retired in the utmost confusion." Steele, for his part, claims that Kelly made his charge after the rebels were routed from the field. Franc Wilkie, Union reporter, supports Rains's account of the incident—either way the results were the same; the rebels were driven from the field in confusion. *O.R.,* 3:49, 51; Banasik, *Missouri In 1861,* 133.

86. According to Franc Wilkie, a Private Devlin was killed, not a Sergeant Devlin. Audley S. H. Boyd, in the letter following, states that Sergeant Devlin did not die, but recovered. Banasik, *Missouri In 1861,* 134.

you cowardly rebels; surrender!" He fell riddled with buckshot within twenty feet of us and in advance of the squad. They halted and business commenced. We had to move around lively to keep from being trampled to death.

They had their pistols drawn and sabers dangling by the wrist. I did not see one of them fire—the work was done very quick, from six to ten feet distant. We fired six shots with shotguns, eleven with pistols and every one of that squad, I believe, was on the ground. I know five were shot dead. Edley Boyd and I alone were left—nothing to sight but

Two Horses Galloping Away

Edley Boyd and I grabbed a saber and pistol and left the scene, meeting the company mounted 200 or 300 yards distant. I ordered Lieut. Reagor to move forward, look after the wounded and secure the arms, my horse being hitched, where we dismounted. He moved forward and dismounted, finding eleven pistols, some sabers, two guns strapped on saddles of wounded horses.[87] Gus Lewis, putting a wounded Dutchman on one of the horses, started to the rear, but left him soon, as he could not travel fast enough. Just before I reached the ground Totten's Battery[88] opened on us and we retreated not in the best order. Moving back about a mile we reformed, threw out advance guard and went into camp that evening; in good order, near headquarters.

One man was missing; never heard of, one almost scalped with saber, and one died from exhaustion. During this fight Gen. Rains on horseback half a mile west of us was firing at long range. His horses were very disorderly and could scarcely be kept in ranks. When the artillery opened on him his command gave way, and being nearer the road than we were; beat us to it. There was no more fighting that evening that I heard.[89] Gen. Lyon moved on down and camped on my old camp ground three or four miles from Gen. McCulloch. Next morning as the advance guard of Gen. McCulloch's army I saw in passing Gen. Lyon's encampment evidences of a very hasty retreat. There were several butchered beeves and

---

87. After Kelly's charge the skirmish abruptly ended. Steele did not follow up the retreating rebels, being ordered by General Lyon to fall back to a new position. The Confederates, for their part, regrouped and continued to monitor the front. Captain McIntosh, who was called upon for support, never arrived, as he "respectfully declined," to support Rains, because Rains had "unadvisedly" engaged the enemy. *O.R.*, 3:50–52.

88. Totten's Battery was Company F, Second U.S. Artillery, commanded by James Totten. The battery consisted of six 6-lb. guns. Banasik, *Missouri In 1861*, 377–378.

89. Losses on both sides at Dug Springs were minor; the Federals reported losing four killed and seven wounded; Rains lost six wounded. However, in Dyer's *Compendium*, Federal losses were reported as 4 killed and 37 wounded. News reporting at the time put the Confederate losses at "twenty-five killed and sixty to one hundred wounded." Additionally, General Frémont, the department commander, reported the Federal losses as 8 killed and 30 wounded while causing the rebels 40 killed and 44 wounded. Since the Federals gave up the field immediately after the battle this last comment seems a bit far-fetched, considering General Rains's report of the affair. Ibid., 134; *O.R.*, 3:47, 50–51; Dyer, 798; Janet Hewett, ed. *Supplement to the Official Records of the Union and Confederate Armies*, 100 vols. (Wilmington, NC, 1994–2001), pt. 1, 226–227, hereafter cited as *O.R.S.*

an unfinished breakfast left. I followed on and had quite a skirmish a mile north of Oak Hills battle ground; afterwards we moved to the old camp ground west of Sharp's house.[90]

A. V. Rieff.

* * * * * * *

Item: Battle of Dug Springs, Missouri, August 1, 1861, by Audley S. H. Boyd, Company C, Third Missouri Cavalry (Confederate). At Dug Springs, Boyd was a member of "Dick" Campbell's Company E, First Cavalry Battalion, Seventh Division, Missouri State Guard.[91] **Published:** November 13, 1886.

Dug Springs.

Hurricane, Crittenden Co., Ky., Oct. 20

Editor, *Republican*

I notice in your issue of September 25 a sketch of the Dug Springs fight by Capt. A. V. Rieff. Edley Boyd is alive and hearty and endorses all he said about this affair. Sergt. Devlin, whom we left for dead with six others, recovered from those wounds. I saw him after in the hospital at Springfield.

Capt. Rieff is the coolest and bravest man I ever saw. He talked to me all the time we were surrounded by the cavalry, urging me to stand firm. One fellow stuck his revolver in my face. I kept him from shooting with my gun, which was empty, till the captain shot him. There has been a great deal said about Gen. Mc-Culloch

Not Having Any Information

in regard to Lyon's forces in and around Springfield. The day after McCulloch's army encamped at Sharp's farm our company (Capt. Dick Campbell's) were encamped on the west side of the farm. Capt. Campbell came up to the quarters and

---

90. Joseph D. Sharp's farm was a prominent feature on the Wilson's Creek Battlefield, comprising a total of 1,272 acres of largely unimproved land. The farm consisted of a large two-story house, a barn and assorted pens; it typically produced corn, wheat and oats with some potatoes, butter, cheese and other lesser items. In 1860 the farm was valued at $11,000. Piston, 152.

91. Audley S. H. Boyd was born in Carrsville, Kentucky, and moved to Springfield, Missouri, in 1840. He was the son of Marcus Boyd, a strong Unionist, and brother to Edley and Poney Boyd. The Boyd family consisted of eight sons and one daughter; the majority of the sons fought for the Confederacy. Just prior to the beginning of the Civil War, Audley returned from California and joined Campbell's Company of "Scouts." Joanne C. Eakin, *Missouri Prisoners of War From Gratiot Prison & Myrtle Street Prison, St. Louis, Mo. and Alton Prison, Alton Illinois Including Citizens, Confederates, Bushwhackers and Guerrillas* (Independence, MO,1995), "Boyd, Audley S. H." entry, hereafter cited as Eakin, *Missouri Prisoners of War*; Wayne Schnetzer, *More Forgotten Men: The Missouri State Guard* (Independence, MO, 2003), 28, hereafter cited as Schnetzer, *More Forgotten Men*; *Pictorial and Genealogical Record of Greene County*, 215; *History of Greene County*, 404.

called Marion Fullbright[92] to one side and told us Gen. McCulloch wanted us to go as spies to Springfield. We went and reported to Gen. McCulloch the next morning the true situation of Lyon's forces about Springfield. He was satisfied with our report and the arrangement was made

To Attack

on the night of the 9th. The army was to move in three divisions to the attack. Marion Fullbright and myself were to pilot one division up Wilson's Creek and it was to attack on the west. Fullbright was at Gen. McCulloch's quarters that night when the march was abandoned and I returned to camp, and Marion Fullbright will say this is true. So will his brother-in-law, Joseph Catheral. My greetings to all surviving members of Campbell's Company, Rieff's of Fayetteville, Ark., and also to Martin E. Green's Brigade,[93] and especially Samuel's Battalion[94] and Gate's First Missouri[95]. Any member of Co. B, Third Cavalry (dismounted) would confer a favor by addressing me at Hurricane, Crittenden County, Ky.

---

92. Marion Fullbright, like Boyd was a member of Campbell's Scouts, though not listed in any book or record on the MSG. *History of Greene County,* 404.

93. Martin E. Green commanded the Second Missouri Brigade and was later killed at Vicksburg, Mississippi, on June 27, 1863. The brigade consisted at various times of the Fourth and Sixth Missouri Infantries, the First and Third Missouri Cavalries (Dismounted) and Guibor's, Jackson's (also known as the 7th Missouri Light), King's (also known as the 2nd Light), Landis's and the St. Louis Batteries (also known as the 3rd Missouri Light). After the fall of Vicksburg, which resulted in the capture of the First and Second Missouri Brigades, the two brigades consolidated into the First Missouri Brigade. *O.R.,* vol. 10, pt. 1:789; *O.R.,* vol. 17, pt. 1:374; Joseph R. Crute, *Units of the Confederate States Army* (Midlothian, VA, 1987), 195, 208–210, hereafter cited as Crute; James E. McGhee, *Missouri Confederates: A Guide to Sources for Confederate Soldiers and Units 1861–1865* (Independence, MO, n.d.), ix; R. S. Bevier, *History of the First and Second Missouri Confederate Brigades. 1861–1865* (St. Louis, 1879), 79, hereafter cited as Bevier.

94. Samuel's Cavalry Battalion (also known as the Third Missouri Cavalry Battalion or the Third Missouri Cavalry Regiment) was formed in early 1862, and sent to the east side of the Mississippi River under the command of Leonidas St. Clair "Dick" Campbell (commander, Company E, First Cavalry Battalion, Seventh Division, MSG—Campbell's Scouts). Campbell resigned on August 12, 1862, and returned to the Trans-Mississippi Department; D. Todd Samuel then became the commander of the battalion. Samuel was severely wounded at the Battle of Peachtree Creek on July 21, 1864, and died in Atlanta on August 30, 1864 (Note: the *O.R.S.* has the date as September 27, 1864). The battalion was consolidated with the First Missouri Cavalry (Gates's), in November 1863, following its capture and subsequent exchange during the Vicksburg Campaign. Peterson, 200; Crute, 197–198; Joanne C. Eakin, *Confederate Records From the United Daughters of the Confederacy Files, Volume Six: Mitchell–Saye* (Independence, MO, 1999), 207, hereafter cited as Eakin *Confederate Records; O.R.S.,* pt. 2, vol. 50:179.

95. Elijah Gates's First Missouri Cavalry was organized on December 30, 1861, at Springfield, Missouri, and the unit was mustered in on January 16, 1862. It initially served in the Trans-Mississippi, being engaged at Elkhorn Tavern, Arkansas (March 6–8, 1862), before being transferred to the east side of the Mississippi River in April 1862. It subsequently fought at Corinth and Iuka, Mississippi, participated in the Vicksburg Campaign, the Atlanta Campaign, the Nashville Campaign and the Siege and Capture of Mobile, Alabama in 1865. The regiment was surrendered with the Department of Alabama, Mississippi and East Louisiana in May 1865. Bevier, 77, 86; *O.R.S.,* pt. 2, vol. 50:114, 116, 118–119, 121, 123, 125–126, 128, 130, 132; Crute, 195–196.

A. S. H. Boyd.
Co. C, Third Cavalry (dismounted), Green's
Brigade, A.W., C.S.A.

* * * * * * *

Item: Incidents of the early actions in Missouri including comments on pillaging by Missourians; the Skirmish at Dug Springs (August 2, 1861); the opinion of General Ben McCulloch on Missouri troops; and sketches of Generals McCulloch and Nathaniel Lyon, by J. F. Snyder, M.D.; Field & Staff, Eighth Division, Missouri State Guard.
Published: August 14, 1886.

The Fight for Missouri

Virginia, Cass Co., Ill., Aug. 4
Editor, *Republican*

The now wrinkled visage of the veteran was illuminated with a broad smile as the fogs of a busy quarter of a century were gently wafted from a memory long in repose, by reading in Col. Musser's admirable paper[96] on "The War in Missouri," (read before the St. Louis Southern Historical and Benevolent Society) this passage in his study of "the idiosyncrasies of the Missouri soldier;" "Courage was his birthright, and personal integrity, always the concomitant of courage, marked his career with few instances of pillage, and no instance of deliberate outrage."

Pretty good, that: A Missouri soldier myself, I gratefully accept—cum grano salis,[97] however—this deserved encomium from the high authority of another Missourian who was there himself. The courage of the Missouri soldier is fully attested by the history of the hundred hard-fought battles; and with pride I add the testimony of my observation and experience that his self-respect and early moral training kept him reasonably honest in the absence of strict military and civil restraints, and, I may add, in the absence, also, of anything worth taking. His integrity would bear supervision, but was perhaps of as high standard as the spirit of the times would permit. I am glad to know that his instances of pillage were few; perhaps his chances were not very numerous. I will always remember the trouble he gave me after the surrender of Col. Mulligan at Lexington,[98] when

---

96. Doctor Snyder was referring to a paper that was subsequently published in the *Southern Bivouac* and was republished in 1993, by Broadfoot Publishing in North Carolina. Richard H. Musser, "The War in Missouri," *Southern Bivouac*, 6 vols. (reprint ed., Wilmington, NC, 1993), 4:678–685, 745–752; 5:43–48, 102–107, hereafter cited as Musser.
97. Cum grano salis—Latin for "with a grain of salt."
98. Lexington was the county seat of Lafayette County, Missouri, and the site of a siege in September 1861. It was located about 300 miles from St. Louis by river. Its population at the beginning of the war was near 5,000 inhabitants, who participated primarily in the hemp growing industry. The city consisted of some manufacturing (hemp) with two colleges. The Masonic College, which embraced some fifteen acres, served as the Federal defensive point during the siege in September 1861. McElroy,

the captured accouterments, cavalry equipments, etc., had been transferred from the entrenchments at the Missouri College to the courthouse, and there placed in my care. I had a strong detail made to guard the valuable property, and fancied that I had it safe; but before the next morning I discovered to my dismay that every man of my squad, through the reliefs, had helped themselves to the choice of arms, saddles, bridles, etc., and in the exuberance of his "commitment of courage," was rapidly passing out the second choice to his friends on the outside. I went immediately to Gen. Price and, explaining the status quo, asked him to have another guard detail to watch those I already, or to at once order the distribution of the goods in my care, otherwise he might soon have nothing to distribute but old shotguns and worn-out saddles, left in exchange by the possessors of the aforesaid "concomitant." The grand old man

Was Sorely Vexed,

and told me to shoot the first man and every man I caught stealing; but, as I had not enlisted for the purpose of killing off our own army, I saved my ammunition, and a pro rata distribution of what was left was soon made.

I recall another instance in those days that well illustrated the common instinct of frail man to "absorb" things when favorable opportunities are presented. On Sunday August 4, 1861, two days after the fight at Dug Springs, our army broke up camp at Cassville and had commenced its forward move on to Springfield. Our division of M.S.G. [Missouri State Guard], the Sixth, under Gen. James S. Rains,[99] was in advance, in high spirits, confident of the speedy vindication of our cause and of soon regaining our left homes. By the road side, near some farm buildings, with its closed doors and window-shutters strongly suggested of hidden booty, was a storehouse belonging to a man named McCulla.[100] As the head of the column sighted this modest mercantile establishment now deserted, the patriots incontinently broke ranks and made a rush for it. The first impetuous assault of our celebrated Blackberry Cavalry carried it, but their success was well nigh barren, as the prudent proprietor had previously removed or otherwise disposed of his stock of staple goods, leaving in the building only a few articles that, in the distracted condition of the country, he had failed to sell and thought no one would want or could make any use of. Gen. Rains and myself happened at the time to be riding leisurely along together in pleasant chat, a little in rear, when we suddenly became aware of an unusual commotion at the front. We knew that Gen. Lyon's army had been in this immediate vicinity only thirty-six hours before. Could it be

---

206–207.

99. Rains commanded the Second Division, MSG at the time between the Battles of Carthage and Wilson's Creek; he never commanded the Sixth Division. *O.R.,* 3:20, 127; Peterson, 172.

100. Alexander McCullah or McCulla owned a local storehouse near a spring that bore his name. The area consisted of the storehouse, a church, McCullah's farm and a post office. The area was located on the Wire or Telegraph road near the county line between Christian and Stone Counties. It was about twenty-four miles from Springfield. Snead, 254; Ingenthron, 78, 317.

possible that the enemy had returned and that we had fallen into an ambuscade. Alert to every exigency of the situation we plied our spurs and were directly in the midst of a scene of wild confusion and disorder. The Missouri soldier had not found the enemy—in fact wasn't looking for him; but the little storehouse, with its doors and windows smashed in, was filled and surrounded by a scrambling mob eager for plunder, as a few of the more murky ones were decamping with such fruits of the raid as they had been able to secure. As we came up we observed one soldier of the legion proudly making off with a bunch of "spun cotton" tied to the pommel of his saddle. Another hero had mounted his horse and was hurrying away with an old side-saddle slung over his shoulder. A third light dragoon dug his heels into the flanks of his charger as he moved off galloping with his left arm and hand a large

Old Fashioned Spinning-Wheel,

while with his right hand held his bridle-reins and his long squirrel rifle. A fourth one had just mounted his horse and was in the act of shouldering a cross-cut saw about seven feet in length, and still another defender of Southern rights was emerging from a window with an old eight-day clock under his arm. The general, grasping the condition of affairs, dashed furiously into the crowd, but for a moment was speechless. Like the traditional teamster who lost the tail-gate out of his wagon as he was going up a steep hill with a load of potatoes, language sufficiently impressive to adequately express his emotion, utterly failed him. Recovering himself presently he unceremoniously uncorked the vials of his wrath and fairly made things lurid with healthy and vigorous Missouri invectives. Quelling under the sting of his mighty words, the raiders, in repentant shame, replaced in the building the useless stuff they had taken, and refastened the doors and shutters. The culprits were ordered to report "under arrest" at the next camp, which they forgot to do, and, after resting awhile, the column was reformed and moved on.

At that date, with the exception of very moderate control exercised by our military officers, the portion of the state in our possession was very nearly in the condition of complete anarchy, and beyond the precincts of the army there was absolutely no semblance of legal authority whatever. Such incidents as I have related were regarded only as matters of jest, dwarfed to insignificance, as the war progressed, by far greater crimes and calamities for which private soldiers were not individually responsible. All of which tends to prove that man, in natural freedom, is not an honest animal. But for the dread of public censure, and all the other restraining influences of civilization—education, law with its correlative fear of punishment have and hereafter, &c.—our ideas of justice and rights of property would perhaps still be gauged, as in the days of the Federal barons by the numbers and strength of our retainers. The curriculum of the Spartan youth's training comprised instruction in the art of stealing—more properly stated—in developing a natural propensity more or less inherent in all races of men.

Human Nature—

especially American human nature—is about the same all around. Courage, honor, integrity and other qualities that constitute true manhood, were not the birthright of the Missouri soldier exclusively, but he could justly lay claim to his share in common with all American soldiers. And, considering the license offered by lax military government and total abrogation of civil law, and the blunting of moral perceptions, resulting from the chaos of war, the Missouri soldier's record will suffer nothing by comparison with that of the soldier from any other state of the Union.

Six miles farther up the Telegraph road we arrived at Dug Springs, and Dug Springs were two or three holes that had been dug by the roadside to retain and economize during the dry, hot season, the water of as many feeble springs that sipped in from the clay and gravel ridges which hemmed in a narrow, parched valley. It was at this place two days before 100 men of our division had a sharp little skirmish with the advance guard of Gen. Lyon's army, resulting to us one man killed, one died of sunstroke and seven wounded. The enemy lost four killed, one mortally and several slightly wounded.[101] We found the ghastly remains of the dead soldiers as the victors had left them, rudely thrown together in trenches so shallow and covered with so little earth that the feet, encased in their travel worn boots and shoes and other parts of their bodies were exposed to the burnings rays of the sun. Completing their burial in the best way we could under the circumstances, we continued our march to Wilson's Creek.

Several widely differing versions of this unimportant skirmish have appeared in the histories of the Missouri campaign, but none of them agree in every particular with the facts as I remember them. (I will here remark if this paper chances to be read by any comrade who was with us in that affair, I will be pleased to hear from him through this department of the *Republican,* and feel grateful to have him verify my recollections of it or correct any mistakes of memory.)

In Greely's *American Conflict*—a book by the by, chiefly noted for its numerous inexcusable blunders and mistakes—we are told (vol. 1, p. 577): "At length (Lyon), hearing that the enemy were advancing in two strong columns, from Cassville on the south and Sarcoxie on the west, to overwhelm him, he resolved to strike at the former before it could unite with the latter. He accordingly left Springfield, August 1, with 5,500 foot, 400 horse and eighteen guns, and early next morning encountered, at Dug Springs, a detachment of the enemy, whom he lured into a fight by pretending to fly, and speedily routed and dispersed. The rebels, under McCulloch, thereupon recoiled, and, moving westward, formed a junction with their weaker column advancing from Sarcoxie to strike Springfield from the west."

---

101. Not true—for losses at Dug Spring see Note 89.

There Was No Encounter

of to two armies proper at Dug Springs, and it is ridiculous to attempt magnifying the brush we had there to the dignity of a battle.

Gen. Price had formed a junction[102] with McCulloch, and the united army was encamped in and about Cassville, the county seat of Berry County, scattered along the main road leading from Arkansas to Springfield for several miles,[103] waiting on the whimsical indecision of Gen. McCulloch. We knew that Gen. Lyon had left Springfield with all of his available force, but we were uncertain as to his destination or intentions.[104] Price had not then yielded the command of his Missouri State Guard to McCulloch, and no plan for effective concert of action had been agreed upon by the two commanders.[105] On Thursday, the 1st of August, our scouts reported the Federal Army moving down the road in our direction,

---

102. Price reached Cassville, Missouri, on July 28, where he joined 650 armed men of General McBride's MSG, who were already in place. On July 29, General McCulloch arrived with his brigade, followed by General Pearce, thus uniting what General McCulloch styled the "Western Army." *O.R.*, 3:98; Piston, 134; Moore, *Missouri, Confederate Military History*, 53; Snead, 246; Joanne C. Eakin, *Missouri State Guard Doctor Leaves a Diary in 1861* (Independence, MO, 1999), 1–2, hereafter cited as Eakin, *Diary.*

103. On the night of August 1, the day prior to the engagement at Dug Springs the rebel forces were deployed as follows:

Advance Force (General James S. Rains)—Dug Springs (Hayden Farm)
First Division (General Ben McCulloch)—Crane Creek, Missouri; about seven miles from the advance.
Second Division (General N. B. Pearce with General Price)—Camp Pearce, twelve miles northwest of Cassville, Missouri at Flat Creek.
Third Division (General Steen)—Cassville, Missouri
Unarmed men of the army—Cassville.

Note: In the *Official Records*, Price states that a General Steel commanded the Third Division—There was no General Steel in the MSG. This was clearly a misprint—it should have been Steen as noted in the *Confederate Military History. O.R.*, 3:50, 98–99; *O.R.*, 53:719; Moore, *Missouri, Confederate Military History*, 54; Piston, 139.

104. The troops received their orders to leave Springfield late on the afternoon of August 1; at 6 p.m. (about sundown) the troops broke camp and marched until about 3:00 a.m. on August 2, when they went into camp on Terrell Creek, about ten miles from Springfield. General Lyon believed that the rebels were advancing on Springfield in three columns and he intended to destroy the largest column before the others could come up to support their threatened comrades. Lyon's forces consisted of 5,868, broken down into four brigades:

First Brigade (Major S. D. Sturgis)—884
Second Brigade (General Franz Sigel)—1,420
Third Brigade (Lieutenant Colonel G. L. Andrews)—1,264
Fourth Brigade (Colonel G. W. Deitzler)—2,300

Banasik, *Missouri In 1861*, 130–131; *O.R.*, 3:47–48; Ware, 270–271.

105. Price would yield command of the Missouri troops to General McCulloch on August 4, 1861. *O.R.*, 53:720.

but McCulloch discredited the report. Gen. Rains was ordered by Gen. Price to ascertain the enemy's movements, and we started the next morning with three mounted companies.[106] We cautiously advanced to a point a little beyond or north of McCulla's store—or Curran, as the county post office there had been called— and had stopped there to get breakfast, when, in the midst of our repast, we were startled by the boom of two six-pounders stationed somewhere in the bushy hills ahead of us. We concluded that this salute was not altogether a matter of military courtesy, but meant business; so Gen. Rains immediately dispatched an orderly to Gen. McCulloch, whose camp on Flat Creek was two miles nearer to us than Gen. Price was,[107] announcing that we had heard from the enemy and asking him to send up reinforcements. The shot of the two six-pounders fell short of us, and, not being further molested, we quietly, though rather nervously, finished our frugal meal and waited for the assistance we expected would be sent to us, when we could proceed and find out just how much of the enemy was before us and ascertain what he wanted. Gen. McCulloch took no pains to conceal his disbelief of Rains's message, but at once ordered Col. [James] McIntosh,[108] with three or four companies of mounted Arkansans, to go, not to re-enforce Gen. Rains, but to reconnoiter and report to him (McCulloch) if there was any truth in Rains's wild communication.[109] We spent several hours

In Looking Around

over the hills, with the exercise of a good deal of that rascally virtue—prudence— until at last McIntosh arrived. He was a good looking young man, about the proportions of Emmett McDonald [MacDonald],[110] only not quite so tall and didn't

---

106. Rains's immediate force consisted of 400 men from six companies of his command. Additionally, Captain Harbin commanded a battalion of three companies and Campbell's Company of scouts. Dr. Snyder belonged to this latter unit. McGhee, *Letter and Order Book,* unnumbered pages 18–19 (entries pages 35–37).
107. On the morning of August 2, McCulloch's command was camped on Crane Creek—not Flat Creek, about seven miles from Rains, and Price was on Flat Creek about ten miles behind McCulloch, with the command's "Second Division." See note 103 above. George B. Davis, et al., *Atlas to Accompany the Official Records of the Union and Confederate Armies* (Washington, DC, 1891–1895), plt. 160, hereafter cited as *Atlas to Accompany the Official Records*; *O.R.,* 3:51, 99.
108. James M. McIntosh was born at Fort Brooke (modern-day Tampa), Florida in 1828, graduated from West Point, last in his class, in 1849. Initially serving in the infantry, McIntosh transferred to the cavalry in 1855. At the beginning of the Civil War, McIntosh was a captain in the First U.S. Cavalry, from which he resigned on May 7, 1861. McIntosh was promoted to brigadier general on January 24, 1862, and commanded a brigade in Ben McCulloch's Division at the Battle of Pea Ridge, Arkansas. He was killed on March 7, 1862. See Michael E. Banasik, *Duty, Honor and Country: The Civil War Experiences of Captain William P. Black, Thirty-seventh Illinois Infantry* (Iowa City, IA, 2006), 447–448 for a complete biography; Boatner, 533; Heitman, 1:669.
109. McIntosh was both a captain of Confederate troops and a colonel of Arkansas troops at the time of Dug Springs and commanded 150 men; probably from the Second Arkansas Mounted Rifles. *O.R.,* 3:51–52; Piston, 140.
110. Colonel Emmett MacDonald was born in 1837, in Steubenville, Ohio, and moved with his parents to St. Louis in the 1850s. A resident of St. Louis at the beginning of the Civil War, MacDonald com-

have as long hair as Emmett had, and was certainly in no respect Emmett's superior, excepting that he was a graduate of West Point and had been a lieutenant in the regular army. He bore himself like [Michel] Ney or [Joachim] Murat[111] and made no attempt to disguise the honest contempt he entertained for "Mr." Rains's ragged and poorly-armed Missourians and their uncouth, ununiformed officers. He didn't seem to see us "rabble" at all as we stood around staring with blank admiration at the beautiful festoons of gilt braid on his neatly-fitting gray uniform, and barely making a few inquiries of "Mr." Rains, he rapidly rode on with his cavalry a mile or two up the road, and after looking around a little with his field glasses, leisurely returned to his camp and reported to Gen. McCulloch that it was only "a scare of those—Missourians."[112]

Gen. Rains was justly indignant at his treatment, and when they again met in the evening he told McIntosh in very plain Missouri vernacular what he thought of it. Among other opinions forcibly expressed he informed McIntosh that he McIntosh: was a "[damned] fool," and that he believed that McCulloch and his fac torum[113], whom he was addressing, were

Afraid to Meet the Yankees.

Determined to satisfy himself as to what rifled or smooth-bored obstructions might be in the way of our peaceable journey homeward, Gen. Rains struck out up the Telegraph road and we slowly and very watchfully proceeded to Dug Springs. It was a very hot, sultry afternoon, the air in the narrow, pent-up valley was as stifling as a furnace blast, and the fierce glare of the sun was, to man and beast, almost intolerable. We halted at the springs and had just commenced a rush on the little reserving of hot, muddy water, when we were again startled by the thrilling roar of Totten's guns and the rattling of grapeshot; and at the same time a com-

---

manded a squadron of cavalry during the Camp Jackson affair. After his capture, MacDonald refused parole and subsequently obtained his unconditional release. Illinois judge, Samuel Treat, ruled that MacDonald could not be a prisoner of war since he was legally assembled at Camp Jackson. Next, MacDonald joined Brigadier General James S. Rains's MSG unit, participating in the Siege of Lexington, the Battle of Pea Ridge and numerous skirmishes in northwest Arkansas and southwest Missouri. By the Battle of Prairie Grove (December 7, 1862), MacDonald had risen to the rank of colonel, commanded a brigade of cavalry and had been appointed Provost Marshal General of Missouri. At Hartville, Missouri (January 11, 1863), MacDonald received a fatal wound and died a short time later. *O.R.*, 3:25, 186, 189; *O.R.*, 8:310, 319, 324; *O.R.*, vol. 22, pt. 1:208–210; Special Order No. 45 (August 5, 1862), Special Orders Letter Book (June 1–Dec. 18, 1862), Hindman's command, Peter W. Alexander Collection, Columbia University, hereafter cited as Special Orders Book No. 1; Winter, 119.

111. Michel Ney and Joachim Murat were cavalry officers who served in Napoleon's army. Ney was most famous for taking command of the French Army at Waterloo after Napoleon became incapacitated for a time. Murat, like Ney was a French Marshal and served as the King of Naples from 1808–1815. David B. Guralnik, *Webster's New World Dictionary*, 936, 959, hereafter cited as Guralnik.

112. Neither McCulloch or McIntosh had any respect for Rains or his Missouri troops; McIntosh refused to support Rains at Dug Springs, leaving the Missourians to fend for themselves; while McCulloch condemned Rains and his troops in front of the rest of his command. The affair at Dug Springs became known as "Rains's Scare." Piston, 140–142.

113. Fac torum—Latin for handymen. Guralnik, 501.

pany of blue-coated United States dragoons and a lot of infantry,[114] in the same colored clothes, have in sight a few hundred yards ahead. We had been ordered by Gen. Price not to fight, but to "feel of the enemy." What the enemy's orders were[115] I have never ascertained, but he lost no time in feeling for us, with canister and minnie ball, in a very uncivil and, to us, uncomfortable way. Some of us left precipitately, just then remembering we had urgent business at camp, but the majority of us deployed to the right and

Made A Stand

on the ridge, east of the road, under the cover of the dense growth of blackjacks that crowned the hills, and as we stuck to our position, blazing away as fast as we could load, until driven out by the regulars, on foot. The brush was so thick on the hill that the opposing line were almost in contact before we could distinctly see each other, and so closely were we engaged that one of our men, at the edge of the thicket, received a severe scalp wound from a saber wielded by a dragoon in blue, who in turn was gently persuaded by a load of buckshot to desist from such rude sport. The booming of cannon and the whizzing of grapeshot among the craggy branches of blackjacks, neither hurt nor alarmed us, but when that confounded infantry in blue persisted in crowding on through the undergrowth with the evident intent to do us great bodily harm, and came so unpleasantly close that we could look down in the muzzles of their muskets and plainly see prospective funerals in them, we concluded that, as it was pretty nearly supper time anyway, we had better get back to camp. And we got. The skirmish lasted less than an hour, but was strong and hot in every sense while it did last.[116]

Gen. McCulloch and McIntosh received our account of this affair with derision and pronounced it another of Rains's scares. They could not yet believe that any considerable part of Lyon's army was so near us, and only became convinced of the fact when, the next morning, they received, through a source they could no longer doubt, information that the entire Union Army had reached Curran, only six miles from their guard lines.[117]

114. The cavalry belonged to Captain D. S. Stanley's Company C, First U.S. Cavalry, commanded by Lieutenant Michael J. Kelly, while the infantry was Captain Steele's battalion of the Second U.S. Infantry. Banasik, *Missouri In 1861*, 133.

115. The Union advance was commanded by Captain Frederick Steele, who was to seek out the enemy. After the rebels were found near Dug Springs, Lyon halted his command for the day and left Steele to screen his front. Steele was not expected to bring on a general engagement, but to warn of any rebel advances. Following the confused action of August 2, Lyon pulled back his advance, not caring to press the situation as his infantry column was in no condition to fight an extended battle. *O.R.*, 3:47, 49–50.

116. The skirmish at Dug Springs began at 9:00 a.m. by most accounts and ended about 6:00 p.m., sunset. Ibid., 3:49; Ware, 276.

117. General Rains's performance at Dug Springs did little for his reputation or that of the Missouri troops. The term "Rains's Scare" was first associated with Dug Springs and later used with the opening of the Battle of Wilson's Creek on August 10, 1861. McCulloch doubted the abilities of the Missouri troops, and further that Rains had exaggerated the presence of Lyon's entire army at both Dug Springs

Says Col. Snead in his accurate and remarkably well-written history of the *Fight for Missouri,* page 254: "The loss on either side was trifling in this skirmish at Dug Springs, but the conduct of Rains's command on this occasion caused McCulloch and McIntosh to lose all confidence in the Missouri troops and laid the foundation for that distrust and ill-felling which eventually separated the combined armies and frustrated all their hopes." In this statement Col. Snead correctly represents the feelings and opinions of the distinguished Confederate commanders.[118]

The Contempt

entertained for Price's "rabble," particularly by Col. McIntosh, who had been trained in the rigid regulations of the national military school, was a matter of familiar knowledge to us all at the time.[119] But, inasmuch the Arkansas troops with us were about as much of a mob as we—in point of discipline[120]—and we knew that Gen. Price was a far better general than McCulloch and McIntosh together, the views of the latter concerning us or our officers caused no diminution of appreciation, or loss of sleep or confidence, in our ranks. If they would only help us fight our way back to Missouri River, they were welcome to hold and enjoy

---

and Wilson's Creek. Moore, *Missouri, Confederate Military History,* 56; Piston, 201.

118. Neither McCulloch or McIntosh had any respect for the Missouri troops, even after they vindicated themselves at the Battle of Wilson's Creek on August 10, 1861. On November 8, 1861, McCulloch wrote the Confederate Secretary of the War that the Missouri troops were "under the control of politicians, who know not the value of discipline, and consequently can never make an army that would be but little better than a city mob." McCulloch further believed that someone, other than a Missourian should command Missouri troops, even suggesting General Braxton Bragg for the command. *O.R.,* 3:733–734.

119. Immediately following the engagement at Dug Springs both McCulloch and McIntosh were heard lambasting the Missouri troops. McCulloch for his part was seen dashing up the road among the routing Missourians "fairly foaming with rage, exhausting his whole vocabulary of vituperation (no meager one) in denunciation of Rains's Missouri Cavalry." McIntosh was rumored to have been killed but, reappeared "'Cussin the Missourians.'" W. H. Tunnard, *A Southern History. The History of the Third Regiment Louisiana Infantry* (Baton Rouge, 1866), 65, hereafter cited as Tunnard.

120. True—Arkansas had seceded from the Union on May 6, 1861, and promptly began organizing troops to serve for a one year period of time. In the western part of the state, Fort Smith, on the Arkansas River, was set as the rendezvous point for the Arkansas troops. N. Bart Pearce was commissioned a brigadier general and assigned to command the Arkansas troops at Fort Smith, where he arrived on May 16, 1861. By early June 1861, Pearce had moved his 900-man command to Maysville in the northwest corner of Arkansas to what was dubbed "Camp Walker." General McCulloch, who was now in command of the Arkansas, Texas and Louisiana troops in northwest Arkansas, subsequently issued a call for more Arkansas troops to assemble at Fayetteville, Arkansas, about twenty miles from Pearce's position—this latter group comprised Dandridge McRae's Arkansas Battalion. By the engagement of Dug Springs, the Arkansas state troops under Pearce numbered about 2,500 men and were no better trained than the Missourians. Pearce would ultimately release his troops at the end of August 1861, and allow them to return to their homes. *O.R.,* 3:583, 622, 694–695; *Confederate Military History,* vol. 10: *Arkansas,* by John M. Harrell, 15, hereafter cited as Harrell, *Arkansas, Confederate Military History;* Edwin C. Bearss, "Fort Smith Serves General McCulloch As A Supply Depot," *Arkansas Historical Quarterly* 24 (Winter, 1965): 319, 322, 325, 329, hereafter cited as Bearss, "Fort Smith."

any opinion of us they chose, and we would submit to the sneers and still heartily render them the meed of our praise and sincere gratitude.

In the intense and comprehensive book written by my fried, Col. Thos. L. Snead, to which I have referred, the most cautious critic will find, either in diction or facts, but little to correct or carp at. But errors will creep into any written history; some can be absolutely perfect. A few lines above the extract I have quoted, the colonel says: "Hardly had we left, however, when Steele attacked Rains vigorously, opening upon him with two of Totten's guns, and put the Missourians to flight with the utmost confusion." In justice to Col. Snead and the aforesaid Missourians, that the statement does not accord altogether with the facts. That—as I have said—some of us left "in the utmost confusion" at the first sound of Totten's guns, it is true; but the result of the fray—four of the enemy killed and several wounded—prove conclusively (or, rather corroborates my testimony), that some of us remained and faced the music like men.

I failed to see at the time, nor can I now after the lapse of a quarter of a century comprehend how or why our conduct at this skirmish could or should have shaken the confidence of McCulloch in the courage or reliability of the Missouri troops. Gen. Rains had but a scouting party, and was twelve miles from the main army, with but little ammunition, and positive orders from Gen. Price not to engage the enemy; and was, as he believed, and subsequently proved to be true, facing Gen. Lyon's entire force. But few of our men ran away at the start. With the loss of two dead and seven wounded, and inflicting upon our antagonists double our own loss, we were forced from the field by superior numbers—and retired. When we saw that we could not stay we left the field, perhaps not in the best order—I admit right smart of confusion then—but at that time war was a new business to us, and we were not in the habit of executing many military maneuvers—especially retreats—in first-class West Point style. With hostile muskets almost punching us in the ribs and 5,000 or 6,000 more of them hurrying up and trying to get at us we had no time to consult Hardee's tactics[121] to learn

The Regulation Method

of taking leave of such company, but left of a sudden. The conduct of our Missourians two days later, in sacking McCulla's store, was indeed reprehensible and may have been calculated to disgust and weaken the confidence of the West Pointer, but there was surely nothing reprehensible in what we did at Dug springs. Everyone of our men would have cheerfully returned to renew the fight that night if Gen. Price had consented for them to do so, and all were eager to push and meet the Federal on a fair field.

That same night of the 2nd, Gen. Lyon advanced to Curran, or McCulla's

---

121. The writer was referring to Confederate General William J. Hardee, who wrote a book entitled *Rifle and Infantry Tactics* in 1861. The book was a standard guide, for both the North and South, on how to fight and organize for combat.

store. It can only now be conjectured what the result might have been if the plucky little Yankee had pushed right on and attacked us before daylight next morning.[122] A concentrated assault of his 6,000 well-armed and well disciplined soldiers upon our scattered and unprepared mob would have undoubtedly created consternation and more or less stampeding. By many, his failure to then and there pounce upon us is regarded as the great mistake of his life. Be that as it may, on the next morning, Saturday, 3rd, he commenced a retrograde movement and reached his old camp at Springfield on Monday, 5th.[123]

On Sunday, the 4th, Gen. Price formally conceded the command of the Missourians to Gen. McCulloch, and before daylight the next morning the combined army, with Gen. Rains's division in advance, had commenced its march to Springfield.[124]

At this distance of time from these anxious and trying days, it seems incomprehensible why our generals were so deficient in means of securing correct information regarding what was taking place beyond our lines. We were constantly groping in the dark while our adversaries were well posed in every detail of our affairs, excepting our plans—for of these we had none. As an illustration of this, Col. Snead says, page 258: "Believing that Lyon was still at McCulla's farm, McCulloch marched at midnight (Sunday), expecting to surprise and attack him at daybreak. He was already some distance on the way when he learned that Lyon had left twenty-four (really thirty-six) hours previously and was retreating to Springfield." It was with difficulty that McCulloch was finally convinced that Lyon had approached to within six miles of him, and by the time that he did find this out and got ready to give him battle the vigilant Federal general was almost back at his base. There is no room to doubt that had Lyon made no stop at Curran, but pushed on southward, he would have astonished McCulloch, about dawn on Saturday morning, fully as much as he did on the next Saturday at a little later hour.

The Union Army arrived in Springfield on Monday, and we reached Wilson's Creek, ten miles from that place, on Tuesday;[125] and, not knowing what else to

---

122. Following the engagement at Dug Springs, Lyon advanced to McCulla's or McCullah's store, halted, and reevaluated his situation. From reports that he received, Lyon believed that the rebels were flanking his position with a view to take Springfield via another road. With his command on scanty rations, Lyon deemed it "impractical to advance" and retreated to Springfield. *O.R.*, 3:47.

123. Lyon began withdrawing to Springfield on the morning of August 4, and arrived at the city near sundown on August 5. Ware, 286, 293; Banasik, *Missouri In 1861*, 138.

124. Following the affair at Dug Springs, McCulloch concentrated his forces at Crane Creek. During the day of August 4, McCulloch expected an attack but none ever came. Meanwhile, McCulloch decided to make a night march and attack Lyon at dawn on August 5. In accordance with orders, and with "general satisfaction," the army marched at midnight August 4, with the Third Louisiana Infantry leading the advance. (As the advance element the Third Louisiana left camp at 11:00 p.m.). *O.R.*, 53:720–721; Tunnard, 47; Eakin, *Diary*, 4–5.

125. On August 6, the Confederate Army broke camp at Big or Moody Springs, about twelve miles from Springfield, and marched a short mile or two where they arrived at their Wilson's Creek camp. *O.R.*, 3:99; Eakin, *Diary*, 5; Tunnard, 49.

do,

Stopped There.

While in camp in this funnel-shaped creek valley during the next four days, again quoting Col. Snead, p. 261, "McCulloch would every day sling his Maynard rifle[126] across his shoulder and reconnoiter towards Springfield, sometimes in force, and sometimes almost alone. But as adventurous, daring and skillful as he was, he could learn nothing positive as to either Lyon's strength, or as to the defenses of Springfield. He could not even ascertain whether Lyon had fortified his position at all, or not. To all the entreaties of Price and the Missourians that he would advance, he only replied that he 'would not make a blind attack upon Springfield;' and, blaming them for his want of success in reconnoitering, told them at last that he would order the whole army back to Cassville rather than bring on an engagement with an unknown enemy.'" On our own ground, where many of us were familiar with every hog-path, and acquainted with the majority of citizens, not a word could we hear of what was transpiring in or about the enemy's camp, only ten miles away.[127] No expedient or stratagem of ours could circumvent Lyon's excessive precautions. Mr. R. I. Holcombe remarks in his *Account of the Battle of Wilson's Creek*, 1883, p. 13: "A vigilant guard was at once set upon all roads and avenues of approach to Springfield. No one was allowed to go out except physicians, although everybody was admitted. Never, perhaps, in the history

---

126. The Maynard Carbine, not rifle, was invented by a Doctor Edward Maynard, a dentist from Maryland, in 1851. The breech loader employed a cap firing system similar to the modern day cap-gun, that allowed the user to rapidly cap his weapon and fire. The Maynard also had interchangeable barrels, though "few long barreled Maynards of military form suitable to be called 'rifles' are known." In the Confederate Army, the Maynard came in two basic calibers—.50 or .35—with a twenty inch barrel. At the beginning of the war, the weapon had a primer magazine attached to the right side of the carbine. In all likelihood this would have been the weapon that McCulloch had at the time, since the model without the primer magazine attached did not come out until after the war began. William B. Edwards, *Civil War Guns: The Complete Story of Federal and Confederate Small Arms: Design, Manufacture, Identification, Issue, Employment, Effectiveness, and Postwar Disposal* (Secaucus, NJ, 1962), 16–17, 101–103, hereafter cited as Edwards, *Civil War Guns*; Jeffrey Patrick, "Remembering the Missouri Campaign of 1861: The Memoirs of Lieutenant William P. Barlow, Guibor's Battery, MSG," *Civil War Regiments: A Journal of the American Civil War* 5, no. 4, (1997): 35, hereafter cited as Patrick, "Remembering the Missouri Campaign."

127. According to Richard H. Musser, a member of J. B. Clark's, Sr. staff at Wilson's Creek, Snyder's statement was not correct. Musser wrote:

> General Price had accurate information from many and reliable sources of the condition of Lyon's forces at Springfield. The means of this accurate information was astonishing. He had daily communications, in one shape or other, with the enemy's camp. Ladies visiting camp brought letters in cipher or verbally; newspapers, and the almost daily arrival from all parts of the State of recruits and visitors, made the situation known to him. The knowledge of Frémont being in command and of the disposition of General Lyon, the expiration of the term of service of his troops...

Musser, 682.

of war was a camp so well guarded, and all knowledge of its character kept so well from the enemy as was Gen. Lyon's at Springfield."

On the other hand, our camp daily swarmed with Federal spies, who came in every guise. Old, innocent-looking farmers hunting stray or stolen stock, or proposing to sell us supplies of all kinds; hucksters, peddling milk, fruits and vegetables; recruits loudly reciting their wondrous experiences and dangers in escaping to our lines, and even the ladies from town visiting old friends among us, vociferous in their touching professions of sympathy and unbounded expressions of good will and wishes for our success. They were all surprisingly ignorant of what was going on in Lyon's camp; but told us many widely conflicting stories, and, of course, with little basis of truth in them. So well did these aiders and abetters of the Union cause do their work that, as its fruit there was found, after the battle, on the 10th, in Gen. Lyon's haversacks, among other papers, a well-drawn plan of our encampment and its topography and roads, with the position and strength of each division and several of the separate regiments, noted down with great approximate accuracy. When, on Friday evening, the 9th, the long-expected and much wished-for general order was issued for us to be in readiness to start at dark to surprise and take Springfield, there was not a man among us, from the commanding general down to the drummer, who knew whether or not the place was fortified, or who had the slightest idea of where Gen. Lyon was, or could guess within 5,000 of the actual number of his effective force.

The Two Generals

commanding the opposing armies at the Battle of Wilson's Creek had both seen active military service before. Lyon had been initiated by several years' rough usage in conflicts with the Seminoles, mosquitoes and malaria of the Florida Everglades; and for credible conduct to Gen. Scott's campaign from the coast to the City of Mexico, he was promoted from a second to first lieutenancy, and subsequently to the rank of captain. From the close of the Mexican War to the commencement of our civil troubles he had never been heard of outside of the circles and literature of the Regular Army. McCulloch had taken an active part in the struggle of Texas to gain and maintain her independence, and under Gen. Taylor in our war with Mexico had achieved wide renown for reckless daring, and his name and story of his exploits were familiar in every household throughout the land. When they both met at Wilson's Creek they were both in the full, vigorous prime of life. Lyon, a native on Connecticut; was 43 years of age. McCulloch, born in Tennessee, was 47. Both were members of the Democratic Party. Lyon was a thoroughly educated man, having graduated at West Point in 1841, ranking eleventh in his class of fifty members; and he had devoted his life to the profession of arms. McCulloch's education was limited. He had migrated from his home in Tennessee when a mere boy to the turbulent colony of Texas, where, unhampered by school or conventionalities of cultured society, his buoyant nature found free scope for development. Peace having been declared with Mexico he laid aside his arms and engaged in business, chiefly politics, and served as United States marshal, sheriff of Sacramento, Cal., and United States Commissioner for Utah. Both were impulsive, nervous and rash, but years of experience in the conflicts of life had given to each perfect control of his impetuous nature. Both were brave, and, by their utter contempt of danger, both met death[128] as true soldiers, at the head of their men, in the thickest of the fight, urging them on in the desperation of impending defeat.

The career of both generals in the Civil War was brief, but sufficiently long to fully disclose the ability and weakness of each as a military leader. When Sumter was fired on but few had heard of Nathaniel Lyon or knew of his existence; but all knew of the gallant Gen. McCulloch, and his name alone was weighty as a well-equipped regiment, and his presence among us inspired confidence and enthusiasm.[129]

In all the great mass of literature concerning the Civil War that has poured, and is pouring, upon the public in steadily increasing quantity, there cannot be a more perfect and life-like portrait of any individual actor in it—drawn by words alone—than the description of Gen. Lyon presented to us by Col. Snead, in *The Fight For Missouri*. Every characteristic of the man has been faithfully and impartially delineated, no feature has been exaggerated, no fault extenuated. He stands before us in the pages of that masterly little book, a born soldier, sternly loyal to his convictions, inflexible in purpose, determined, firm to obstinacy, undaunted by insuperable obstacles, with keen penetration and unlimited self-reliance—a military genius, full of promise and possibilities of future greatness. Though an enemy of unrelenting rancor, his splendid courage, eagerness, ability and valor, that self-lifted him out of obscurity to high distinction, compel the homage of our sincere respect and admiration.

The mortifying failure of McCulloch in generalship is treated by Col. Snead with courageous frankness. In charitable kindness he evades the discussion of its real cause at the same time giving to the distinguished Texan full and candid credit for all of the many sound and brilliant qualities that he possessed. For the dilatory, vacillating and apparently pusillanimous conduct of his campaign in Missouri our author apologizes by every plausible explanation, and is magnanimously mild in his criticism. The chief reason of the general's hesitancy and seeming timidity, Col. Snead states, as before quoted, was his loss of confidence in the Missouri troops, and he says further (pp. 255-6): "While the two armies lay facing each

---

128. Lyon died on August 10, 1861 at the Battle of Wilson's Creek, while McCulloch died at Pea Ridge Arkansas on March 7, 1862. Boatner, 498, 530.

129. By the beginning of the Civil War, Ben McCulloch was a folk hero throughout the United States, largely for his exploits during the Mexican War. Following the war with Mexico, Samuel Reed wrote a popular book on Zachary Taylor's campaign in northern Mexico and southern Texas entitled *The Scouting Expeditions of McCulloch's Texas Rangers*. The book launched "McCulloch's name into national prominence." Thomas W. Carter, "Ben McCulloch," *Confederate General*, 6 vols. (Harrisburg, PA, 1991), 1:117–118.

other (at Curran), Gen. Price begged McCulloch to attack, but McCulloch, who had now made up his mind not to co-operate with the Missourians any longer unless Price would

Yield to Him the Command

of the combined armies refused to advance any further, alleging as an excuse that the Confederate Government had declined to give him leave to move into Missouri except for the defense of the Indian Territory; and that to advance further into the state might endanger the safety of that territory and subject himself to the censure of his government. While this was a very good excuse it was not McCulloch's main reason for refusing to attack Lyon. He had in truth no confidence in the Missouri troops and none in Gen. Price or in any of his officers except Col. [Richard H.] Weightman.[130] Rains he had disliked from the beginning, and now he was embittered against him by an open quarrel which had taken place between him and McIntosh for whose opinions and soldiery accomplishments McCulloch had a veneration, which made him distrustful of his own capacity and which often hampered his own action."

In this passage Col. Snead suggests the real cause of McCulloch's failure; he distrusted the Missourians. Conscious incapacity was the secret of his inaction. His fame was not based on acts of generalship. He had won distinction as a dashing bush-ranger and scout and for victories gained in fights with the squalid mongrels of Mexico. In our civil conflict his fame might have been preserved and made more lustrous had he been placed in the independent command of a regiment or two of cavalry, untrammeled by too much accountability to superiors. In such a position he would have felt at ease and would have exercised all his peculiar powers. But made brigadier and given command of an army comprising the different arms of the service, hampered with all the exactness and restraints of army regulations and caprices of the Richmond war office, the man was confused and lost. His

---

130. Richard Hanson Weightman was born in the District of Columbia (Peterson has it as Maryland and Bartels says it was Virginia) in 1818, attended West Point from July 1, 1835 to April 28, 1837, at which time he was expelled for knifing a fellow student in the face. Moving to Missouri, Weightman commanded the St. Louis Artillery Battalion during the Mexican War and was honorably discharged in May 1848. He later moved to the New Mexico Territory where he edited a local newspaper, and served as the Representative to the U.S. Congress for the New Mexico Territory. Sometime thereafter, Weightman returned to Missouri and took up residence in the vicinity of Independence. At the beginning of the Civil War he joined the MSG, being elected colonel of the First Cavalry Regiment, Eighth Division, MSG, on June 11, 1861. Weightman, who had a reputation "'of a gallant, high-spirited daredevil such as one rarely encounters in life,'" was elevated to brigade command on June 30, following the death Edmund Holloway, who was killed by friendly fire at Rock Creek, Missouri. At Wilson's Creek, near the end of the battle, Weightman received a fatal wound. As "he lay dying…he asked those around him" what the shouts of exultation meant. "'We have whipped them—they have gone,' he was told. 'Thank God,' he said. In another moment he was dead." See Chapter 2, "The Battle of Oak Hills," John F. Snyder letter (October 10, 1885) for more on Colonel Weightman. Heitman, 1:1014; Bartels, *Forgotten Men*, 384; Peterson, 14–15, 212, 244; Moore, *Missouri, Confederate Military History*, 60–61; Bartels, *Trans-Mississippi Men*, 159.

abilities were not suited to such restrictions or to the field of action. His energies were crippled and his usefulness destroyed. His friend, Col. McIntosh, who had been sent from Richmond to oversee and instruct him, was an educated soldier, who had resigned his office as lieutenant in the old United States Army, and was presumed to know a great deal of the art of war, or, perhaps its science. Of this science, as a science, McCulloch was profoundly ignorant, consequently he relied upon McIntosh implicitly, and sacrificed to his distastes his own

Common-Sense and Judgement.

In state legislature as well as in our national congress it sometimes happens that a member knowing nothing of parliamentary law or usages is selected as speaker to preside over the deliberators of the house, and by tact and prompt-ings of a shrewd page acquits himself well in the discharge of his duties and succeeds in concealing his ignorance. In statesmanship this sort of charlatanism can sometimes be sustained, but in war its exposure is inevitable and its failure canot be retrieved by any amount of personal bravery. Gen. McCulloch occupied a similarly false position. He was eminently the right man in the wrong place. The prestige of his accomplishments in and before the Mexican War had secured for him a command which in no manner adapted. Pride and ambition impelled him to attempt the discharge of his new and intricate duties by relying altogether on the promptings of Col. McIntosh, and he failed.

Let us suppose, in this Missouri campaign the conditions to have been re-versed, with Lyon in place of McCulloch, is there any who can believe that the fiery little Yankee general would have hesitated an hour on account of distrust of Missouri troops, or allowed any considerations of Richmond red tape to deter his progress toward Springfield on the Missouri River? Is there any reason to doubt the course that Col. John S. Bowen or Cols. [Louis] Hébert, [Thomas J.] Churchill or [Elkanah B.] Greer[131] would have pursued had any of them been

---

131. Louis Hébert was born on March 13, 1820, in Iberville Parish, Louisiana. He graduated from Jefferson College, St. James Parish, and entered West Point in June 1841. Graduating number three in the Class of 1845, Hébert was appointed a second lieutenant of engineers. Prior to the Civil War, he was elected to the Louisiana State Senate, served as the Chief Engineer of Louisiana and held a commission as colonel in the Louisiana Militia. Hébert organized the Third Louisiana Infantry in May 1861, fought at Wilson's Creek and Pea Ridge, where he was captured. Exchanged, Hébert fought at Corinth and Iuka, Mississippi, and was again captured at the fall of Vicksburg in July 1863. After be-ing again exchanged, Hébert completed his war service as a brigadier general in charge of the heavy artillery at Fort Fisher, North Carolina. He returned home after the war, where he edited a newspaper and taught school. See Appendix B for a complete biography. Tunnard, 27–29; Warner, *Generals in Gray,* 130–131.

Thomas J. Churchill was born on March 10, 1824, near Louisville, Kentucky, educated at St. Mary's College and studied law at Transylvania College. He served in the Mexican War as a lieutenant of mounted rifles in Marshall's Kentucky Regiment, was captured, but exchanged during the latter part of the war. Moving to Little Rock, Arkansas, in 1848, Churchill married and became a local plantation owner. In 1859–1860, Churchill organized a militia cavalry company, armed with lances and sabers. At the beginning of the Civil War he organized the First Arkansas Mounted Rifles and fought at Wil-

substituted for McCulloch?

De mortuis nil, etc.[132] Ben McCulloch was not much of a general, but a superb fighter. In Texas and Mexico; at Wilson's Creek and Pea Ridge he displayed the mettle of a true soldier. His dauntless courage and wonderful self-possession in the presence of danger were unsurpassed; his honor and integrity were spotless. His devotion to duty, intense loyalty to state, to friends, to the cause he considered right; the purity of his private life, his generous benevolence and genial kindness, his patriotic service and heroic death have enshrined his memory in the hearts of our people and made his name illustrious in history.

J. F. Snyder, M.D.

* * * * * * *

---

son's Creek and Pea Ridge. Transferring to the east side of the Mississippi River as a brigadier general, Churchill served under Kirby Smith in Kentucky. In the latter part of 1862, Churchill was given command of Arkansas Post, which he surrendered in January 1863. After his exchange, Churchill commanded a division and a corps in the Trans-Mississippi Department, participating in the Red River and Camden Campaigns. He was promoted to major general on March 18, 1865. After the war, Churchill returned to Arkansas where he was elected governor in 1880. He died on May 14, 1905. Warner, *Generals in Gray*, 49–50; Harrell, *Arkansas, Confederate Military History*, 395–396; Stewart Sifakis, *Who Was Who in the Civil War*, 2 vols. (New York, 1988), vol. 2: *Who Was Who in the Confederacy: A Comprehensive, Illustrated Biographical Reference to More Than 1,000 of the Principal Confederacy Participants in the Civil War*, 53, hereafter cited as Sifakis, *Confederacy*; W. E. Woodruff, *With the Light Guns in '61–'65: Reminiscences of Eleven Arkansas, Missouri and Texas Light Batteries, in the Civil War* (Little Rock, AR, 1903), 7, hereafter cited as Woodruff.

Elkanah B. Greer was born on October 11, 1825, at Paris, Tennessee. He moved to Mississippi and volunteered as a member of the First Mississippi Rifles in the Mexican War. In 1848 he moved to Marshall, Texas, where he became a planter. At the beginning of the Civil War he was elected colonel of the South Kansas and Texas Regiment (also known as the Third Texas Cavalry). Greer led his command at Wilson's Creek and Pea Ridge, and was promoted to brigadier general on October 8, 1862. The Governor of Texas considered Greer "a gentleman worthy of the highest confidence." At war's end Greer was the Chief of the Conscription Bureau of the Trans-Mississippi Department, a post he had held since his promotion to general officer. He died at DuVall's Bluff, Arkansas on March 25, 1877, while visiting a sister, and was later buried in Memphis, Tennessee. Warner, *Generals in Gray*, 118; *Confederate Military History*, vol. 11: *Texas*, by Oran M. Roberts, 233, hereafter cited as Roberts, *Texas, Confederate Military History*.

132. Demortuis nil nisi bonum—Latin; of the dead say nothing but good. Guralnik, 376.

Item: The march to Wilson's Creek; Confederate uniforms; and a description of the Wilson's Creek area, by Capt. Thomas H. Bacon,[133] late private, Captain William F. Carter's Company B, Colonel John Q. Burbridge's Regiment, Third Division, Missouri State Guard. **Published:** August 21 1886.

Introduction

The *Republican* today begins the publication of a series of papers on the Oak Hill Campaign read before the Southern Historical Society by Thos. H. Bacon, late captain artillery for Ord. P.A.C.S.A. Capt. Bacon writes of the Confederate movements as the "Campaign of the Three Standards," and in this paper gives only reminiscences of service as a private in Capt. [William F.] Carter's Company[134] of Col. [John Q.] Burbridge's Regiment[135] of Gen. [John B.] Clark's Division, M.S.G.[136] in August 1861. The references in the sketch are to United States

---

133. Thomas Bacon was born on July 10, 1839, in Palmyra, Missouri. As a Democrat, he voted for Stephen Douglas in the 1860 Presidential Election and supported Governor C. F. Jackson. He enlisted in Company B, First Infantry Regiment, Third Division, MSG on July 12, 1861, at Cowskin Prairie in southwest Missouri. At the Battle of Wilson's Creek he was wounded in the groin and departed the Guard when his enlistment ran out. Bacon reenlisted in the Confederate service on April 10, 1863, and was elected a lieutenant in Company D, Pindall's Sharpshooter Battalion on June 6, 1863. He transferred to the artillery in February 1864, and in October was made a captain of artillery. After the war he returned to Missouri, studied law and married in 1876. Bacon was the judge of the Missouri Sixteenth Circuit (1886–1892) and died at Hannibal, Missouri, on September 1, 1908. Bartels, *Forgotten Men,* 9; Eakin, *Confederate Records, Volume 1, A to B,* 42–43; Mudd, "What I Saw At Wilson's Creek," 100.

134. Carter's Company was organized on July 3, 1861, at Spring Creek, Missouri, with John Q. Burbridge elected as captain and William F. Carter third lieutenant. Burbridge was subsequently elected colonel of the regiment, leaving a vacancy for captain. When the company reached Cowskin Prairie on July 9, they elected William F. Carter the captain of Company B (also known as the Jackson Guards), First Infantry Regiment, Third Division, MSG. Carter's new command considered him "a master of tactics and discipline," and were happy to have him as their commander. Following Wilson's Creek, Carter joined the Second Missouri Infantry as captain of Company F on January 12, 1862. Carter would later become a major in the Second Missouri Infantry. He was killed at the Battle of Franklin, Tennessee, on November 30, 1864. *O.R.S.,* pt. 2, vol. 50:427; Peterson, 115; Mudd, "What I Saw At Wilson's Creek," 92.

135. John Q. Burbridge commanded the First Infantry Regiment, Third Division, MSG. He was born about 1830 and lived in Louisiana, Missouri, at the beginning of the Civil War. During the course of the war, he led troops in the MSG and commanded regular Confederate troops, serving mostly in the Trans-Mississippi. One old veteran described Burbridge as "a man of less than medium height, very erect and graceful...[and] made a notable appearance on the" battlefield. After the war he moved to Alabama. For his complete military service record see Michael E. Banasik, *Serving With Honor: The Diary of Captain Eathan Allen Pinnell of the Eighth Missouri Infantry (Confederate)* (Iowa City, IA, 1999), 378–380; Eakin, *Confederate Records,* 2:186; Mudd, "What I Saw At Wilson's Creek," 91.

136. John B. Clark, Sr. commanded the Third Division MSG. He was born on April 17, 1802, in Kentucky, moved to Missouri in 1818, became a lawyer and a successful politician. At the beginning of the Civil War he was appointed a general in the MSG, was wounded at Wilson's Creek and subsequently became a senator from Missouri in the Confederate Congress. After the war, Clark fled to Mexico, but later returned to Missouri, where he resumed his practice of law. He died in October 1885 in Fayette, Missouri. See Banasik, *Serving With Honor,* 282–283 for a complete biography; Peterson,

War Records, Series I, Volume 3.

[Note: The next two parts will be found in Chapter 2.]

The Chase.

At midnight we arose and fell into line along the banks of Crane Creek.[137] The stars had swung over into the weird positions of the smaller hours. As we noiselessly moved out towards the main road some soldier managed to discharge his fowling piece. The report invoked the echoes and filled us with dismay. Soon we were tramping on the march. Unused to such experiences I became drowsy and as we walked along I fell sound asleep. After awhile strange voices awoke me. Strange shuffling of the feet grated on my ears. I found I had dropped back out of my place. Then I hastened forward only to repeat my experience. Finally a comrade named Mason,[138] entertained me. He was one of the most assiduous patrons of my canteen. He showed me his star. It was Lyra, the brilliant, bluish beacon, then declining from the region of the zenith Alpha Lyrae.

In Mr. Holcombe's sketch[139] there is a testament leading to the theory that the Battle of Wilson's Creek was fought under the same constellation—the Lyra. It is a quarter of a century ago. Nearly all those I mention are dead. Many in battle died the soldier's death. Conscious of the mendacities of the day, I have cautiously waited till others have rendered their accounts, or passed away, leaving me comparatively

Free From Detection.

In view from the prevalent inspiration, I crave allowance. A memoir calls for personal experience, even though its recital appears tinged "with color of romance." The world is tolerant with a soldier who "shoulders his truth and tells how fields were won."

My comrade Mason was an army acquaintance. Years afterwards we casually met, both in the Confederate Service of the line. I trust his good, true heart is beating yet.

As we glided like shadows through the woods the distance seemed interminable. Morning dawned and still no enemy. We were passing the scene of the Dug

---

107; Allardice, 59–61.

137. The chase began at 11:00 p.m. on August 4, 1861, as the advance guard led by the Third Louisiana Infantry piloted out the army in pursuit of the Federals. Eakin, *Diary,* 5; Tunnard, 47.

138. There were two Masons who served in the Third Division, MSGs—George and Tyler Mason, both were from La Plata, Macon County, and served in Company A, Fourth Infantry Regiment. However, the company that the Masons belonged too did not organize until August 7, 1861, and did so, according to Peterson, in Macon County. Peterson, 123; Schnetzer, *More Forgotten Men,* 149.

139. The writer was referring to a small book written by R. I. Holcombe and Adams (no first name) and originally published in 1883, on the Battle of Wilson's Creek. R. I. Holcombe and Adams, *An Account of the Battle of Wilson's Creek or Oak Hills* (Springfield, MO, 1883; reprint ed. Springfield, MO, 1961), viii, hereafter cited as Holcombe.

Springs fight. Bullets had struck the dark trunks of the small oak trees exposing the inner fiber. These scares were low and frequent, scarcely one above the dangerous space. Our comment was that a sharp engagement had taken place and some effective shooting had been done. In broad daylight we reached a deserted camp of Gen. Lyon. The inevitable fragments of blue uniform cloth remained as loyal souvenirs. We must have passed through the McCalla farm camp before day. The camp site we saw was probably the place occupied by Gen. Lyon when he fell back from Gen. Rains. It was in a defile with long swelling ridges of treeless hills on each side. Somewhere along here we came to a spring. Here we crowded to assuage our thirst and fill our canteens. Almost in the spring was a new and plethoric mound. From it issued an offensive odor of

Blue Bottle Flies.

A soldier scraping away a few inches of earth exposed a blue blanket. We surmised that some of the victims of the late fight were buried here. We were not deterred for we were told that we would go twenty miles that day without more water. Gen. Lyon had secured twenty hours' start. He did not stand upon the order of his going. He simply went at once. This incivility entailed on us extreme privation, for when Gen. McCulloch found that the enemy would rather escape than attack, we redoubled our exertions to overtake the fugitives. Our road followed up the defile till we reached a divide. As we hurried along in the cool of the morning a small troop of well-armed horsemen galloped by, not by the road, but on the open ground. Word was passed that Gen. McCulloch was the leader and the men were some of his Texans.[140] We had heard of Gen. McCulloch's Maynard rifle, and here he was in true Indian fighting style. Great was our enthusiasm at the sight of our general forging ahead to find the enemy. His real incentive was probably his indignant disappointment in so stealthily slipping up on a vacant camp. No doubt he felt that if the Missourians could not do any better he would himself be on the warpath. During our march that forenoon we also saw our mounted men on each side out in the rolling prairie attending our advance. They had been originally thrown out to flank the enemy. They bore several large Confederate flags. Nothing could be more inspiring than this casual

Unfolding of Their Colors

as the morning winds, aromatic with the breath of prairie life, lazily lifted the bars of canadine. All that day we raced along. The dust was thick and gritty. It was a fearful march. I remember one well of sandstone water, but the soldiers soon exhausted it. Masses of them swarmed and crowded around that well, new candidates arriving as others departed, and I moved on in despair.[141]

---

140. The cavalry that Thomas Bacon saw was probably Captain A. V. Rieff's independent company of Arkansas cavalry, General McCulloch's body guard. Piston, 157.
141. The rebel march on August 5 was further exasperated due to the lack of foodstuffs. The Federals,

Toward afternoon we saw a large body of unarmed soldiers in homespun garb, sitting along the fence that lined the road. They were shaking their fists and yelling their regrets. In Gen. McCulloch's last report on this matter (p. 744, 745) he said much about such unarmed men. He stated that Gen. Price's argument was that these non-combatants should be left behind. Then Gen. McCulloch was dismayed to find these camp followers, as he unjustly terms them, still attending our march. He said Gen. Clark's unarmed men were the last we shook loose. But Gen. McCulloch claimed that Gen. Rains camp at Wilson's Creek was full of such camp followers when Gen. Lyon passed his compliments. In another place Gen. McCulloch taxes our reprobates with robbing his killed and wounded men of the 300 stand of muskets (p. 672). The field was tolerably well patrolled. Our unarmed men did not see what use a dead Confederate had for his weapon. The Federals claimed that they themselves used the cartridges of their own dead and wounded (63, 69). Nothing could repress the enthusiasm of our unarmed troops. When left behind at Cassville they appropriated Confederate tents, and with them followed in the wake of the army. Gen. McCulloch cited this illustration of

Their Intrepid Thievery

(p. 672). His compliments materially tend to tarnish the glory of Missouri heroism.

As I panted through the dust my borrowed hunting rifle kept settling its narrow stock into my shoulders with the menace of severing my collar bone. At sundown we reached Moody Spring, but the approach was blocked by great masses of men, our Southern allies waiting their turn. They had precedence, but we were famished. We formed in line and waited but darkness came on and found us waiting still. Our officers raved and stormed but their imprecations had no effect. The Confederate officer in charge was cool and obdurate. In spite of the obligations of hospitality it would not have taken much to start a fratricidal fight for access to the spring. Finally we broke ranks in despair with nothing to eat. I found and appropriated a piece of moldy bread which someone had thrown away. We built our camp fires by the side of a muddy creek which slaked our thirst. The details brought in a large quantity of roasting ears taken from adjacent fields. The foragers said that we were patronizing the farms of Sample Orr[142] and the Hon. John S.

according to Dr. James Wiatt, laid waste to everything. "Thousands of bushels of corn being burned up. Oats, wheat and corn all the same." Eakin, *Diary*, 5.

142. Sample Orr was a probate judge (1857), Greene County farmer, strong Unionist and late candidate for Governor of Missouri in 1860. Labeled "nobody's nominee," the red haired, freckled-faced Orr ran under the banner of the Constitutional Union Party. A period newspaper described Orr as "A man medium in height, white eye-lashes, nervous, short step, sloping shoulders, long neck—another Ichabod Crane." Orr was a forceful speaker, and though largely unknown, garnered 66,583 votes to C. F. Jackson's 74,446. At the beginning of the Civil War, Orr was elected a major in the "Phelps County Regiment." He later relocated to Jefferson City and was considered one of three candidates for Provisional Governor of Missouri in July 1861, but lost to Hamilton R. Gamble. During the course of the war, it appears that Orr ran afoul of General Ben Loan, who arrested Orr for "uttering disloyal senti-

Phelps.[143] Then I lay on a root of a tree which overhung the pool of the creek. That night there was a thunderstorm and a stampede. Take a place where thousands of horses are rested, let them be seized with the temporary hysteria that congregates them into a galloping mass. If you are on the ground and they come your way they will run over you and trample you to death. They cannot be stopped or turned. When I awoke with the alarm and confused cries in the darkness I rolled over

Into the Pool.

Men were scampering in every direction. Some were plunging headlong into the water but the impulse was to claw for a tree or a sapling. But the horses did not come our way and we resumed our sleep.

Somewhere on the march our division was reenforced by a company of Vernon County Infantry,[144] transferred from Gen. Rains' command. The Kansas border troubles had no doubt educated these men to familiarity with warlike pursuits. They wore homespun suits, and swallowed their share of dust. One of them especially attracted attention. He carried the only musket in his company. He was tall and broad-shoulder and sinewy, but inclined to stoop. His eyes were white and staring, particularly so when a ring of sandstone dust adored each optic. He had a bayonet. It was evidently a treasure. The soldier knows that his musket is made with an exact poise on the shoulder, a balance of which a bayonet destroys. Hence no soldier cares to fix his bayonet. It is to be carried in his scabbard, and even then it is such a nuisance that the average solder will manage to lose it unless he is serving a solvent government, that deducts from his pay the value of the lost implement. But our Vernon County warrior always kept his bayonet fixed. He may have had no scabbard, but wherever you might see him, tramping along a lane or tuning a point of timber,

---

ments" and being a member of the "Order of the American Knights"—a radical group that opposed the draft. A short time later, then Governor Gamble, ordered Orr's release, with no reason given. *O.R.,* 13:806–807; *O.R.,* Series 2, 4:687, 7:753; C., "Affairs in Missouri," *Chicago Daily Tribune,* July 10, 1861; Ryle, 134–135, 149, 153; Ingenthron, 30–31; *History of Greene County,* 249, 270, 285.

143. John S. Phelps was born on December 22, 1814, in Simsbury, Connecticut, educated at Trinity College in Hartford, after which he moved to Springfield, Missouri in 1838. He was elected to the U.S. Congress in 1844, and served for eighteen years. He organized the Phelps County Missouri Regiment (six months) in October 1861, and fought at the Battle of Pea Ridge. President Lincoln made Phelps the Military Governor of Arkansas in July 1862, and in November, Phelps was promoted to brigadier general to date from July 18, 1862. Phelps's commission was never confirmed by Congress and his military rank expired on March 4, 1863. After the war, Phelps returned to Missouri where he was elected Governor in 1876, and served one term. He died in St. Louis on November 20, 1886. Warner, *Generals in Blue,* 367–368.

144. The Vernon County Company was organized in June 1861 and commanded by Captain James M. Gatewood. The unit was also known as the "Montevallo Company" and later became Company G, Seventh Cavalry Regiment, Eighth Division, MSG. In addition to Wilson's Creek, the unit also fought at Carthage (July 6, 1861) and Dry Wood Creek (September 7, 1861). Peterson, 117, 270.

There Was His Bayonet

coquetting with the sunlight. I was told he had killed a man in a personal difficulty shortly before he enlisted. Perhaps his patriotism was an afterthought. When the Battle of Wilson's Creek was over this man turned up with a bayonet wound. His zeal in ramming cartridges had caused him to impale his hand on his own bayonet.

Refreshed and stimulated by our nocturnal adventures, we formed the next morning and recommenced our chase. After going about two miles we descended from a plateau down into a valley. The road came to the edge of the plateau and then made a steep decent of about seventy feet. Here about a hundred yards to our right a creek, coming from the north, struck the bluff line which formed the edge of the plateau from which we had descended. We went northwest on the main road a little distance, till we came to where the creek approached the road, thus forming a triangle, having the bluff line on the south, the creek on the northeast and the road on the west.[145] Here suddenly we turned to our left up into the dense brush and undergrowth that lined the left side of the road and rose off gradually northwest in a long, ascending slope. Here on the second bench we halted.[146] This was a surprise. We had supposed ourselves in hot pursuit with every moment precious. At the point where we turned from the main road there was an old disused road leading up the ridge. It was soon explained that Gen. Lyon had gone eastward

Toward Rolla

and we were to cut across the country by neighborhood roads so as to gain on him.[147] However, we did not move, and we began to form a camp thus early in the morning. The whole affair was a mystery. Gen. [Mosby M.] Parsons' men[148] and our men always camped near together, so here the two camps were bounded on

---

145. Bacon was describing the Wilson's Creek battlefield. When his unit descended into the Wilson's Creek Valley, they had Skegg's Branch off to their left and Wilson's Creek to their right at the bottom of the bluff. The triangle area that Bacon describes was formed by the intersection of Skegg's Branch with Wilson's Creek. Boatner, 933; Snead, 259–260.

146. Bacon's unit halted at the base of what was Oak or "Bloody Hill." Boatner, 933; Snead, 259–260.

147. Lyon had not retreated to Rolla, but stopped at Springfield to contemplate his next move. Considering his situation, Lyon seriously considered abandoning Springfield and retreating to either Kansas or St. Louis, via Rolla. Lyon was "'gripped by indecision,'" according to William Piston, hardly the hallmark of a confident commander. *O.R.,* 3:48; Piston, 146.

148. Mosby M. Parson's command, the Sixth Division, MSG, consisted of the First Infantry Regiment (Colonel Joseph M. Kelly), First Cavalry Regiment (Colonel William B. Brown), with three companies attached, and Guibor's four-gun battery—in all 660 men. Parsons, a resident of Jefferson City, was born in Virginia in 1822, moved to Missouri at age thirteen, and was a veteran of the Mexican War. On November 5, 1862, he was commissioned a brigadier general in the Confederate Army. Parsons spent most of his Civil War years in the Trans-Mississippi Department. At war's end he went to Mexico, where he was killed on August 17, 1865. See *Missouri Brothers in Gray* (146–148) for a complete biography and photo. Banasik, *Missouri In 1861,* 380–381; Snead, 313.

the east by the main road and divided by the old disused road leading up the hill. I think this was known as an old mill road. At its intersection with the main road was stationed what we called Parsons' battery, meaning Capt. [Henry] Guibor's battery.[149] Farther west the woods became tall and open as if a fire had cleared the undergrowth. Nearer to us a dense thicket of brush and blackjack adhered to the slope and crowned the crest of the hill. This hill and the rising ground father west sloped southward to a dry branch which preserved its site among tall woods at the foot of the bluff line which ran nearly east and west. We were camped on a tongue or terrace of land between the dry branch and the creek, which received the dry branch near the bluff line. The affluent always turns away when it acquires a tributary. Our men thought that the open woods behind us would be a splendid place to fight. It was not long before some of their associates tried it. This creek was

Wilson's Creek,

and this site was soon to be our battle-ground. On the crest of the long slope rising behind us and within the dense thicket of stunted trees and brush was soon to stand the Federal line, was soon to open Totten's Battery.

On the plateau south of the bluff line and east of the main road by which we had come was Sharp's farm, and Sharp's barn stood close in the angle. This barn was composed of two log cabins built apart and connected by a roof forming a hallway shed. On this farm near the bluff line would be posted and taken Sigel's field pieces.[150] North of the bluff and east of the main road, was the creek bottom densely wooded with tall timber and undergrowth. Eastward beyond was the opposite bluff, not visible to us except on the northeast. Here would promptly respond [William E.] Woodruff's Battery.[151] About a mile up the dry branch was

---

149. Henry Guibor, a St. Louisian and member of the Volunteer Militia, commanded an artillery company at Camp Jackson in May 1861. After his parole, Guibor joined Sterling Price's army, where he commanded a four gun battery. He participated in the Missouri battles of Carthage (July 5, 1861), Wilson's Creek (August 10, 1861), Lexington (September 19, 1861), and Pea Ridge. Captured at Wilson's Creek, Guibor escaped shortly before the battle had ended. Guibor finished his military service on the east side of the Mississippi, serving in the Army of Tennessee. Guibor's command at Wilson's Creek consisted of four 6-lb smoothbore cannon (model 1841), with 104 men. Banasik, *Missouri In 1861*, 381; Mudd, "What I Saw At Wilson's Creek," 101; Snead, 217; *O.R.,* 3:32, 101, 186; *O.R.,* vols. 17, 1:24, 32, 38, 39; *O.R.,* Series 2, 1:556; William L. Shea and Earl J. Hess, *Pea Ridge: Civil War Campaign In the West* (Chapel Hill, North Carolina, 1992), 162–164, hereafter cited as Shea and Hess.
150. Sigel's Battery was Backoff's Missouri Artillery, which consisted of two 12-lb howitzers and four 6-lb smoothbore cannon. The Sharp farm was located to the rear of Bacon's command on the bluff they had descended on to reach their Wilson's Creek camp. Boatner, 933; Banasik, *Missouri In 1861*, 378.
151. Woodruff's Arkansas Battery was commanded by William E. Woodruff, Jr., a native of Little Rock, born on June 8, 1831. Woodruff commanded an Arkansas Militia Battery known as the Totten Battery in 1860. In May 1861, when the battery reorganized, he was again elected captain of what was known as the Pulaski Light Battery. At Wilson's Creek, the battery consisted of two 12-lb howitzers and two 6-lb smoothbore cannon. The battery reorganized again in December 1861, as the Weaver Light Artillery, with Woodruff as captain. Later, in 1862, Woodruff commanded a battalion, rising to the rank of major of artillery in 1863. Woodruff completed his service to the Confederacy, serving as a clerk in various quartermaster sections in the Trans-Mississippi Department. Following the war,

a spring whence we secured our drinking water. From Col. Snead's book I learn that the muddy creek, near Moody's Spring was Tyrel's [Terrell] Creek, and the dry bed I described was Skagg's Branch. We soon were told that Gen. Lyon had camped at Pond Spring, near Springfield. For five days we remained in one camp, feasting on roasting ears. In the succeeding days in autumn when corn was somewhat hardened, I have been told that Gen. Price's soldiers had to use a piece of stovepipe, punched in the style of a nutmeg grater which an ear of soft corn was rubbed by hand. This they called

Armstrong's Mill.

With condiments added the same receipe is good for corn oysters.

Our Wilson's Creek camp was soon adorned with parallelogram frameworks made of four forked sticks set upright in the ground, to support a framework of horizontal rods on which slices of beef were smoked and dried by the slow fire underneath. This was called jerked beef. While this was exposed it was occasionally jerked in a more expedient way by prowlers who were more attentive than the owners. The use of these and similar applications gave our deserted camp a woebegone and barbarous appearance, an unpleasant indication of a relapsed from civilization. Crusoe's savage would have made precisely such a showing.

One night my turn came to stand guard, and as I was posted beside one of the yellow, old-fashioned six-pounders, I thought of the familiar pictures of the sentry beside the cannon under the shadows. I could strike the attitude of support arms and the cannon was correct in ardent pattern. We had not then learned that the explosive impact of the cargo is expended in the dislodging start of the projectile and the heavy muzzle rings are useless. We had all confidence in our artillery and ignorance was bliss. Guard mounting at night had its weird fascinations. You must stand guard two hours out of four. Presumably you keep awake, and you

Have No Company

on post except your own thoughts. At the guardhouse strange, dreamy tunes are hummed by reminiscent reliefs, when muffled tones will scarcely break the silence. The officer catches the solemn inspiration and gives the command "Order arms!" with a pressure monotone that suggests the burial of the dead. On sentry duty apparitions emerge from the darkness, low words are muttered, and then, with rustling garments and stealthy tread, they disappear in the shadows as the

---

Woodruff became the owner and editor of the *Arkansas Gazette,* one of the oldest newspapers west of the Mississippi River. Labeled a man of "enterprise," Woodruff would later serve as the Arkansas State Treasurer (1881–1891), but would do so under a cloud of corruption. Tried for corruption, Woodruff was acquitted, but not before one Little Rock newspaper called the treasury shortages under Woodruff "the worst thing of its kind in the history of Arkansas." Margaret Ross, *Arkansas Gazette: The Early Years 1819–1866* (Little Rock, AR, 1969), 284, 401, hereafter cited as Ross; John L. Ferguson and J. H. Atkinson, *Historic Arkansas* (Little Rock, AR, 1966), 180; Woodruff, 9, 18, 42–43, 56, 80, 96, 105–107.

guard goes around. In such moments the gravity of a soldier's life reveals itself. Then he communes with his own heart and is still. In fancy's realm he views afar the lighted homes of peace and love.

Private Mason had a Mississippi rifle[152] which he petted. Out of a sardine box he had made a cartridge-box, covered with rubber taken [illegible] material for a first class cap-pouch. The[se] from a worn out waterproof, which also fur-car-tridge-box was well filled with fixed ammunition. Its owner had taken exquisite pains to rig himself for slaughter. But he was unexpectedly appointed a hospital steward and I fell heir to his fighting outfit. Had I known that my marching days were over for the present I would have retained the ponderous back-woods rifle. Perhaps it might have fouled after a few discharges, but I had become attached to its crescent guide sight and its long silvery front sight, on which, in the pioneer dialect, I could "drawer" as fine as a hair. But we all supposed that we soon would be on a tour of investigation, and I was tired of lugging a crowbar through the country, so I took the Mississippi rifle. This is yagger made expressly for military use. The caliber is 52.[153] The sights are low and coarse, but

Good for Rapid Firing.

This arm came into use as a military rifle irrespective of the expanding pro-jectiles. My cartridges contained elongated balls. The caps were a real treasure— regular musket caps, combining all the virtues of a cap with the exact shape of a hat.

While in camp, either at Moody's Spring or Wilson's Creek, the Louisiana regiment marched by us.[154] These were rather slender looking men, arrayed in uniforms of solid neutral gray.[155] They were well armed, well provided, well

152. The Mississippi Rifle was the U.S. Model 1841 Rifle, the first U.S. rifle to use percussion caps. The weapon as first manufactured was .54 caliber, about 49 inches long and weighed about ten pounds. The first model had no mount for a bayonet. In 1850 the weapon was changed to .58 caliber to cor-respond with the introduction of the minie ball; the weapon was also refitted to handle a bayonet. This modified weapon was probably the one carried by Mason. The weapon was called the "Mississippi Rifle" in honor of Jefferson Davis's First Mississippi Regiment, which was armed with the rifle during the Mexican War. Boatner, 556, 860; Edwards, *Civil War Guns*, 381.

153. The .54 caliber Mississippi Rifle was not equipped to handle a bayonet, so the writer must be mistaken as to its caliber. The term "yagger" was applied to the Mississippi Rifle because of its smaller size and resemblance to the German "Jäger" (hunting) rifle . However, at least one unit—the Third Louisiana—which was partially armed with the Mississippi Rifle had another opinion, calling the weapon "worthless, often exploding, and so inefficient that the enemy boldly exposed themselves, and taunted the men for their unskillful shooting." Boatner, 860; Tunnard, 53, 226, 242; Piston, 11.

154. This was the Third Louisiana Infantry Regiment—the only Louisiana unit in the Confederate Army at Wilson's Creek; it was commanded by Louis Hébert. Tunnard, 27; Banasik, *Missouri In 1861*, 378–381.

155. The Third Louisiana would receive an assortment of uniform changes through its history. In Oc-tober 1861, they received clothing made of a material referred too as "jeans," of a grayish blue color, except for Company K which received dark brown; all manufactured at the Louisiana State Peniten-tiary. In January 1863, they received their much hated "white jeans," which many soldiers refused to wear until ordered to do so by a superior officer. And finally in January 1864, the Third Louisiana

equipped and accoutered. As they passed us they exchanged glances with us, their large black, kindly eyes regarding us with curious interest, as if we were more amused at our appearance than they cared to reveal. They looked as if their home libraries might contain the best selections of English, French and Spanish literature, while I regret to say that we knew little about belle-lettres. But neither their mental or physical elevation suggested any of the lofty condescension attributed to the giraffe. It was reported that they brought their own rations—viands that we did not dream of. Coffee grounds had been seen where they had camped.

So much had been said about their array that I feel compelled to discuss the Confederate uniforms. The Confederate coat was made of material called cadet gray, a name referring perhaps more to the substance then to the shade. Cadet gray is really a grayish light blue. The Confederate Army regulation will show that in pantaloons the Confederate uniform involved the

Bluest of the Blue.

The tint or shades varied with the arm of the service. One, I think, the infantry of the line, had the ultra-marine, the most pure and delightful of all blues. The different fastenings, red for artillery, blue for infantry, buff for the cavalry and green for riflemen, made the Confederate soldier, with his cap to match, in true Confederate uniform as gray as a tropic bird. The officers' trousers were accented by the Prince Albert skirts of their double- breasted coats. All know the sub-civilized production for long-tailed coats and the complimentary tendency to equestrian boots. Hence, when a Confederate officer appeared in full uniform his person was so enveloped by his magnificently tinseled coat as to leave visible nothing else except his cap and boots. The existence of any other garment has been strenuously and persistently disputed. Considering the meager Confederate wardrobe, this question must be relegated to the domain of conjecture. Lexicographers, as usual, differ about the gray. Worcester and Webster both say that "gray" is the correct orthography, while Richardson and Johnson impliedly prefer "grey." All derive the word from Teutonic and Scandinavian origin, though Webster allies the word to graios—aged, and hence gray. One lexical definition of gray is "a mixture of black and white." Black and white alternating in figures or stripes small enough to produce a grayish appearance, give a superb effect in the apparel of any type of human beauty. So with steel-gray or pearl-gray, or ashen-gray. Webster expressly mentions ashes as a gray. Neither black nor white is a color. Hence artists and art critics were

Two Kinds,

or classes of gray, one not composed of colors, and the other composed of nothing but colors, and the lexicons are reproached for making no discrimination. The

---

received a complete uniform of Confederate gray cloth, which was received with great "excitement and rejoicing." Tunnard, 92, 220, 332.

profession designates the black and white gray as neutral gray. There are certain hues produced by combinations of fixed proportions of the three primary colors, yellow, red and blue. These are called tertiaries, or colored grays, to-wit: Citrine, russet and olive, according to the predominate primary. The art critics go farther, and use gray only for the neutral gray and gray only for the tertiaries. (See Sampson's Art Criticism, p. 483). Art critics are not happy in verbal expression. When they mean economic arts, they say useful arts, but they recall from the inevitable antithesis, which suggests the useless arts where they say fine arts. There is but one gray, and it cannot be properly called an epicene. The tertiaries should never be called colored grays. The expression colored gray should be abandoned.

As gray never composed any part of the Confederate uniform the Confederate cause should never have been associated with gray, but Providence otherwise appointed. The southern people are ever ruled by Greek philosophy. Thus they preserved their system of helotry [slavery] and their contempt for luxury. They are the Greeks of the New World. Prof. Sampson cites Hesiod to prove that gray is from Graios, referring to the colorless complexions of the ancient Greeks (p. 483). The same characteristic attends our Southern face.

The rich name "butternut" is also related to gray. the scientific name of the tree is Juglans Cinerea, referring to the ashen appearance of the bark as distinguished from Juglans Nigra, the black walnut.

* * * * * * *

Chapter 2

Battle of Oak Hills or Wilson's Creek

Item: Prelude to Oak Hills; from the organization of Company B, Fifth Infantry Regiment, Eight Missouri State Guard, in May 1861, through the Battle of Oak Hills, by Dr. Flavius J. Lindsey, late member of Company B, Fifth Regiment, Eight Division, Missouri State Guard.
Published: March 20, 1886.

Cowskin Prairie and Wilson's Creek.

Round Top, Benton County, Ark., Feb. 21, 1886.
Editor *Republican*

I have been much interested in "Tales of the War." Though nearly twenty-five years have past since the struggle began, the "Old Reliable" in her sketches brings many familiar faces to memory—none more than that of Dr. [John F.] Snyder who contributed an interesting article some time since. The writer was the escort of Dr. Snyder when sent from Gen. Price's headquarters on Cowskin Prairie to Gen. Ben. McCulloch, on Baltie, near Maysville, Ark., to invite him with his Texans to join the Missouri State Guard to assist in repelling Lyon & Co. from old Missouri.[1] Our company was organized in 1861, at Bolivar, Mo.,[2] Capt. [Benjamin F.] Mitchell, Lieuts. [John F.] Calloway, [Charles H.] Nichols and [William H.] Lemon [Lemmons].[3] The same Charlie Nichols was afterwards lieutenant-colonel

---

1. Federal forces under Colonel Franz Sigel occupied Springfield, Missouri on June 24, 1861, followed in subsequent days by assorted regiments that constituted Lyon's command at Wilson's Creek. Lyon arrived at Springfield with about 4,600 troops on July 13, having successfully driven the rebel command before him into the southwest Missouri. Prior to Lyon's arrival, Colonel Sigel had departed Springfield with about 1,000 men and two batteries of artillery in an attempt to cut off rebel troops who were retreating from Lyon's advance. On July 5, Sigel became engaged in a running fight with the forces of General Price at Carthage, Missouri, and was driven back to Springfield. As to communications, cooperation between General Price, Governor Jackson and General McCulloch had begun in early June 1861. This would eventually culminate in the joining of the two commands in late July, just before the Battle of Wilson's Creek. The incident that Dr. Lindsey described probably occurred sometime between July 9–25, 1861, when the two forces moved to unite at Cassville, Missouri. *O.R.*, 3:17, 394; Ingenthron, 42, 48, 51; Snead, 230–231, 239; Bearss, "Fort Smith," 325.

2. This was Company B, Fifth Infantry Regiment, Eighth Division, MSG. The unit elected its officers in the first week of June 1861. Peterson, 237. [Note: At Wilson's Creek the Eighth Division, MSG was known as the Second Division. This will be true throughout this book for any person or unit that was noted as part of the Eighth Division.]

3. Captain Benjamin Franklin Mitchell commanded Company B, Fifth Infantry Regiment, Eighth MSG. He was from Bolivar, Polk County, Missouri, and was murdered by Federal soldiers sometime after he was mustered out of the MSG. Mitchell fought at Wilson's Creek, Dry Wood Creek and Lexington. Schnetzer,

of [Sidney D.] Jackman's regiment[4] and was killed by one of the Younger brothers[5] while sheriff of Dallas County, Texas.[6] Our company consisted of seventy-
four members, raised for the artillery. Our uniform was brown jeans with a red
calico strips one inch wide on the outside seam, there were only four married men
in the company. You may guess there was some red striped strutting when we got
on drill. There was one boy in the company, "Foster Nichols," who had seen some
service on the border of Kansas

In The Ball's Mill Expedition.[7]

More Forgotten Men, 164; Peterson, 237.

Second Lieutenant John F. Calloway or Calaway was born about 1840 in Missouri and lived near Bolivar
in Polk County at the beginning of the Civil War. Elected a lieutenant in Company C, Fifth Infantry regiment, Eighth Division MSG, on June 1, 1861, Calloway resigned his commission on August 25, 1861,
following Wilson's Creek. Calloway would later rejoin the Guard and was wounded at the Battle of Pea
Ridge in March 1862. Bartels, *Forgotten Men,* 45–46; Peterson, 237.

Charles H. Nichols was born in Missouri and lived in Bolivar. He was eighteen years old when elected
captain of Company A, Fifth Infantry Regiment, Eighth Division, MSG, on August 20, 1861. It appears
that Nichols left Company B, in which he served as a lieutenant, after Wilson's Creek. In late 1862, Nichols
was elected major of S. D. Jackman's Infantry Regiment, but was later relieved by General T. C. Hindman,
for unknown reasons. During Price's 1864 Missouri Raid, Nichols commanded a cavalry regiment as a
lieutenant colonel and served with distinction throughout the raid. On August 24, Nichols captured a Federal standard at Jones's Hay Station, Arkansas, which under the standards of the time, would have earned
him the Medal of Honor if he had been serving in the Union Army. *O.R.,* vol. 41, pt.1:671–678; Richard
L. Norton, *Behind Enemy Lines: The Memoirs and Writings of Brigadier General Sidney Drake Jackman*
(Springfield, MO, 1997), 131, hereafter cited as Norton.

First Lieutenant William Hughes Lemmons or Lemmon was born in Missouri and lived in Bolivar. At the
age of 21, Lemmon joined the MSG on June 3, 1861, being elected first lieutenant of his company. While in
the Guard, Lemmon fought at Oak Hills, Dry Wood Creek and Lexington. He later enlisted in McCowan's
Missouri Infantry Battalion of the Fifth Infantry Regiment on the east side of the Mississippi River. Bartels,
Forgotten Men, 216; Schnetzer, *More Forgotten Men,* 140.

4. Sidney D. Jackman raised two regiments during the Civil War; the first, an infantry unit was organized
in the fall of 1862, and the second, a cavalry command was raised in late spring of 1864. Sidney D. Jackman was born in Jassamine County, Kentucky, on March 7, 1826, moved to Howard County, Missouri,
in 1830, where he was educated. He married in 1849, then relocated his family to near Pappinville, Bates
County, Missouri in 1855. Caught up in the border wars of the late 1850's, Jackman raised a company of
defense forces to counter the raids from Kansas. At the beginning of the Civil War, Jackman reluctantly
joined the Confederate cause as the years of border warfare had taken its toll on his support of the Union.
During the war, Jackman was basically a guerrilla leader, participating in only two major engagements:
Lone Jack (August 16, 1862) and Westport (October 22–23, 1864). He moved to Texas following the war,
where he died on June 2, 1886. Crute, *Units of the Confederate Army,* 201, 208; *More Generals In Gray,*
133–135; Norton, v, 3–9.

5. There were five Younger brothers; Richard, Cole, James, John and Robert. The eldest brother Richard
died in 1860. Of the remaining four Younger brothers, only Cole and James participated in the Civil War.
Cole Younger, *The Story of Cole Younger: An Autobiography of the Missouri Guerrilla, Confederate Cavalry Officer, and Western Outlaw* (Reprint ed., Springfield, MO, 1996), 10, 30.

6. In recalling the incident on January 17, 1871, Cole Younger stated that his brother John and another man
by the name of Russell, confronted Sheriff S. W. Nichols of Dallas, Texas, over an incident that took place
the previous day. In the ensuing melee John Younger was wounded, and it appears that Nichols was killed.
Our writer seems to be saying that Charlie Nichols and S. W. Nichols are one in the same man, or maybe
Cole Younger got the sheriff's name wrong. Ibid., 72–73.

7. The "Ball's Mill Expedition," better known as the "Southwest Expedition," occurred in late 1860. In ear-

He knew how to shoulder and present arms, but there was so much difference in the length of our guns that the line did not present much uniformity. We were the bravest set of boys, no doubt, in our own estimation, that walked the earth: could whip any amount of men who would attempt to drive us from home and sweethearts, but on the 18th of May, 1861, the news arrived that [Franz] Sigel[8] was coming and no mistake[9]. Our captain held a council of war and concluded that as Sigel had several more men than us, and was a Dutchman, that maybe if we fell into his hands, his troops not understanding our language, would come the Alamo on us. The argument was conclusive. By 8 that night we were on a general run to meet Rains in the West. We left without tent, grub or anything, but a few old rifles and shotguns, some of them borrowed from our neighbors and not yet returned. The first night's ride brought us to Stockton,[10] in Cedar County, where the young ladies headed by Miss Lou Hill (now Mrs. Haines of Bentonville, Ark.), volunteered to make tents, the courthouse being the place selected. While the young ladies cut and sewed we soldiers sang "Dixie" and "Sweet Home," which place

ly November 1860, James Montgomery, Kansas Jayhawker and later colonel of the 3rd Kansas Infantry, entered Missouri and rounded up six or eight pro-slavery men near Ball's Mill and killed them. In response, Missouri Governor Robert M. Stewart called out Daniel M. Frost's St. Louis Missouri Militia Brigade. Frost's mission was simple, to "protect the lives and property of the people of the border." Arriving at the Kansas-Missouri border in late November 1860, Frost's small brigade positioned itself about twelve miles from Montgomery's headquarters, in Kansas, awaiting Montgomery's next move. Within days Montgomery disbanded his command, followed by Frost disbanding the militia save two companies, who were left near Ball's Mill in northwest Vernon County to patrol the border. Moore, *Missouri, Confederate Military History,* 10; Nicole Etcheson, *Bleeding Kansas: Contested Liberty in the Civil War Era* (Lawrence, KS, 2004), 221; Donald L. Gilmore, *Civil War on the Missouri-Kansas Border* (Gretna, LA, 2006), 100–104, hereafter cited as Gilmore.

8. Franz Sigel was born November 18, 1824, in the grand duchy of Baden (Germany), graduated from the military academy at Karlsrule in 1843, and fought on the losing side in the German Revolution of 1848, also known as the Hecker-Struve Insurrection. Emigrating to the United States in 1852, Sigel was living in St. Louis in 1861, when the Civil War began. During the early months of the war, Sigel proved to be a recruiting magnet for Federal troops of German ancestry in Missouri, as the phrase "I fights mit Sigel" became a rallying cry for the German population. Non-German troops had another opinion, with most not liking the man, seeing him as a "weasel." For his performance at Wilson's Creek, one Iowan wrote that Sigel "was no good; he was timid and inefficient." Still, Sigel was made a brigadier general on August 7, 1861, and for gallantry at Pea Ridge he was promoted to major general. After Pea Ridge, Sigel was reassigned to the Eastern Theater of operations, where he completed his Civil War service. He died in 1902, in the state of New York. For a complete biography see Banasik, *Missouri In 1861,* 362–364; "Francis Sigel, the Hero of Carthage," *Chicago Daily Tribune,* July 17, 1861; Ware, 336.

9. Following the capture of Camp Jackson on May 10, 1861, both sides began preparations for the expected war. However, no advance on Jefferson City took place at this time; indeed, General Harney, commander of the Department of the West invited Sterling Price, commander of the Missouri State Guard to come to St. Louis to discuss the situation. While the two opposing commanders parlayed in St. Louis, the MSG began arriving in Jefferson City and the Federal forces secured St. Louis. The meeting of Harney and Price resulted in a quasi cease fire, until General Lyon, who replaced Harney, repudiated the Price-Harney Agreement. Following a subsequent meeting between Governor Jackson, General Price, General Lyon and Frank Blair, Lyon declared war on Missouri, initiating an advance on Jefferson City on June 13, 1861, not May 18 as the writer notes. Snead, 202–203, 208.

10. Stockton was about twenty-four miles northwest of Bolivar. It was the county seat of Cedar County, Missouri.

many of us have never visited yet. From there we traveled west in search of Gen. James S. Rains, who we heard had a great many men. We found him at last on Cowskin River, or rather the prairie.[11] Here we went into a kind of organization. Our regiment was the Fifth Missouri State Guard.[12] [James J.] Clarkson,[13] an old Mexican War veteran, was our colonel; Robert Crawford[14] of Mt. Vernon, Mo., our lieutenant-colonel; Miles [Michael] Buster[15] of Greenfield, Mo., our major; Camel Lemon[16] of Polk County, our adjutant. A braver set of officer never graced the history of any cause, but it seems that the part that regiment took

---

11. Cowskin Prairie was located in McDonald County, about twelve miles from Maysville, Arkansas, in southwest Missouri and the point where Sterling Price organized the Missouri State Guard. Snead, 235.

12. The Fifth Infantry Regiment, Eighth Division, MSG was primarily raised in Dade County, Missouri. It participated in the Missouri engagements at Carthage, Wilson's Creek, Dry Wood Creek, Lexington and at Pea Ridge, Arkansas. Peterson, 239.

13. James J. Clarkson was born in Kentucky in about 1812, and moved to Missouri prior to the Mexican War. He fought in the Mexican War, after which he relocated to Leavenworth, Kansas, and during the mid-1850's, got involved Missouri-Kansas border war on the pro-slavery side. Returning to Missouri, Clarkson was elected colonel of the Fifth Infantry Regiment, Eighth Division, MSG. He later transferred to the Confederate Service, was captured at Locust Grove and exchanged in 1864. Clarkson returned to the Trans-Mississippi Department and in early 1865, he was murdered by Mississippi River pirates. See Appendix B for a complete biography. Bartels, *Forgotten Men*, 61; J. J. Clarkson Letter, February 29, 1864, J. J. Clarkson Collection, Missouri Historical Society; Hale, 59; Heitman, 2:47; Peterson, 236.

14. Robert W. (or N.) Crawford was born in Virginia in about 1812, attended West Point for two years, then dropped out. A resident and lawyer of Mt. Vernon, Lawrence County, Missouri, Crawford represented his county at the March 1861 Secession Convention, held in Jefferson City Missouri. On July 12, 1861, Crawford was elected the Lieutenant Colonel of the Fifth Infantry Regiment, Eighth Division, MSG. After service in the Guard, Crawford escorted his family to Texas and then offered his services as a recruiter for the Confederate Army. In recommending Crawford for the recruitment mission in Missouri in 1862, Waldo P. Johnson called Crawford a "sober man, of decided courage & good judgement," one who was "capable in an emergency of deciding promptly, and executing with energy." *O.R.*, 53:824; Bartels, *Forgotten Men*, 75; Hale, 72; Ryle, 214; Waldo P. Johnson letter (October 24, 1862), Miscellaneous Correspondence, Peter W. Alexander Collection, Columbia University; C. F. Jackson letter, October 24, 1862, Miscellaneous Correspondence, Peter W. Alexander Collection.

15. Michael W. Buster was born in Tennessee and lived in Greenfield, Dade County, Missouri, at the beginning of the Civil War. Appointed adjutant of the Fifth Infantry Regiment, Eighth Division, MSG on July 12, 1861, Buster was wounded at Wilson's Creek. During the summer of 1862 he helped organize J. J. Clarkson's Cavalry Regiment, which was routed at Locust Grove, Indian Territory on July 3, 1862. Buster later commanded the reformed regiment, now a battalion, which fought at Newtonia, Missouri (September 30, 1862) and Old Fort Wayne, Indian Territory (October 22, 1862). His unit combined with other companies to form Clark's Missouri Regiment (Ninth Missouri Infantry) in November 1862. Buster later left Clark's command and raised a battalion of cavalry in late 1863, final disposition unknown. *O.R.*, 13:299; *O.R.S.*, pt. 1, vol. 3:65–67; National Archives, Record Group M322, roll no. 172, Confederate Compiled Service Record, Clark's Missouri Infantry Regiment; Peterson, 236; Bartels, *Forgotten Men*, 43.

16. Alexander Campbell Lemmon was born about 1838, in Missouri and resided near West Bend, Polk County, at the beginning of the Civil War. He organized a seventeen-man company from his local area, which upon joining the army appears to have been consolidated with other units. Lemmon subsequently became the major of the Fifth Infantry Regiment, Eighth Division, MSG on July 12, 1861. During his service with the Guard, Lemmon was engaged at Oak Hills, Dry Wood Creek and Lexington. Latter, Lemmon commanded Company D, Fifth Missouri Infantry (Confederate), was wounded at Corinth, Mississippi, in October 1862 and lost an arm. Lemmon completed his war service as a major, returned to Missouri where he settled in Bolivar and became the county clerk. Peterson, 236, 289; Hale, 188; Bartels, *Forgotten Men*, 215; Schnetzer, *More Forgotten Men*, 138; Eakin, *Confederate Records*, 5:54.

Has Been Left Out.

This was the regiment that supported Bledsoe's battery,[17] the battery being a part of us. We were a mixed regiment; part mounted and part infantry. After living on wheat flour, bran, all ground together, for sometime on Cowskin, we became restless and longed for the flesh pots of old Polk and Cedar, but we were in for six months. So we grinned and wanted to repel the invader. As we consolidated our brigade commander was Gen. Wakeman or Waltman [Weightman]. While we were on the prairie we witnessed one of the most stupendous stampedes on record. About 7,000 horses took fright after dark; it seems they were all running at once. I said that I saw the stampede. I did not see it, only the part that was closest to us, but I think I heard it all. A great many of us had our horses lariated. In the run the sticks came up and away went the horses, each with a forty-foot rope. We were camped on the edge of the timber. Someone yelled out "the Yankees are upon us!" "To arms!" "Run for the brush!"

One of the lieutenant said, "It's only Rains's Blackberry cavalry stampeded. If you want to save yourselves climb these black jacks."

And up we went. After the excitement was somewhat over there was more than one sitting flat on the ground with his arms and legs locked around a tree, thinking he was safe ten feet up. Some of these horses were found the next evening thirty-five miles from camp. Some were never found. A short time after this we were ordered up and north we went. On Crane Creek we met the enemy

And Were Dispersed

after a few shots. Here was the first dead soldier we saw. A few days later we marched to Wilson's Creek, where on the morning of the 10th, that memorable battle was fought. At precisely 6 o'clock by Dr. [John M.] Dunn's[18] watch we sat down around a table-cloth at headquarters. That was about all we had, except one pint cup of coffee and nine roasting ears. We were passing the cup, each man taking a sip, when bang! boom! boom!. The four corners of the cloth were suddenly drawn inward. A grape, not the kind we eat, but one of those hard indigestible, had struck the center of our festal board. We were up quicker than it takes to write

---

17. Captain Hiram Bledsoe commanded a three gun battery, consisting of one 12-lb howitzer and two 6-lb smoothbores. The howitzer was a bored out 9-lb gun, named "Old Sacramento," which had supposedly been captured by Bledsoe in the Mexican War. The battery was also known as the "1st Lexington Light Artillery Battery." Additionally, the battery saw action at Pea Ridge, before being transferred to the east side of the Mississippi River in April 1862. Banasik, *Missouri In 1861*, 381; Peterson, 287; W. L. Webb, *Battles and Biographies of Missourians or the Civil War Period of Our State* (Kansas City, MO, 1900), 317, hereafter cited as Webb; William Riley Brooksher: *The Civil War Battle of Wilson's Creek* (Washington, DC, 1995), 122, hereafter cited as Brooksher.

18. Captain John M. Dunn was the regimental surgeon of the Fifth Infantry Regiment, Eighth Division, MSG and later of the Thirteenth Cavalry Regiment of the same division. He was born in Virginia in about 1834, and lived in Greenfield, Dade County, Missouri, at the beginning of the Civil War. Bartels, *Forgotten Men*, 96.

it. Our division was on the southeast hill.[19] The battery, Bledsoe's, on the most elevated ground. It was unlimbered immediately and turned on the advancing foe.[20] After the Yanks got our range the first shot killed three horses and tore one leg off a fifteen-year old boy rider. Here the enemy seemed to concentrate their aim. Our horses were soon all disabled. The guns were then run by hand. Thus the battle went on. Our balls gave out, when [Hiram] Bledsoe[21] would take a sack of No. 1 buckshot and cram them down that memorable old gun "Sacramento";[22] at 200 yards such loads did such execution that we were the terror to their lines, so much so that Sigel sent a round

To Silence Us.[23]

19. Weightman's Brigade, including the Fifth Infantry Regiment, was positioned near Manley's Spring, on a high hill between the Manley and Ray houses. The unit was on the east side of Wilson's Creek, while the remainder of its division (Rains's) was on the west side of the creek. Banasik, *Missouri In 1861*, 379–380; Edwin C. Bearss, *The Battle of Wilson's Creek* (Bozman, MT, 1988), 65–66, hereafter cited as Bearss, *Wilson's Creek;* Brooksher, 185.

20. After the battle began, Clarkson's Regiment and its brigade moved about a mile west to the base of Bloody Hill and was positioned next to the remainder of Rains's Division. Bledsoe's Battery took a position on the Springfield road to the rear of Weightman's Brigade and threw about five shells into Plummer's Battalion of U.S. Regulars, who were operating in the vicinity of Ray's Cornfield. The battery, now located near Skegg's Branch, faced about and played a role in the rout of Sigel's column, which was attacking the rear of the Confederates on Bloody Hill. The initial battery, that was in line with Clark's command on Bloody Hill, was Guibor's Missouri Battery, not Bledsoe's. The battery on the hill was probably Woodruff's Arkansas Battery, which unlimbered in place, and commenced firing. *O.R.*, 3:128; Woodruff, 40, 45–46, 113–114; Brooksher, 184, 192; Bearss, *Wilson's Creek*, 85.

21. Hiram Bledsoe was born on April 25, 1825, in Bourbon County, Kentucky, moved to Missouri, in 1839 and settled in Lafayette County, near Lexington, in 1839. During the Mexican War, he joined Company B, First Regiment of Missouri Mounted Volunteers and participated in Doniphan's Southwest Expedition. At the beginning of the Civil War, Bledsoe organized a mounted command, but took on a battery of three guns from Lexington in May 1861. He fought at Carthage, Wilson's Creek, and Dry Wood Creek, where he was wounded. Bledsoe returned to duty in the final days of the Siege of Lexington and subsequently commanded the battery at Pea Ridge. The battery, with Bledsoe in command, moved to the east side of the Mississippi River in April 1862, where they completed their military service. Returning to Lexington, Bledsoe married in 1869, and was elected presiding judge of Cass County in 1872; he served three terms. In 1878 he was elected County Collector and died at his home in Pleasant Hill, Missouri, on February 7, 1899. Webb, 316–321; Bartels, *Trans-Mississippi Men*, 136–139, 160; Peterson, 287.

22. "Old Sacramento" was a gun often written about by Missourians following the Civil War and admired during the conflict. The cannon, supposedly cast from the church bells of Chihuahua, Mexico, using some silver in its construction, was captured at the Battle of Sacramento in 1847. When the piece fired, it had a peculiar ring to it that was far different from any other piece of artillery; some say the ring came because of the silver used in its forging. Webb says that when the piece was rebored from a 9-lb to a 12-lb howitzer, "the chase was turned off smooth, thus reducing the thickness of the metal, which gave the piece a peculiar sound when fired." When the battery moved to the east side of the Mississippi River in April 1862, Old Sacramento participated in its final battle at Farmington, Mississippi, before being recast. Webb, 121, 318–319; Jay Monaghan, *Civil War on the Western Border 1854–1865* (New York, 1955), 38, hereafter cited as Monaghan; Peterson, 310.

23. When Bledsoe's guns engaged those of Colonel Sigel, it proved to be the pivotal moment in the engagement on the Confederate rear. Two guns of Backof's Federal Battery (Wiley Britton says the battery was commanded by Lieutenant G. A. Schaefer) fired in response to the rebel artillery, but they hardly had time to reload as the Third Louisiana Infantry came charging over the hill, fired a volley and captured the

He had no obstruction, for we had no support on our southeast. A detachment was brought up within sixty yards of us. Col. Clarkson sent Maj. Buster to see what command it was. As he rode he was ordered to dismount. As he did so he motioned to Col. Clarkson and fell to the ground, when a Dutchman stabbed him with a bayonet, which went through his shoulder and grated on the rocks below. While this was going on Clarkson gave the word to "fire! charge bayonets!" which was immediately executed. As the Dutchman aimed to withdraw his bayonet Buster caught the gun and was pulled to his feet. Being a very large and stout man, he held unto him until several of the boys were upon him and gave him a taste of bayonets, which ended him. It was said that there were but three of this detachment Federals who ever got out from there except the mounted officers.[24] Be this as it may, the report of cannon began to abate about this time and at 12:20 p.m.[25] the last gun was silent. All of our officers were horseless. Buster was badly wounded, but he recovered and was on the Pecos River, in Texas when last heard from. In this battle many of Missouri's best young men were slain, nearly all shot in the head. Out of the seventy-two skirmishes and battles the writer was in during the war, this was by far the most sanguinary, according to the number engaged.

Dr. Flavius J. Lindsey

* * * * * * *

battery. Within moments Sigel's column was in flight, followed by Confederate cavalry in hot pursuit. Piston, 254–255; Bearss, *Wilson's Creek*, 88–92; Wiley Britton, *The Civil War on the Border A Narrative of Military Operations in Missouri, Kansas, Arkansas, and the Indian Territory* (New York, 1899), 87, hereafter cited as Britton.

24. The incident related by Lindsey occurred about 9:00 a.m. and is fairly accurate in its account. About this time General Price launched an assault on Bloody Hill, employing among the many units Clark's Fifth Missouri, which occupied the far left of the charge. Countering Price's move, General Lyon ordered Colonel Deiztler to charge the oncoming rebels with three companies of the First Kansas Infantry. The Union charge stabilized the Federal lines, but wounded Deiztler in the process and caused his Company E, commanded by Captain Powell Clayton, to be separated from the retreating command. Clayton saw an approaching unit and believed it was a Federal command, when in fact it was Clarkson's Missourians, and aligned his command with it. Clayton subsequently recognized Clarkson, separated his bluecoats from Clarkson's grayclads, and challenged them. Michael Buster, Clarkson's Adjutant, was sent to investigate the matter and in the ensuing conversation was ordered to dismount and order his unit not to fire. Dismounting Buster refused to give the order so Clayton shot him at point blank range while Sergeant Patrick Brannon pinned Buster to the ground with a bayonet. Buster miraculously survived the attack, Clarkson gave the order to fire, and the Federals were routed from the field. Piston, 243–244; W. S. Burke, *Official Military History of Kansas Regiments During the War For the Suppression of the Great Rebellion* (Leavenworth, KS, 1870), 457–459, hereafter cited as Burke.

25. The Battle of Wilson's Creek began about 5:30 a.m. and lasted, by most accounts until 11:30 a.m., when the fight for Bloody Hill ended. *O.R.*, 3:63, 69, 105–106; McElroy, 175; Britton, 104.

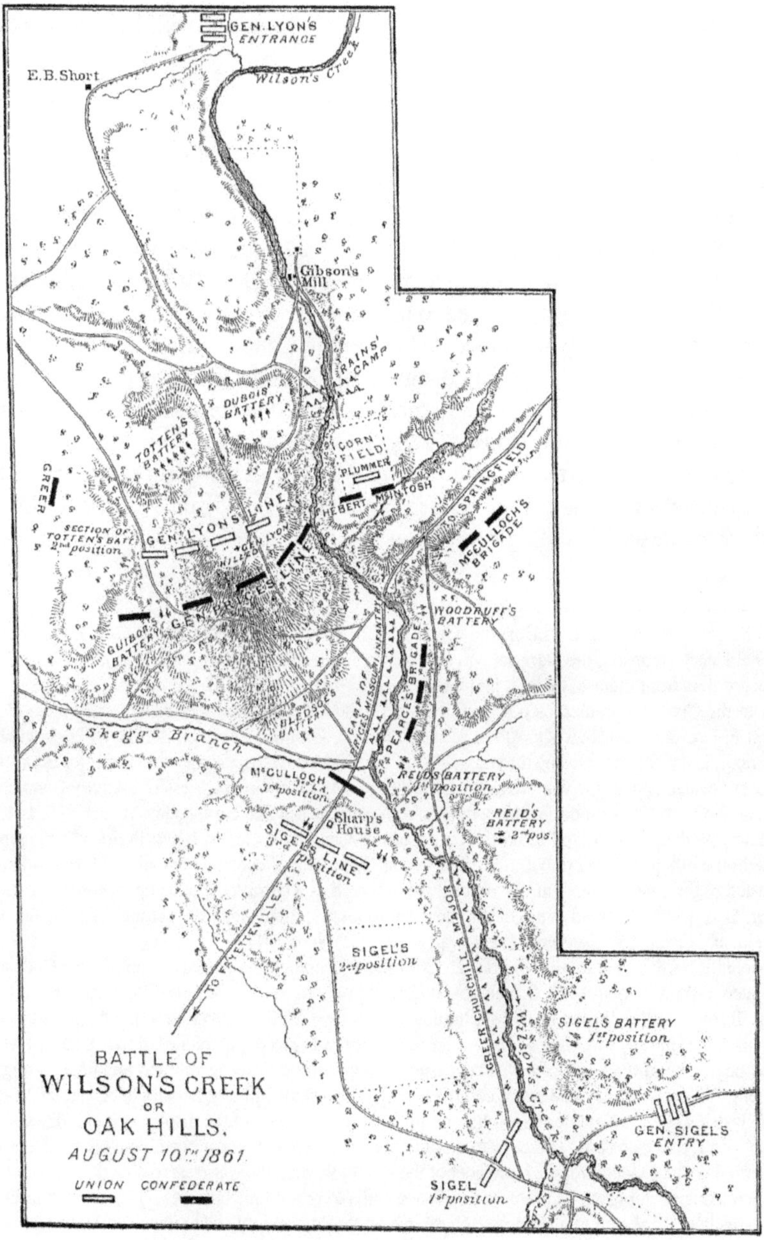
GEN. LYON'S ENTRANCE
Wilson's Creek
E.B. Short
Gibson's Mill
RAINS' CAMP
DUBOIS' BATTERY
TOTTEN'S BATTERY
CORN FIELD
PLUMMER
HEBERT
McINTOSH
GREER
SECTION OF TOTTEN'S BATT. 2nd position
GEN. LYON'S LINE
GEN. LYON KILLED
GEN. PRICE'S LINE
TO SPRINGFIELD
McCULLOCH'S BRIGADE
WOODRUFF'S BATTERY
GUIBOR'S BATTERY
BLEDSOE'S BATTERY
CAMP OF PRICE'S MISSOURI INFANTRY
PEARCE'S BRIGADE
Skeggs Branch
McCULLOCH 3rd LA. 3rd position
REID'S BATTERY 1st position
REID'S BATTERY 2nd pos.
Sharp's House
SIGEL'S LINE 3rd position
TO FAYETTEVILLE
SIGEL'S 2nd position
GREER, CHURCHILL & MAJOR
Wilson's Creek
SIGEL'S BATTERY 1st position
GEN. SIGEL'S ENTRY
SIGEL 1st position
BATTLE OF
WILSON'S CREEK
OR
OAK HILLS.
AUGUST 10TH 1861.
UNION
CONFEDERATE

Item: Arkansas troops at the Battle of Wilson's Creek, by General N. B. Pearce.
Published: August 15, 1885.

Gen. N. B. Pearce, known at West Point and through the war as "Nota Bone" Pearce, is one of two living Confederate generals who took part in the Battle of Oak Hills, known among the Federals as the Battle of Wilson's Creek, John B. Clark, Sr. being the other one. Gen. Pearce graduated from West Point in 1850 and reported for duty in September of that year to Gen. Bragg at Jefferson Barracks[26] St. Louis. He was assigned to the Seventh Infantry. He resigned before the outbreak of the Civil War and located in Benton County, Arkansas, where he now resides, having married the only daughter of Dr. John Smith of that place. When Arkansas passed the ordinance of secession Gen. Pearce was given command of the First Division of the Army of Arkansas. He organized his army with great dispatch, his headquarters being at Camp Walker[27] in the northwest corner of the state. Gen. Pearce was complimented on the field at Wilson's Creek for his gallantry.[28] He describes the fight as follows:

---

26. Jefferson Barracks was established in what would be south St. Louis County on October 23, 1826, by Colonel Henry Atkinson; the barracks was about eight miles south of Civil War St. Louis. Established to protect settlers from Indians, the post participated in the Black War in 1832 and the Mexican War in 1846. Prior to the Civil War numerous personalities were stationed at the barracks including William Harney, Robert E. Lee, Winfield Hancock, Albert Sidney Johnston, Joseph E. Johnston, Nathaniel Lyon and Braxton Bragg, to name a few. During the war Jefferson Barracks served as a rendezvous point for troops in the Western Theater, and, as the war progressed, a military hospital run by the Western Sanitary Commission. In 1863, the Barracks were designated a national cemetery, which still exists today. Winter, 4–7, 144.

27. Camp Walker was located in northwest Arkansas near Maysville, on Beaty Prairie. The camp was located on a 500 acre farm, previously owed by the "Harmonial Vegetarian Society." The main building consisted of three stories, with ninety rooms, which served as a barracks. The camp, according to the *Van Buren Press*, was "well fitted as an encampment for troops, as regards sanitary measures, having fine water convenient." Piston, 98; *Van Buren Press* (Van Buren, AR), June 5, 1861.

28. Nicholas Bartlett Pearce was born on July 20, 1828, in Kentucky, educated at Cumberland College and appointed to West Point in 1846. Graduating in 1850, number twenty-six of forty-four, Pearce served in the Indian Territory and in Western Arkansas until he resigned on April 20, 1858. Entering the business world with his father-in-law, in Osage Mills, Arkansas, Pearce was elected a colonel in the Arkansas Militia. At the beginning of the Civil War, Pearce, despite his opposition to secession, was appointed a brigadier general of Arkansas troops and given command of Northwestern Military District of Arkansas. Wilson's Creek was his only battle, after which he sent his men home, much to the displeasure of Arkansas State officials. In December 1861, Pearce was appointed a Confederate major in the Commissary Department and served in that capacity for the remainder of the war. Following the war, Pearce obtained a pardon from President Andrew Johnson, and returned to Osage Mills to rebuild his business. He became a teacher in 1872, was later employed in a wholesale house in Kansas City, and moved to Texas after the death of his wife, where he worked as a land examiner. He died in Dallas, Texas, on March 8, 1894, at the house of a daughter-in-law. Heitman, 1:778; Allerdice, 179–180; Michael B. Dougan, *Confederate Arkansas: The People and Politics of a Frontier State in Wartime* (University, AL, 1976), 65, hereafter cited as Dougan, *Confederate Arkansas*; Woodruff, 17.

Oak Hill Or Wilson's Creek.

The time agreed upon by the Missouri ex-Confederates for holding the reunion was August 10 to commemorate the action that took place between the Union and Confederate forces at Oak Hill or Wilson's Creek, Mo., this being one of the first and most sanguinary battles that was fought west of the Mississippi River.

The forces engaged on the Confederate side were the Missouri State Guards— commanded by Maj.-Gen. Sterling Price, consisting of the brigades[29] of Rains, Parsons, [James] McBride,[30] [William Y.] Slack,[31] Clark and Weightman, consisting mainly of newly arrived raw material, with such arms as they owned, but made up of as brave and daring man, as their acts on many a hard fought field fully demonstrated, as ever shouldered a gun.

The First Division of the Army of Arkansas,[32] which I commanded, consisted

---

29. The Missourians called their commands divisions, because that was how the state was divided to recruit the MSG. In reality, the commands were closer in size to brigades or regiments as Pearce implies. Only the Eighth Division, MSG, ever attained enough strength to be considered a "division" in military terms, with more than one brigade. Peterson, 22–24.

30. James Higgin McBride was born in Kentucky in 1814, moved to Paris, Missouri, and later relocated to Springfield. A lawyer by profession, McBride was appointed a circuit judge in 1860, and lived in Houston, Missouri, at the beginning of the Civil War. Governor Jackson appointed McBride brigadier general of the Seventh Division, MSG on May 18, 1861, where he served until resigning on February 23, 1862. In the summer of 1862, General Hindman temporarily appointed McBride a general in the Confederate Service, subject to the approval of the Richmond government. Not receiving his commission, McBride resigned in September 1862, and returned to the Missouri State Guard. McBride contracted pneumonia in March 1864, and died at his home in Yell County, Arkansas. See Banasik, *Serving With Honor*, 388–389, for a complete biography.

31. William Yarnel Slack was born on August 1, 1816, in Kentucky and moved to Missouri at the age of three. His family settled near Columbia, where the young Slack was educated. A lawyer by profession, Slack moved to Chillicothe, later commanding a company under Sterling Price in the Mexican War. At the beginning of the Civil War, Slack was appointed a brigadier general, heading the Fourth Division, MSG. He was severely wounded at Wilson's Creek and did not command his division during the Siege of Lexington. Slack was wounded at Pea Ridge on March 7; seeming to be recovering, Slack was moved to another location some seven miles from the battlefield, where his condition deteriorated rapidly. He died on March 21, 1862. Of General Slack, one Confederate veteran recorded, "he was a man of much more than ordinary ability, cool and clear-headed, and a more gallant soldier never lived." *O.R.*, 8:285; James E. McGhee, ed., *Service With the Missouri State Guard: The Memoir of Brigadier General James Harding* (Springfield, MO, 2000), 67; Warner, *Generals in Gray*, 278; Peterson, 136.

32. The First Division, Army of Arkansas began assembling at Osage Mills in Benton County in mid-May 1861, and consisted of State Troops as enumerated by N. B. Pearce. Per their organizational agreement, the men were allowed to determine if they wished to stay in the army after their initial enlistment of six months, or transfer to the Confederate Army. After Wilson's Creek, the Arkansas State Troops left for Arkansas, where a vote was taken on the status of their enlistments. The men were barely clothed, not paid, and according to General Pearce, one of his men stated—"We are as good Southern men as any persons. We have fought the enemy and driven him away. We are needy and will go home, and when another call is made, we will have clothes and shoes and will again do battle for the South." The State Troops were mustered out of the army on August 31, 1861, and their equipment turned in by September 2. *O.R.*, 3:121, 576, 689, 691, 715–716; Woodruff, 54–56; Bearss, "Fort Smith," 336, 338.

of the Third Arkansas Infantry (Gratiot's),[33] Fourth Arkansas Infantry (Walker's),[34] Fifth Arkansas Infantry (Dockery's),[35] Senior First Regiment of Arkansas Cavalry (Carroll's),[36] and Woodruff's and Reed's [Reid's] batteries[37] of artillery. The com-

33. The Third Arkansas Infantry (State Troops), sometimes called Second Arkansas Infantry, was organized in June 1861, with John Rene Gratiot of Washington, Arkansas, being elected colonel. Gratiot was a native of St. Louis and a graduate of West Point, who served with Clark's Battalion of Missouri Volunteers during the Mexican War. By profession Gratiot was both a surgeon and a civil engineer. Following the Mexican War, he relocated to Washington, Arkansas, where he practiced law. His unit participated at Wilson's Creek before being disbanded at the end of August 1861. Many of the companies subsequently joined the Seventeenth Arkansas Infantry (Confederate), while Gratiot remained behind in Arkansas. Heitman, 2:53; Harrell, *Arkansas, Confederate Military History,* 284–285; *O.R.S.,* pt. 2, vol. 2:589, 598; Bearss, "Fort Smith," 338; Charles Edward Nash, *Biographical Sketches of Gen. Pat Cleburne and Gen. T. C. Hindman Together With Humorous Anecdotes and Reminiscences of the Late Civil War* (Little Rock, AR, 1898; reprint ed, Dayton, OH, 1977), 125, hereafter cited as Nash.

34. The Fourth Arkansas Infantry (State Troops) was organized in the late spring of 1861, with Jonathan D. Walker as its colonel. Walker was a circuit judge at Fayetteville, Arkansas, when elected colonel of the Fourth and known as "Little Dave" to distinguish him from Judge David Walker who chaired the Arkansas Secession Convention. Wilson's Creek was the Fourth's only battle, after which it was mustered out of the service. J. D. Walker never entered the service again. After the war, and following reconstruction, Walker was elected U.S. Senator from Arkansas. The Fourth, like the other Arkansas State Troops, was mustered out of the service on August 31, 1861. Harrell, *Arkansas, Confederate Military History,* 286; Piston, 98; Holcombe, 83; Bearss, "Fort Smith," 338.

35. The Fifth Arkansas Infantry Regiment (State Troops) was organized sometime in late spring 1861. Wilson's Creek was the unit's only battle, after which it was disbanded, with several of its members enlisting in the Nineteenth Arkansas Infantry. The commander of the Fifth Arkansas, Colonel Tom P. Dockery, was born on December 18, 1833, in North Carolina. At the beginning of the Civil War, Dockery was a resident Lamartine, Magnolia County, Arkansas. After the Fifth disbanded, Dockery was elected colonel of the Nineteenth Arkansas on May 12, 1862, and moved to the east side of the Mississippi River. Captured at Vicksburg, Dockery was exchanged and returned to the Trans-Mississippi. He was promoted to brigadier general on August 10, 1863, and commanded a brigade during the Camden Expedition. Following the war, having lost his family holdings, Dockery became a civil engineer and moved to Houston, Texas. He died in New York City on February 27, 1898. *O.R.S.,* pt. 2, vol. 2:625; Harrell, *Arkansas, Confederate Military History,* 286; Warner, *Generals in Gray,* 73–74; Sifakis, *Confederacy,* 79.

36. There is little if any information on the First Arkansas Cavalry (State Troops), commanded by Colonel DeRosey Carroll. The regiment was also known as the Third Arkansas Cavalry (State Troops) and was organized in northwest Arkansas. Like the other state troops under General Pearce's control, this unit was disbanded on August 31, 1861, though Harrell in *Confederate Military History,* listed the muster out date as September 19, 1861. Colonel Carroll was born in Maryland, lived for a time in Huntsville, Alabama, and was an "elderly planter" at the beginning of the Civil War. He served as a delegate to the Baltimore Convention for the Southern Democrats in June 1860. Carroll initially served as commandant of Fort Smith in May 1861, and was elected colonel of his regiment a short time later. William Woodruff called Carroll "a brave soldier and an excellent gentleman." After Wilson's Creek, Carroll left the army when his command disbanded and was killed or "assassinated" by a band of Union guerrillas under a Captain Hart, in January 1863, near Fort Smith. Dougan, *Confederate Arkansas,* 29–30, 98; Michael B. Dougan, ed., *Confederate Women of Arkansas in the Civil War Memorial Reminiscences* (Fayetteville, AR, 1993), 85, hereafter cited as Dougan, *Confederate Women*; Harrell, *Arkansas, Confederate Military History,* 286; Woodruff, 21–22; Bearss, "Fort Smith," 338.

37. John G. Reid's Arkansas Battery (also known as the Ft. Smith Battery) consisted of four guns of unknown type and caliber, though they were probably 6-lb smoothbores. The men, according to one observer, were of "excellent material," who were well drilled in the operation of the battery. After Wilson's Creek the battery was disbanded, just like all the other units of Pearce's command and Reid left the army. Reid returned to the army in July 1862, to command a two gun battery at Prairie Grove. The battery and

mand of Gen. Ben. McCulloch, composed of the Third Louisiana (Hebert's),[38] McRae's Battalion,[39] Churchill's Cavalry Regiment,[40] and Greer's Texas cavalry.[41] The whole (by consent of Gen. Price and myself in order to ensure concerted action) was under the chief command of Gen. McCulloch of the regular Confederate Army; a noted Texas Indian fighter, who had won his first laurels under the hero of San Jacinto in the Texas War of Independence.

For several days before the battle took place efforts had been made by spies

---

Reid would disappear from the official records sometime thereafter. Bearss, *Wilson's Creek*, 75; Banasik, *Embattled Arkansas*, 516, 526; Telegram (July 19, 1862), Hindman to Carroll, Copy Book of Telegrams, Telegram file, Peter W. Alexander Collection, Columbia University; Letter (July 17, 1862), Newton to Carroll, Hindman's Command (June 1–December 18, 1862), 90–91 (hereafter cited as Copy Letter Book No. 1); Special Orders No. 29 (July 17, 1862), Special Order Letter Book No. 1, 40–41; Woodruff, 24–25; Bearss, "Fort Smith," 338.

38. The Third Louisiana Infantry (also known as the Pelican Rifles) was organized in April and May 1861, and entered Confederate Service on May 17 with 1085 officers and men, largely from northern Louisiana. The unit fought at Wilson's Creek and Pea Ridge before moving to the east side of the Mississippi River. Again bloodied at Corinth and Iuka, Mississippi, in 1862, the Third was captured at Vicksburg on July 4, 1863. The Third Louisiana was paroled and returned to Louisiana where it awaited exchange. On July 21, 1864, the Third Louisiana was officially exchanged, while stationed in Shreveport, Louisiana, but it never participated in another battle. Louis Hébert, a Louisiana native, commanded the unit until his promotion to brigadier general on May 26, 1862. See Appendix B for a biography of Louis Hébert. Boatner, 391; Tunnard, 26–29, 319; *Confederate Military History: Louisiana*, by John Dimitry, 305–307, hereafter cited as Dimitry, *Louisiana, Confederate Military History*; Ingenthron, 145.

39. McRae's Arkansas Battalion was mustered into the Confederate Service on July 15, 1861, at a camp near Bentonville, Arkansas, by James McIntosh. The battalion contained four companies, with Lieutenant Colonel Dandridge McRae in command. The battalion added six companies in the fall of 1861, making it a regiment, being numerated the Twenty-first Arkansas Infantry. The battalion fought at Wilson's Creek and the regiment at Pea Ridge before being transferred to the east side of the Mississippi River in April 1862, where it completed its military service. Dandridge McRae was born on October 10, 1829, in Alabama, graduated from the University of South Carolina in 1849, and moved to Arkansas to manage the family plantation. At the beginning of the Civil War, he was living in Searcy, Arkansas, where he practiced law. In addition to the Battle of Wilson's Creek, McRae also fought at the Arkansas battles of Prairie Grove (December 7, 1862), Helena (July 4, 1863) and participated in the Camden and Red River Expeditions. By war's end, he had been promoted to brigadier general. After the war, McRae returned to Searcy and resumed his law practice and in 1881, was elected the Arkansas Secretary of State. He died on April 23, 1899, at Searcy, where he was buried. *O.R.*, 3:112–113; *O.R.*, 8:728, 746; *O.R.S.*, pt. 2, vol. 14:563, 566, 567–570, 572–573, 575; Warner, *Generals in Gray*, 206.

40. Churchill's Cavalry Regiment, also known as the First Arkansas Mounted Rifles, was commanded by Thomas J. Churchill. The regiment was organized in May 1861, at Fort Smith, Arkansas, with 768 officers and men. Participating at Wilson's Creek and Pea Ridge, the First Arkansas Mounted Rifles was transferred to the east side of the Mississippi River in April 1862, where it was dismounted. The unit never returned to the Trans-Mississippi Department, surrendering on April 26, 1865. Banasik, *Embattled Arkansas*, 8–10; Crute, 42.

41. Greer's Texas Cavalry Regiment was also known as the "South Kansas-Texas Regiment" or the Third Texas Cavalry. The unit was organized at Dallas, Texas, on June 13, 1861, and moved to Missouri, where it fought at Wilson's Creek. Later, 350 men of the unit participated in the Battle of Chustenahlah, Indian Territory, on December 26, 1861, where they routed their foe. In March 1862, Greer's Regiment was at Pea Ridge, after which it was transferred to the east side of the Mississippi River. Arriving in Memphis, Tennessee, in April 1862, the regiment completed its military service as part of Ross's Texas Cavalry Brigade, surrendering in May 1865. *O.R.*, 8:28–29; Harold B. Simpson, *Texas in the War 1861–1865* (Hillsboro, TX, 1965), 112, hereafter cited as Simpson; Banasik, *Embattled Arkansas*, 8–10.

and otherwise to get information of the strength and position of the opposing forces commanded by Gen. N. Lyons of the United States Army, which was then at or near Springfield, Mo. Finally, some ladies of Springfield obtaining a pass to go outside the Federal lines, drove by a circuitous route and came to Gen. Price's headquarters and furnished the desired information. Gen. Price and the Missouri generals had been clamorous and unjust in their demand on Gen. McCulloch for an immediate advance on the enemy. McCulloch wanted to ascertain more fully what was in front of him.[42] Now that this information was obtained Gen. McCulloch on the evening of the 9th of August after a council of war had been held, composed of the general officers before mentioned, issued an order for an advance on Springfield that night at 9 o'clock.

As soon as the order was issued the whole camp was in a state of activity and excitement, largely making out preparations for the long-wished-for opportunity to meet the foe—to take revenge for having forced them from their homes and firesides and punish them for their impudence and temerity. The universal feeling in the command, produced by the order to advance, was one of joy. Everything was made ready; knapsacks—of those having such an important article—were packed; haversacks filled; bullets molded and powder and cap issued, so that all might be in readiness. As the evening approached the skies became overcast and low, threatening of distant thunder was heard. The big drops of rain began to fall and as a large part of the command had no cartridge boxes in which to carry their ammunition, Gen. McCulloch decided not to move until later. So just before 9 o'clock an order was sent to the various division and brigade commanders that no movement would be made until "further orders," but to sleep on our arms and be ready to move at a moment's warning. This order

General Ben McCulloch

---

42. According to Richard Musser, who was serving as the Judge Advocate General of the Third Division, MSG, the Confederate forces were well aware of the conditions in Springfield. Musser wrote:

> General Price had accurate information from many and reliable sources of the condition of Lyon's forces in at Springfield. The means of this accurate information was astonishing. He had daily communications, in one shape or other, with the enemy's camp. Ladies visiting camp brought letters in cipher or verbally; newspapers and almost daily arrival from all parts of the State of recruits and visitors, made the situation known to him.

Peterson, 108; Musser, 1:682–683.

did not arrive, was not given and just at an early dawn a sergeant of my body-guard of Capt. Carroll's company,[43] named Hite, dashed up to my headquarters, without hat, and with great excitement said:[44] "General, the enemy is on us."

"How do you know?" said I.

"They shot at men when I was up at the spring, where I had gone after water, and where I lost my hat."

I directed the sergeant to go at once to Gen. McCulloch and give him the information.[45] I at once proceeded to put my command in readiness for action, my position being in the center of the camp. I placed Woodruff's battery on an eminence to command the lines of approach from the west and the north. Reid's battery was placed so as to command the east and south.[46] Gratiot's regiment was stationed as a support to Woodruff's battery, and Walk-

General Sterling Price

---

43. Charles A. Carroll commanded an independent company of Arkansas Cavalry, raised in Fayetteville, Arkansas. The forty-man company acted as McCulloch's bodyguard at Wilson's Creek. Like the other militia companies, this one probably disbanded in the end of August 1861. Prior to the war, Charles A. Carroll, a resident of Conway County, Arkansas, was a Democratic candidate for the Arkansas State Legislature and a close friend of Governor Henry Rector. After his militia service, Carroll was assigned to duty as a Confederate colonel, commanding northwest Arkansas on June 3, 1862, and later commanded a cavalry brigade, which he led at the Battle of Cane Hill on November 28, 1862. Carroll was relived of command following Cane Hill, pending an investigation. Returning to Conway County, Carroll never reentered to the army. Ross, 339, 373; Piston, 207; Special Orders No. 6 (June 3, 1862), No. 20 (October 22, 1862), No. 23 (October 26, 1862) and No. 60 (December 3, 1862), Special Orders Book No. 1, 4, 87–89, 91–92.

44. Sergeant Hite, with another man of Carroll's command had, against orders, left camp and went down to the Ray springhouse to get water, and detected Lyons's column, which was approaching the battlefield from the northwest. *O.R*, 3:121, 126–127; Brooksher, 183; Bearss, *Wilson's Creek*, 73.

45. McCulloch received information on the impending attack from multiple sources. At the time, about 6:00 a.m., McCulloch was at breakfast with General Price when Colonel John Snyder, of Rains's Division, came in from General Rains, reporting the Federals approaching from the north. Within minutes another courier arrived announcing the Federal advance, but Sigel's move was not discerned until gunfire from the south announced his presence. McCulloch makes no mention in his official report of when Pearce's courier arrived, I suspect, because at the time, it was a moot point. *O.R*, 3:100; Snead, 271–272.

46. During the previous night Woodruff's Battery, like the other troops in the rebel army, rested on their arms; the artillery horses were harnessed and separated for marching on the morn. At 6:00 a.m. Captain Woodruff observed a Federal battery, Totten's, deploying on Bloody Hill and firing its first shot. Without orders or any direction, Woodruff's Battery went into action where they had rested the previous night. General Pearce would appear a short time later and approve the disposition of the battery. Reid's Battery was ordered into position by James McIntosh, not Pearce. [Note: Woodruff's unpublished report on the Battle of Wilson's Creek was printed in his book *With the Light Guns*, 39–43.] Woodruff, 39–41.

er's to Reed's.[47]

Ready For Action

Gen. Price having also been informed that the enemy was approaching down the creek, where they had attacked Gen. Rains, soon had his command in line of battle and ready for action. Gen. McCulloch in person, with Herbert's [*sic*] and Wm. Rea's regiment, met the advances of the enemy in a cornfield north of the creek, when, after a desperate hand-to-hand struggle, in which Gen. Price's command took an important and active part, succeeded in driving Logan back.[48] Guibor's[49] and Bledsoe's batteries of Missourians doing the enemy great damage and making for themselves a name in history that will long be remembered.

On the left Gen. Sigel had advanced around the extreme left of the Confederates and surprised Churchill's regiment in their tents just after daylight, and a volley from his artillery was the first information they had of Sigel's approach. Col. Churchill moved to the south and west part of the field in which he was encamped. When out of the reach of the enemy he formed his command and did gallant service throughout the day.[50] Sigel moved up in the rear of my command and placed

47. Gratiot's and Walker's commands moved to their assigned positions on the east side of Wilson's Creek, and remained in place through most of the battle. Toward the end of the contest, Gratiot's Third Arkansas Infantry Regiment (State Troops) were ordered into the fight on Bloody Hill, but Walker's command remained in place supporting Reid's Battery. Walker would suffer no losses in the battle, while Gratiot lost 23 killed and 83 wounded; total 106. Woodruff, 42–43; *O.R.*, 3:123.

48. The battle in the cornfield took place at about 7:00 a.m. on the east side of Wilson Creek, between Plummer's battalion (not Logan's) of U.S. Regulars and Hébert's Third Louisiana Infantry, with McIntosh's Second Arkansas Mounted Rifles; Bledsoe's Missouri and Woodruff's Arkansas Batteries provided support. The Confederate cornfield force was commanded by Colonel McIntosh. Dandridge McRae's (not William Rea's) Arkansas Battalion had been ordered to the Confederate flank with McIntosh's force, but became split when a cavalry command ran through the battalion; McRae, with a part of his command ended up supporting Woodruff's Battery while the other men in his battalion were leaderless for a time, rejoining McRae after Sigel's artillery had been captured. The Federal battalion numbered about 300 men while the Confederates countered with about 1,000 men. *O.R.*, 3:112–113; Bearss, *Wilson's Creek*, 75–76, 82, 84–85; Snead, 277–278.

49. Guibor's Missouri Battery was part of the Sixth Division MSG. The battery was organized in June-July 1861, with four 6-lb smoothbore guns while heading to Carthage, Missouri. The battery fought at the Missouri battles of Carthage, Wilson's Creek, Dry Wood Creek, Lexington, and Pea Ridge, Arkansas. In April 1862, it was transferred to the east side of the Mississippi River, where it completed its military service in the Army of Tennessee. Henry Guibor was born in Alsace, France, in 1823, and by the beginning of the Civil War had settled in St. Louis. Prior to the war, Guibor was a carpenter, served as a deputy sheriff and was part of the St. Louis Militia. Captured at Camp Jackson, Guibor did not believe his capture or parole were legal so he joined the MSG, being appointed captain on June 28, 1861. He later enlisted in the Confederate Army and was wounded on March 30, 1863, during the Vicksburg Campaign. Again wounded at Kennesaw Mountain, Georgia, in 1864, Guibor survived and was present at the surrender of General Johnston in North Carolina. Guibor lived out his remaining years in St. Louis, dying of cancer on October 17, 1899. Snead, 217; Peterson, 191; Winter, 137–138.

50. After Churchill reformed his command, he moved his men northward toward Oak or Bloody Hill, where an aid from General Price asked the colonel to reinforce the Missouri line. With no further direction, Churchill formed his 600-man regiment on the left of Price's line and remained in that position throughout the day. By the end of the battle on Oak Hill, Churchill's First Arkansas Mounted Rifles had lost 42 killed

his artillery in position immediately in front of Reid's battery, unlimbered and prepared for action, lighting linstocks and port-fires, but for some cause changed his notion and ordered the battery to change so as to front west which gave Reid's battery an enfilading fire on his battery.[51] In order to ascertain what troops were forming south of my position I sent two of my staff officers—Capt. Tom Jefferson and Col. Emmett MacDonald (both subsequently killed in action during the war) to find out. Capt. Jefferson darted up to the troops near Sharp's house, and demanded to know what command that was. A soldier covered him with his gun and demanded his surrender. Jefferson replied: "I want no foolishness; Gen. Pearce has sent me here to find out what troops these are." The soldier replied: "Dismount, we are Federals, and you are my prisoner." Poor Jefferson was carried to Rolla with the enemy on their retreat, before he was exchanged.[52]

Col. MacDonald seeing the trouble in which Jefferson's rashness had involved him, wheeled his horse, made good his escape and returned to my headquarters, with the desired information. But with a glass I had already discovered that the troops were Federals—the flag bearer in climbing the fence let go its folds, and the wind extending the flag, I saw that it was the stars and stripes, and at once ordered Capt. Reid to open on them, which was done with such unerring aim that they were literally cut to pieces.[53] When in dire confusion from the effects of Reid's cannon Gen. McCulloch advanced with a portion of the Third Louisiana Regiment and captured the battery, excepting one piece, which being in the brush

and 155 wounded—about one third of the command. *O.R.*, 3:109–110; Banasik, *Missouri In 1861*, 378.

51. After driving the Confederate cavalry out of Sharp's cornfield, Sigel moved his command forward and established a blocking position on a bluff near Sharp's house and overlooking Skegg's branch. Backof's Battery had four guns on the bluff facing the main road off to the northeast, with the another two facing northward. Sigel for his part did not detect the presence of Reid's Arkansas Battery on the bluff to his east and simply waited for the Confederates on Oak Hill to retreat or rout in his direction. Piston, in his book on Wilson's Creek, has Bledsoe's Missouri Battery enfilading the Union line, while Bearss has Reid's command enfilading the line. Sigel in a piece published after the war had Reid's Battery enfilading his right flank. Based on the various descriptions of the Federal line both batteries enfiladed some portion of the Union position, which was poorly positioned. Brooksher, 192–193; Snead, 278–280; Piston, 250, 253–255; Bearss, *Wilson's Creek*, 88; Franz Sigel, "The Flanking Column at Wilson's Creek," *Battles and Leaders of the Civil War*, 4 vols. (New York, 1887–1888), 1:305, hereafter cited as Sigel.

52. In other pieces that Pearce wrote on the Battle of Wilson's Creek, including his official report, he makes no mention of sending Jefferson and MacDonald to investigate the Federals about the Sharp house. Author William Piston was mystified as to why Peace did nothing while Sigel sat idle. Piston called Pearce's explanation of inactivity as "hardly credible" and further wrote: "Pearce did nothing to remind the army commander of their presence. He seems to have been content with a largely passive role." The sending of staff officers to investigate the situation may explain the matter, but it still appears that Pearce was trying to cover up his inactivity while Lyon was engaging Price, and Sigel was sending cannon balls into the rear of the rebel lines on Oak Hill. *O.R.*, 3:121–122; N. B. Pearce, "Arkansas Troops in the Battle of Wilson's Creek," *Battles and Leaders of the Civil War*, 1:298–303, hereafter cited as Pearce; Piston, 254.

53. According to Federal accounts, the artillery fire of Reid and Bledsoe did little material damage to Sigel's formation. However, the surprise firing of the artillery, followed immediately by the sudden assault of the Third Louisiana and supporting troops unhinged the Unionists, who went fleeing in every direction. General Sigel described the situation as "frightful confusion," with the troops "throwing themselves into the bushes and by-roads, retreating as well as they could." Brooksher, 202; *O.R.*, 3:87.

the cannoneers and drivers escaped with, by going around the entire army and getting back to Springfield.[54] As McCulloch was advancing on this battery a Federal soldier, not thirty yards away, covered him with a gun. McCulloch raised his hand and waved it back and forth in front of his face to disconcert him. The man lowered his gun, and before he could raise it one of the Third Louisiana planted a ball square in the forehead, killing him instantly.[55]

During the action which Price and McCulloch had sustained with Lyon, mention should have been made of the part taken by Woodruff's battery. This command was made up of the elite of Little Rock and had been drilled by Capt. Latien[56] of the United States Army whose command had been stationed at the arsenal at that place. As fate would have it Billy Woodruff (as everyone called the youthful commander of this company of gallant boys) was to win his first laurels in artillery drill with their former instructor and with my guns that had formerly constituted Totten's battery. In this duel Lieut. Omerweam [Omer Weaver] of Little Rock fell mortally wounded from a grape shot in the shoulder, dying before the action was over, and this brave and chivalrous boy not permitted to rejoin in the victory he had so gallantry contributed toward gaining.[57] This battery, not only here, but in

54. Not true. The Third Louisiana captured four guns in the assault, while the fifth gun was captured by Greer's Texas Cavalry, who pursued the fleeing bluecoats toward Springfield. The fifth gun was captured at the crossing of the James Fork of the White River, where Sigel's half of the retreating column was ambushed. In all Sigel lost 64 killed, 147 captured and the fifth artillery piece at the James Fork crossing. Sigel, himself with one other man, arrived back in Springfield about 2:00 p.m., and according to William Wherry, an aid to General Lyon, went to bed. *O.R.*, 3:119; Sigel, 1:305; Brooksher, 208–209; Monaghan, 177–178; Piston, 260–261; Peckham, 337.

55. As the Third Louisiana was advancing to the attack, General Sigel sent a Corporal or Private Charles Todt, Company K, Third Missouri Infantry (Three Months) to check on the identity of the advancing column. After an exchange of words, Todt realized the advancing troops were rebels, raised his weapon to fire, but Henry H. Gentles, Third Louisiana Infantry, emptied his piece first, killing Todt. General McCulloch turned to Gentles, who had just saved his life, remarking, "That was a good shot." Piston, 253; Tunnard, 53.

56. There is no "Captain Latien" listed in the *Historical Register*, nor is there any reference to a man of that name in the *Official Records* or *Supplement to the Official Records*. At the time that Woodruff's Battery was organized in Little Rock the arsenal was garrisoned by "Military Store Keeper" Richard H. Fathery, of Arkansas, followed by Captain James Totten with his artillery company in November 1860. In further statements, Pearce seems to imply that Totten was responsible for teaching Woodruff's command to drill. According to Woodruff, the only substantial training that the battery got in artillery drill occurred at Fort Smith after the battery moved to that place in mid-May 1861, and at Camp Walker in June. Prior to the move, Woodruff had some rudimentary training under Bushrod Johnson which proved "barely sufficient to qualify a gun squad to officiate in firing a salute, at some 'important' college function." The Pulaski Battery, as the unit was known, was proficient in infantry drill, but little more, until July 1861. Heitman, 1:415, passim; Harrell, *Arkansas, Confederate Military History*, 4; *O.R.S.*, passim; Woodruff, 21–25, 28–29.

57. Omer Rose Weaver was born in Kentucky in 1837, and his family relocated to Little Rock in 1838. A child of privilege, Weaver lived in one of the most expensive mansions in town, graduated from the University of Nashville in 1856, and worked for the U.S. Surveyor General in Little Rock. By all accounts, Weaver would be called a "dandy," being expensively and impeccably dressed. A member of the local debating club, Weaver was elected the first lieutenant of the Pulaski Light Artillery in 1860 and was considered an excellent officer. He met his fate in the opening hour of the Battle of Wilson's Creek. Weaver was struck with a cannonball in the right shoulder, which also crushed his chest. He died a short time later,

many other bloody fields gained undying laurels.[58]

Sigel's Overthrow.

Sigel having been completely routed, his command retreating on the "same quipent" principal was pursued by Greer's Texas rangers and run down and shot in the cornfields like cowboys after jack rabbits, Sigel himself escaping to Springfield unattended by anyone excepting a single orderly.

This terminated the first part of the battle, when the contending forces seemed to withdraw in order to gain strength for the impending struggle that was to decide the yet doubtful victory. Gen. Lyon concentrated his forces up the creek and mostly on the south side above or west of the Springfield road. Gen. Price with his gallant Missourians was on the hill known as Bloody Hill, from the carnage that took place on it. Gen. McCulloch being east of Price's command with his infantry regiments (His cavalry having made many desperate and effective charges on the enemy, at one time driving the men from the guns of a battery; but failing to carry it off, it was again taken possession of by the enemy, Col. Carroll thinking that our infantry would do so. Thus lost the battery after having gallantly taken it).[59] Col. McIntosh, adjutant general on McCulloch's staff, rode up to me and informed me that Gen. McCulloch needed reinforcements for the portion of our army in front of Lyon. I sent a section of Reed's battery and five companies of the Fifth Infan-

---

the first death in Woodruff's Battery at Wilson's Creek. Woodruff, 44–45; Piston, 112–113.

58. After Wilson's Creek, Woodruff's Battery spent another eleven days in Missouri, departing Springfield on August 21, 1861, to be mustered out of the service in Arkansas. At Elm Springs, Washington County, Arkansas, Woodruff's men took a vote to determine if they would remain in state service or become regular Confederates. By a large majority the unit decided that they had served their time and voted to go home. On September 2, at Fayetteville, Arkansas, Woodruff turned over all his property and guns to Colonel Thomas C. Hindman and disbanded his command. Woodruff would recruit another battery between November 1861, and January 1862, with thirty of his former men as a nucleus, while many joined other commands, or, in the case of William Blocher and Henry West, formed their own batteries. Woodruff, 54–56, 64; Bearss, "Fort Smith," 334; Britton, 119.

59. About 10:00 a.m., Colonel Greer with five companies of his cavalry regiment was ordered to attack the Union right flank. Greer moved his command, undetected, across the front on Oak Hill, picking up Carroll's Arkansas Cavalry Regiment as he went and successfully positioned his command in the Union rear and on their right flank. Having no sabers, Greer ordered his men to draw pistols and charge. With a loud "shout for Texas," the Texans charged up Oak Hill, completely surprising the Federals in that quarter. Unfortunately for the rebels, the attack was poorly executed, even though it did scatter some of Totten's men and a Union company which was skirmishing on that flank. Greer's attack quickly evaporated following a devastating volley from Company K, Second Kansas Infantry, commanded by Lieutenant Gustavus Schroyer, and Totten's artillery. Carroll, who was following, did little better. Both units subsequently rallied and redeployed on the Confederate left flank to continue the battle. Of the attack, Captain Totten wrote: "It was so *effete* and ineffectual in its force and character as to deserve only the appellation of child's play." An Iowan called the attack "disorderly" and made by a "crowd of cavalry." The assault had the potential to have seriously affected the Union forces, but the lack of proper preparation and control resulted in a non-event. *O.R.*, 3:74, 118–119, 126; Bearss, *Wilson's Creek*, 103–104, 117–118; Piston, 270–271; Ware, 322; Alice L. Fry, *Kansas and Kansans in the Civil War: First Through the Thirteenth Volunteer Regiment* (Kansas City, KS, 1996), 22, hereafter cited as Fry; Samuel J. Crawford, *Kansas in the Sixties* (Chicago, 1911), 34, hereafter cited as Crawford.

try (Dockery's) with McIntosh to McCulloch's assistance—and taking Gratiot's Third Arkansas, went with them to reinforce Gen. Price, leaving Woodruff's battery unprotected.[60] In descending to the creek to cross, a shell from Totten's battery passed under my horse or near his fore legs, causing him to fall. Many of the soldiers seeing me go down supposed that I was killed, and such was the report at the time. I led this command to the position nearby Gen. Price. In doing so I passed by old Gen. John B. Blark [Clark], who had been hotly engaged with the enemy—He was wounded in the leg—a flesh wound—painful, but still the gallant old hero stayed on the field until victory was declared in favor of the Confederates. On reaching Gen. Price he informed me of the position of the enemy, and of the contemplated movement to be made by our entire force on him—which was to be done at once—I moved my command forward, and had not advanced more than 100 yards when I

Discovered The Enemy

in force in two lines of battle in my front. I at once ordered the charge which was made with great energy and gallantry by Gratiot's Third Arkansas Infantry in advance, and followed up by Gen. Price's Missourians and McCulloch with his infantry on the right. This attack was so sudden and so vigorous that nothing could stand before it. Lyon's first line gave way,[61] hotly pursued by the Confederates and before they could pass the second line it also gave way. Gen. Lyon, in his superhuman efforts to rally the troops, was killed,[62] falling from his horse into the

---

60. The action described by Pearce occurred about 10:00 as the battle was coming to a conclusion. Lyon was already dead, and, the Confederates nearing exhaustion, were buoyed by the enthusiastic arrival of Pearce's reinforcements. For the Confederates on Oak Hill, Pearce's arrival with fresh troops turned the tide and secured victory for them on this day. However, according to Pearce's official report on the battle, he sent seven companies of the Fifth Arkansas Infantry Regiment (State Troops), not five as he mentions in his article. *O.R.*, 3:121; Bearss, *Wilson's Creek*, 126.

61. In about thirty minutes, Gratiot's Third Arkansas Infantry Regiment (State Troops) lost 110 men of 571 engaged or about twenty percent of his command. As they moved to the attack, thus spearheading the final Confederate assault on the Federal lines, they were cheered by their Confederate brethren on Oak Hill. After about fifty paces, Gratiot's boys went to the ground, being raked by artillery and musket fire from the Federals on the hill; but they held their ground. This last assault "proved to be the decisive engagement" in the battle. About 11:30 a.m., with their ammunition nearly exhausted, the Unionists began to pull back; they had been ordered to withdraw and were not pushed back as Pearce implies. Bearss, *Wilson's Creek*, 127–128, 130; 302–303; Pearce, 1:302–303.

62. By most accounts General Lyon was killed about 9:30 a.m., well before the events described by General Pearce. The most credible accounts have Lyon directing Captain Thomas W. Sweeny to lead a portion of the First Iowa Infantry forward, while he and Colonel Robert Mitchell led the Second Kansas Infantry into the fray. As the Second Kansas crested Oak Hill, they were met by a crushing volley; Lyon was hit in the chest and died within seconds, while Mitchell took rounds in his thigh and calf. Mitchell survived the battle, but turned command of his regiment over to Lieutenant Colonel Charles Blair, who finished the battle unscathed. Some accounts have Lyon leading the First Iowa forward, which on the surface could easily be misunderstood, as Lyon was close to the First Iowa Infantry when the final Union advance began. One of the best accounts comes from Samuel Crawford, who commanded a company in the Second Kansas. According to Crawford, who was only ten paces away when Lyon was stuck, his unit fired a volley into the rebels, "over Lyon's body." Still another account by William Wherry, Lyon's aid-de-camp, has

arms of Col. [Robert] Mitchell[63] of the Second Kansas, who then took command, but he was shot through the thigh with a minnie ball and taken off the field. The retreating army was then taken command of by Maj. Sturgess [Sturgis][64] of the old United States Army, and the fight was over, the enemy leaving their dead general in the field. Capt. Tom McKinney, seeing the body of an officer in uniform, reported the fact to Gen. Price, who, as soon as he saw it, exclaimed "'Tis Gen. Lyon' I knew him well!" And calling to a sergeant directed him to take charge of the body and have it removed to his headquarters. This was done. The remains were called for by a party under a flag of truce that evening and delivered to the Federals by order of Gen. McCulloch.[65] During the hottest of the fight Woodruff's battery (which had been doing efficient service against Lyon's infantry while the

---

Lyon leading both the Second Kansas and two companies of the First Iowa forward. Banasik, *Missouri In 1861*, 149; Holcombe, 36; Piston, 265, 268–269; Brooksher, 213; Burke, 17; Crawford, 32–33; William H. Wherry, "Wilson's Creek, and the Death of Lyon," *Battles and Leaders of the Civil War*, 1:295; McElroy, 171; Britton, 98.

63. Robert Byington Mitchell was born on April 4, 1823, in Mansfield, Ohio. He attended college in Ohio and Pennsylvania and later practiced law in his home town. During the Mexican War, he served as a lieutenant in the Second Ohio Infantry. Returning home, Mitchell was elected mayor of Gilead, Ohio, in 1855, but left Ohio in 1856, for Linn County, Kansas. A Democrat, Mitchell espoused the Free Soiler cause, and served in the Kansas Territorial Legislature prior to the Civil War. He raised the Second Kansas Infantry and was appointed colonel on May 23, 1861. He received a brigadier general's commission on April 8, 1862. Following his promotion, Mitchell served on the east side of the Mississippi River, and in 1864, returned to the Trans-Mississippi to command first in Nebraska (January 1–April 11, 1865) then Kansas (April 11–June 28, 1864). Following the war, Mitchell served as Governor of New Mexico (1865–1867), after which he moved to Washington, D.C., where he died on January 26, 1882. Warner, *Generals in Blue*, 328–329; *The Union Army A History of Military Affairs in the Loyal United States 1861–1865—Records of the Regiments in the Union Army—Cyclopedia of Battles—Memoirs of Commanders and Soldiers*, 8 vols. (New York, 1908; reprint ed., Wilmington, NC, 1998), 8:178 (hereafter cited as *Union Army*); Boatner, 557–558; Sifakis, *Union*, 276–277.

64. Samuel D. Sturgis was born on June 11, 1822, in Pennsylvania, graduated from West Point in 1846 (number 32 of 59), and served in the Mexican War. At the beginning of the Civil War, he evacuated Fort Smith, Arkansas, and proceeded to Fort Leavenworth, Kansas, where he assumed command. Sturgis led a brigade at Wilson's Creek, and took command of Lyon's wing of the army upon the latter's death. After Wilson's Creek, Sturgis served for a time on the staff of General David Hunter before being transferred to the east side of the Mississippi River, where he completed his Civil War service. Sturgis was promoted to general officer in March 1862, to date from August 10, 1861, and to major general by war's end. He retired from the army in 1886, and died on September 28, 1899. See Banasik, *Missouri In 1861*, 364–365, for biography. *O.R.*, 3:62; Boatner, 816–817.

65. Following the Battle of Wilson's Creek, the Federal Army failed to take the body of General Lyon with them. It was discovered a short time later and taken to the Ray house on the battlefield. As to who first identified the body, Holcombe, in his short book on the battle, stated that more than a dozen people claim to have been the first to identify Lyon's body. Piston writes that Colonel James McIntosh was the first to identify Lyon's remains. Be that as it may, after the body was cleaned up, it was placed in a wagon and sent to Springfield under an escort of four Confederates and Doctor S. H. Melcher, of the Fifth Missouri Infantry (Union, Three Months), who had remained behind on the battlefield to tend to the wounded. En route to Springfield the escort party, passed Lieutenant Charles W. Canfield and his company of Federal cavalry, who were sent to the battlefield, under a flag of truce, to recover Lyon's body. The remains were delivered to Major John M. Schofield at about 9 p.m. at Lyon's old headquarters. By far the best account of the aftermath of Lyon's body is presented in Holcombe's book on Wilson's Creek. Piston, 302; Holcombe, 96–100; Peckham, 339; Musser, 4:679.

charge was being made in front) suddenly ceased firing. I noticed this, and having taken away the support of the battery to reinforce Price was fearful that the enemy had captured the battery. I at once started with the intention of taking Walker's regiment to recapture the battery. But on reaching the position I saw Capt. Woodruff limbering up to move his battery to some other point. I called to the captain to know the object, and was told that Gen. McCulloch had ordered the change. This was just

At The Critical Moment.

My reply was, "Dog on it, unlimber, and open on that blue retreating column;" which was done quickly, and soon the battle was over and the Confederates victorious.[66]

Gen. McCulloch at this time also arrived at Woodruff's battery, and on being complimented by me on the victory he had just achieved, responded in his usual trim and emphatic manner "The d—d [damned] rascals had me whipped; your coming saved me and won the battle; you deserve and shall have the credit of it."[67]

In the fight fell Gen. Weightman, commanding a Missouri brigade, a graduate of West Point, brave and chivalrous. He early in the war proved his earnestness to the cause he had espoused and with his life sealed his devotion to it. No braver or more gallant man fell then Weightman. Many other brave and gallant heroes, though perhaps not so noted, still as true and devoted, were left on the bloody field, and, while the survivors are permitted to live and meet in grand reunions we should remember the brave men who rest under the sod; we should remember the loved ones they left and see that the widow is cared for and the child educated and given a chance to be useful as a member of society and of a free and generous country.

N. B. Pearce

* * * * * * *

---

66. Pearce was mixing up and combining events in the battle to make it appear that his orders to Woodruff had a significant impact. During the course of the battle, Woodruff only moved his guns once, about one hundred yards to the right; this occurred early on, between 6:30–7:00 a.m., and at the direction of General Pearce. As the battle was closing, Woodruff did indeed pepper the retreating Union command with artillery rounds, but by all accounts Pearce was no where near the battery, being with the Third Arkansas Infantry (State Troops), which he led to Oak Hill on the Confederate left. Pearce gives no indication in his other accounts of the battle that he directed Woodruff to fire into the retreating Unionists. *O.R.*, 3:121–122; Pearce, 1:302–303; Woodruff, 42–43, 45–46; Bearss, *Wilson's Creek*, 81–82.

67. In his official report on the Battle of Wilson's Creek, General McCulloch wrote: "General Pearce, with his Arkansas brigade (Gratiot's, Walker's and Dockery's regiments of infantry), came gallantly to the rescue when sent for, leading his men into the thickest of the fight. He contributed much to the success of the day." *O.R.*, 3:106.

Item: The Battle of Wilson's Creek or Oak Hills, August 10, 1861, by Dr. John F. Snyder, Eighth Division, Missouri State Guard; Ordnance Officer/Chief of Staff of Rains's Division.[68]
Published: October 10, 1885.

[Editor's Note: In the two articles following this one R. I. Holcombe and Thomas Snead both respond to Snyder's piece, concerning the opening announcement of Lyon's arrival on the battlefield of Wilson's Creek. Holcombe says he got the information that Snyder commented about from Snead and a writer by the name of "Gath," who wrote for the *Cincinnati Enquirer.* Snead, for his part, somewhat supports Holcombe, but leaves the reader wondering by the following statement which closes out his article.]

I am not responsible for all the statements quoted as mine by Dr. Snyder [actually, R. I. Holcombe made the statements]. Some of them are very absurd. Many of them I never made and never could have made. They found their way into print through the reports of an interview to which I unsuspectingly subjected some eight or ten years ago and about which I knew nothing till after its publication.

Overall, Dr. Snyder's article does add some interesting items on the Battle of Wilson's Creek, while leaving the reader to ponder what really happened in the early part of the battle.]

Recollections of Wilson's Creek

Virginia, Cass Co., Ill, Sept. 30—When we all were at Springfield, Mo. in Aug. 1883, attending the reunion of the veterans of the Wilson Creek battle, I purchased—as many others did—a copy of a small volume entitled, "An Account of the Battle of Wilson Creek, or Oak hills," etc.; written and complied from authentic sources by Holcombe & Adams, and published at Springfield by Dow & Adams, 1883. As a history this little book contains a great deal of valuable information regarding the "famous victory," but is lamentably deficient in incidents and details and is in some of the statements is very loose and disjointed; but altogether, it is a credit to the enterprising spirit of its compilers and publishers, who, I was sorry to learn, lost money in the venture.

Incidents of the war, however trifling in importance at the time, gain in interest and value by the lapse of years; hence, while popular taste is demanding and relishing these old tales, I think it is well that those of us who were actors in that great drama and are yet spared should place upon record our personal reminis-

---

68. Bearss has Snyder as Rains's Chief of Staff, while Snyder, later in his article, writes that he was Rains's Ordnance Officer. As previously seen in note 73 of the first chapter, Snyder occupied a number of positions while serving in the MSG. Bearss, *Wilson's Creek*, 59.

cences before we, too, are summoned to answer to the last roll-call and stack our arms forever.

So thinking, I open Messrs Holcombe & Hill's [Adams] "Account," at page 52, and read as follows: "Col. T. L. Snead states that on the night of the 9th he sat up all night at Gen. Price's headquarters, which were on the side of the creek, at the foot of the sloping, rocky, blackjack hills on whose summit the main battle was fought. About daybreak Gen. Price got up in great impatience and set for Gen. McCullough [McCulloch], who soon afterward arrived, accompanied by Col. James McIntosh (of the Second Arkansas mounted riflemen), his assistant adjutant-general.[69] 'Gen. Price and I were just sitting down to breakfast,' says Col. Snead, 'and they sat down with us.' As the officers were eating a messenger came running up from the front where Gen. Rains' division was posted, a mile or more away, and said that the Yankees were advancing, a full 20,000 strong and were on Rains' lines already, peppering his camp with musketry. 'Oh pshaw!' said Mc-Culloch, 'that's another of Rains' scares, alluding to the Dug Spring affair. 'Tell Gen. Rains I will come to the front myself directly,' he added. The three officers went on eating, and in a minute or two another messenger came up and reported that the Federals were not more than a mile away, and had come suddenly upon Rains' men as they lay upon their arms and had driven them back. McCulloch again said: 'Oh, nonsense! that's not true,' but just then Rains' men could be seen falling back in confusion. Gen. Price rose up and said to Col. Snead, 'Have my horse saddled and order the troops under arms at once! He had hardly spoken when Totten's battery unlimbered and sent its first shot, and about the same instant Sigel's guns opened."

Quite Otherwise.

Now, I don't know if Tom Snead said all this or not. If he did he must have been slightly "off his base"; or maybe I was. The culinary or domestic department of Gen. Price's headquarters was, as stated, immediately on the creek, on the west side; but the tent in which he slept and received visitors and transacted business was on the "rise" above and to the east of the creek about fifty yards. The Federals did not fall suddenly on Gen. Rains's men while they lay on their arms; nor could our men be seen falling back in confusion. And if Gens. Price and McCulloch were in conversation when the alarm was first given they must have talking to each other by telephone. These are all unimportant details to be sure; but then while we are recording the truth of history we may just as well be sure that we get the facts down exactly right. It so happens that I was that messenger who first carried news of the coming of the invading host to Gen. Price. I didn't catch him eating his breakfast either; nor did I see anything of Gen. McCulloch or

---

69. James McIntosh actually wore two hats at the Battle of Wilson's Creek. He commanded the Second Arkansas Mounted Rifle Regiment and served as McCulloch's Adjutant General. *O.R.*, 3:52, 111; Piston, 102, 202; Holcombe, 53; Snead, 271–272.

Col. McIntosh. This is what I know about it.[70]

Gen. Rains's division, while we lay on Wilson Creek, occupied the extreme west side of the hollow, and our camps stretched along the creek and foothills at the base of "Bloody Hill." As is well known, we had been ordered to march, armed and equipped, the night before the battle to surprise Gen. Lyon at Springfield, and, after standing in line from dark until 11 o'clock, we received a subsequent order to "lie on our arms" until further orders.[71] I was at the time ordnance officer of Gen. Rains's division, and always camped near the general's headquarters. Gen. Rains was usually an early riser and so was I. When the order came to lie on our arms, being very tired, we tied our horses to the blackjacks and rolled into the hazel bush whole—booted and spurred—and slept soundly. In the morning we crawled out of our lairs and were ready for work without the bother of making elaborate toilets. While the general and I were discussing the "surprise" of the previous night, we were suddenly startled by the clatter and rattling of a lot of empty forage wagons thundering down the rocky hill, and the drivers yelling like Indians and urging their jaded teams to the top of their speed.[72] Presently a mounted wagon-master stopped his panting steed before us, and fairly screamed to the general that his wagon train had started before day to the prairie for forage, but had met the Yankees moving down on us in full force. As our pickets had been called in the night before to take a hand in the surprise party[73] and

---

70. All accounts, both modern and contemporary, published on the Battle of Wilson's Creek, have Price, McCulloch and McIntosh eating breakfast or about to eat breakfast when the messenger, identified as John F. Snyder, arrived to announce the arrival of Lyon's command. General Price in his official report of the battle clearly states that McCulloch was at his headquarters when riders arrived announcing Lyon's presence, though not stating who the messengers were. The present article is largely different on how the Confederate command received word of Lyon's advance. Oddly, Piston in his book, clearly shows that he was aware of Snyder's article in the *Republican*, even referencing it. Still, Piston accepted the other accounts of Snyder arriving at Price's headquarters as the three generals were sitting down to eat. Another possibility was that the mentioned officers were in Price's tent when Snyder arrived with the word of Lyon's advance or that they had departed by the time Snyder arrived. However, Snead in his book, makes it clear that McCulloch conversed with Snyder on the subject, while Snyder makes it equally clear that he did not see or talk to anyone else. *O.R.*, 3:100; Piston, 192, 202, 363–364, 389; Brooksher, 182; Bearss, *Wilson's Creek*, 59, 62; Holcombe, 53; Snead, 271–272.

71. General Price recorded that the movement was canceled "just as the army was about to march," which was at 9:00 p.m. General McCulloch stated about the same, and that a light rain caused him to cancel the march at the appointed time. Captain John Wiatt corroborates McCulloch's statements, noting that his command was ready to march when it began to rain, thus canceling the movement. W. H. Tunnard of the Third Louisiana Infantry noted that a light rain began to fall in the afternoon. "At 9 o'clock the order to advance was countermanded, but the troops required to hold themselves in readiness to march at a moment's notice." And William Woodruff, commanding an Arkansas battery, noted that the rain commenced in the afternoon and "continued until after night." *O.R.*, 3:99, 104; Eakin, *Diary,* 7; Tunnard, 49; Woodruff, 38.

72. Brooksher and Snead have Rains sending Snyder off to warn the rebel leaders after James Cawthorn, commanding Rains's lead brigade, reported the enemy to his front. Piston and Bearss write that Rains sent Snyder out to review the situation after he had received reports from his foragers that the Federals were advancing. Monaghan states that Rains had pickets out all night and upon returning to camp, after foraging some corn, they espied Lyon's column and hurried back to camp to report the approach of the enemy. Brooksher, 180; 269–271; Bearss, *Wilson's Creek*, 59; Snead, 269–271; Monaghan, 171.

73. The lack of pickets was clearly a mistake on the Confederates' part and it seems that all units were

Had Not Yet Been Sent

out again, the Yankee surprise of our army seemed by no means improbable. As calmly as if inviting me to take a drink—which he didn't—Rains remarked to me, "Doctor, get on your horse and ride up there and see what is the matter." In the twinkling of an eye I mounted and "lit out," and in a very short time reached the edge of the prairie. Memory will never permit the sight that met my astonished gaze then and there, on that balmy, beautiful August morning, to be dimmed or marred by the flight of years while life lasts. Coming down the prairie right toward me, a little more than a mile distant, were several ranks of blue-coated infantry, marching as if they were in a hurry to get somewhere, in solid columns, with flags flying and their bright muskets reflecting the light of early dawn. And I saw several cannons, each drawn by many fine looking horses; but there was no noise.[74] This was, in fact, a revelation to me. I had seen, since the Civil War commenced, a few soldiers in blue near Sarcoxie,[75] and a few more at Dug Springs, but this was the first army of the ruthless invader that had yet come in range of my visual organs; and magnified by fear or surprise or both it appeared to me that the whole prairie was covered with soldiers and cannon. It was a grand and exhilarating sight, but I didn't tarry long to gloat upon its picturesque beauty. I beat Maud S.'s[76] time back to Gen. Rains and told him in brief words what I had seen. "Go and tell Gen. Price," said he, and I went. I had the real honor of an intimate acquaintance with Gen. Price from the time that he was Governor of Missouri,[77] and had now and then called on him socially and in the way of business at his camp since the fortunes (or misfortunes) of war had thrown us nearer together, and so I knew this morning just where to look for him. My horse leaped the creek like

---

guilty of the offense. A doctor in the MSG wrote "that the picket line had been called in or had not been sent out as usual. We being lulled into security." Willie Tunnard, of the Third Louisiana Infantry, also wrote on the subject providing some insight as to why. According to Tunnard: "The picket guard had been recalled so as to be ready to march with their respective commands, and then in expectation of momentarily receiving marching orders, the different regimental commanders objected to sending them out again. It was a serious blunder." From the Texas command, a Commissioner from the Governor of Texas also reported that the pickets had been recalled and never replaced. And General Pearce of Arkansas recalled that the pickets had been removed and were not returned. Eakin, *Diary*, 7; Tunnard, 50; Willard E. Wright, ed., "An Unofficial Account of the Battle of Wilson Creek, August 10, 1861," *Arkansas Historical Quarterly* 15 (Winter, 1956): 363, hereafter cited as Wright, "Wilson Creek"; Pearce, "Arkansas Troops in the Battle of Wilson's Creek," 301.

74. Captain Joseph P. Plummer's 300-man battalion of the First U.S. Infantry led Lyon's advance, followed by Major Peter J. Osterhaus's 150-man battalion of the Second Missouri Infantry and James Totten's Artillery. *O.R.* 3:60; Banasik, *Missouri In 1861*, 377.

75. At the beginning of the Civil War, Sarcoxie, Missouri, located in the southeastern corner of Jasper County, was the second largest city in the county, boasting about four hundred residents. It was also the home of MSG General James S. Rains. Ward L. Schrantz, *Jasper County, Missouri in the Civil War* (Carthage, MO, 1923; reprint ed., 1992), 23, 27, hereafter cited as Schrantz.

76. "Maud S." was a champion harness racing horse in the 1880s. Hamilton Busbey, *Recollections of Men and Horses* (New York, 1907), 5.

77. Price served as governor of Missouri from 1853–1857. Warner, *Generals in Gray*, 247.

a deer, and with a few bounds I reined him up at the grand old commander's tent and "hollered." By this time Gen. Rains's division was in motion and commotion, and things over there were getting pretty lively generally. Now, when I issued my vocal notes at the tent of Gen. Price I failed to see him and Tom Snead just sitting down to breakfast, nor were Gen. McCulloch or Col. McIntosh in sight, but Gen. Price came out of his tent looking to me very much like a man who had just got up out of bed, or imitating a person of that kind. He was bareheaded and in his shirt-sleeves; in fact his shirt, pants and boots were all the clothes he had on so far as I could discover, and was buttoning his suspenders as he emerged. I gave him no time to ask questions, but told him what I firmly believed at the time to be true—that about 20,000 Federal soldiers with at least

A Hundred Cannon

were moving down the prairie on a run, and that in less than half an hour he would see them coming down that hill over there. "Did you see them yourself, doctor?" he asked. "Yes sir," I replied, "I have just come from the border of the prairie and was ordered by Gen. Rains to come and report to you." He said no more to me, but called for his horse and was soon in the saddle. The tumultuous agitation soon spread from our division and pervaded the whole encampment. Bugles filled the air with their brazen summons to "boots and saddles"; the long roll of tenor drums everywhere sounded the thrilling summons to arms, and orderlies and officers dashed wildly from point to point, pale with determination or flushed with enthusiasm. Everybody yelled, and hundreds of panic-stricken men, some wounded, many on foot and many others in all sorts of wheeled vehicles, rushed madly down the telegraph road in desperate confusion to get out of the way and escape certain death. Many of this herd continued their flight until they reached Arkansas.[78] But above all this unearthly racket the voices of command could be heard, and in obedience thereto cool, brave men rapidly found their places in line and were soon ready to meet the foe in deadly affray.

The realization of all the probable horrors of the impending conflict, to novices, in war, as we nearly all were—to me individually I freely admit—was truly appalling; but the fray once begun, the awful feeling of dread and despair was soon lost in the frenzied eagerness for success. That's what aided me on that occasion anyway.

I remained on the east side of the creek long enough to see the first line of animated blue filing along among the blackjacks on the western summit; and simultaneously the bright guns of Totten's battery wheeled into position nearby and, with a roar that shook the hills, opened the ball. The uncivil salute was answered

---

78. As the teamsters, camp followers, unarmed men and others fled southward, down the Wire or Telegraph Road, they eventually ran into Sigel's force. Sigel reported taking 100 prisoners, who were fleeing from Lyon's advance and others who were found in the enemy's camp near Sharp's cornfield. *O.R.*, 3:87; Bearss, *Wilson's Creek*, 71; Brooksher, 199.

almost immediately by Woodruff's Little Rock battery that was planted a short distance to the northeast of Gen. Price's tent.[79] The guns of this battery, if I mistake not, were taken from the United States arsenal at Little Rock, and were some of the identical pieces[80] commanded by Capt. Braxton Bragg at Buena Vista,[81] at the time Gen. [Zachary] Taylor[82] rode up to him and delivered that memorable speech, beautiful for its brevity and impressiveness, "A little more grape Capt. Bragg." A little beyond Woodruff's big guns was Col. Herbert's [Hébert's] splendid Third Louisiana regiment—the only really military organization, besides the batteries, in our whole outfit—standing like a living rampart and waiting the word to move to the front.

It looked to me as if the well-directed galling fire of Woodruff's battery checked the Federal advance. Perhaps Gen. Lyon purposely halted on the crest of that ridge, awaiting preconcerted signals from Sturgis and Sigel. Let that be as it may, the fact remains that he halted when Woodruff opened on him, and then and there lost his opportunity for success. His delay was fatal, for it gave for our men a chance to recover from their surprise, to rally and form and fall upon him. It was some little time after this artillery duel had commenced before Sigel began to send us tokens of affection from our rear, and his rude behavior was another astonishing surprise to us.[83] About this time I concluded to take a hand myself,

---

79. Woodruff's Battery was located on a bluff near the Guinn house (Piston calls it the Winn house), on the east side of Wilson's Creek and near the Telegraph Road. The property, in 1860, was owned by Larkin D. Winn, but was abandoned by August 1861, and, apparently, according to Piston, farmed by John A. Ray. Piston, 153–154, 194; Bearss, *Wilson's Creek*, 36; Brooksher, 183.

80. Lieutenant Colonel James Pritchard, First Infantry Regiment, Fourth Division, MSG, in his account of Wilson's Creek, says that the guns were the same ones Bragg had used at the Battle of Buena Vista, Mexico, in 1847. Bevier, 47; Peterson, 143.

81. The Battle of Buena Vista, Mexico took place on February 22–23, 1847, near Saltillo, Mexico. Zachary Taylor commanded the American force of 4,700 men while General Santa Anna, of Alamo fame, commanded a Mexican Army that numbered 20,000. The battle began on February 22 in the late afternoon and continued until dark with no result obtained. On the morning of the twenty-third the Mexicans attacked in overwhelming numbers, and pushed back the American left flank in confusion. About 9:00 a.m. Taylor arrived on the field with fresh troops from Saltillo and stabilized the situation. Several more attacks and counterattacks would punctuate the remainder of the day, even as a rain storm pelted the two armies. Nightfall put an end to the battle, after which Santa Anna withdrew, declaring victory. The battle was the last major fight in northern Mexico. Singletary, 48–53, 164.

82. Zachary Taylor (born 1784) was commissioned a lieutenant in the Seventh U.S. Infantry on May 3, 1808. He fought in the war of 1812 and the Seminole War, for which he was promoted to brigadier general on December 25, 1837. During the Mexican War, he fought and won the Battles of Palo Alto (May 8, 1846), and Resaca de Palma (May 9, 1846) in Texas, and Monterrey (September 20–24, 1846) and Buena Vista in Mexico. After being elected President of the United States in 1848, Taylor resigned from the army on January 31, 1849. Taylor was the twelfth President of the United States, but only served a little more than one year, dying on July 9, 1850. Ibid., 163–164; Heitman, 1:949.

83. Sigel opened fire on the Confederate cavalry camps in Sharp's corn and stubble fields at 5:30 a.m., which sent the camps into chaos. Failing to rally the troops, the rebel leaders retreated their men into the woods out of harm's way, prompting Sigel to move his command forward. About 7:15 a.m. Sigel's artillery again deployed and scattered another Confederate force that was attempting to form in the lowlands of Wilson's Creek. By 8:00 a.m. Sigel's command came to their final resting place, near the Sharp house, blocking the main road. Firing into the rear of the MSG troops on Oak Hill, caused the rebels to about-

and, though an "officer," in the celebrated Blackberry Cavalry, I lost time in securing my carbine and cartridge box, and taking place in the ranks fought the battle through as a private.

A Sharp-Shooter's Fate.

In the midst of the fight, while in the ranks, I noticed far off across the ravine a Federal sharpshooter stationed behind a large hollow tree, from which apparently safe shelter he cautiously edged every few minutes and deliberately fired at such of our unguarded patriots as chanced to come within range of his rifle. The tree that served as his fort was duly the decayed and blasted remnant of a once mighty monarch of these hills. The tornado's wrath and lightning's shock of the centuries had shivered and prostrated its top and burned out its trunk so that but a mere shell remained to support a few wide-spreading branches. The rifleman had taken his position on the convex and sound-looking side of this once grand old oak, and doubtless thought himself securely protected by a large solid tree. From our point of vision, however, the deep, charred and blackened hollow—of which he was ignorant—was plainly in view. While I was watching him Gen. Parsons, with a part of his command, moved up to our right,[84] and for a time we were all in pretty active business. In a temporary lull of the carnage I called the general's attention to the blue coat who was having his own fun at our expense. Parsons saw him fire a round or two, and then pointing him out to one of his artillery men suggested the experiment of catching that shooter with a cannon shot. The gunner grasped the situation at once and said he thought he could do it. A six-pounder was wheeled around and carefully loaded and sighted, with proper elevation for the computed distance.[85] The blue coat again peeped around and fired, and just as he dodged back out of sight the cannon answered his manly puff of smoke with a thundering admonition to quit that kind of nonsense. Having no field glasses we could not tell if the iron shot had hit or missed the mark; but we saw nothing more of the sharpshooter so long as we remained on that part of the field. After the battle was over Gen. Parsons and myself went to the old tree to see if the cannonball had hit it and we found that it had, and nearby we also found what was left of the marksman who, perhaps, had little thought of death lurking around in that shape. The

---

face one of their regiments, with Bledsoe's Missouri Battery, to engage Sigel. The Confederate Army was pinned between Lyon and Sigel, but Sigel did little to aid Lyon and simply waited for the battle to come to him. Piston, 222–31; Bearss, *Wilson's Creek*, 72.

84. In the various histories written on Wilson's Creek, Parsons's Division with Kelly's Regiment and Guibor's Artillery, deployed to the right of McBride's Division and to the left of Clark's command. Rains's Division was on the far right of the Confederate line, adjacent to Slack's Division on their left. The writer seems to be indicating that the Confederate lines were more integrated than previously thought or he possibly forgot who was next to whom or what command he joined to fight the battle. Piston, 210; Bearss, *Wilson's Creek*, 83; Brooksher, 248, 264.

85. The artillery piece probably belonged to Guibor's Battery, though no mention of the incident was indicated in the memoirs of Lieutenant Barlow of Guibor's command. Patrick, "Remembering the Missouri Campaign," 34–40.

six-pound ball had made only a small hole on the side of its entry, but on the side of its exit, just where the soldier stood at the time, the tree was torn and splintered for a foot or more in extent. The ball, with riven fragments of bark and wood, had struck him about the middle of the body and literally blew him to pieces. The poor fellow had evidently not had time to feel surprise or to be conscious of what had hurt him. I do not know if the artilleryman who fired that shot survived the battle of the war, but if still living; I would be pleased to learn his name and add it to this concise history in order that fame may catch up and sound it down through the avenues of time.

Col. R. H. Weightman.

Can anyone tell me where I can find a reliable sketch of the life of Col. Richard Hanson Weightman, who was sacrificed at Wilson's Creek as part to the pay for the brilliant victory achieved there? Has any account—full in details—of his death ever been published? It was generally conceded among us that he was very able and promising man, and a strong accession to our cause; but his early death left the measure of his military genius unknown. He was born a soldier, and brave to rashness; and as a disciplinarian had few to his superior, and certainly no equal in our mob. He combined in his make-up, to a singular degree, the extremes of unctuous suavity and ungovernable passion. A most courteous and polished gentleman, but as fractious and quick tempered as a wasp. In one moment lavishing the softest blandishments filled with the tenderest sentiments, and the next instant swearing like a pirate. He was a man of fine sense, sound judgement, broad views, and possessed a wonderful fund of general information. In disposition he was exceedingly modest and exclusive, with no fondness for idle talk, or society, or publicity. All in all he was a strange compound. Genial and affable at times, but stern, morose and exciting in every minute of duty. Firm as granite, yet gentle as a woman; charitable and benevolent; kind and sympathetic in the presence of distress or misfortune, but merciless to all opposition. He was the very embodiment of sterling integrity, honor and sturdy manhood. The rudest simplicity characterized his daily life, in dress, in diet and in every habit. At night the earth was his couch, with saddle or boots for a pillow, and his coat and blanket constituted his bed. This was the man during my three months, my acquaintance with him in 1861. I think that Cromwell must have had around him a good many men very much like Col. Weightman. He always suggested to my mind my ideal of Praise God Barebones or Christ-Died-for-Thee Jenkins of the days of Marston Moor[86] and the Rump parliament.[87] In him piety and profanity were in ceaseless conflict

---

86. The English Civil War Battle of Marston Moor occurred on July 2, 1644, between the forces of Oliver Cromwell and Prince Rupert. The royalists were eventually routed with the loss of 4,000 killed and 1,500 captured. Norman Stone, *The Wordsworth Dictionary of British History* (Hertfordshire, England, 1994), 234.

87. An off-shoot of the English Civil War, the "Rump" or the "Long Parliament" remained in effect after Cromwell's victory and declared England a Commonwealth on May 19, 1649. Because the Rump Parlia-

for supremacy. Always, before lying down to sleep at night, it mattered not in what surroundings or under what circumstances, he reverently read or repeated a prayer or some other excerpt from the Episcopal litany. The next minute perhaps, provoked by some trivial mishap, he made the circumambient air blue with wholesome imprecations not found in any book of common prayer.

The concurrent testimony of those who were near him in the battle supports the assertion that he was greatly excited and recklessly exposed himself to the enemy's fire. He fell, wounded in three places, in the advance of his men and with his face to the foe. Rough but kind hands bore him to the rear and essayed to assuage his suffering and soften the awful rigors of death. An army chaplain was bending over him with pitying glances and faltering voice, administering words of consolation. The dying soldier cast his eyes heavenward, and with the look of benign resignation calmly said: "My trust is in the redeeming grace of the Savior." Just then Gen. Rains—one of the tenderest-hearted of men—with a few drinks aboard and tearful eyes, in the excess of kindness, gave the apology of a pillow a shove, so as to slightly change and thereby ease the position of the colonel's head. This pained or annoyed him, and turning his gaze from the ethereal regions earthward, he blurted out: "Damn it, let me alone." He spoke but little more; and in a short time, conscious to the last, quietly passed into that dreamless sleep that knows no awaking.

After the Fight.

Among all of my memories of the battle of Wilson's Creek, about the pleasantest is that of my meeting with our commanding general—that grand old Roman—Sterling Price, a little while after the fight was over.

All who were there, and didn't get killed, will remember that particular 10th of August was a hot day—in more senses than one. The heat in that creek bottom, shut in on all sides as it was by timber-covered hills, was very oppressive and enervating. The reaction, following the super stimulation of all the energies and activities of the system during the battle, was now felt in extreme lassitude and prostration. That was my fix considerably. I had no breakfast that morning, and not much supper the night before; and the prospect for dinner was not encouraging. For ten days or more before the battle, we had been living on tough roasting-ears and tougher beef with creek water and spartan sauce—plenty of the latter. Coffee and whiskey were and had been for a long time unattainable luxuries to all but a favored few. The excitement of the fight over I felt as weakened and gaunt as Dr. Tanner after his fast and would have given a horse for a drink of whisky without caviling about its quality.[88] In this frame of mind and body I was wander-

ment was "corrupt and ineffective," Cromwell dissolved it in April 1653, replacing it with what became known as the "Barebones Parliament" on July 4, 1653. This latest parliament got its name from "Praisegod Barbon, or Barbones," one of its members. After six months the Barbones Parliament was dissolved and Cromwell was proclaimed the Lord Protector of England. Ibid., 31, 88, 313.
88. Henry S. Tanner was a Minneapolis physician who gained national notoriety for conducting a

ing around, as we all were, seeking to learn who were killed and wounded and who had escaped when I came to Gen. Price's camp by the creek-side and was overjoyed to see, sitting in the shade with his shirt-collar open, the general himself safe and sound and in unusual good humor. A few friends were there also and we shook hands all around and exchanged fervent gratulations and congratulations. To my inquiry as to how he got through the scrimmage the general showed me the cut on his side still bleeding a little and said he was all right and ready to go right on to Springfield. After taking a minute or so I think he must have noticed my look of "goneness" and haggard fatigue; for dropping his voice to the sweetest tones, he suddenly propounded to me the startling interrogatory, "Doctor, will you take something to drink?" Our proximity to the creek naturally suggested to me its warm, muddy water—the only fluid that had passed down my neck for many days—as all that his question comprehended, and I was about to shrink back in dismay and decline with thanks. Regarding a negative answer to his interrogation as only a little short of impossible, he waited for none, but turned to his keeper of the great seal and remarked, "Jo, fix up a toddy for the doctor." I now fully understood his meaning and realized the magnificence of his hospitality. If Mr. Cleveland[89] should

Send Me A Commission

as inspector of consulates I wouldn't be more surprised or gladder than I was then. I was mute with amazement and tried to look as if I didn't care anything about it. Jo was always slow and methodical, but I know that no mortal could again be as exasperatingly deliberate as he was on this occasion. It appeared as if he never would find the right key, and when he did find it the lid of the chest hung firm, and when it at last yielded to his persuasions, a glass had to be washed and then a corkscrew hunted up and a fossil bottle uncorked. And all this time I was standing there with mouth watering in tantalizing expectancy. But even agony cannot last forever, and mine terminated with the liquid inspiration that Uncle Jo finally handed me. It proved to be a powerful receiver and struck with subtle touch the sprigs of human bliss. Together with the exhilaration of our victory it floated me up to a higher level, from which the future looked bright and rose-tainted—a heap more so than it did about two years later.

> Kings may be blest, but Tom was glorious,
> O'er a' the ills o' life victorious.

And I felt triumphant over the combined tyrannies of heat, hunger and the

---

6-week fast in 1880. James Grant Wilson and John Fiske, eds. *Appleton's Cyclopædia of American Biography*, 6 vols. (New York: 1889), 6:32.
89. Grover Cleveland, the twenty-second and twenty-fourth President of the United States (1885–1889, 1893–1897).

Lincoln administrations.

Nearly the quarter of a century has passed since then, and for the last many years I have been a rigid teetotaler—almost a disciple of the modern St. John; but that cordial greeting and hearty shake of the hand by Gen. Price in the hour of our success is still as fresh as on that memorable day, and the memory of that soul-cheering toddy even now tingles and reverberates with exuberance of ecstasy to the uttermost fibers of my anatomy.

John F. Snyder, M.D.

* * * * * * *

Item: A response to Dr. John F. Snyder's piece on Wilson's Creek; includes a portion of a letter from Colonel Thomas Snead on the opening guns at Wilson's Creek, by R. I. Holcombe.
Published: October 17, 1885.

First Alarm at Wilson's Creek

Kingston, Mo., Oct. 12.

Editor, *Republican*

I desire to assure Dr. John F. Snyder of Virginia, Ill., that Col. Thos. L. Snead did say "all of this" that I quote him as saying in my *Account of the Battle of Wilson's Creek, or Oak Hills,* referred to by Dr. Snyder in the *Republican* of last Saturday [October 10]. As I complied every word and line of that account myself (Mr. Adams's name on the title-page was gratuitously added), I feel bound to defend, or at least explain, the statements therein made.

Dr. Snyder's reminiscences of the Battle of Wilson's Creek are very interesting, and quite well related. His recollection that he was the first to inform Gen. Price of the approach of the Federals is—as was often said of rumors and reports during the war—"important if true." The weight of authority has long been against his statement—at least to its report that neither Gen. McCulloch, Col. McIntosh or Col. Snead were "in sight" when he delivered his information.

Col. Snead was Gen. Price's Assistant Adjutant-general before and after the Battle of Wilson's Creek, and his relations with the general were of course very close and intimate. This no one will dispute. Under date of February 26, 1883, Col. Snead wrote me from New York City, where he then resided and I believe he now resides,

Almost Word For Word

what is stated in the account regarding the opening of the battle. Regarding the presence of McCulloch and McIntosh, the breakfast scene, etc., Col. Snead says:

About daybreak the general (Price) got up in great impatience and sent for

McCulloch, who soon afterwards came, accompanied by McIntosh. Gen. Price and I were just sitting down to breakfast, and they sat down with us. In a few moments an officer from Rains, who was in our front, and probably one and a half miles from where we were breakfasting, rode up in great hast, and said that the enemy was upon Rains in great force—20,000 strong—and that the latter was in pressing need of reinforcements. McCulloch and McIntosh, who had the greatest (and most undeserved) contempt for Rains smiled incredulously, and McCulloch merely told the officer to say to Gen. Rains that he himself would go to the front directly, remarking, "It is only another of his scares." While we were still breakfasting another officer rode up and said that Rains had been overpowered and driven back, and at the very instant we saw his men falling back in confusion over the hill in front. Dispositions for the battle were quickly made, etc.

In the summer of 1877 Col. Snead made substantially the same statements to Mr. George Alfred Townsend ("Gath") that he wrote me. As published in the *Cincinnati Enquirer* and republished in Switzlers *History of Missouri,* page 378, "Gath's" account of the breakfast scene at Price's headquarters, August 10, 1861, based on Snead's statements is as follows:

At 4 o'clock, on the morning of the battle, McCulloch rode over to Price's headquarters, which were pitched in a sort of cow yard, by a small farm house down in a hollow. McCulloch's was back on a hill.[90] While Price, McCulloch and Snead were taking breakfast at the earliest dawn, a man came in from the front where Rains was posted and said he had an important message. The Yankees were advancing, fully 30,000 strong, and were on Rains's line already. "Oh, pshaw," said McCulloch, after a minute, "that's another of Rains's scares." They went on eating until a second man came in and again reported that the Federals were not more than a mile away, and right on Rains's column as they lay on their arms. McCulloch again said, that it was nonsense; but Price was excited, etc.

In preparing my account of the incident I drew upon Col. Snead's

Report To "Gath,"

as well as his written version to me, and though one was made six years prior to the other there is no variation as to the main point, that Price, McCulloch, Snead and McIntosh were all together and eating breakfast when word was brought to Gen. Price that the Federals had attacked him. I trust that Dr. Snyder is now satis-

---

90. McCulloch's headquarters was near the Winn house (Bearss calls this the Guinn house; Piston has the Guinn house located about a mile south of Wilson's Creek on the Telegraph Road), while Price's was near the Edward's farm. Piston, 154–155; Bearss, *Wilson's Creek,* 36.

fied that Col. Snead said "all of this." The issue of veracity between the gentlemen is one in which I am neither called upon to interfere or to decide. It only concerns me to show that I did not misquote Col. Snead, although if he is wrong or mistaken I am interested in learning the fact, alike with many other students of the history of our state.

I admit the justice of Dr. Snyder's criticism that my little book is "lamentably deficient in incidents and details." If there had been room in the little volume for any of them it would have been difficult to decide what incidents to have inserted and what to have omitted; and, of course, there was not room for all that occurred. Except as to certain facts I had to deal in generalities, but I deny that any of its statements are "loose and disjointed." No statement is made loosely or without good authority; nothing is assumed or guessed at. The story is told very poorly, no doubt, but it is told connectedly. And both sides of the story are given too.

I do not wish to advertise the little book. It is out of print and I understand that all the copies were long since disposed of to speculators and others. I do not know whether or not the publishers made a profit on their investment. I only know that I never received a single cent for compiling the work.

R. I. Holcombe

* * * * * * *

Item: Another rebuttal of Dr. Snyder's account of Wilson's Creek, by Thomas L. Snead.
Published: October 24, 1885.

One of Gath's Victims

It will be remembered that a card from Mr. Holcombe was published last week [October 17], stating that he trusted to one of "Gath's" interviews for certain statements regarding the Battle of Wilson's Creek. The subjoined letter from Mr. Snead explains itself:

New York, Oct. 16, 1885

Editor, *Republican*

I dislike to find fault with the very interesting reminiscences of the Battle of Wilson's Creek, which my old friend Dr. Snyder, contributed to the *Republican* of the 10th, but I am constrained to notice his rather flippant contradiction of a statement which I have often made and which I know to be true—that Gen. McCulloch and Col. McIntosh were breakfasting with Gen. Price and myself when the fact of Lyon's attack was made known to them.

I would not speak so confidently as to anything which happened nearly a quarter of a century ago if I had only to rely upon my own memory, but there is abundant contemporaneous evidence to sustain my statement. The best—and there could be no better—is the testimony of Gen. Price. In his official report, written forty-eight hours after the occurrence, he says:

About 6 o'clock I received a messenger from Gen. Rains that the enemy were advancing in great force from the direction of Springfield and were already within 200 or 300 yards of the position where he was encamped with the second brigade[91] of his division, consisting of about 1,200 mounted men under Col. [James] Cawthorn.[92] A second messenger came immediately afterwards from Gen. Rains to announce that the main body of the enemy was upon him, but he would endeavor to hold him in check until he could receive reinforcements. Gen. McCulloch was with me when these messengers came, and left at once for his own headquarters to make the necessary disposition of our forces.

While this establishes conclusively the truth of my statements, it does not necessarily contradict anything that Dr. Snyder says as to what he himself saw and did on that occasion.

I am not responsible for all the statements quoted as mine by Dr. Snyder [actually, R. I. Holcombe made the statements].[93] Some of them are very absurd. Many of them I never made and never could have made. They found their way into print through the reports of an interview to which I unsuspectingly subjected some eight or ten years ago and about which I knew nothing till after its publication.

My desire to retain the good opinion of the people among whom I used to live is my only motive for asking you to publish this note.

Thomas L. Snead.

* * * * * *

---

91. James Cawthorn's Second Brigade, Rains's Division, MSG, consisted of six regiments of cavalry, total 1,210 men. Banasik, *Missouri In 1861*, 379–380.

92. James Cawthorn was born in Virginia in about 1809, and at the beginning of the Civil War lived near Claplinger, Cedar County, Missouri. He was elected captain of Company D, Fourth Cavalry Regiment, Eighth Division, MSG on May 31, 1861, and on July 4 was selected colonel of his regiment. At Wilson's Creek, Cawthorn commanded the cavalry brigade in Rains's Division, and was severely wounded in the foot; his leg was later amputated. Cawthorn died on August 18, 1861, in Springfield, Missouri. Peterson, 243, 256, 258; Bartels, *Forgotten Men*, 53.

93. Doctor Snyder never claimed that Snead ever made the statements concerning the breakfast messengers. R. I. Holcombe made the statements using a composite of a letter he had received from Snead, dated February 26, 1883, and an earlier interview supposedly given by Snead to "Gath" of the *Cincinnati Enquirer* in the summer of 1877.

Item: A soldier in the Third Texas Cavalry traces his regiment's history from its formation through the Battle of Wilson's Creek, by Henry L. Lewis.
Published: December 12, 1885.

Third Texas Cavalry at Wilson's Creek.

Grapevine, Tex., Nov. 8

Editor, *Republican*

I am a subscriber to your paper and take great interest in the war tales as they appear, and having never seen anything regarding the Battle of Oak Hill or Wilson's Creek except by Missourians, concluded I would give my experiences as an eye-witness of that memorable conflict. I belonged to Greer's Third Texas regiment of cavalry, the only Texas regiment on the field, the first one that left the state and the first one that fired a gun in the late Civil War. We left Dallas the last of June, 1861, and marched leisurely along through North Texas and the Indian Nation, and when at Van Buren, Ark.,[94] we received intelligence that the Federals were pressing Gen. Price and his troops toward the Arkansas line, and for the command to push forward to render the necessary aid in such a crisis.[95] The regiment was stripped to light marching order, details made to guard the wagon train and Capt. [John] Good's splendid battery[96] left with the train. It did not get up in time to take part in the battle. We marched rapidly to Cassville in Barry County, Mo., and there rumors were rife of the daring bravery of the Federals and that they only wanted us to stand still long enough for them to crush and destroy us from the face of the earth. My command was almost entirely made up of boys from 16 to 20 years of age and knew nothing of military life. We had drilled some while

---

94. Van Buren was located on the Arkansas River in Crawford County. With Fort Smith, Van Buren served as a supply depot for the Confederates in western Arkansas. Banasik, *Embattled Arkansas*, 249, 255–257, 467; Michael E. Banasik, *Reluctant Cannoneer: The Diary of Robert T. McMahan of the Twenty-fifth Independent Ohio Light Artillery* (Iowa City, IA, 2000), 94–101, hereafter cited as Banasik, *Reluctant Cannoneer*; Bearss, "Fort Smith," 315–347.

95. Greer's Texas Cavalry Regiment departed Dallas, on July 9, 1861, and arrived at Fort Smith on July 29, 1861. Resting two days to recruit horses, Greer force-marched his command to McCulloch's headquarters, at Crane Creek, Missouri, arriving there on the evening of August 4. *O.R.*, 3:614, 633; Piston 123–124, 148.

96. Good's Texas Battery began service in early 1861, as a State Militia unit, and was accepted into Confederate Service on June 13, 1861. Initially, the battery consisted of fifty men from Dallas, with no guns. The unit completed its organization by combining with another fifty-man unit from Smith County and receiving four 6-lb. smooth bore guns pulled by mules. The battery fought at Pea Ridge before being transferred to the east side of the Mississippi River, where it completed its military service. It was the only Texas battery to serve east of the Mississippi. John J. Good was born in Mississippi on July 12, 1827, moved to Dallas in 1851, fought in the "Hedgecoxe War" in 1852, and was a representative at the Texas Secession Convention. After his unit transferred to Mississippi, Good gave up his command and was latter appointed a colonel and military judge. After the war, he returned to Texas, briefly became a judge, then a lawyer and finally, mayor of Dallas in 1880. He died on September 17, 1882. *O.R.S.*, pt. 2, vol. 68:492–493; *O.R.*, Series 4, 2:395; Piston, 123; Simpson, 131–133; Roberts, *Texas, Confederate Military History*, 36.

In Camp

at Dallas, but were by no means proficient and many were the questions asked how a battle was fought. Some thought all of one side had to be killed or wounded before a victory was claimed. How green we were in those glorious days of '61. Each company was ordered when in line to stay and fight to the bitter end, and this order was obeyed on that sanguinary field of Oak Hill.[97]

We reached Price and McCulloch's army at Crane Creek in Southwest Missouri August 5. That night the order was given for the whole army to advance upon the Federal forces under Lyon and Sigel, four miles away. At 3 o'clock on the morning of the 6th Price's and McCulloch's troops were in line ready to move. The Third Texas was in the advance.[98] The first battalion under Lieut.-Col. W. P. Lane[99] was on the left of the main road, and the second battalion under Maj. [George W.] Chilton[100] was on the right. The infantry and artillery followed

97. Greer's regiment was made up largely of amateurs, as were most Civil War commands. With the exception of a few officers, like Walter P. Lane, a veteran of the Texas War for Independence and Mexican War, Greer's officers were "'blissfully ignorant of the ruthless nature of war, as the men they commanded'." Additionally, Greer, according to William Piston, did not "burden his men with excessive training or discipline" during their initial military indoctrination, which would explain their haphazard performance at Wilson's Creek. Piston, 123.

98. The writer is wrong on several points. By August 5, the army had already departed Crane Creek, and Greer's regiment did not lead the way. Greer's regiment arrived at Crane Creek on the evening of August 4, just before the army moved forward. When the army departed, between 11:30 p.m. and midnight, the advance was led by the Third Louisiana. Greer's command was with the cavalry column which brought up the rear, just in front of Price's MSG Cavalry—in fact, no cavalry were permitted in the nighttime advance, except for mounted officers. However, the writer's errant comments may be explained by Willie Tunnard, of the Third Louisiana Infantry. Just after dawn (August 5), according Tunnard, "Greer's Texas Cavalry joined us…They were a splendid body of daring, dashing Texas Rangers, magnificently armed and mounted. The army moved steadily forward, with cavalry on both flanks." These flanking units would be Greer's Texas Cavalry, who deployed after dawn. Tunnard, 47–48; O.R., 53:720–721; McGhee, *Letter and Order Book,* unnumbered pages 22–23 (entries pages 41–43).

99. Walter Paye Lane was born in Ireland on February 18, 1817, moved to the United States in 1821, and to Texas in March 1836. He fought in the War for Texas Independence, the Mexican War and was a resident of Marshall, Texas, at the beginning of the Civil War. Elected lieutenant colonel of Third Texas Cavalry Regiment, Lane fought at Wilson's Creek, Chustenahlah, Indian Territory, and Pea Ridge. In mid-1862, Lane organized the First Texas Partisan Cavalry Regiment and led that unit in the West Louisiana Campaign of 1863. On April 8, 1864, he was severely wounded at Mansfield, Louisiana. On March 17, 1865, Lane was confirmed as a brigadier general. Following the war, Lane returned to Texas and spent his remaining years writing his memoirs, and pursuing a mercantile business. He died, an unmarried man, on January 28, 1892, being buried in his hometown of Marshall. See Appendix B for a complete biography. O.R., vol. 26, pt. 1:218; O.R., vol. 34, pt. 1:618; Boatner, 471; Walter P. Lane, *Adventures and Recollections of General Walter P. Lane, a San Jacinto Veteran, Containing Sketches of the Texian, Mexican and Late Wars, with Several Indian Fights Thrown In* (Marshall, TX, 1928), 7, 9, 124, 146, hereafter cited as Lane; Warner, *Generals in Gray,* 173–174; Simpson, 85–86.

100. George W. Chilton was born in Elizabethtown, Kentucky, on June 4, 1828, attended college in Marion, Alabama, and joined Hay's Texas Cavalry Regiment at the beginning of the Mexican War. Returning to Alabama after the war, Chilton obtain a law degree and practiced law for a time, before moving to Tyler, Texas, in 1850. He was elected to the Texas Legislature in 1857, and served as a representative at the Texas Secession Convention in January 1861. He became major of the Third Texas Cavalry Regiment in

closely and every moment we listened for the enemy's guns to open upon us. Gen. Lyon not knowing the number of reinforcements received by McCulloch, and fearing to risk an engagement, decided to retreat upon Springfield. We found his camps deserted, and one regiment pushed rapidly on to strike his rear and force him to turn about and give battle. We did not overtake them, however, and they reached Springfield in safety.[101] Our army encamped on and around the now famous battlefield of Oak Hill. Gen. Rains's division of Missouri troops was in the advance, camped on both sides of the Springfield road, just in his rear were the balance of the Missouri troops. Woodruff's Arkansas battery was camped on the east side of the creek

On A High Hill

overlooking the whole field, and was supported by the Third Louisiana Infantry. This famous battery did not move from this position during the whole battle, and its services I think went far toward winning the great battle for the South. The Sharp house was situated about half way between the points where Lyon and Sigel attacked. Just in the rear of the house, and in a field, the Third Texas Cavalry was camped, and farther back in the same field all the Arkansas troops under Gen. Pierce [Pearce] were camped. Every day the enemy were seen maneuvering in our front, and an engagement was constantly looked for. The troops were kept in readiness, and this precaution saved us. The enemy made a heavy demonstration in our front on the 8th, and McCulloch took the Third Texas regiment out to ascertain their object in approaching so near our position. As soon as they saw us deploying they gradually withdrew. Our entire force consisted of 4,000 Missouri, 3,000 Arkansas, 1,000 Texas and 1,000 Louisiana troops, with several batteries.[102] With Price were about two or three thousand unarmed men. On the evening of the 9th the army received orders to prepare to move on Springfield. The night was cloudy and dark, and looked as if the rain would come down in torrents. The troops cooked rations and had everything in readiness for the advance, but on account of the threatening weather and the troops having no cartridge boxes to protect their ammunition, Gen. McCulloch revoked the order to advance, and ordered the troops to

---

June 1861, fought at Wilson's Creek, received a head wound at Chustenahlah, Indian Territory (December 1861), and served with note at Pea Ridge. When Hamilton P. Bee was promoted to brigadier general, Chilton transferred to his staff, rising to the rank of colonel by war's end. Following the war, he was elected to the U.S. House of Representatives, but that body refused to seat him. Chilton died in 1883, and was buried in Tyler. *O.R.*, 8:23, 299; Simpson, 76; Roberts, *Texas, Confederate Military History*, 36.

101. Lyon's army reached Springfield in the early evening of August 5. *O.R.*, 3:57.

102. The rebel force at Wilson's Creek consisted of 5,298 Missouri infantry, artillery and cavalry, with two batteries of seven guns; the Arkansas troops numbered 3,544 men of all types with two batteries of eight artillery pieces; the Third Louisiana Infantry had 700 men; and the Third Texas Cavalry numbered 800 men. The total Confederate force numbered 10,342 troops of all types. Banasik, *Missouri In 1861*, 378–381.

Lie on Their Arms.

This precaution seemed providential from the fact that the enemy had conceived a similar plan and ordered it carried out at the same time. If the two armies had met in the darkness of night one or the other would have been annihilated. It has been said we had no pickets out,[103] and if we had they did us no good for the first intimation we had of the enemy was the booming of cannon and bursting of shells. Gen. Lyon marched down the main or Wire road and fell upon Gen. Rains with great fury, but his gallant troops did not waiver. At the sound of the first gun the unarmed Missouri troops and wagon train were ordered to the rear. Their retreat caused great confusion, but with their absence quiet was restored. Simultaneously with Lyon's attack came that of Sigel, who had marched down a road leading southeast from Springfield and to our rear right flank, where the troops under Col. Churchill of Arkansas were camped. This regiment was confused and somewhat scattered by the sudden attack, but soon rallied. The Arkansas troops fell back and formed in the woods at the edge of the field. The Third Louisiana regiment was ordered from the support of Woodruff's battery and formed on the left of the Arkansas troops. Sigel now marched down from the hills and formed in the field, facing nearly north with his battery planted in front of the Third Louisiana Infantry.[104] Meanwhile

Gen. Price

had got his troops into line, his batteries in good position awaiting the advance of Lyon. Woodruff's battery kept up an incessant roar from the hill east of the creek. At this time Price's army was facing north with Lyon in his front while McCulloch's army was facing nearly south with Sigel in his front. It was now about 8 o'clock and the battle was becoming general along the line and the work getting warm. The rattle of musketry and thunder of artillery were deafening as the Arkansans, Louisianans, and Texans engaged Sigel in a hot contest. As the fight progressed the hoarse shells groaned their solemn warning high in the air and the whistling minie ball sounded many a soldier's requiem; yet the shouts of the combatants rose often above the pandemonium of battle. Sigel was sorely pressing the Arkansas and Louisiana troops, and their lines were beginning to waiver when Gen. McCulloch rode up to Col. Greer of the Third Texas Cavalry

---

103. Confederate pickets were pulled in on August 9 in preparation for the night march. When the march was canceled, the pickets were not returned. General Rains stated in his official report that he had sent out pickets, but in all likelihood it was nothing more than the forage wagons sent out by Colonel Cawthorn. These foragers initially discovered the advancing Federals, not a picket force put out by General Rains. *O.R.*, 3:127; Piston, 192, 196; 169; Brooksher, 169; Bearss, *Wilson's Creek*, 57; Moore, *Missouri, Confederate Military History*, 56.

104. The writer's statement is an abbreviated version of Sigel's early maneuvering in the battle from 5:30 a.m. until he took his final position near Sharp's house, about 8:00 a.m. Bearss, *Wilson's Creek*, 60, 82, 104.

and pointed out the state of affairs and ordered him to charge the advancing enemy. Col. Greer gave the order: "Forward!" and it was greeted with a "rebel yell." Before the Federals had time to fix a bayonet the Texans were on them, and over the routed columns they swept with the force of an avalanche.[105] Sigel's army was vanquished and flying before the victorious Confederates. McCulloch now hastened with his entire command to the assistance of Gen. Price, who was hard pressed by Gen. Lyon, who made

Charge After Charge

upon Price's lines at the head of his troops in person. Hearing of Sigel's defeat[106] he fought with tremendous energy to snatch the victory ere Gen. McCulloch could render Gen. Price the necessary assistance, and had he not fallen back we know not what the result might have been. The second battalion of the Third Texas regiment was sent in pursuit of Sigel's retreating army and captured his last gun and a battle-flag.[107] Private Duke Zachary captured the flag. He belonged to Co. G, Third Texas. From 9 o'clock to 10 the fighting was terrific indeed. Col. Weightman of the Missouri troops was mortally wounded and many line offices and privates killed. About 10 o'clock there was a lull in the engagement: Gen. Lyon was now making his last effort, putting every available man into line and getting his batteries into good position.[108] On our side, every effort was being made to repel

---

105. Editor's Note: The three main books on the Battle of Wilson's Creek all have slightly different takes on the role of Greer's Regiment. This is my best look at it:
After the initial warning, that the Federals (Lyon's column) were advancing on the Confederate position from the north, McCulloch ordered Colonel Greer to investigate the matter. Greer formed five of his companies and moved out on the Springfield road; the remaining five companies, under Lieutenant Colonel Lane and Major Chilton, were still forming in Sharp's fields, when Sigel let loose scattering them. These broken companies did not join Greer's main column until after Greer had led the abortive attack on the Union right flank about 10:00 a.m.
About 8:30 a.m., McCulloch, with a portion of the Third Louisiana Infantry, with some Arkansas and Missouri troops, launched his devastating assault on Sigel's poorly organized line. Sigel's command broke, split in two, with part heading west while the others went east. Greer's Texans were not part of the assault. About 10:30 a.m., Greer received word that a band of Sigel's command, with some artillery, was retreating to the east. Greer sent Lieutenant Colonel James P. Major, of the MSG, in pursuit with a mixed command of Texans and, Missouri troopers. The Third Texas provided Hinche P. Mabry's Company G (the Deadshot Rangers) and Company H (the Cypress Guards) commanded by Jonathan Russell. *O.R.*, 3:118–120; *O.R.*, 53:425–426; *O.R.S.*, pt. 2, vol. 67:704; Piston, 201, 224–225, 260; Bearss, *Wilson's Creek*, 68, 104; Brooksher, 197 231–232.
106. Lyon's column never heard of Sigel's defeat until after the battle had been decided. Major John M. Schofield, of Lyon's staff, recorded: "Nothing had been heard from Colonel Sigel for a long time. No one could tell where he was or what he was doing." The time was about 10:30 a.m. At 11:30 a.m., a messenger finally reached Lyon's wing, telling of Sigel's rout, but by then a retreat had already been ordered by Major Sturgis, then commanding Lyon's column. *O.R.*, 3:62–63, 69.
107. The pursuit unit contained Companies G and H of the South Kansas-Texas Regiment, commanded by Major Chilton, the Windsor Guards of the First Cavalry Battalion, Third Division, MSG, and a detachment of cavalry from Parsons's MSG Division, all under Lieutenant Colonel James Major, Third Division MSG. *O.R.*, 3:118–120; *O.R.*, 53:425–426.
108. Lyon was already dead by 10:00 a.m.; he was killed about 9:30. Bearss, *Wilson's Creek*, 104.

the enemy's charge which all knew was coming. Just before the lull in the battle the Third Texas charged the Kansas jayhawkers and drove them from the field in great confusion.[109] We followed them a mile capturing and killing numbers of them. Three shots from Totten's Federal battery was the signal for the tragic scene about to be enacted on the soil of Missouri. All the Southern batteries replied and, in a magnificent splender [sic], the Federal lines came on,

Led By Gen. Lyon,

with their bright sabers and bayonets shining in the sun making a dazzling display. Just in front of the Third Texas regiment was a battery of four guns which the gunners were moving forward with their hands. When the enemy were about 100 yards away the order to charge was given and at us they came. All along the Southern line came the shout, "Charge!" and these two mighty armies came together like the jaws of a steel-trap. The fighting was bloody and desperate. The smoke was so thick you could not see five feet, whilst the roar of cannons, bursting shells and rattle of musketry drowned all other sounds; in some places the opposing lines were so close that they used their guns as clubs. At last the heroic Lyon was killed. Then the Federal lines began to waiver, and with one desperate effort the rebels broke the ranks, poured through the gaps and ended the hard fought battle. In this last struggle the Third Texas charged over the battery in front of them and through the infantry that supported it, and about face and charged back through to the Southern lines. The Federal gunners ran under their gun carriages to get out of our way. The Missouri, Arkansas, Louisiana, and Texas troops all did their duty nobly and deserve alike the glory of this great victory.

Henry L. Lewis, M.D.

* * * * * * *

Item: Comments on the Battle of Wilson's Creek with an official report, by T. J. Churchill.
Published: January 9, 1886.

Arkansas Riflemen at Wilson's Creek

Little Rock, Ark., Dec. 30, 1885
Editor, *Republican*

As much has been said and written about the Battle of "Wilson's Creek," I thought that I would send you a copy of my official report of that engagement, written the night after the battle when everything was fresh in my memory. My regiment was 400 or 500 strong, at least that was about the number I took into

---

109. This was Greer's and Carroll's 10:00 a.m. assault on the Union right that ended badly for the rebel troopers. Confederate reports have little to say on the attack save that it temporarily distracted the Unionists and gave time for Price to reform his lines for yet another attack on Oak Hill. *O.R.*, 3:105, 119.

action.[110] In conversation with Gen. Price he told me that my regiment undoubtedly saved the battle. Coming to his assistance at the time I did, when he had been forced back by superior numbers, gave his men renewed courage, and time to reform his line and fill up his broken ranks.[111] This movement on my part prevented the junction of Lyon and Sigel, which, if accomplished, would have resulted in our defeat. Checking the rapid advance and progress of Gen. Lyon gave Gen. McCulloch time to take the Louisiana regiment, or part of it, to oppose Sigel, whose battery he captured, and put to flight the remainder of his forces. Even after Sigel's defeat, the battle raged furiously for several hours. Two-thirds of my officers were either killed or wounded, and my loss was as great as the combined losses of the Texas, Louisiana and Arkansas state troops.[112] I well remember the remarks of Gen. Price, as my regiment came marching down the road.

Without A Single Break

in their ranks, and moving by the left flank into line of battle, he turned around to his soldiers and said: "Now, boys, stand your ground like men; the Arkansas troops have come to help you." I never saw a cooler or more fearless man upon the field of battle than Gen. Price. He took no care of his person, but was seen riding up and down his lines, giving words of encouragement to his soldiers. The loss of the Missourians was quite heavy—in fact, more than half the entire army.[113] Our whole loss was in front of Gen. Lyon's command. Sigel made but a feeble resistance and inflicted but little injury upon our lines; I doubt whether five men were killed or wounded before his advance. I lost only two or three men when he fired upon my camp in the open field. My entire loss was in the front of the forces of Gen. Lyon, and he fell about seventy-five or a hundred yards in front of my

110. Most sources have Churchill's First Arkansas Mounted Rifles carrying 600 men into the Battle of Wilson's Creek. However, it appears that all of the sources, including my own, used Snead's *Fight For Missouri* as the basis for Churchill's strength. Additionally, Snead also says that only 500 men of Churchill's command were engaged in the fight on Oak Hill, suggesting that the other 100 men had scattered from Sigel's first fire at 5:30 a.m. or that these 100 men held the horses of the command and were not counted as "engaged." Brooksher in his account of the battle cites the U.S. Army Command and Staff College as his source. Banasik, *Missouri In 1861*, 378; Piston, 335; Brooksher, 239–240; Snead, 312, 314.

111. In his official report of the battle, Price did praise Churchill for his support. He wrote: "Where all behaved so well it is invidious to make any distinction, but I cannot refrain from expressing my sense of the splendid services rendered under my own eyes by...Colonel Churchill's regiment of mounted rifles." *O.R.*, 3:100.

112. During the battle Churchill lost 42 killed and 155 wounded. Greer's Texans lost 4 killed, 23 wounded; Hébert's Louisiana regiment lost 9 killed 48 wounded; and the Arkansas State Troops lost 36 killed and 188 wounded; total 49 killed and 259 wounded. However if the comparison is limited too just those Arkansas State Troops who fought on Oak Hill, Churchill's command lost 197 men while the other mentioned commands lost 193; in which case Churchill would be correct in his comment. Banasik, *Missouri In 1861*, 378–379; Snead, 314–315.

113. Price's Missouri command lost 162 killed, 528 wounded and 112 missing; total 802. Pearce's Brigade of Arkansas State Troops lost 36 killed and 118 wounded, while McCulloch's Brigade posted losses of 68 killed and 276 wounded; total 498. Out of 1,300 men lost, Price's Missourians suffered 62 per cent of the total rebel losses at the Battle of Wilson's Creek. Banasik, *Missouri In 1861*, 381.

command and the Missourians. I am inclined to believe that he was either killed by the Missourians or my regiment.

Yours truly,
T. J. Churchill

[Note: Following his initial comments General Churchill included a copy of his official report on the Battle of Wilson's Creek, which has been omitted here. See *Official Records,* 3:109–110.]

* * * * * * *

Item: The Battle of Wilson's Creek; the combat on Bloody Hill; backwater of the battle; treatment of wounded, by Capt. Thomas H. Bacon, late private, Captain William F. Carter's Company B, Colonel John Q. Burbridge's Regiment, Third Division, Missouri State Guard.
Published: September 11 and 18, 1886.

[Note: The following pieces constitute parts 2 and 3 of Captain Bacon's tale of the Wilson's Creek Campaign. For Part 1 see the previous chapter. All Bacon's references in the sketch are supposedly from the *O.R,* Series I, Volume 3; however, I've noted discrepancies where found.]

[Part 2]

The Surprise

With the Afternoon of August 9 came orders to march that night to surprise and attack Gen. Lyon. We busied ourselves to be ready, but soon after dark a light rain set in. A rain would disarm us. The percussion caps of shotguns and squirrel rifles were too small to stand any wet. The tubes were too small to readily communicate fire. Flintlocks were no better. Our ammunition was exposed. If we had marched and had encountered a hard rain there would have been no battle, we would have simply maintained our reputation for Missouri time. I believe if a hard rain had attacked us in camp that night our charges would not have fired next morning, for every man had his gun ready loaded. When 9 o'clock came the orders were that on account of the rain and the attendant danger to our ammunition we should sleep on our arms till the rain was over. I did this literally. The rain continued. I went to the draught mules and robbed them of some hay. On this I placed my Mississippi rifle, my cartridge-box, with about thirty cartridges, and my cap-pouch full of percussion caps. Over the hammer of my gun I put my pliant brown felt hat. Then I laid myself face downward on my gun and ammunition and let the rain fall on my back. I did not sleep soundly, for I did not dare to turn over and we were momentarily expecting cessation of the rain and the sequent marching orders.[114] The night wore drearily away. Morning broke and the rain was over, but a night march or a surprise party was now out of question, and we set to work get breakfast. With our rations of coarsely ground wheat, we had cooked our bread in the skillet. At that moment,

Col. John Q. Burbridge

came around, and in a level tone of voice, as in ordinary conversation, said: "Capt. Carter, form your men immediately. Gen. Lyon is on that hill," pointing to the hill just behind us, soon to be called Bloody Hill. Our cook hastily broke up the bread into pieces for mess distribution. It was all we had ready. With a piece of bread in one hand and a gun in the other we formed in line. Meanwhile, Col. Burbridge passed on to other companies, that had to leave their breakfast unprepared. We did not believe a word of the news. Still their was haste in gathering up the camp [illegible] and dumping them into the company wagon, and some invalids took hasty passage but scarcely a man fit for duty showed any concern. Our wagon soon sped down the main road and fell in with the rushing tide of similar vehicles clearing the arena. The drivers yelled and cracked their whips, and their vehicles sailed like schooners, southward bound. No doubt a cynic like Gen. McCulloch or an intercepting column like that of Gen. Sigel, on seeing the confused hurry of this motley crew might think that the Missourians were braking and fleeing from their camp, but our fighting men had come to stay.

Our butcher, Private [David M.] Schultz [Stultz][115] of Lincoln County, was in the act of slaughtering a sheep when he received the alarm. He was urged to wash his hands, but he would not wait, and with his hands covered with blood he rushed back to the mess, secured his gun, and fell into line, soon to receive a wound from which he did not recover. When we formed I was in the rear rank. Right face. By file left march. Double-quick march. By file left march. Halt, front! This put me in front rank. We then stood complacently eating our bread and awaiting further orders. Then from the indicated woody crest came the roar of a cannon waking the morning echoes. Over the valley of Wilson's Creek to our right flew a cannon ball, a shell singing

A Battle Dirge.

We saw it curving through the air and saw it descend. From the place where it alighted there simultaneously came a counter explosion, and with the same tra-

---

114. Prior to Wilson's Creek, Burbridge's command was located at the base of Oak Hill on the west side of Wilson's Creek, on the Edwards farm. The unit had McBride's Division to their left and Slack's division to their left front. By the time the battle began Slack's command was on Burbridge's right, Guibor's Battery, with Kelly's Missourians in support, would place themselves on the left of Burbridge, followed by McBride's command. Piston, 155; Brooksher, 184, 187, 218; Bearss, *Wilson's Creek*, 64, 105.

115. David M. Stultz (not Schultz) was a member of Company B, Burbridge's Regiment, MSG. He was wounded in the right groin and died six days after the battle. Mudd, "What I Saw At Wilson's Creek," 100; Bartels, *Forgotten Men*, 348.

jectory a cannon ball went howling back to the Federal position. Totten's Battery had opened on Woodruff's Arkansas Battery and had received acknowledgement. Then the two antagonists exchanged four or five more shells. The Southern battery sent its compliments, whizzing gun for gun. Although it did not do any substantial damage to the enemy, it no doubt inspired wholesome awe, and certainly made us feel at home. With curious interest I stood and watched the ponderous missiles. This was my first experience in battle's consecrated hour. I took one look at the sun. It was slightly above the horizon and just emerging from a light rift of yellow clouds. The morning was vaporous, but the sky was clear.

Gen. Lyon's men were somewhere up in those woods. Had they, without any artillery practice, marched on at once, perish the thought, we would have been put into the utmost confusion. They would have captured our wagons with all their valuable contents; they would have probably taken our artillery and we would have been driven helter-skelter across the creek, where the thick woods might have enabled us to rally, every man for himself. There would have been no organized commands on our side. Col. Sigel's Battery would not have been captured, but we would have drawn to the east, leaving all the Federal forces west of us. The chances are we would have witnessed

A Regular Missouri Panic,

grading fully up to the McIntosh standard; Gen McCulloch's contemptuous estimate of our fighting capacity would have been fully confirmed. His views would have been profoundly corroborated and his command, abandoned by our scattered forces, might have struck a bee line for Arkansas, trumpeting at every jump the demerits of the panic-breeding Missourians. All the exposure arose from our being a horde of barbarians swarming together without any videttes, pickets or outposts. The camp on Vinegar Hill could never have been so disgraced. When, in seeking Gen. Price's army, I came in two days' march of the Cowskin camp, I was halted by a cavalry picket, who, in sepulchral tones, propounded the interrogatory: "Who goes there?" Yet Gen. Lyon's whole army was allowed to camp in a few hours' march of us and was permitted to march all around us and intrude into our camp without exciting any especial comment. This was a discrimination demanding the severest of censures. The Federal troops could say with the apostle, "the barbarous people showed no little kindness."

Little hand-books on outpost duty, primers that could be carried in the pocket unfold the whole science of protection from surprise. An army is like a bug. It has its long antenna and its feelers testing every approach, and acquiring valuable information. Without such aids the bug could not exist. But picket duty is arduous. It is the service that most severely tests the soldierly qualities. Here is where raw troops certainly do fall. Fighting is a minor incident in soldiering. The soldier's trade, like any other art, must be learned by apprenticeship and slow experience. I respectfully suggest that every outpost ought to have some detonating bombs or hand grenade to give alarm and prevent anarchy in a protected camp.

The late Capt. Quantrill[116] assured me that he never kept out any pickets. It was too much trouble and the men preferred to run the chances. Gen. McCulloch says he never did learn whether our pickets on the night of August 9 came in with or without orders, and he never did learn, who, if anyone, caused them to come in (p. 746).[117] The Missouri mounted men were camped

Both North and South

of the army.[118] Gen. Rains says that on the evening of the 9th, he received a General Order detailing the order of march and the mode of attack on Springfield, and in accordance with verbal instructions drew in his pickets with a view to take up the line of march that evening by 9 p.m., and that on the following morning he, at the break of day, sent out pickets who reported the enemy in force west of Wilson's

---

116. William C. Quantrill was born in Ohio in 1837, and moved to Kansas in 1857. During the Civil War he became one of most infamous guerrillas on the frontier border. For additional information on Quantrill's band see Michael E. Banasik, *Cavaliers of the Brush: Quantrill and His Men* (Iowa City, IA, 2003), passim; see also Banasik, *Serving With Honor,* 391–392, for a complete biography of Quantrill.

117. In writing about the lack of pickets, General McCulloch recorded in December 1861:

> I have never been able to learn who ordered these pickets to leave their posts, or if they left without orders when the time arrived to march the night before at 9 o'clock. Be that as it may, the fault was theirs, and not mine, that the enemy was allowed to approach so near before we were notified of it.

As shown before, the removal of the pickets was a universal event and not limited just to the Missouri troops (See note 76 of this chapter). Further investigation shows that McCulloch, himself, was probably responsible for the pickets being pulled in, whether directly or indirectly. Writing after the battle a representative of Governor Edward Clark of Texas recorded:

> The order was that our horses should be saddled and the army ready to move on Springfield by 1/2 past 10 o'clock at night—The same order commanded that the pickets should return to join the main body at 12 o'clock. The horses were saddled—The Pickets came in and the army was ready to move and would have done so immediately had not a rain storm come up—and our troops having few cartridge boxes it was deemed prudent to commence the movement until the rain ceased. It was expected that the movement would commence every minute and in consequence of this the Pickets were not placed out again.

The only comments found on the withdrawal of the pickets in the *Official Records* comes from General Rains, who stated that he "drew in" his pickets prior to the march on August 9, with a comment that he restored them in the morning. William Piston, for his part, dismisses Rains's comments on restoring pickets, but credited Cawthorn's forage party for notifying the rebel army of the approach of Lyon's command. Snead in his account says as much, though he says Cawthorn sent out pickets, but made no mention of the forage wagons. *O.R.,* 3:127, 746; Piston, 192, 196; Snead, 268–269; Wright, "Wilson Creek," 363.

118. Cawthorn's Brigade, a cavalry command of six regiments with 1,210 men, including staff, was the most advanced unit of the army, being located on a hill to the north of Oak Hill. Of the other Missouri cavalry commands, Rive's Regiment camped near the southern crest of Oak Hill; Brown's Regiment and Majors's Battalion camped south of the army in Sharp's fields; and several independent companies of mounted Missourians camped on the east side of Wilson's Creek, below Woodruff's and Reid's Arkansas batteries. Piston, 144–156; Brooksher, 184.

Creek, and three miles from camp. Then as foraging parties returned he further reported the advance to Gens. McCulloch and Price. Here seems to have arisen a fortuitous circumstance. Greene County was noted for its predominance of Union sentiment. As soon as our army camped on Wilson's Creek the local Unionists made themselves thoroughly acquainted with our positions and numbers, and the exact locations of our outposts. Gen. Lyon knew more about ourselves than we did. This to him was rain in the desert. Seeing his opportunity he determined to attack us the very first night of our camp at Wilson's Creek (p. 59).[119] Knowing the exact stations of our pickets, and having a shoal of neighborhood guides he proposed to cut off and take prisoner our pickets and then run over our entire camp. But as it happened, his attack was several days delayed, and when he started we had arranged to try a surprise on his camp. The same coincidence occurred at the Revolutionary War Battle of Camden, with the difference that both armies met in the road, about half way, to engage in their equally hard fought battle.[120] When Gen. Lyon cautiously slipped up on our pickets they were not there. (See Maj. Schofield's report, p. 60). Then the column halted and waited until dawn (I.B. [ibid]). Gen. Rains, as stated, had

Drawn in Our Pickets

during the night, and at daybreak he sent them out again (p. 127). When Gen. Lyon's troops made their final advance they met these out-going pickets. The meeting was as unexpected on one side as the other. This was about 4 o'clock a.m. (p. 60). Our pickets were out of their place, and therefore, were not captured. Therefore our pickets hurried back to bring the news, while the enemy attended them by way of corroboration. Lieut. Col. [George] Andrews[121] of the First Mis-

---

119. True. According to Major John M. Schofield, Lyon's command was "well informed through our scouts and spies of the movements and strength of the enemy." After Lyon's army arrived back in Springfield, on August 6, the day the Confederates encamped about Wilson's Creek, Lyon planned to attack the rebel advance. However, having received the information on the enemy's position and strength too late in the day Lyon called off the advance. *O.R.*, 3:58–59.

120. On August 15, 1780, Horatio Gates made a night march on Camden, South Carolina, with 3,000 men, in the hopes of surprising the British garrison. Lord Cornwallis, hearing of the Continentals' advance, moved out of Charleston with several hundred British Regulars and ran into Gates's command during the night. Nothing happened as both sides pulled back and waited on the dawn. The next morning the battle began, proving disastrous for Gates, as his army was routed, losing 750 men to Cornwallis's 350. James Kirby Martin, et al., *A Respectable Army: The Military Origins of the Republic, 1763–1789* (Arlington Heights, IL, 1982), 157–158.

121. George L. Andrews was born in Rhode Island and moved to St. Louis prior to the war. In 1860, Andrews was elected a lieutenant in the Second National Guard Company, St. Louis Missouri Militia. Just prior to the Camp Jackson Affair, Andrews was elected captain of his militia company, but he was denied his promotion because of his political views. Andrews resigned from the militia and became the lieutenant colonel of the First Missouri Infantry (Three Months). His command was at the capture of Camp Jackson, Boonville, and Wilson's Creek. When his time with the First Missouri expired, Andrews became a major in the Seventeenth U.S. Infantry. Andrews completed his Civil War service as a lieutenant colonel, commanding the Thirteenth U.S. Infantry. Following the war, he remained in the army, retiring as a colonel in 1892. Peckham, 86–87; McElroy, 165; James Hardy, Missouri Militia Report (January 18, 1861), Missouri Mi-

souri[122] says his skirmishers commenced the action at 5:10.[123] It is probable that Gen. Rains's reports were regarded by Gen. McCulloch as simply manifestations of Missouri effervescence. No wonder Gen. Rains's pickets were scared, this was the second time they had seen the enemy's line of battle. There never was a grander sight than the deployment and advance of this embattled bannered host across the virgin prairie. Our pickets with kaleidoscope vision saw 20,000 men advancing on our camp.[124] We were thus surprised but not entirely victimized. As it happened we were compelled to depend on Gen. Lyon for reliable news of his approach. With the friendly conviviality that characterizes military life, he had invited himself to breakfast and brought his friend along. Courtesy to Col. Sigel demanded some delay to enable him to participate. But when patience was exhausted, Gen. Lyon gladly fired a few signal guns to inform the laggard that the banquet was awaiting him. Happily for us their breakfast bells received a share of our attention. It took a salvo of artillery to arouse us to the situation. The idea that our fugitive enemy would hunt our camp was preposterous. Yet there was his artillery tossing us certificates to prove it.[125]

In the following autumn I rehearsed my experience to Dr. Gustavous M. Bower[126] of Monroe County, Missouri, one of the survivors of the massacre of the

---

litia Papers, Missouri Historical Society, 7; Scrapbook of St. Louis Missouri Volunteer Militia, "National Guards," page 18 of unnumbered pages; Scrapbook of St. Louis Missouri Volunteer Militia, "Military," page 28 of unnumbered pages.

122. The First Missouri Infantry (Three Months) was organized on April 27, 1861, under the President's call for 75,000 troops and was commanded by Frank P. Blair. The regiment contained 1,020 officers and men. During its short history, the First Missouri participated in the capture of Camp Jackson, Boonville, Dug Springs, and Wilson's Creek. Even as their term of service was nearing completion, the command began training as an artillery unit and was again mustered into the service, this time as an artillery regiment for three years. *O.R.*, 3:13, 48, 75–78; *Union Army*, 4:257; C., "Affairs In Missouri," *Chicago Daily Tribune*, August 7, 1861.

123. Colonel Andrews stated that his command, remained at rest until 4:15 a.m., at which time the march resumed. Moving forward, Andrews deployed Company H, under Captain Theodore Yates as skirmishers with the rest of the regiment following in column by companies. At 5:10 a.m. Yates's command commenced skirmishing with D. C. Hunter's Regiment, from Cawthorn's Brigade. *O.R.*, 3:75–76, 815; Snead, 269.

124. Colonel John F. Snyder was the one who made the report. See Snyder's article on Wilson's Creek in this chapter. Holcombe, 53.

125. The Federal attack was by no means coordinated. Sigel for his part had a considerably longer distance to march than Lyon's column and was directed to attack at dawn upon hearing Lyon's guns from the north. As the situation turned out, Sigel marched through the rains and dark of night and was in position at dawn, awaiting Lyon's firing. When muskets began to pop to the north Sigel let loose with four of his cannon, causing a "stirring effect" in the enemy camp. Sigel, 1:304.

126. There were two men named Gustavous M. Bower or Bowers in the MSG; Bower, Sr. and Bower, Jr, both from Paris, Monroe County. Gus Bower, Jr. enlisted as a member of Joseph Porter's First Cavalry Regiment, Second Division, MSG in 1861. He served for six months, after which he returned home due to illness. In 1923, Bower, Jr. was still alive and residing in Paris. In this case the writer was referring to Dr. Gustavous M. Bower, senior, who came from Kentucky and settled in Paris. Bower had been a member of the Kentucky Militia and was present at the Battle of River Raisin or Frenchtown, Michigan, in 1813. He later participated in the Blackhawk War. At the beginning of the Civil War he helped organize the first company from Paris to serve in the MSG. Bower served but a brief time in the Guard and appears to have

River Basin, otherwise known as the Frenchtown Massacre.[127]

(In the Western Annals, page 627 is embodied his letter of April 24, 1813, describing that butchery, the resulting penalty of timid management.)

The veteran, interrupted us with indignant disapprobation. "What," said he, "was there no long roll beaten?" I replied that we knew nothing about a long roll and would not have understood it if we had heard it. We had one square drum and one fife which occasionally entertained us. But if we sounded any alarm we have invited the enemy to descend on us before we formed.[128]

Bloody Hill.

Swarming in the bushes on each side of us came other companies, springing out of the ground like clansmen of Roderdic Dhu.[129] Again we went at double-quick up the hill, through the maze of scrubby undergrowth. Soon I came to the corpse of an unarmed man. No pickets or foragers had run on us. We were told that Gen. Rains's men were already fighting up the road, but we did not credit it, as we had heard no firing whatever, except shotted salutes of the two opposing batteries. Yet here was a lethal gunshot wound. I had to step over the body. The man's shirt was open and his bosom showed a torn and blood hole large enough for a grape-shot. But no cannon had been turned that way. He had been probably been shot through the back by some Federal skirmisher who had come down through the copse wood. With the enemy were numbers of men armed with .69 caliber muskets. That means an elongated projectile nearly three-quarters of an inch in diameter. A man can really stick his thumb into the bore of such a rifle. But

---

never left the vicinity of Paris. During the course of the war he was later arrested and tried for treason, though nothing appears to have come of the trial. The elder Bower like his namesake survived the war, but his other three sons did not; A. J. Bower [or Jack] was listed as missing and presumed dead at Corinth, Mississippi; James C. Bower was severely wounded at Wilson's Creek and later died of his wounds; and Cricket Bower was killed at Vicksburg. Bartels, *Forgotten Men*, 29; Bartels, *Trans-Mississippi Men*, 62; Eakin, *Confederate Records*, 1:121; Peterson, 83–86; Schnetzer, *More Forgotten Men*, 27; C. M. Farthing, *Monroe County, Missouri: "Chronicles of the Civil War In Monroe County"* (Independence, MO, 1997), 19, 22, 24, 44.

127. In January 1813, General Henry Harrison sent 850 men into eastern Michigan, under General James Winchester to protect setters from the Indians in the vicinity of Frenchtown (modern day Monroe, Michigan) on the River Raisin. Winchester's command was attacked by a combined force of 1,100 British regulars and Indians on January 21, 1813, and defeated. On the day following the British departed the area leaving the wounded Americans, about 30 in number, to the mercy of the Indians. The drunken Indians then massacred the wounded Americans, burning many alive in the houses of Frenchtown. Including the wounded killed, the Americas suffered the loss of over 300 killed with the remainder of the command captured. Donald R. Hickey, *The War of 1812* (Urbana, IL, 1989), 85–86.

128. According to Joseph Mudd, another veteran of Burbridge's unit, the long roll was sounded in the regiment. The long roll was also sounded in Pearce's Arkansas Brigade (State Troops), while the Second Arkansas Mounted Rifles responded to a combination of artillery fire and bugle calls. *O.R.*, 3:111; Pearce, 1:299; Mudd, "What I Saw At Wilson's Creek," 94.

129. Roderick Dhu or "Black Roderick" was a character in Sir Walter Scott's *Lady of the Lake*. Jean L. McKechnie, *Webster's New Universal Unabridged Dictionary* (New York, 1979), supplement 71.

it does not appear that any .69 caliber men were opposite our front.[130] The sight of the fearful collapse of death and its too efficient cause profoundly influenced all who witnessed the spectacle. The ghastly hopelessness of his filmy eyes inspired us with sudden horror. We thought that our wounds would be like that. But

We Rushed On

through the brush and up the slope until we were about two-thirds of the way to the top and then by common consent we halted. I found all my caps had been scraped off from the nipples of my leather disk, but I had plenty more in my pocket and in my cap pouch. We had no skirmishers out, we knew nothing about a skirmish line, but the Federals did. Their sharp-shooters, hidden in the dense retreats opened fire on us. Their bullets sang of the horrible abyss of sudden death, the demise deplored by the prayer-book. Here I swallowed a lump in my throat and resigned the hope of life. Could the scene be laid on the carpet-like sward that enamelled my home-land hills, or amid the majestic columns of their ancient trees, or under the shimmering canopy of their massy foliage, or could I have been summoned to expire on some grassy field where purling stream murmurs of nature's joy, where meadow wild flowers expand their souls to worship the summer sun and commune with heaven's blue, or where like violet blossom, the bright winged butterflies should dot the green with varied decoration, on such a bed I could have died content. But here was parched and thirsty ground, eager for human gore. Here ugly stones projected from the sandy earth, and rank, forbidden herbage suggested converts for wild beasts instead of dying patriots.

Prof. [G. C.] Swallow's[131] geology affirms that the blackjack grows on the poorest soil in the state (p. 224).

Totten's Battery was on my right. The First Missouri Volunteers went in on the right of Totten's Battery. Maj. [Peter J.] Easterhaus's [Osterhaus][132] Battalion [133]

---

130. It is entirely possible that Burbridge's troops faced an enemy armed with .69 caliber weapons. Missouri and Iowa volunteers were armed with muskets from the St. Louis Arsenal, the majority of which were converted .69 caliber flintlocks. *O.R.*, Series 3, 1:1; Snead, 157; Banasik, *Missouri In 1861*, 34–35.

131. Considered an authority on the geology of Missouri in the late 1800's, G. C. Swallow was also a contributing author to an *Illustrated History of Missouri*. William F. Switzler, *Switzler's Illustrated History of Missouri From 1541 to 1871* (St. Louis, 1879), ii.

132. Peter J. Osterhaus was born in Coblenz, Prussia, on January 4, 1823. He received a military education in Prussia and fled to the United States following the German Revolution of 1848. Eventually settling in St. Louis, Osterhaus rose to fame in the German community, being elected major of Second Missouri Infantry (Three Months) in April 1861. Osterhaus served in the Trans-Mississippi until late 1862, after which he transferred to the east side of the Mississippi River. He was wounded during the Vicksburg Campaign, returned to duty, commanded a division at Missionary Ridge, and rose to the rank of major general, commanding a corps in Sherman's march to the sea. Boatner, 613; Warner, *Generals in Blue*, 352–353; McElroy, 162–163.

133. The Second Missouri Infantry (Three Months), commanded by Colonel Henry Boernstein, was organized on April 22, 1861, in St. Louis. Boernstein, an Austrian by birth, arrived in the United States in 1849, and at the beginning of the Civil War was the editor of the German St. Louis newspaper *Anzeiger*

and two companies of the First Missouri Volunteers[134] were deployed as skirmishers, the former to the right the latter to the left.[135] These men were part of Gen. Lyon's

Force At Boonville.[136]

The inference is that the skirmishers in front of us were deployed from Col. Blair's Regiment, First Missouri, which regiment must have been the one facing us. The First Missouri was composed largely of natives of this country, and Irishmen (per Col. Snead, p. 165). In this regiment the casualties were 295 out of a total present 775. In Maj. Osterhaus's battalion the casualties were 55 out of a total present 150. These figures indicate that the extreme right wing of Gen. Lyon's army encountered somebody. Our extreme left ultimately flanked Gen. Lyon's right, where, as I believe our firing never stopped, until the enemy abandoned this position (pp. 66, 67). We cleaned out the First Missouri, and they were replaced by First Kansas, which came up according to official report, in time to prevent the First Missouri from being destroyed (pp. 61, 67). The First Kansas, after losing 284 out of 800 present, had enough, and retired in confusion (p. 81), and were succeeded by the First Iowa (p. 67). When Col. Churchill's Arkansas dismounted men reenforced us just in time (p. 110). According to Mr. Holcombe, Col. Churchill first came up on the extreme left, and afterwards came in on Gen. Slack's left (Col. Snead p. 281). This placed his regiment on Gen. Clark's right.[137]

---

des Westens. During its three months service, the Second Missouri Infantry participated in the capture of Camp Jackson, the engagements of Boonville, Dug Springs, and Wilson's Creek. Its most memorable, or infamous action, occurred on May 10, 1861, when Colonel Boernstein ordered his command to fire into a protesting St. Louis crowd following the capture of Camp Jackson (see note 164). The regiment was mustered out of the service on August 31, 1861. Peckham, 113–114, 149; *O.R.*, 3:13; 48; Dyer, 1322; Webb, 314; Gerteis, 74; Winter, 43.

134. This was Plummer's two company battalion of the First U. S. Infantry, not First Missouri Infantry. Bearss, *Wilson's Creek*, 60.

135. After the initial contact with Cawthorn's Brigade, Lyon deployed his command to drive the rebels back. The First Kansas Infantry moved to the left of the main Federal line while the First Missouri was to the right; Totten's Battery was positioned in the center between the two infantry commands. Plummer's First U.S. Infantry moved off to the far left near Gibson's Mill. As the line pushed Cawthorn back across Oak Hill, Osterhaus's Second Missouri Battalion deployed to the right of the main Federal line. The First Kansas and First Missouri maintained their relative positions, while Totten's Battery moved to the top of Oak Hill, which placed the First Kansas Infantry to their right front. Bearss, *Wilson's Creek*, 60–61, 82–83.

136. The Federal command at Boonville consisted of portions of the First, Second and Third Missouri Infantries (Three Months), Totten's Battery and two companies of the Second U.S. Infantry. *O.R.*, 3:11–14; Phillips, 217–220.

137. There is a lot of confusion as to where Churchill's command deployed for combat. Churchill and Snead both say that he deployed to the left of Slack and remained there for the rest of the battle. Major J. B. Clark, Jr., commanding Burbridge's Regiment stated that he deployed to the left of Slack. After the first charge, and upon receiving fire in their rear, Burbridge's Regiment became disordered and withdrew down Oak Hill to reorganize. Meanwhile, General Price had ordered Guibor's Battery to reinforce the rebel center. When the situation sorted itself out Guibor's Battery was between Burbridge's Regiment and Slack's Division. John T. Hughes, who took command of Slack's Division after Slack was wounded, makes no

Our original position placed Capt. [Lloyd P.] Hallack's company[138] across the old by-road or mill-road. Then came about a half a dozen men comprising Capt. [Hays] Farris' company[139] of Howard County—men with whom was Lieut. [Bennett H.] Clark,[140] the general's son, the Clark's being battle epicures. Then came a company, perhaps Capt. [H. A.] Martin's,[141] and then our company. This is the way I recollect the disposition. It seems to me that I remember the open space where the old road ran. Many of my impressions are doubtless derived from the talk immediately after the battle. But Capt. Hallack's company suffered

A Fearful Mortality,

the heaviest of any company in our regiment. Both he and his son Alonzo[142] fell, not far separated, one pierced through the head, the other through the heart. From

---

mention of either Guibor's Battery or Churchill's Regiment. As previously shown, both Piston and Brooksher have Churchill to the left of Guibor's Battery, while Bearss has Churchill to the right. To make matters even more confusing, William Barlow, an officer in Guibor's Battery, whose recollection "was clear," places Churchill's command on his left toward the end of the battle and not Burbridge's Regiment. I suspect that when Churchill received the messenger from General Price to support Slack, that Churchill marched his command to the sounds of the guns and to a position on the left of the Confederate line. It is difficult to believe that Churchill would have marched up his regiment and pushed in between Burbridge and Slack, thus lending more confusion to the situation. *O.R.*, 3:110; *O.R.*, 53:426, 429, 431–432; Mudd, "What I Saw At Wilson's Creek," 95; Patrick, "Remembering the Missouri Campaign," 35–37; Snead, 281.

138. Lloyd P. Halleck or Hallack commanded Company G, First Infantry Regiment, Third Division, MSG. A resident of Macon City, Missouri, Halleck was the Register of the U. S. Land Office in Palmyra from 1850–1853 and was considered a "gentleman of education and refinement." On June 26, 1861, he was elected captain of the Marion County Company, MSG. Departing for the army, Halleck took his sons Alonzo (age nineteen) and William (age thirteen) with him. The two elder Hallecks were both killed at Wilson's Creek on August 10, 1861, after which William took up arms and entered the line to finish the battle. After the battle Sterling Price sent William Halleck home. William was captured in Marion County by Federal troops in September 1861, sent to Gratiot Street Prison in St. Louis and then to Alton, Illinois, Prison in August 1862. His final disposition was unknown. Bartels, *Forgotten Men*, 142; Bartels, *Trans-Mississippi Men*, 26; Mudd, "What I Saw At Wilson's Creek," 97; Peterson, 100, 116.

139. Company C, First Infantry Regiment, Third Division, MSG, was organized on May 14, 1861, with John B. Clark, Jr. elected captain. Upon Clark's promotion to major, Farris was elected the new captain of the company on May 21. Hays or Haze Farris, a resident of Fayette, Howard County, Missouri, was beheaded by a cannonball at Wilson's Creek, "while advancing upon the enemy." Following the battle, Company C was "reconstituted as Company B." Peterson, 115; *O.R.*, 53:427; Thomas H. Bacon, "Sigel's Disaster," *Missouri Republican*, September 18, 1886.

140. Bennett or Ben Hilliary Clark was born in Fayette, Howard County, Missouri and was the son of John B. Clark, Jr. In 1860, he joined the Richmond Grey's, Missouri State Militia, and at the beginning of the Civil War was elected third lieutenant, Company C, First Infantry Regiment, Third Division, MSG. He was captured on October 23, 1861, exchanged and subsequently fought at Pea Ridge, where he was wounded. After the war he settled in Austin, Texas. Clark never married and died sometime before 1920 from the effects of his wound. Eakin, *Confederate Records*, 2:56; Peterson, 115

141. H. A. Martin commanded Company D, First Infantry Regiment, Third Division, MSG. Peterson, 116.

142. Alonzo Halleck was the first sergeant in Company G, First Infantry Regiment, Third Division, MSG. He was shot in the heart and killed at Wilson's Creek. He was the son of Lloyd and brother of William Halleck. Bartels, *Forgotten Men*, 142; Mudd, "What I Saw At Wilson's Creek," 97.

rather recent conversation with Capt. D. H. McIntyre,[143] late Attorney-General, I concluded that his company was on our left. A year or more ago, while in the Supreme Court room at Jefferson City, I noticed present three attorneys, who not far apart at Wilson's Creek, became the subjects of surgery. Mr. McIntyre's visage still showed his martyrdom. Mr. [B. R.] Dysart[144] of Macon County limped in testimony of a broken limb. I do not know where our Vernon County butternuts[145] were posted. They may have been found with Gen. Parsons in Col. Kelly's command. They were in somewhere as their casualty list fully attested. One of them who was wounded on the knee so as to permanently stiffen his leg was nicknamed Abraham Lincoln, and as such we afterwards knew him in the hospitals. A day or two after the fight he received a visit from his father, who happened to be camped at the spring up the dry branch,[146] when the Federals appeared there and killed perhaps knifed, the unarmed old man. The current story of the day was that the

143. Daniel Harrison McIntyre was born in Callaway County, Missouri, on May 5, 1833, moved to Audrain County in 1834, and was educated at Westminster College in Fulton, Missouri. At the beginning of the Civil War, while a senior at Westminster College (he received his degree from Westminster in absentia in the summer of 1862), McIntyre was elected captain of a company, which eventually became Company A, First Infantry Regiment, Third Division, MSG. At Wilson's Creek McIntyre was severely wounded, taking a round in the jaw. He recovered, was captured at Blackwater River or Milford, Missouri, on December 19, 1861, and was sent to Alton Prison, then Camp Chase and Johnson's Island Prison. After nine months, McIntyre was exchanged at Vicksburg on September 1, 1862. Returning to duty, McIntyre completed his military service serving under General Price in the Trans-Mississippi Department. During the war he was engaged at Carthage, Wilson's Creek and Blackwater River in Missouri. After the war, McIntyre returned to Mexico, Missouri, married, became a farmer, and, in 1871, studied law. Admitted to the Missouri Bar, he opened a law office in Mexico. He was elected to the Missouri Senate in 1874 and from 1876–1880 represented Audrain County in the Missouri Legislature. McIntyre became the Attorney General of Missouri (1881–1885) after which he again served in the State Legislature (1887–1891), representing Cole County. Later in life, he had to give up the practice of law, as the wound he suffered at Wilson's Creek affected his eye sight. He retired to Mexico and was still living in 1900. Bartels, *Forgotten Men*, 247; Eakin, *Confederate Records*, 5:119; Eakin, *Missouri Prisoners of War*, "McIntire, Daniel" entry; Hale, 214–215; *History of Audrain County*, 271–272, 343, 352, 695; Peterson, 96, 100, 114; Schnetzer, *More Forgotten Men*, 157; Kathleen White Miles, *Bitter Ground: The Civil War in Missouri's Golden Valley Benton, Henry and St. Clair Counties* (Warsaw, MO, 1971), 65–66, hereafter cited as Miles.

144. B. R. Dysart, a resident of Macon, Missouri, was born about 1834. His father John Dysart was a colonel in the Missouri militia prior to the Civil War. B. R., a member of the Third Division, MSG, was wounded at Wilson's Creek, survived the war and died on April 14, 1922 at the age of 88. Eakin, *Confederate Records*, 2:216; Bartels, *Forgotten Men*, 98.

145. The Vernon County company, of the First Infantry Regiment, Third Division, MSG was commanded by Captain James M. Gatewood. The unit was temporarily assigned to the First Regiment, from the Seventh Cavalry Regiment (D. C. Hunter), Eighth Division, MSG, just prior to Wilson's Creek and returned to their original command following the battle. The company joined Burbridge's Regiment on August 5, 1861. Peterson, 117, 270; Thomas Bacon, "The Chase," *Missouri Republican*, August 21, 1886.

146. Bacon was probably referring to the Skegg's Branch and spring. The spring was located about a mile west of Wilson's Creek on the Skegg's Branch by the Skegg's house. Bearss in his book on Wilson's Creek, implies that water was flowing in Skegg's Branch at the time of the battle, while Bacon says it was dry. A period correspondent also noted that for August that the "streams…though traceable on the maps" were "only distinguishable by their dry rocky beds." Piston, 194; Bearss, *Wilson's Creek*, 87; "The Fight at Dug Springs, Mo.," Frank Moore, ed., *The Rebellion Record: A Diary of American Events*, 12 vols. (New York, 1861–1868; reprint ed. New York, 1977), 2: DOC 468, hereafter cited as *Rebellion Record*.

Federals that morning did some massacring: at the expense of those who were so unfortunate as to be surprised at the spring.[147]

According to Mr. Holcombe (p. 78 [34])[148] our extreme left was composed of Gen. McBride's 605 men, next were Gen. Parsons' infantry, Col. Kelly's 142 men with Capt. Guibor's Artillery, four guns and sixty-one men.[149] Then Gen. Clark's infantry, Col. Burbridge's 270 men, the Vernon County Company being omitted. Then Gen. Slack's 720 men[150] around the hillside toward main road and then Gen. Rains's 1320 men[151] farther north (ib., p 51). The numbers are from Col. Snead's Appendix. As far as the infantry was concerned, I think we had the advantage of position as we were not so liable to overshoot, but the battle

Was Practically Lost

to us because Gen. Lyon obtained choice of position and set his batteries on Bloody Hill—the top being a plateau and the sides being a gentle declivity, all around foretelling nature's own glacis and enabling Totten's Battery to command and sweep any part of the approach to his position, and also enabling these pieces to sweep the plateau so that our men could not flank the Federal line or turn its position. When the First Missouri was transferred, Capt. Totten in person, under Gen. Lyon's orders, moved a section of his battery to its support (p. 74 top) and played through the undergrowth (p. 61). Our men could not take Totten's Battery. At times they approached to within thirty or forty yards of it (p. 61 foot, p. 67). Maj. Sturgis says that "the enemy could frequently be seen within twenty feet of Totten's guns and the smoke of the opposing lines was often so configured so as to seem but one" muzzle to muzzle (p. 68) In their advance in so dense a thicket had our men been provided with the celebrated Roman cold-chisel of the pattern handled by the Tenth Legion, the key of Gen. Lyon's position might have been captured. Gen. Gaius J. Caesar scorned to tell how many he killed. He chronicled merely how many he left. Still, the Roman bowie knifers never tried to take a

---

147. There was no evidence that the Federals massacred any rebel troops on their approach to the Wilson's Creek battlefield. However, Federal comments on the battle do note that they captured Confederate foragers as they approached the battlefield. *O.R.*, 3:86; Sigel, 304.

148. Not true. Holcombe implies on page 34 (not 78), that McBride's command, composed of 605 men, was on the far left of the rebel line. Holcombe, 34, 63.

149. In General's Price's report on the Battle of Wilson's Creek he lists the infantry (Kelly) and artillery (Guibor) strength of Parsons's command as 256 men. In Parsons's report on the battle he lists Kelly's strength as 142 men, which leaves 114 men for Guibor's Battery, while Snead lists the battery strength as 61 and Kelly's strength as 142. William Barlow, a lieutenant in Guibor's Battery, recalled that the battery had lost "fourteen men, out of about sixty engaged. *O.R.*, 3:101; *O.R.*, 53:433; Patrick, "Remembering the Missouri Campaign," 38; Snead, 313.

150. Slack's Division consisted of a cavalry regiment (234 men), commanded by Col. Benjamin A. Rives; and a combined infantry regiment and infantry battalion (650 men), commanded by Colonel John T. Hughes. Banasik, *Missouri In 1861*, 380; *O.R.*, 3:101; Snead, 313.

151. Snead lists Rains's two brigades as containing 1,320 men. General Price's official report lists Rains's strength as 1,306 men for Colonel Weightman's brigade and 1,200 for Colonel Cawthorn's brigade, total of 2,506 men. Banasik, *Missouri In 1861*, 379–380; *O.R.*, 3:101; Snead, 313.

battery of artillery. All gunners are aimers. An infantryman may fire his shot at the nearest clouds, but a gunner knows that he cannot afford to waste a quart of ammunition. Moreover, when a cannoneer repels infantry courage he has his easiest aim. Point bank range is about 200 yards. All that distance the gunner sights without elevation. Hence the gunner is not troubled with calculations of the curve of the projectile's flight. The enfilading blast of a cannon at such range will

Blow An Infantry Line

out of existence, and no human courage can be of any avail against such machinery. Men massed against cannon are like men against a steam engine. There mere force cannot prevail. Two years later in such a thicket we would have thrown out a battalion of skirmishers who would have crawled into range and flattened themselves on the ground and murdered every cannoneer that tried to ram a cartridge.[152] While standing in line I heard Col. Burbridge riding along behind us saying in a low voice, "Don't shoot, don't shoot: wait till you are ordered to fire." Meanwhile the skirmishers' balls were singing close to us, cutting leaves, breaking limbs, and doing some damage. But we obeyed orders, and under our company officers we occupied ourselves in trying to form a line of battle. There were too many of us for the ground. This probably was because to form a line of battle we had converged towards the crest of the hill. First it would be side step to the left, and we would side step until we crowed too much that way; then side step to the right till we swayed and surged about and could not find the room. We squeezed and squeezed until I turned sideways, and to the best of my knowledge and belief, every man was squeezed up sideways. Meanwhile, I was never more jammed or crowded in my life. My shape is such that turning sideways did not afford me much relief. Even then the surging line would curl up and wrap and twist, and here and there the line would break and overlap so as to be in places four deep in line. All the time the enemy kept up an irregular skirmisher's fire into our ranks. But we never got into bunches. When a battle line gets into bunches it is gone. I heard Col. Burbridge now addressing some

Pointed Remarks.

"Go back! " said he, "Go back," or "I'll shoot you." A wounded soldier was

---

152. During the battle an interesting incident occurred opposite Guibor's Battery, that goes counter to what Bacon says they would have done later in the war. Lieutenant William Barlow of Guibor's command recalled:

> We were very close, and one of the enemy's guns was soon silenced, when we saw a man walk up on his knees and insert a cartridge in the muzzle of the gun. Rock Champion, seeing this, called out "My God, don't kill that fellow. He is too brave a man." And this within probably less than thirty minutes from the time we were all in a sound sleep.

Patrick, "Remembering the Missouri Campaign," 34.

endeavoring to leave the field and the officer thought the private was skulking and did not propose to see his men stroll off that way.

We were ordered to squat down, and so far as I saw, all the privates obeyed but three of us, who did not come there to do obeisance. Some reclined. On one side of me stood Thomas Lally, a tailor from Hannibal, though I first met him in camp. On the other side stood a little New Yorker; we called him Yank. "Stand up my boys," was his adjuration. I turned my head and saw Gen. John B. Clark, Sr. sitting on his horse, not twenty feet behind us, facing square to the firing and motionless, except an occasional bat of the eyes. He kept this distance. His son, Maj. John B. Clark,[153] then newly shaved, was riding and looking about surveying the general line. All our field officers were, mounted and close up behind us. I could see how we might escape casualty, but I could not see how these officers could avoid stopping some of the missiles that flowed so thickly overhead. These projectiles had a sonnet ring totally unlike the sibilant hiss of the bullets of Confederate days. I had to learn the lesson over.

About twenty feet in advance of us was a single brass field piece, a six-pounder, one of Capt. Guibor's guns. The horses were there and the artillery men were stolidly awaiting their time to fire. Meantime, the Federal skirmishers were still at work. Soon one artillery horse caught it full in breast and when they released him he turned to us reared and raced down to us in agony with the imprint of one of those big bullets and the blood gushing from the wound. This horse was so frantic we had to dodge around and open a wide space to let him through. Some of the men cried out "shoot him," but we had not such heart. Then another artillery horse got a bullet through the face. They set him free, and he held his face down with the blood dripping fast and turned to us. We opened a way and let him through. The other horses

Stood There As Quietly

as if at a drinking trough. The tumult had not disturbed their nerves.[154] They ap-

---

153. John B. Clark, Jr. was born in Fayette, Missouri, on January 14, 1831, educated at the University of Missouri (Columbia) and received a law degree from Harvard in 1854. At the beginning of the Civil War, Clark was elected captain of Company C, First Infantry Regiment, Third Division of the MSG in May 1861. At Wilson's Creek, while leading Burbridge's Regiment, Clark was wounded. He subsequently rose in rank, commanding his regiment and then the Third Division, MSG. While serving in the Guard, Clark also fought at Lexington, Missouri, and Pea Ridge. Clark was appointed a colonel in the Confederate Army on June 28, 1862, and assigned, in November 1862, by Thomas C. Hindman to command the Ninth Missouri Infantry in northwest Arkansas, which he led at Prairie Grove. He was promoted to brigadier general on March 8, 1864, having fought in most major engagements west of the Mississippi River. After the war, Clark was elected to the U.S. Congress (1873–1883) from Missouri. He died on September 7, 1903. See Banasik, *Serving With Honor,* 380–381, for a complete biography of Clark. Moore, *Missouri, Confederate Military History,* 206–208; Special Order No. 38 (November 10, 1862), Special Orders Book No. 1, 111–112; Peterson, 107, 113, 115; Warner, *Generals in Gray,* 52; National Archives, Record Group M861 (roll no. 36), Records of Confederate Movements and Activities, Ninth Missouri Infantry.

154. Guibor's Battery was originally pulled by mules, but by the Battle of Wilson's Creek the mules had been replaced with horses. With the experience gained at Carthage in July 1861, and from assorted prac-

peared in deep meditation. The sight of the artillery men grimly standing there waiting their turn did much to inspire our line with equal resolution. It seemed to me that war horses were entitled to more sympathy than the men, because the men were volunteers. All this time the enemy's skirmishers were practicing on us, but still we would not fire.

Then ensued an interval of silence. Their skirmishers had retired. Then from the whole Federal line came a volley. It seemed that such a storm of missiles would destroy us. The air was thick with fluttering coupons of oak leaves. They fell like snowflakes all around us. On the ground ahead the bullets danced like occasional hailstones. They glanced from the trees; they buried themselves in the trucks; they hurtled over head, but we were silent. Another volley, and each time I held my breath. Then at last our cannon belched its thunder and its supposititious grape or canister. It spoke our epithets for us; it expressed our sentiments; it cleared a path and inspired us with the sound of defiance. With a tolerably fierce yell we rushed forward, and the field piece went off again just as I was abreast of the muzzle. The concussion stunned me just enough to cut short my artificial and tentative war-whoop, but not enough to arrest my progress.[155]

Lieut. Col. Andrews speaks of his regiment, the First Missouri, unmasking a battery (p. 76) [Guibor's Battery]. The other pieces were farther west, with Gen. Parsons's command, where they belonged. What business that cannon had there I never did know. Artillery should be stationed on the wings to deter flanking columns, but, nevertheless, as Gen. Lyon was

Not Strong Enough

to flank us our cannon was of utmost service until we got by it, and after that I cannot tell what became of it, for we closed up immediately in front. Here we had two moral effects; one was the blasphemous voice of the Mexican trophy,[156] the other the infantile-rebel yell, the product of too much political excitement. For me

---

tices, Guibor's Battery, including livestock, was well prepared for the tumultuous sounds of battle. Patrick, "Remembering the Missouri Campaign," 28–34.

155. Price's initial line on Oak Hill was formed by 6:30 a.m.; the remnants of Cawthorn's Brigade occupied the far right, next came Slack's command, then Clark's Division, including Burbridge's Regiment, followed by Parson's small division and finally McBride's men. In all, the initial line contained about 2,000 men. By 7:00 a.m., Weightman's Brigade had joined Price's line, closing a gap between Slack's and Cawthorn's commands and increasing the rebel numbers to about 3,300 men against about 2,800 Federals atop Oak Hill. About 7:30 a.m., Price launched his first of many assaults, to take Oak Hill. Most accounts have McBride's over anxious division leading the assault, which in turn caused Price to commit the rest of his line. Bacon's account, as will be seen shortly, shows that Price's line, minus McBride's men began the assault, followed by McBride's boys a short time later. Be that as it may, this rebel move halted the Federal advance, and forced it back; however, the Confederates were themselves halted and pulled back to regroup. Banasik, *Missouri In 1861*, 379; Bearss, *Wilson's Creek*, 66, 82; Piston, 206–207, 232, 239–242.

156. Bacon was referring to "Old Sacramento" and its distinctive ring when fired. Men in the MSG and from Louisiana reported hearing this sound, even though they could not see the gun. It seemed to reassure them. Tunnard, 67; Flavius J. Lindsey, "Cowskin Prairie and Wilson's Creek," *Missouri Republican*, March 20, 1886.

this latter factor had no special charm. It was terribly dry yelling.

Perhaps it was proper to duly notify the enemy that we were thirsting for their gore. Perhaps we thought to intimidate. If so, it was apparent that our visitors refused to take a civil hint. More likely it was perfunctory yelling, artificially rendered, merely because it was considered the correct thing for the occasion. But at least it was spontaneous and it served our purpose. It showed Gen. Lyon that though he could march into our camp before we knew it, and though we were the despised raw militia, the terror of his advent had not stampeded us, the bellowing of his batteries had not impaired our stamina. We at least appraised him that he had waked up a pitched battle instead of a panic.

As we drew up one of our men named McGinnis sprang from the ranks, and in a half stooping position ran forward into the brush about twenty feet. He evidently saw something. He went like a hunter after a wild turkey. I kept with him to see. When he stopped he fired and then got behind a blackjack and began to reload. I could not see anyone and got behind another tree and held my fire. Capt. Carter made us come back to place in line. After the battle McGinnis told me that he saw a Federal in the bushes just as we halted, and McGinnis fixing his eye on the spot ran up on him and killed him. McGinnis was a swarthy man, his eyes were the color of licorice and his system seemed saturated with nicotine. His teeth matched his complexion and seemed to have been worn off by insatiable attrition. He had the name of being a dead shot. I afterward heard that at Lexington, Mo.[157] he fired sixty rounds.

[Part 3]

Sigel's Disaster

After we resumed our place in the line I held my rifle at arm's port so as to interpose some protection, though this was hardly fair to the owner. Occasionally a slight shuffling somewhere in the ranks indicated that someone had gotten a hole burnt in his hide, but no exclamation was heard.

Suddenly on our extreme left cheers and rifle-shots announced our long-delayed response. Away out in the tall open woods McBride's men were running and firing uphill, the smoke from their country rifles spitting out six feet on the grade of the slope. Our men in running did not carry themselves upright, but bent double, partly to run uphill more easily, and principally to remain as close to the ground as possible and thereby evade the enemy's missiles.

The previous firing had been at too great a range and the enemy was now probably advancing. In the thicket our men could not see them, hence our men on the

---

157. Lexington, Missouri, a town of roughly 5,000 inhabitants in 1861, surrendered on September 20, 1861, to the MSG after a short siege. In addition to the loss of Colonel James Mulligan's command, the Federals surrendered 5 pieces of artillery, 2 mortars, 3,000 stands of arms, 750 horses, $100,000 worth of commissary supplies, the great seal of Missouri and the state's public records. *O.R.*, 3:188; McElroy, 206–207.

extreme left first obtained a view of the enemy first opened our fire.[158] This fire communicated itself like a fuse. It ran along through the open woods toward us till it descended into the deep ravine, where the brush set in, and then rattling through the brush, it came up out of the ravine like a whirlwind and sped along to where I was. The chariot rolled past me and went on across the old by-road or mill-road and thence around the side of the hill towards the main road and in front of the enemy's battery. Once opened this fire was un-intermittent. Our men were making up for lost time. Still I did not fire because I did not see anything to shoot; and therefore I stood still and kept peering into the now smoky woods whence volleys came. Presently I dimly saw three men standing together, and abreast, some distance up the hill. I raised my yagger, but the barrel trembled so that I could not hold on any object running up the hill, and the concussion of our cannon had rendered my head unsteady so I lowered the barrel and rested. Then

I Tried Again

to draw a bead, but again I failed. After resting a little more I levelled up all right and drew on the center man and fired. When my smoke cleared away so had the trio. Possibly I winged one of them. In reloading I tried to bite off my cartridge according to the books, but the paper was so thick and tough that I was compelled to violate the regulations on that subject by untying the string. This done, I poured in the powder, inserted the ball, rammed the charge and resumed my lookout. But I could not see any foe. I could see smoke and hear the opposing fire and take account of the firing missiles. Suddenly I saw that the smoke had lifted, and under it was a line of Federal soldiers, much nearer to me, than the men I had aimed at. I distinctly saw their blue blouses, their belts and their belt-plates. These were the men who had been doing the volley-firing. I had been overlooking them. Col. Snead mentions an out-cropping of rock in some places near the crest of the hill. Perhaps my three men were above this and the battle line below it. To use the expression of Dr. Lucius Mudd of Lincoln County, they were "banked up" in line. They appeared like wooden men and not over sixty yards away. I raised my rifle and this time I had no trouble. I drew a line bead on a belt-plate. I had always considered those belt-plates desirable targets. Here was a chance. I was at last tasting the sweets. But there is many a slip. Confederate luck betide to me. Just as my finger was contracting on the trigger I received a terrible blow, apparently from behind. Dr. Mudd says I

---

158. After McBride's men advanced they were first greeted by some rounds from Totten's Battery, became momentarily disorganized, rallied and advanced to the summit of Oak Hill. Cresting Oak Hill, McBride found himself on the flank of the First Missouri Infantry (Union), where he delivered a well "directed and effective fire in the enemy's ranks." George L. Andrews, commanding the Unionists, seeing McBride's flanking move shifted half of his regiment to confront the rebels and "drove them back." William Piston sees this move by McBride, though unsuccessful, as the turning point in the battle for Oak Hill, as the Federals had stopped advancing and for the remainder of the battle would essentially be fending off Confederate attack, after attack, until the battle closed. *O.R.*, 3:76; *O.R.*, 53: 434–435; Piston, 240–242.

Jumped Like A Deer.

I am ashamed to say how high. I know I jumped some and fell forward on all fours and did obeisance after all.

I declared that I was shot from behind by some of our own men. Just such casualties did happen that day. Our men were crowded up so that those in front were in danger from their friends. It seemed as if someone behind me had hit me with the full force of a brickbat. My undischarged gun flew out of my hands with the concussion. I scrambled through the line of battle and sat down in the rear. Then I became sensible that something had hit me in front; but whether in the right thigh or in the inguinal or abdominal region I could not tell. The shock was so severe that I could not make any better diagnosis. I saw the blood welling up from the region of my right groin, and I found I was sitting in a pool of blood. I sat there expecting to grow feint and then sink over and expire. That was the only fault that I found with my record that day. I did very well until knocked over, but when hit I expected only the worst. I felt sure the femoral artery had been opened, and that I could live but a few moments. I always envied those soldiers whose apprehensions departed with the first fire. I have a friend who was a Federal officer. When he was in battle he felt as if no gunshot could kill him. When he was severely wounded he ignored the honor and bolted along as if nothing happened. He thought a bullet through the brain would not hurt him. This is probably the A. Jackson[159] type of courage, and I was not so constituted. But as I sat I seemed to become no weaker and dismissing the idea of a collapse I spoke to one of Gen. Clark's aide-de-camps, a shrilled voiced Capt. [William B.] Cox,[160] who happened near, and I asked permission to retire. He asked me if I was wounded. I said I was and he let me go. The next day at the hospital he voluntarily asked pardon for his question on the ground that I showed no indication of having been hurt. It had not occurred to me that his question involved the reflection which he disclaimed.

When I set out for the war so many young men were seeking position that I preferred to

Serve In The Ranks.

But on that day the splendid courage of our officers, and the invaluable ser-

---

159. "A. Jackson" is a reference to Andrew Jackson, the seventh President of the United States.

160. William B. Cox, a resident of Saline County, Missouri, was appointed the Acting Adjutant General of J. B. Clark, Jr.'s First Infantry Regiment, Third Division MSG on August 5, 1861. During the Battle of Wilson's Creek, Cox had two horses shot out from under him and received the "highest of praise" of his commander for his actions. By the Battle of Pea Ridge, Cox had been promoted to lieutenant colonel and again earned the praise of his commander for his actions in the battle. While in service with the Guard, Cox was at the engagements of Carthage, Wilson's Creek, and Lexington in Missouri and Pea Ridge in Arkansas. It appears that Cox later entered Confederate Service as part of the Ninth Missouri Infantry. He was captured at Little Rock on September 10, 1863, and sent to Gratiot Street Prison in St. Louis, then to Camp Chase Prison in Ohio in October 1863. Final disposition was unknown. *O.R.*, 8:320; *O.R.*, 53:427; Peterson, 114; Schnetzer, *More Forgotten Men*, 55; Eakin, *Missouri Prisoners of War*, "Cox, William B." entry.

vices they rendered in holding the men down to their work, added substantial glory to the inventory of the honors of official station. All through the war the Confederate field officers maintained places as close to the front as practicable. If they wanted a place carried they left no room for mistake in their directions. They went and put their hands on the objective point. When I arose to leave the fight my entire right side seemed drawn down and distorted, and I staggered down the slope. Blood was freely flowing from my right breeches pocket, coursing down into my shoes, and charging the air with its unwelcome steamy and sickening odor. Then it was that I sincerely felt that after all this was a poor way to settle political issues. I forgot about Camp Jackson's provocation.[161] My course was not back to our camp, but towards an almost barren spur leading to the dry branch.[162] Wounded men with ghastly faces were being helped away in the same direction. It seemed, that except for myself, every wounded man was now conveyed by one or two comrades. I say it to the eternal honor of my company, not one man assisted me or paid the slightest attention to me except to step in my place. The men of my company were preoccupied with important business. I hope that the greater part of the helpers immediately resumed their posts. I know that some did not. I do not remember seeing a single one going back. For us it was evidently better to have a man killed outright.

What A Cunning Trick

it was to watch for a wounded man and spring to his relief and share with him the sweets of retirement from the hail-storm. These attendants knew very well that they could not leave without an excuse, but honestly they circumvented Col. Burbridge's revolver by detailing themselves for hospital duty. It was a painful sight, a pitiable sight to find so many tender-hearted souls heartily wandering off with one hand supporting a wounded soldier and the other grasping a precious rifle. It occurred to me that with all our camp fire laws we had omitted to provide an enactment against helping wounded men from the field. Had we foreseen this ill we would have talked up a public sentiment that would suppressed it. Skulkers would have had notice they could not thus indulge their propensities without exposing their disgrace. Unless absolutely disabled no patriot volunteer should be allowed to retire from action. In our case the loss was not very material as we were so crowded that our ranks need considerable thinning.

Reaching an exposed part of the spur I was in more danger than ever. Charges of canister seemed to sweep the spot so that I felt sure that I could not stand it

---

161. The "Camp Jackson provocation" was more than the capture of Camp Jackson on May 10, 1861. Following the capture of Frost's Missouri Militia Brigade, the prisoners were marched off to the St. Louis Arsenal. En route, a mob attacked the Federal troops, resulting in the killing of 25 civilian men, women and children along with 3 unarmed prisoners from Camp Jackson. This then became known as the "St. Louis or Camp Jackson Massacre." Adamson, 62–64; Banasik, *Missouri Brothers in Gray*, 12; Bevier, 25; Philips, 192.
162. This was probably Skegg's Branch.

any longer and I lay down at full length behind a friendly blackjack. Just then a wounded soldier came impetuously charging down on my post of refuge. He gave me a hard look and thought he was going to dislodge me, but another shower started him and he scurried away down the grade. Here several times the missiles kicked the dust into my face. From the time I first looked back at our line of battle I noticed our men in good alignment with their ramrods

Perpetually Twinkling

and firing over their heads. They were hard at work. McGinnis was there and the others of his type. They were killers putting in their time. All along their line men were dropping out under the influence of casual perforations. Still the ramrods twinkled like lightening overhead. As I look up I saw that our line, though still firing, was slowly backing down the hill.

When in Richmond in 1863 I asked our C.S. Senator, Gen. John B. Clark, Sr.,[163] what made our line give ground. He said that he saw that our men were too much in range, and he ordered them back to improve their position. On seeing the sag, Gen. Price came down on him galloping like a tornado and saying: "Gen. Clark, what the L. [Lord] do you mean sir?" The latter explained the object of the new adjustment, the men stopped backing, and the fight went on.

The sight of our men retiring aroused in my mind the direct apprehensions. I think our line had good reasons for yielding ground. This was the time probably when Capt. Totten, in support of the First Missouri, moved a section of the battery to participate in the fight raging in the thick woods to the front and right of the position occupied by that battery.[164] Here these cannons partially enfiladed our line with canister. One round shot or shell came feeling around that way. It took off the head of Capt. Farris and went through the body of Lieut. [John] Hoskins[165] from

---

163. John B. Clark, Sr. was appointed a Confederate Senator in late December 1863, when Robert L. Y. Peyton, the sitting senator died on December 19, 1863. Clark served out the remaining days of the term until May 1, 1864, when he was replaced by George Vest, and Clark became a representative in the Confederate Congress for Missouri. The other Confederate Senator from Missouri was Waldo P. Johnson, who served throughout the war. Marcus J. Wright, *General Officers of the Confederate Army* (New York, 1911), 165, 175, hereafter cited as Wright, *General Officers*; Bartels, *Trans-Mississippi Men*, 2.

164. By 6:30 a.m. both sides had established their lines about Oak Hill, and Lyon ordered his men to advance. They were met by a crushing volley from Price's Missourians, which brought the Federal movement to a halt. For thirty minutes, the two sides traded volleys, even as James McBride was moving on the right flank of Lyon's main line anchored by the First Missouri Infantry. Lieutenant Colonel Andrews, commanding the First Missouri, sent word to Lyon of the rebel movement on his right flank. Lyon directed Totten to move George Sokalski's section of artillery to support Andrews's right flank. Between 7:30–8:00 a.m. Lyon's charge and Price's counter charge had petered out and both sides adjusted for the continued action. Piston, 207, 234, 242; Bearss, *Wilson's Creek*, 79–80, 82; *O.R.*, 3:74, 76.

165. Prior to the Civil War, in 1855, John S. Hoskins or Haskins participated in a military intervention into Nicaragua, under William Walker, after which he returned or moved to Missouri. At the beginning of the Civil War, Hoskins became a member of Company A (Calloway Guard), First Infantry Regiment, Third Division, MSG, being elected the unit's first lieutenant. At Wilson's Creek, according to another account, Hoskins was attempting to scatter some of his men, who had bunched up behind a tree, when a cannon ball took the heads of two of the men and "tore Haskins nearly in two." Peterson, 114; Piston, 236; R. Boyd

side to side, and killed two other soldiers. Sergt. Maj. Clinton Burbridge[166] heard the concussion and asked his brother if that was a shell bursting. His brother—the colonel— replied: "No; It was those men."

Lieut. Hoskins had been one of Walker's men in Nicaragua.[167] His favorite boast was that he had fought in eighteen pitched battles and bullet was never run that could hit him. Cannon balls were under advisement. At Cowskin Prairie I often noticed his vigorous drilling as, sword in hand, he

Humped His Shoulders

and bent forward, and like a stream tug through a chopped sea ploughed [plowed] the tall prairie grass, his mouth half open and his white incisors gleaming under the shoe-brush mustache.

Totten's Battery kept the start of us [*sic*]. Out of eighty-four present it lost only four killed and seven wounded.

Capt. Dubois reported that many of his company, himself included, were struck and slightly injured by spent musket and canister shot, but only two were wounded and one missing. Here came in our inadequate munitions. Artillery is the skeleton supporting the entire framework of the army. Our original thoughts of fighting did not take into account the terrible machine power of the ponderous battery.

When I saw our men pressed back I thought we were whipped: We had always

---

Murphree, "William Walker," *Encyclopedia of the Civil War*, 2053–2054, hereafter cited as Murphree.

166. Clinton D. Burbridge, a brother to John Q. Burbridge, was a resident of Louisiana, Missouri, at the beginning of the Civil War. Appointed sergeant major of the First Infantry Regiment (Burbridge's), Third Division, MSG in July 1861, Burbridge was praised for "his gallantry and bearing throughout" the Battle of Wilson's Creek. While serving in the Guard, Burbridge participated at Carthage, Wilson's Creek, and Dry Wood Creek. Leaving the Guard, Burbridge became a Second Lieutenant in what became Company A, Second Missouri Infantry (Confederate) on December 8, 1861. The unit fought at Pea Ridge and was transferred to the east side of the Mississippi River at the end of March 1862. On May 8, the Second Missouri reorganized and Burbridge was "thrown out" as the lieutenant of his company. Clinton returned to Missouri as an aid to his brother, John, who declined to run again for colonel of the regiment. During the summer of 1862, the Burbridges raised the Fourth Missouri Cavalry Regiment. Clinton was reported in Ralls County in September 1862, raising troops, subsequently branded a guerrilla and was captured in Audrain County on June 8, 1863, while in civilian attire. Tried as a spy, Burbridge was convicted, sentenced to Gratiot Street Prison and placed in irons. He was transferred to the state penitentiary at Jefferson City in December 1864, and was supposed to be exchanged in January 1865, though his disposition was never known. *Branded as Rebels*, 52; *O.R.*, 13:271; *O.R.*, vol. 22, pt. 2:272; *O.R.*, 53:427; *O.R.*, Index: 1230; *O.R.*, Series 2, 6:173; *O.R.*, Series 2, 7:1040; *O.R.*, Series 2, 8:86; *O.R.S.*, pt. 2, vol. 38:414–415, 421, 437; Peterson, 113–114; Schnetzer, *More Forgotten Men*, 33.

167. William Walker was born in Nashville, Tennessee, on May 8, 1824, studied law in New Orleans and in 1848, became a newspaperman for the *Daily Crescent*. Following the death of his wife in 1849, Walker moved to California where he began a life of an adventurer leading first an invasion of the province of Sonora, Mexico, in 1853, and subsequent interventions into Nicaragua or Honduras in 1855, 1857, 1858, and 1860. His most successful invasion occurred in 1855, when he led 58 men, deemed his 'Immortals," into Nicaragua and eventually secured the presidency of the country. He was subsequently deposed in mid-1857, but led other invasions in the region. He was finally captured in 1860, and executed on September 12, 1860, at Trujillo, Honduras. Murphree, 2053–2054.

estimated the enemy's forces at over 10,000 men. Soon our line would retreat over me, perhaps break and run away. Soon the victorious, the anarchistic Dutch,[168] as we appraised them, would be prodding me with their bayonets. But where was my rifle? Just where I pitched it forward when I fell. If I had it I could defend myself. Moreover, I had promised Mason that I would return his property. I arose and waddled back to our line, which was now flourishing ramrods as fast as ever. Then I pushed through and wandered out in front, peering about for my lost yagger. I could not find it. Presently I saw the brass butt projecting from under the body of a 16-year-old Lincoln County boy named [Robert W.] Tanner.[169] Identification being easy I pulled out the arm, but

Tanner Did Not Move.

I thought he was dead, and I suppose he thought so too. He lay on his face with arms outspread. His thigh was broken by a bullet, but he ultimately recovered. Perhaps he simulated death to escape the inquisitive probe of the bayonet. When I secured my rifle I found the hammer drawn back at full cock, precisely as I had dropped it. Here was a chance for another shot, but the original thought of using it now for personal defense, absorbed my intent. I turned and repassed the smoke-spitting line of battle and again moved down the exposed slope, but in less danger than before. When I reached the dry branch bottom, I sat behind a large cottonwood tree and inspected the wound. I found in my right groin a round ball about the size of a dime. Blood had ceased to flow and the muscles had closed the opening. An indurated lump behind showed that I had stopped the ball. I arose and fell in with the stream of wounded fugitives down the branch.

Sigel's Disaster

When I came to the main road I saw just across and under the bluff line, and behind the main road and Wilson's Creek, a hospital flag. Straw was scattered over the ground and wounded men were gathered there. Soon appeared other men from my company. Private [W. L.] Wingfield,[170] who had filled my place, came

---

168. Dutch (from German "Deutsch") was the moniker associated with German troops, who were part of the Union Army. Non-German Missourians generally viewed the Dutch as "infidel, Sabbath-breaking, [and] beer-drinking," thus Bacon's characterization. McElroy, 14–15, 38.

169. Robert W. Tanner was a private in the Third Division, MSG and was a member of Company C, First Infantry Regiment. He was born about 1835, lived in Lincoln County, Missouri, and was considered one of the youngest members of the company. Wounded at Wilson's Creek in the right thigh bone, Tanner refused to be carried from the battlefield, stating to his sergeant "Put me down! put me down! I want to kill some more yankees." Tanner survived the war, returned to Lincoln County, where he died sometime in the late 1890's. Bartels, *Forgotten Men*, 353; Mudd, "What I Saw At Wilson's Creek," 100.

170. Private William Lewis Wingfield was born on December 17, 1836, in Lynchburg, Virginia, and moved to Missouri. On June 6, 1861, he enlisted in Company B, First Infantry Regiment, Third Division, MSG. He was wounded at Wilson's Creek on August 10, 1861, and "paroled out of service" on August 30, 1861, on account of the wound that he received. After the war he married, but never had any children. Wingfield never owned slaves, but his mother did. Bartels, *Forgotten Men*, 397; Eakin, *Confederate Records*, 8:88.

nursing a perforated arm. Several then came bearing the apparently lifeless body of Col. Burbridge. The back of his head was missing, and his brains were oozing out over his hair. He was in profound collapse, and his body looked as limber as a rag. Yet he recovered, and became known as a restless fighter. Matters assumed a desperate shape. We were receiving too many accessions. Still, the pounding of the opposing field pieces jarred the air with ponderous defiance. Still, the continuous rattle of musketry prevailed on the smokey hill. It was not a roar. It was more like the grinding of heavy wagon-wheels on a macadam road. Presently excited cries were heard around us among the surgical staff. "Tell those men to get away from here; this is a hospital!" said one. "What battery is that," said another. "Is that our battery?" "Yes," said another, "they are our men." "No, they are not; they are Federals."[171] Thus a loud jarring and wrangling went on. Meantime, the obnoxious battery proved to be on the bluff above us, and it began to fire over our heads, and we could hear its shells sailing over to curve down on some devoted target. But at once the boom of opposing cannon responded, and its adverse shell came over from some northern points.[172] As I lay on the straw I thought

The High Shelling

would do very well. It seemed as if Woodruff's Battery was answering, but it was Reid's Battery on the east bluffs of Wilson's Creek and farther down the stream. Shells flew high and fast, and our hospital was beginning to quiet down when a storm of canister came plunging from the hostile bluff. The hail was upon us. By the time I could arise, every tree was pre-empted, and all who could move were hustling out of the way. I hurried across Wilson's Creek and passed on to the bottom on the east side. Amid the tall dark woods everywhere, I found wounded men, like stricken deer, and too often I saw the pop-eyed convoy. His human impulses had prevailed upon him to abscond from glory's harvest. Pale, anxious faces, and bodies pierced with cruel wounds were there. Helpers vainly tried to pilot their friends to places of permanent safety. As I followed the creek southeastwardly[173] I found myself between two lines. A small body of our home-spun troops had passed down between the creek and the bluff to meet a small body of the enemy. I took refuge behind a log, which caught too many bullets for chance firing, but our men cheered and spit our horizontal streaks of smoke and rushed forward pell-mell in good style. Their adversaries cowered and staggered back. They then fled

---

171. The medical staff were commenting on the arrival of Sigel's battery which posted itself on the bluff overlooking Skegg's Branch and near the Sharp house. The time was about 8:00 a.m. Bearss, *Wilson's Creek*, 104; Piston, 231.

172. From this description, and later comments that Bacon has given, it appears that a hospital tent was established somewhere near Reid's Battery, on the west side of Wilson's Creek, near where Skegg's Branch entered.

173. According to Bacon's direction, he was heading away from the main ford, which was to the north of Skegg's Branch. However, there was a minor ford, crossed by a farm road, southeast of Skegg's Branch that crossed Wilson's Creek near the Sharp cornfield. *Atlas to Accompany the Official Records,* plt. 135, no. 1; Heidler, "Wilson's Creek, Missouri," *Encyclopedia of the American Civil War*, 2126.

and the field was clear.[174] The battery on the bluff over our hospital had ceased firing about the time I crossed the creek. The everinsting [everlasting] rattle of small arms continued on the blackjack hill, but it seemed to be moving away, and I essayed to reach the hospital.

A Ghastly Spectacle.

I approached at the same ford[175] which I had crossed. There, extended up the creek, a ghastly spectacle awaited my eyes. Along the banks lay the corpses of men, in civilian garb, but with white bands around their arms—Arkansas men, who had followed the stream from where they fought and had wandered here to die. They were probably Gratiot's men, who, at the creek, about that time, out of 500 souls had lost 100 men in thirty minutes. Their lips were blots of livid purple. Their faces pallid yellow, their eyes like lamps gone out, their forms like fallen statues, scattered along the gravel bed. The August light glared down in their faces and their features appealed to the sun. Their blood had flowed into Wilson's Creek and its current was bearing back to the bosom of their sunny land the precious offering. "It is a sin," each face did say, "It is a sin to shine on me so. Let me be out of man's sight. My life was sweet. I yield it and I am done. Oh, humanity, give me my grave."

When I again reached the hospital ground I found some Louisiana soldiers. One had lost his good looks. His face was black with powder burns. His eyes were nearly destroyed and he kept them closed. When the moving shadow of an adjacent tree let the sunlight fall on his face he would ask to be moved into the shade again. He had acquired his complexion powder at the canon's mouth. That shower of missiles that drove me out was from four guns of Sigel's Battery. They had been posted too near the bluff line and perhaps in ignorance of its nature. While Reid's Battery aided by Bledsoe's Battery had been pounding Col. Sigel's command as described, the right wing of the Third Louisiana,[176] under Lieut.-Col.

---

174. After Sigel's command took up its blocking position across the main road from Springfield, several of his men went into the rebel camps in Sharp's fields to steal what they could. The Federals being driven out of the field were probably just a few stragglers who had wandered into the area and quickly vacated the premises when they were confronted by some of the rebels. However, according to Jay Monaghan, some of Churchill's command accomplished the deed and killed or captured all the looters who were in the camp. Sigel, for his part, denies that any looting took place, but the evidence suggests otherwise. Sigel, 304–305; Piston, 247; Ware, 336; Monaghan, 177; Brooksher, 199–200; Shalhope, 177.

175. After Bacon departed the hospital, crossing Wilson's Creek, he went southeastward down the creek. This would have put him at the farm road ford near Sharp's cornfield. Generally speaking, Wilson's Creek was fordable by troops at most any point; however, the steep banks allowed wheeled vehicles to cross only where the bank had been broken down, thus providing a ford for their use. In this case, only one place was labeled a suitable ford over Wilson's Creek and that was near the Guinn house (Piston calls this the Winn house). Piston, 151–152, 194; Bearss, *Wilson's Creek*, 36; *Atlas to Accompany the Official Records,* plt. 135, no. 1.

176. The right wing of the Third Louisiana, at the time, consisted of Companies A, B, C, D, E, F, G, and K, with a portion of Company H, the whole commanded by Lieutenant Colonel Hyams. Company I and the remaining men of Company H, under Major W. F. Tunnard, constituted the left wing of the regiment and

[Samuel M.] Hyams[177] attended by Gen. McCulloch in person and probably led by him

Crept Up The Steep Bluff

and when on top they found themselves in easy reach of the hostile battery.[178] Upon it they charged and the Federals at so short of distance had not time to do much execution. Some seventy Missourians directly participated in this assault and capture, but in the general camp, the talk of the day, Louisianans alone were mentioned as the successful assailants.[179] Doubtless the Louisianans were the best armed troops we had. They must have had bayonets, and as bayonets were the exception the Third Louisiana was naturally selected for the charge.[180] Much as one may criticize Gen. McCulloch for his general mistrust no one can refuse to applaud him for this brilliant stroke, the turning point in the battle. He perceived the enemy's plan. He saw that we were surrounded. Here was a hostile battery playing in the rear and in easy range of our infantry line. When Gen. McCulloch went to Sharp's barn he went for death or victory.

The official reports of the capture of this battery require reconciliation.[181]

---

lagged behind the main column. The left wing did not arrive in time to participate in the assault on Sigel's guns, which occurred about 8:30 a.m. *O.R.*, 3:115–117; Tunnard, 27–28; Bearss, *Wilson's Creek*, 104.

177. Samuel Myers Hyams was born on September 16, 1813, in Charleston, South Carolina, attended Charles College, and moved to New Orleans in 1830. Continuing his education at Centenary College, Jackson, Louisiana, Hyams earned a law degree and settled in Natchitoches in 1834. Prior to the Civil War, Hyams served in a variety of government positions, including U.S. Deputy Surveyor, Clerk of the District Court, sheriff, U.S. Marshal of the Western District of Louisiana and Register of the Land Office. During the Mexican War, he raised a company and was elected captain of a company in the Fifth Louisiana Infantry. At the beginning of the Civil War, Hyams raised Company G, Third Louisiana Infantry and was mustered in on May 17, 1861, as the regiment's lieutenant colonel. Hyams was well thought of by his command and served in the Third Louisiana, despite being nearly crippled with rheumatism, until he left the army in October 1861, on furlough; he never returned, being "disabled by disease." Final disposition unknown. *O.R.S.*, pt. 2, vol. 23:740; Heitman, 2:56; Tunnard, 29–30, 324, 529.

178. After the situation in Ray's cornfield had been contained, General McCulloch led off the right wing of the Third Louisiana to assault Sigel's guns which were placed on the bluff overlooking Skegg's Branch and blocking the Springfield road. When they arrived at the bluff, McCulloch surveyed the situation and directed the assault, which was made by Companies A and K under Lieutenant Thomas G. Stringer and Captain John P. Viglini, respectively; the remaining companies of the Third Louisiana following closely behind. *O.R.*, 3:117–118; Tunnard, 27–28, 52–53, 97–99, 503, 557.

179. The seventy-man Missouri unit was commanded by a Captain Johnson. Piston believes that there were three possibilities for Johnson: J. Johnson, commanding Cedar County Company in the First Cavalry Regiment, Rains's Division; Thomas P. Johnson, commanding Company C, Second Cavalry Regiment, Rains's Division; and James Johnson, commanding Company A (Osage Tigers), First Cavalry Regiment (William Brown), Parsons's Division. However, Lieutenant Colonel Hyams in his report on the battle clearly states that Missouri infantry, not cavalry, assisted him in the movement against Sigel's guns. *O.R.*, 3:115; Piston, 198, 251, 371.

180. According to Willie Tunnard, the Third Louisiana did have bayonets, and used them in the assault on Sigel's Battery. Tunnard, 53.

181. The next several paragraphs present various pieces dealing with the capture of Sigel's Battery. The "reconciliation" mentioned by Bacon has taken place with the various books which have been presented on the Battle of Wilson's Creek. All the modern accounts credit the Third Louisiana Infantry with the capture

Gen. Rains credits the exploit to the Louisiana regiment and other infantry, among whom was Maj. Thomas Murray's Battalion.[182] He also says that Bledsoe's Artillery under Lieut.-Col. [Thomas H.] Rosser[183] about 11 a.m. silenced Sigel's Battery.[184]

Col. [John R.] Graves[185] says Bledsoe disabled Sigel's guns, also at the same time Col. Rosser, with a part of his (Gen. Rains's) infantry with the Louisiana

---

of Sigel's Battery, with supporting roles provided by McRae's Arkansas Infantry Battalion, Greer's Texas Cavalry, Reid's Artillery Battery and Bledsoe's Artillery. The only part that is not clearly defined is the role that Missouri troops played. As previously shown, William Piston provides some units, commanded by various Captains Johnson, but nothing is definitely known of the part the Missouri troops played. Rains's report on the battle actually throws another wrinkle into the picture—Rains has Major Thomas Murray's Infantry Battalion, not cavalry, participating in the capture of Sigel's guns. A close review of Murray's command provides another Johnson—A. A. Johnson of Company A, Murray's Infantry Battalion. Little is known of this Johnson, save that both his captain and the lieutenant of his company were disabled at the Battle of Carthage and not present at Wilson's Creek. Was A. A. Johnson in command of the company? And was he the Captain Johnson, that Lieutenant Colonel S. M. Hyams mentioned in his report? *O.R.*, 3:115, 127; Peterson, 232–233.

182. Thomas H. Murray's unit was known as both the Fourth Infantry Battalion and the Fourth Infantry Regiment, First Brigade, Rains's Division. The battalion was organized on July 4, 1861, and contained men from St. Clair, Henry and Benton Counties, Missouri; the regiment was subsequently organized in October. Murray was born in Kentucky about 1833, and lived in Warsaw, Missouri, where he was editor of *The Southwest Democrat* and the Chief Clerk for the Missouri House of Representatives. On May 6, 1861, he enlisted in Company E (Warsaw Grays), Fourth Infantry Battalion, Rains's Division and was at the engagement at Cole Camp on June 18, 1861. Murray was elected major and commander of the battalion on July 4, 1861, which he led at Wilson's Creek. Murray resigned from the Guard on August 13, 1861, following the Battle of Wilson's Creek. In 1862, he entered Confederate service and was elected major of the Eleventh Missouri Infantry on September 15, 1862, promoted to lieutenant colonel on March 24, 1863. Murray was wounded at Helena, Arkansas (July 4, 1863) and at Pleasant Hill, Louisiana (April 9, 1864). He died in McKinney, Texas, in 1884. *O.R.S.*, pt. 2, vol. 38:686; Bartels, *Forgotten Men*, 266; Bartels, *Trans-Mississippi Men*, 250; Peterson, 232–235; Hale, 230; Miles, 34, 40–42, 53, 385; Wayne H. Schnetzer, *Men of the Eleventh: A Roster of the Eleventh Missouri Infantry Confederate States of America* (Independence, MO, 1999), 6.

183. Thomas H. Rosser was born in Virginia in about 1818, and lived in Westport, Missouri, at the beginning of the Civil War. While in Virginia, Rosser had served in the Virginia Militia. On June 11, 1861, he was elected lieutenant colonel of the First Infantry Regiment, Eighth Division, MSG. He fought at Wilson's Creek and Pea Ridge before being transferred to the east side of the Mississippi River. In June 1862, he was the commandant of the Port of Memphis and in 1863, he was transferred to Selma, Alabama, where he completed his military service. After the war, Rosser remained in Selma, where he died in the 1870's. Bartels, *Forgotten Men*, 315; Peterson, 214; *Branded as Rebels*, 376.

184. When Sigel's guns began firing into the rear of Price's command on Oak Hill, Colonel Richard Weightman directed Rosser to move his command to support the cavalry in Sharp's fields. With his own command, Bledsoe's Artillery and Murray's Infantry Battalion, Rosser faced Sigel's guns overlooking Skegg's Branch. *O.R.*, 3:127; Piston, 252; Bearss, *Wilson's Creek*, 66; Brooksher, 199.

185. John (or Jonathan) R. Graves was born in Kentucky about 1831, and lived near Lexington, Lafayette County, Missouri, at the beginning of the Civil War. He was elected captain of Company A, Second Infantry Regiment, Eighth Division, MSG and on June 19, 1861, was elected colonel of his regiment. Following the death of Colonel Weightman, Graves was made brigade commander of Rains's First Brigade. His name was stricken from the rolls, date unknown, per General Order No. 8, dated October 8, 1861, which stated that any officer who absented themselves, without permission, for ten or more days, shall be dropped from the rolls. Peterson, 213, 221–222; Bartels, *Forgotten Men*, 133; McGhee, *Letter and Order Book MSG*, unnumbered pages 30–31 (entry page 59).

regiment captured five pieces, etc. [*O.R.*, 3:128].

Gen. Pearce says that Reid's Battery opened on Sigel and that he himself gave information that enabled Herbert's [Hébert's] Louisiana Regiment to take the battery. Gen. Pearce had a field glass and as soon as Sigel went into position, Gen. Pearce saw the immortal barber-pole unwind itself to the breeze and at once directed Capt. Reid to open. This explains at once the promptness of Capt. Reid's response [*O.R.*, 3:121].

Gen. McCulloch says that Reid's Battery opened on Sigel's Battery and disabled it; also, that he himself took two companies of the Third Louisiana and ordered Col. McIntosh to bring the rest. Also, that Greer's Texans and Lieut.-Col. Major's Missourians, joined in the pursuit of Sigel [*O.R.*, 3:105].

Col. Herbert [Hébert] says that Col. McIntosh and Gen. McCulloch with his right wing moved on Sigel's Battery, Lieut.-Col. Hyams leading [*O.R.*, 3:113-115].

Lieut.-Col. Hyams says that seventy Missourians, under Capt. Johnson, and seven companies of the Third Louisiana and a detached company of Monticello Rifles[186] took the battery [*O.R.*, 3:115-116].

Capt. [John P.] Vigilini[187] of the Third Louisiana says that Reid's Battery was firing on Sigel's Battery. He shows that Sigel's guns were too close to the bluff [*O.R.*, 3:117-118].

Col. Greer shows that he pursued Sigel with his Texas Cavalry [*O.R.*, 3:119].

Capt. Reid says

He Disabled Sigel's Battery

in three minutes, and the Third Louisiana then carried it [*O.R.*, 3:120].

Lieut.-Col. Hyams says that his men rolled the captured guns down the hill and took one with the horses to their artillery. After the battle was over I saw some iron guns being idly hauled northward on the main road.

Col. Graves says that three of the captured guns were attached to Capt. Bledsoe's Battery.

Gen. Price says that the forces under his command had possession of three twelve-pound howitzers and two brass sixes; This was true, but no doubt Gen. Price, having only the exuberant reports of Gen. Rains and Col. Graves, was misled as to the means by which the guns were acquired. Because Gen. Price did not give the Third Louisiana proper credit Gen. McCulloch subsequently asked for

---

186. The Monticello Rifles was Company H, which was commanded by Captain John S. Richards. The detachment was commanded by First Sergeant T. G. Walcott not Wolcott. *O.R.*, 3:115; Tunnard, 28, 551, 561.

187. John P. Viglini commanded Company K, Third Louisiana Infantry, being mustered into the Confederate Service on May 17, 1861. At the Battle of Pea Ridge, Viglini was captured and exchanged on March 24, 1862. Failing to be reelected as captain of his company in May 1862, Viglini resigned and returned to Louisiana. He never reentered the military. Tunnard, 147, 561; *O.R.*, 8:231.

the captured cannons, and they were accordingly surrendered.[188]

The Third Louisiana actually only captured four pieces. The other two pieces were not in battery, and when they got away, closely pursued by Col. [William] Brown[189] and Lieut.-Col. [James P.] Majors,[190] Missouri mounted men and by the Texans, one of Sigel's cannons, in going through a farm gate, shaved off a wheel, and thus fell into Missouri hands (See Mr. Holcombe [page 44]). This was according to the camp talk of the day. Capt. [Eugene A.] Carr[191] says the piece was lost by the killing of a wheel-horse [*O.R.,* 3:90]. Col. Sigel began two miles below at Tyrel's [Terrell] Creek and worked his way up, but I saw no one who had any idea of his presence, and I heard nothing from his quarter until his bombardment opened overhead. Gen. Price says that Col. Sigel's attack was almost simultaneous with Gen. Lyon's opening. Gen. Sigel says that having [hearing] the main engagement he moved northward to take us in the rear. He soon struck the Fayetteville road and worked his way

---

188. Initially Price's Missourians claimed the guns for themselves, but upon closer review of events they returned them over to the Third Louisiana, though without horses and harness. A disgusted General Mc-Culloch wrote: "I would not have demanded these guns had General Price done the Louisiana regiment justice in his official report. The language used by him was calculated to make the impression that the battery was captured by his men instead of that regiment." For his part, Price wrote of the captured battery: "The forces under my command have possession of three 12-pounder howitzers, two brass 6-pounders and a great quantity of small arms and ammunition taken from the enemy; also the standard of Sigel's regiment, captured by Captain Staples." *O.R.,* 3:100, 128, 746.

189. Colonel William B. Brown was a resident of Saline County, Missouri, and a Kentuckian by birth. In May 1861, he organized the "Saline Cavalry Company," and was elected the unit's captain. On June 28, 1861, Brown was appointed the colonel of the First Cavalry Regiment, Sixth Division, MSG. When leading his troops into battle, Brown used an old hunting horn that he blew when his command was charging the enemy. He died at the Second Battle of Boonville (September 13, 1861) while leading his command. *Branded As Rebels,* 50; Musser, 4:750–752; Peterson, 30, 174, 176.

190. James Patrick Majors was born on May 14, 1836, in Fayette, Missouri. He attended West Point, class of 1852, where he graduated number 23 of 49, in 1856. After serving on the Texas frontier, fighting Kiowa and Comanche Indians, Majors resigned from the army on March 21, 1861, and joined Earl Van Dorn's staff. At Wilson's Creek, Majors commanded the First Cavalry Battalion, Third Division, MSG. Majors later transferred to the east side of the Mississippi River, where he served for a time as Van Dorn's Chief of Artillery. On July 21, 1863, he was promoted to brigadier general. Returning to the Trans-Mississippi Department, Majors commanded a Texas cavalry brigade and a division during the Red River Campaign, where he received high praise for his actions at Pleasant Hill and Mansfield, Louisiana. After the war, Majors, lived for a time in France, but returned to Louisiana and Texas where he became a planter. He died in Austin, Texas on May 7, 1877 (Heitman and Roberts say May 8). Warner, *Generals in Gray,* 209–210; Boatner, 503; Heitman, 1:685; Roberts, *Texas, Confederate Military History,* 245–246.

191. Eugene A. Carr was born on March 20, 1830, in New York state, attended West Point, where he graduated in 1850 (number 19 of 44). Assigned to Texas, Carr fought Indians, was wounded, and in 1858 was promoted to captain. He commanded Company I, First U.S. Cavalry at Wilson's Creek and was recognized for his gallantry. On August 16, 1861, Carr was commissioned the colonel of the Third Illinois Cavalry. At the Battle of Pea Ridge, he was wounded three times and received the Congressional Medal of Honor for his service. On March 7, 1862, Carr became a general officer, fought for a time on the east side of the Mississippi River, but returned to Arkansas for Steele's Camden Expedition. On March 11, 1865, Carr was breveted a major general. Carr remained in the army following the war, rose to the rank of brigadier general (1892) in the Regular Army, and retired in 1893. He died on December 2, 1910, and was buried at West Point. Boatner, 127–128; Warner, *Generals in Blue,* 70–71; *O.R.,* 3:56, 89.

Through Throngs Of Cattle

and horses and until he reached the slaughtering place, to-wit, Sharp's farm. Then he posted his pieces on the plateau near Sharp's barn. His infantry he disposed across the Fayetteville road and the bag was ready. At 8:30 a.m. the assault on Sigel's guns took place. Maj. Schofield heard the cannonading about 8:30 a.m.; also Maj. Sturgis. The reports of these two officers might as well been consolidated. They bear even date, August 20, near Rolla, Mo., and are full of coincident passages. Language must have been scarce when these two reports duplicate so many expressions.[192] Capt. Carr says his order to retreat came about 10 o'clock a.m. After the capture of the battery the Louisianans appear to have turned the right flank of Col. Sigel's two regiments,[193] causing them to break.[194] There was another cause. Col. Snead says that Lieut.-Col. Rosser with his own men and O'Kane's Battalion[195] had taken position west of the main road and north of Skegg's Branch, where also was posted Capt. Bledsoe's Battery. Also that this infantry followed

---

192. Indeed, there are large amounts of similar passages in the two officers' reports. Schofield, for his part, does provide a great deal of information on the events preceding the battle, while Sturgis writes strictly on the battle, which mirrors Schofield's writings. *O.R.*, 3:57–71.

193. Sigel's final line was organized in a haphazard manner, meant to catch the fleeing rebels or block their retreat. Cavalry covered the two flanks, but Company I, First U.S. Cavalry was deployed so far from Sigel's main line, on the left flank, to be essentially useless. Company C, Second U.S. Cavalry covered the command's right frank, but its position, according to William Piston, placed these horsemen in a poor position to support Sigel's main line. Sigel's six guns were placed up the bluff overlooking Skegg's Branch but they were fifty yards from the military crest of the bluff, which would allow any enemy to advance on the battery without being fired upon by either the battery or its supporting infantry. For infantry support, Sigel placed a scant five companies of the Third Missouri Infantry (Three Months) in the immediate support of the guns—about 250 men. Sigel's remaining infantry, including the remainder of the Third Missouri and the entire Fifth Missouri Infantry (Three Months), were placed in reserve to the rear of the main line. Piston, 246–247.

194. When the Louisiana regiment charged Sigel's guns, they hit the center of the Union line, not the right flank, as McCulloch led them to believe. However, it mattered little, as Sigel's poor positioning of his guns, limited the artillery to maybe one round, that went high, before the Louisianans crested the bluff occupied by Sigel's guns. The Third Louisiana then delivered a crushing volley into Sigel's guns and the supporting infantry sending them into a headlong flight. This in turn caused a general panic throughout the Federal line as even the reserve broke with every man for himself. Piston, 253–255; Brooksher, 203.

195. O'Kane's Battalion was the Fourth Battalion or Regiment, Eighth Division, MSG, commanded by Thomas H. Murray. Walter S. O'Kane was born in Virginia about 1835, and lived in Independence, Missouri. He was sent to Warsaw, by Governor Jackson, to organize the local militia and on May 6, 1861, was elected captain of the Warsaw Grays. On July 4, O'Kane was elected lieutenant colonel of the Fourth Battalion, which he commanded until December 31, 1861. O'Kane became an aid-de-camp for General Rains on January 1, 1862, was captured in June 1862, while recruiting in northern Arkansas and was exchanged in September 1862. O'Kane completed his military service on General John S. Marmaduke's staff, having been passed over for regimental command of the Eighth Missouri Infantry by General M. M. Parsons. While in the Guard, O'Kane fought at Cole Camp, Wilson's Creek, and Pea Ridge. He later participated in the Battle of Prairie Grove, Arkansas, and assorted cavalry raids under General Marmaduke. *O.R.*, 8:328; *O.R.*, 13:45; *O.R.*, vol. 22, pt. 1:77, 736; Peterson, 211, 232, 234; Bartels, *Forgotten Men*, 278; Miles, 34, 40, 214; Bartels, *Trans-Mississippi Men*, 237; Letter (December 26, 1862), Hindman to Anderson, Copy Letter Book, Hindman's Command (June 11–December 30, 1862), 187–188 (hereafter cited as Copy Letter Book No. 2).

the Third Louisiana and went through the brush. Following must imply order of time—not of travel. There was no brush on the eastern side of the road at that point—that was Sharp's farm. But there was brush on the western side of the main road, and it must have been through it that the detachment of Gen. Rains' men charged on Col. Sigel's two regiments.[196] I did not hear Capt. Bledsoe's guns and did not see any other attacking party except the Missourians who went down the creek. The Sigel episode was over in a few moments after he posted his forces at Sharp's farm. From Col. Snead's description it is inferred that Capt. Bledsoe's station was on the spur where, when wounded, I had consulted a tree and that Col. Rosser's and O'Kane's men swarmed over the ground on which I had travelled down the dry branch in fancied safe retirement, and thence they had scrambled up the bluff on the left flank of Col. Sigel's infantry and emerged from the brush

Charging And Firing,

about the same time that the Third Louisiana worked in. This was enough to curl up any two regiments. Of course our men would not walk in the road like the cattle and horses. The road was in the center of Sigel's line of battle. This position was not selected for fighting purposes. It was merely to stop the supposed fugitives. Col. Sigel thought the battle was over. The position he occupied was precisely the place which Gen. Lyon had previously designated for the obvious purpose of capturing our whole command. So when our forces perversely refused to keep [to] the main road and rebelliously crept up and took the battery and charged his flanks the surprise affected him and his men with profound vertigo. Col. Sigel held letters patent of flanking maneuvers. After working all night to circumvent the enemy his trip merely invited the enemy to outflank him.

This was not the first time that the quasi spherical proportions of Maj. Thos. Murray, or the sandy-bearded and ferocious visage of Col. O'Kane, had come through the brush on exposed and innocent Teutons. The tactics of Cole Camp[197] were repeated, though with less slaughter. It was a coincidence that these two leaders should so soon again assist in repeating the same office. Col. Sigel should either have occupied some enfilading position on the extreme edge of the plateau, or else he should have kept entirely away from it. Wherever he was he should have thrown out skirmishers on each flank and in front to find out what he was

---

196. By the time the rebel support troops hit Sigel's line it was already in a state of chaos. The arrival of Rosser's and McRae's men, put an end to any possible resistance of Sigel's command. The Louisiana regiment captured Sigel's guns at the point of the bayonet, while all the supporting troops, with the Louisianans, mopped up the fleeing Federals. Piston, 254–255; Brooksher, 202–203.

197. The engagement at Cole Camp, Missouri, occurred on June 18, 1861 (various accounts have the date between June 17 and 20, 1861). Cole Camp was located in northern Benton County, about fifty miles southwest of Boonville. A Confederate band under Colonel Walter S. O'Kane attacked a Federal Home Guard force under Colonel A. H. W. Cook while they were sleeping. In the ensuing rout, the Unionists lost in addition to about 400 weapons, 15 killed, 52 wounded, and 100 prisoners. The rebels lost about 30 killed and wounded. Dyer, 797; Moore, *Missouri, Confederate Military History,* 46–47; Webb, 68–69; McElroy, 130–132; Miles, 32–63.

brewing. Instead of that his attendants peeped up the same road. His skirmishers were as scared as our pickets. Under such circumstances the excuse that the enemy was mistaken for friends is unworthy or regard.[198] He took our dispersion for granted and tolerated no other theory. Hence any body of well ordered troops was bound to be Gen. Lyon's men. Col. Sigel's views were quite unreasonable. If he expected our men to keep the road why did he

Himself Cut Through The Woods?

In Mr. Holcombe's monograph occurs the following sentence: "It is claimed by officers of both armies that had an avenue of retreat been open, it is highly probable that the result of the day's battle would have been different."

I have shown that Sigel's attempted blockade had no influence on our embattled men, because they could not have known it, and because they did not know it. Even those of us who were under the muzzles of Sigel's guns did not know whether they were hostile of friendly until they opened fire.

So that when the same author says that "It became apparent that some of the Southerners desired to retreat, but they soon learned that they were practically surrounded," I cannot assent. Gen. Lyon was on the crest of the hill. He could see when we could not, and yet Sigel's Battery came up within pistol shot of both lines, and was lost without arousing the suspicions of Gen. Lyon or of any of his officers. The Federals did not give Sigel up until they received the news at the close of the battle. The troops who were fighting Gen. Lyon knew nothing of Col Sigel's diversion until long after the latter had started for Rolla.[199]

When Col. Sigel was temporarily at Carthage, Mo.,[200] a hostile shell burst near him; thereupon a citizen prisoner remarked to him: "Colonel, it's pretty hot!" "Yeah," he replied, "mosht too tamped hot." Of his opinion of the temperature at Sharp's farm no record has been preserved.

* * * * * * *

---

198. As the Third Louisiana moved toward Sigel's position they were spotted, but not fired upon. Sigel believed them to be men from Lyon's column, namely the First Iowa Infantry. As the column drew closer, Sigel sent one man to investigate, and upon challenge he was shot dead. By then it was too late as the rebels were under the brow of the military crest and could not be engaged until the Third Louisiana was only paces away from Sigel's Battery. Sigel's hesitation and his poor position doomed his command to defeat. Sigel, 305.

199. The Federals abandoned Springfield between midnight and 2:00 a.m. on August 11, and by sunrise they had exited Greene County. The Confederates entered the city shortly thereafter, but made no pursuit of the retreating Unionists. Holcombe, 69–70.

200. The Battle of Carthage took place on July 5, 1861. It was actually a running fight of about ten miles that began at the Spring River and proceeded southward into and through the town of Carthage. Nightfall terminated the action. The rebel force, under Sterling Price, numbered about 4,000 effectives while the Federals, under Sigel, fielded about 1,100 men. The Unionists lost 18 killed, 53 wounded, and 5 missing; Confederates lost 12 killed, 64 wounded and 1 missing. David C. Hinze and Karen Farnham, *The Battle of Carthage: Border War in Southwest Missouri, July 5, 1861* (Campbell, CA, 1997), 202, 205, 278; Schrantz, 23, 31–33.

Item: Incidents surrounding the Battle of Oak Hill or Wilson's Creek, August 10, 1861, by Dr. E. McD. Coffey, Surgeon, First Cavalry Regiment, Fifth Division, Missouri State Guard and Surgeon, First Missouri Cavalry Regiment (Confederate).[201]
Published: September 19, 1885.

Two Stories About Gen. Price

Having recently noticed several accounts of the disposition of the body of Gen. Lyon after he fell at Wilson's Creek, I thought it likely that the following incidents, one of which may throw some additional light upon the above mentioned transaction and both of which illustrates in some degree the admirable character of Gen. Price, might be of some interest.

On the 12th of August, 1861, I was, with several other soldiers and citizens, sitting on the long porch or veranda that runs along the front of the hotel situated on the north side of the public square in Springfield, listening (as his soldiers liked to do) to the conversation of Gen. Price when an ambulance containing two or three men wearing the Federal uniform drove up and, one of them, a lieutenant, I think, approached Gen. Price and handed him a letter addressed "To whom it may concern." Gen. Price read the subscription and, without opening the envelope, motioned to the officer, remarking, "I do not receive communication addressed to whom it may concern."[202] The momentary silence that followed was terribly embarrassing to the lieutenant, but Gen. Price, with the magnanimity so characteristic of him, said, "I suppose you have come for the body of Gen. Lyon?" and being answered in the affirmative, continued." Certainly you may have it, and I will see that you have with it a safe escort to your own lines."[203]

---

201. Ephraim McDowell Coffey was a resident of Camden Point, Platte County, Missouri, and a member of the Camden Guards, Missouri State Militia prior to the Civil War. On June 21, 1861, Coffey was appointed surgeon of the First Cavalry Regiment, Fifth Division, MSG and served in the Guard until January 12, 1862. He later enlisted in the First Missouri Cavalry (Confederate) as a surgeon. During his military service, Coffey was in the Battles of Carthage, Wilson's Creek, Dry Wood Creek and Lexington in Missouri and Pea Ridge in Arkansas, before being moved to the east side of the Mississippi River. At Pea Ridge, Coffey was captured, and paroled to tend to the wounded. *O.R.*, Series 2, 3:820; *O.R.S.*, pt. 2, vol. 38:111; Peterson, 156; Schnetzer, *More Forgotten Men,* 50.

202. A Mr. Quilian, a reporter of the *Cincinnati Gazette*, accompanied the retrieval party to Springfield and recorded that General Price "received us haughtily, and as I had anticipated, declined to open our documents." The reporter failed to provide any other details of the encounter, save that they were given a pass to collect Lyon's body at Mrs. Phelps's farm. "Interesting From Springfield," *Rock Island Register* (Rock Island, Illinois), September 11, 1861,

203. Doctor Coffey has this part of the story wrong. On August 22, 1861, not August 12, an ambulance, dispatched by order of General Frémont, arrived at General Price's Headquarters, bearing a metallic coffin for Lyon's body. The party consisted of a driver in uniform, two relatives of General Lyon—Danford Knowlton, a cousin from New York City and John B. Hasler, a brother-in-law from Webster, Massachusetts—and George N. Lynch, a well-known undertaker from St. Louis. Two officers accompanied the party, Captain George P. Edgar of Frémont's staff and Captain Emmett MacDonald, of the MSG, who had escorted the party from Rolla. The note that was delivered to General Price was signed by General Frémont. The party retrieved the body the same day and arrived back in St. Louis on August 26. With a military escort, the

The other incident occurred on the day after the Battle of Wilson's Creek. On that morning, the 11th of August, I had gone into Springfield quite early for the purpose of assisting in preparing hospital accommodations for such of our wounded as could be removed from the field. The first thing I did after getting there was to visit the Federal hospital (in the courthouse), where I found a large number of wounded in the care of Surgeons [E. C.] Franklin[204] and [Samuel H.] Melcher,[205] both of whom I found to be pleasant gentlemen, and very efficient medical officers. Very soon one of the above named gentlemen, I do not remember which, came to me in great distress and said, "Doctor, all our medical stores are being carried away by your men," and asked me to interfere. I promptly complied with the request, and was remonstrating with the captain [end of column missing in original] manner ordered his teamsters to load up the Yankee goods and take them to camp, also saying "I am commanding here." at the same time ordering us away. I saw it was useless to say anything further, and quietly told the surgeon that Gen. Price would soon be there and would have the supplies returned.

Sure enough, it was not long until "Old Pap" came riding in, accompanied by his staff, and I immediately informed him of the acts of Gen. R. [Rains], and to say that he was indignant would convey but a faint idea of his feelings. He was

---

burial party then journeyed to General Lyon's birthplace at Eastford, Connecticut, where Lyon was buried on September 5. Holcombe, 103–104; Phillips, 259–260; Ashbel Woodward, *Life of General Nathaniel Lyon* (Hartford, CT, 1862), 332–334; G. C. C., "Gen. Sigel's Army," *Chicago Daily Tribune*, August 18, 1861; G. C. C., "From Rolla," *Chicago Daily Tribune*, August 23, 1861; Britton, 112–115

204. Doctor Edward C. Franklin was born in New York and was the regimental surgeon of the Fifth Missouri Infantry (Three Months), being mustered into the service on May 18, 1861. After his command arrived in Springfield, in June 1861, Franklin was placed in charge of the General Hospital and remained in the city after its capture, tending the wounded from Wilson's Creek. Franklin left Springfield on September 7, 1861, and returned to St. Louis. On September 30, 1861, he became a surgeon of volunteers, later brigade surgeon in General Grant's army, and Medical Director of the Mound City General Hospital. Franklin resigned from the army on August 5, 1862, and returned to St. Louis, where he died on December 10, 1885. *O.R.*, Series 2, 3:451; *O.R.S.*, pt. 1, vol. 1:236, 268; *O.R.S.*, pt. 2, vol. 9:387; Peckham, 118, 123; Heitman, 1:434.

205. Samuel H. Melcher was born on October 30, 1828, in Gilmanton, New Hampshire, received his primary education in New Hampshire and "graduated from the medical department of Dartmouth College, in 1851." At the beginning of the Civil War he resided in St. Louis and on May 7, 1861, was appointed the Assistant Surgeon of the Fifth Missouri Infantry (Three Months), being mustered into the service on May 11, 1861. Following the rout of Sigel's command, Melcher stayed behind on the battlefield to tend the wounded and later accompanied General Lyon's body to Springfield. Melcher remained in Springfield following Wilson's Creek tending wounded and departed the city on November 11, 1861, with the remaining casualties. After returning to St. Louis, Melcher was appointed a brigade surgeon on December 4, 1861, but shortly thereafter organized the Thirty-second Regiment of Enrolled Missouri Militia for which he was appointed colonel. Melcher left his regiment in the fall of 1862, being appointed the Medical Director of the District of South Western Missouri and the Army of the Frontier on October 26, 1862. In 1864, Melcher served as an aid-de-camp for General Pleasanton, during Price's 1864 Missouri Raid. After the war Melcher moved to Chicago in 1897, where he spent his remaining years. He died on August 1, 1915. *O.R.S.*, pt. 1, vol. 1:236; Peckham, 118, 123; National Archives, Record Group No. 393, General Order Book (October 14, 1862–April 10, 1863), Army of the Frontier, General Orders No. 8 (October 26, 1862), 4; Charles S. Bently, Edward D. Redington, and Jared W. Young, "Samuel Henry Melcher," *Memorial of Deceased Companions of the Commandery of the State of Illinois, MOLLUS*, 13D:255–257.

furious, and turning to one of his aids, he said, "Go to Gen. R.'s camp and tell [him] if he does not return the medical supplies taken from the Federal hospital immediately, I will arrest him for this act of vandalism." Then turning to the surgeon said, "We propose to carry on this war as civilized persons should. I will see that your sick and wounded are treated accordingly." It is useless, perhaps, to say that it was but a very short time until all the medical stores were hauled back and carefully returned to the Federal surgeon.

I learn that both Dr. Franklin and Dr. Melcher reside in St. Louis, and, doubtless one or both of them will recall the incident herein narrated, as it was well calculated to forcibly impress the minds of any one surrounded by similar circumstances. More than twenty-four years have elapsed since then, but the stirring events of four years' service as surgeon during the Civil War and a busy professional life of twenty years since, have not lessened in the smallest degree our admiration for the character of the great statesman and soldier whose memory we love so well to cherish; whose great, warm heart was moved by the appeal made by the Federal surgeons on behalf of their sick and wounded soldiers, and who, on the day afterward, so readily complied with the request made for the body of the brave Gen. Lyon.

E. McD. Coffey,
Late Surgeon First Cavalry, Missouri Volunteers, C.S.A.
Platte City, Mo. August 30, 1885.

* * * * * *

Chapter 3

Fall Campaign of 1861 in Missouri

Item: Engagement against Frémont's Body Guard, near Springfield, Missouri (October 25, 1861), by "One of Them," a late member Lebanon County Company, Third Infantry Regiment, Seventh Division, Missouri State Guard.
Published: December 18, 1886.

Capt. Johnnie Wickersham

Clinton, Mo. Dec. 12.

Editor *Republican*

By request of several comrades I will relate from memory, for the benefit of your many readers, the daring of a boy of 15 in the fight with Frémont's Body-Guard[1] twenty-four years ago at Springfield, Mo.[2] The boy was afterwards known to almost the entire army as Capt. Johnnie Wickersham, and many ladies now living remember kissing the little captain while driving or calling with Gen. Price. They will also remember the company of boys he commanded that were quartered the following winter in Springfield.

In October, 1862 [1861], after the death of Lyon and the retreat of the Federal Army from Wilson's Creek to Rolla, Mo.,[3] leaving all the southwest portion of the

---

1. Major Charles Zagonyi raised a cavalry command in early August 1861, at the request of General Frémont, that became known as "The Guard" or "Frémont's Body Guard." Composed of four companies, the Guard remained in the service as long as General Frémont served in the West. When Frémont headed toward Springfield, he was accompanied by three companies of his Body Guard, while the fourth remained behind in St. Louis. Jessie Benton Frémont, *The Story of the Guard: A Chronicle of the War* (Boston, 1863), 29, 213–214, hereafter cited as *The Story of the Guard*; *O.R.*, vol. 12, pt. 1:35; McElroy, 227–228; U.S. Congress, *Report of the Joint Committee, on the Conduct of the War: Part III—Department of the West* (Washington, DC, 1863), 186–187, hereafter cited as *Report of the Joint Committee*.
2. On October 25, 1861, Major Zagonyi led a scouting expedition to Springfield, during which he charged a superior force of Confederates. Zagonyi was hoping to scatter the rebel command, for whom he had little respect, and take Springfield in the process. The Confederates, estimated at between 1,500–2,200 men, had little difficulty in repulsing "Zagonyi's Charge." Zagonyi claimed a great victory because he had left stragglers behind in Springfield to take possession of the city, which the rebels had already abandoned. On October 27, the Union army occupied Springfield. General Frémont declared that Zagonyi did "handsome and bold service," and that his charge was "too brilliant to be passed over cursorily." Frémont ordered that the War Department and his entire army be informed of what could "be accomplished by discipline and good conduct." Following the engagement, the rebels continued their movement, unmolested, southward, to join the main body of Price's army, which they reached at Jollification, Missouri, on October 25. *O.R.*, 3:250–251; Eakin, *Diary*, 35; *Report of the Joint Committee*, 188.
3. The Federal command abandoned Springfield between midnight and 2:00 a.m. on August 11, and reached Rolla, on August 17, 1861. *O.R.*, 3:63; Ware, 344; Britton, 108–109; Holcombe, 69–70.

Zagonyi's Charge
(October 25, 1861)

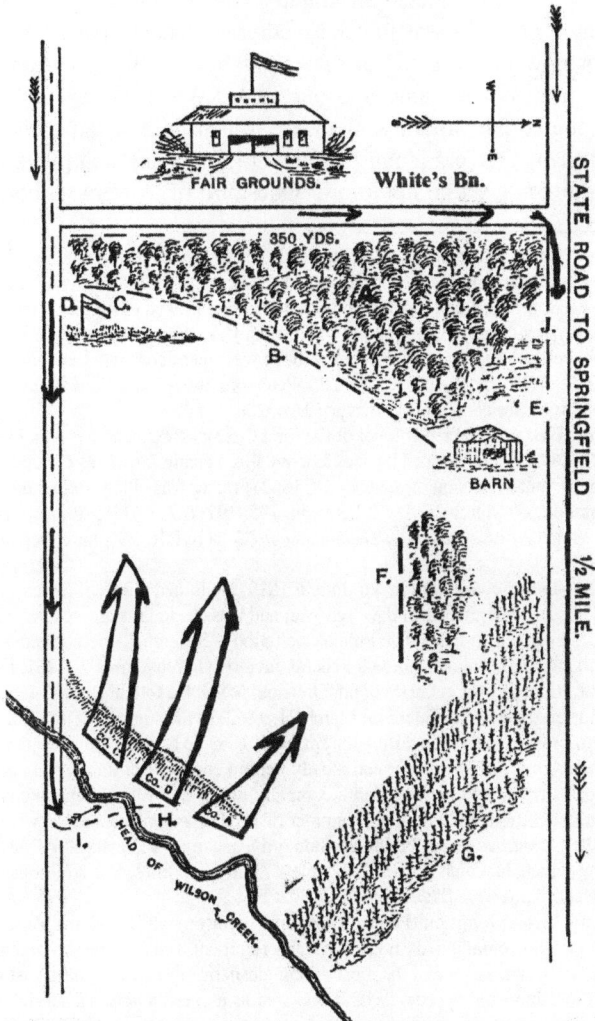

A. Dense woods
B. Rebel infantry
C. Rebel flag
D. Repulse of White's Bn.
E. Wickersham kills Lt. Connelly

F. Rebel cavalry
G. Corn field
H. Charge of Bodyguard
I. Bodyguard reorganizes
J. White's second assault

state free from Federal garrisons, in almost every hamlet and town thus freed, men volunteered for the "Lost Cause" and were organized into companies and started South to join Price's army, which was then at Springfield.

R. J. Wickersham[4] organized an infantry company in Lebanon. The second day on the march South he was joined by other companies, but who commanded them I cannot now remember. But that night little Johnnie Wickersham, having run away from home, came into our camp. When we reached Springfield our force numbered 280 infantry. We were joined by a squad of cavalry commanded by [Julian] Frazier,[5] [John A.] Shavel [Schnable][6] and [Miscal] Johnson [Johnston][7]—how many I do not know.[8] One-third of us were without arms and

4. Captain Richard James Wickersham, also known as James Wickersham, was born in about 1838, lived in St. Louis at the beginning of the war, and in the summer of 1861 enlisted a company from Laclede County, Missouri. The unit assembled at Lebanon and moved south and joined Price's command. Later, Wickersham became the captain of Company A, Wood's Missouri Cavalry Battalion, rising to lieutenant colonel by war's end. He survived the war and relocated to Lebanon, where he died on August 12, 1917. *O.R.S.*, pt. 2, vol. 50:285–286; Peterson, 205; Eakin, *Confederate Records*, 8:57; *Branded As Rebels*, 466; Bartels, *Trans-Mississippi Men*, 226.

5. Colonel Julian Frazier was elected colonel of the First Cavalry Regiment, Seventh Division, MSG, on September 16, 1861. He commanded the Confederate force facing Zagonyi's Charge and was made commander of the Seventh Division on January 18, 1862. Frazier was killed while leading a charge at Humansville, Missouri, on March 26, 1862. Peterson, 195, 197; *O.R.*, 3:355; *Branded As Rebels*, 151; Frank J. White, "Major White's Report," *Rebellion Record,* 3:DOC 236–237, hereafter cited as "Major White's Report."

6. Colonel John A. Schnable was born in Virginia in 1819. He joined the Dent County Cavalry, Seventh Division, MSG, at the beginning of the Civil War, and was elected first lieutenant of his company. In October 1861, Schnable commanded an infantry battalion at Springfield, being second in command of the force which engaged Major Zagonyi's Federal cavalry. On November 2, 1861, he was elected colonel of the Third Infantry Regiment, Seventh Division, MSG. He fought at Pea Ridge (March 6–8, 1862) and was mustered out of the Guard on March 21, 1862. In the summer of 1862, Schnable organized a battalion of MSG cavalry, and during the spring of 1863 he began recruiting another command for the Confederate Army. Schnable operated mostly behind enemy lines until 1864, when he joined the Ninth Missouri Cavalry and commanded a company under Ben Elliot. Schnable participated in the 1864 Camden Expedition, and during the summer of 1864 he organized a cavalry battalion of raw recruits at Yellville, Arkansas. Later, he joined Sidney D. Jackman's Brigade for Price's 1864 Missouri Raid, during which Jackman praised Schnable's fighting abilities. For additional biographical information see Banasik, *Serving With Honor*, 392–393.

7. This was Colonel Miscal Johnston (Peterson calls him Johnson, while Richard Musser says it was a Michael Johnson), who commanded Frazier's cavalry regiment, since Frazier commanded the rebel force at Springfield. Known as "one of the most daring, desperate and troublesome customers in Missouri," in 1861–1862, Johnston appears to have operated as a guerilla after his service in the Guard. In 1864, he was in the process of organizing a cavalry regiment with Thomas R. Freeman, but circumstances changed dramatically. While escorting his family back to his home in the Rolla area in January 1864, Johnston's party was attacked and vigorously pursued by the Federals who captured his family. By the end of January, Johnston had surrendered to Federal authorities, was paroled, and ordered to reside in northern Illinois for the remainder of the war. *O.R.*, vol. 34, pt. 1:61; *O.R.*, vol. 34, pt. 2:176; Peterson, 197; Hale, 165; Ingenthron, 104; "Major White's Report," 236; Musser, 5:103.

8. At the time of the Springfield engagement, Federal authorities estimated Frazier's force at between 1,500–2,200 men. However, Major Frank White, who was captured by the rebels just prior to the battle, had access to their camp and placed their forces at 1,200 men. Richard Musser, a member of the MSG at the time, placed the rebel command at 800 "armed" men. Zagonyi's command consisted of

those who were the proud possessors of a squirrel rifle or shotgun were looked upon as heroes. We were much surprised to find Price had retreated south from Springfield.[9] We camped a mile out of town, up the main road leading west.[10] On either side of the road was a high "stake and rider" fence, forming a lane. Our camp-ground was an old field north of the lane. It was high and sloped to a ravine one-fourth mile towards town. On our west was a thick growth of young oak trees, so thick that a horseman could not ride through. Two hundred yards from the young timber, towards town, we had made a gap in the lane by letting the fence down to go through into the other field for water. Our officers, with few exceptions, were down in town loading wagons with salt to send South. To the south

Colonel John A. Schnable

of the lane, beyond the ravine, towards town, was camped the cavalry, who were performing picket duty for us.[11]

About 4 p.m. on October 25, 1861, the usual monotony of camp life was broken by the sound of many horses' feet running on the hard road. "There's a race," shouted the boys, and, with seemingly one accord, we were on our feet in a moment. Six horses came flying down the lane from the west. Bets were fairly offered. The riders had no guns or hats. There was no jockeying in that race, but every fellow doing his "level best" to come out ahead. Two hundred yards behind and urging their horses to their utmost speed came thirty of Frémont's Body-

172 men of the Frémont Body Guard (Company A—54 men; Company B—66 men; Company C—52 men) and Major White's Battalion, 154 men; total 326. *O.R.*, 3:249, 251; "Major White's Report," 236; Musser, 5:103; Banasik, *Serving with Honor*, 224; James L. Foley, "With Frémont In Missouri," *Sketches of War History 1861–1865. Papers Prepared for the Commandery of the State of Ohio, Military Order of the Loyal Legion of the United States, MOLLUS* 4:81–82, hereafter cited as Foley.

9. Price ordered Springfield abandoned just prior to the arrival of Zagonyi's advanced guard. According to Richard Musser, Price's rear guard, under a Colonel Campbell (probably Lieutenant Colonel L. A. Campbell, Seventh Division MSG—the only Colonel Campbell in the MSG at the time), departed the city on October 25, just prior to Zagonyi's arrival. When Zagonyi arrived he encountered elements of the Seventh Division, MSG, who were marching to Price's camp from Lebanon, Missouri. The Lebanon contingent, under Colonel Julian Frazier, reached Springfield on October 25, and camped a mile southwest of town, on the Mt. Vernon road—the same road that Zagonyi took into the city. Peterson, 196, 346–347; Musser, 5:103.

10. Frazier's command camped on what was known as "Foxbright's pasture." Musser, 5:103.

11. The cavalry command was Colonel Miscal Johnston's First Cavalry Regiment, Seventh Division, MSG. They numbered about five hundred men, according to one Federal account. "Major White's Report," 236; Peterson, 195.

Guard, with drawn sabers, six abreast; down the lane they fled.[12]

Since the late unpleasantness I have seen in our cities many gaudily-dressed military companies; but I think the body-guard could have outshone them all. They carried two of the Colt's dragoon revolvers in holsters attached to their saddles. The stocks to these revolvers contained secret canteens![13] after the fight there were a hundred of them in the lane. We thought them some new kind of firearms.

The Odor Of Peach Brandy

filled the air, but its whereabouts were not discovered until one of the boys accidentally found the secret canteen. We afterwards learned of their raiding a still five miles out. But I am transgressing. They carried these breeches suspended from a four inch fair leather strap worn over the shoulders. Every piece of metal was plated, either gold or silver, and gold braid and cord were used in profusion upon their uniforms. To our ignorant eyes they seemed more like gods than human beings.[14] Many of the boys shouted, "Lawd what pretty men." We had a regular stampede for the fence to get a better view of them. We never thought of war or battle, but gave them a hearty cheer. We all talked at once and wondered who they could be. Many of the boys climbed to the top of the fence and waved their hats in their wild excitement. Every man was at or on the fence when the main body of the body-guard and Maj. White's Battalion of Irish Dragoons[15] charged down the

12. According to Federal accounts the rebel command was well aware on the oncoming assault and were prepared to meet it, having been previously warned by their pickets. The rebel cavalry was formed in the field, while the infantry, under Colonel Schnable formed next to a "Virginia rail fence." The Confederate infantry and cavalry were in a "hollow square" according to the Union account, with skirmishers scattered throughout the woods on either side of the open field. "St. Louis 'Democrat' Narrative," *Rebellion Record*, 3:DOC 237–238, hereafter cited as "St. Louis 'Democrat' Narrative"; *O.R.*, 3:251; Britton, 154.

13. Frémont's Body Guard was armed, according to Zagonyi, with "sabres, Beale's revolvers, and Colt's carbines with stock attached;" only about two-thirds of his command had carbines. *The Story of the Guard*, 38; *Report of the Joint Committee*, 187.

14. Frémont's Body Guard "wore plumed hats and a distinctive blue uniform" and were mounted on matching horses. According to Zagonyi, their uniform was "simple" with "not a bit of cord" on it and was made by the Quartermaster, Justus McKinstry. The troopers were "men of education and means," of the same basic height and age and according to Zagonyi "each to be as [an] officer." The Guard was intended as a nucleus for training future cavalry officers, according to Jessie Frémont, a staunch supporter of Zagonyi and his command. However, the soldiers of the time saw the guard differently, ridiculing them with titles like "'Carpet Knights,' 'Kid-glove Dandies,' and 'Parlor Pets.'" Gerteis, 146; *The Story of the Guard*, 29, 34, 63; Charles Treichel, "Major Zagonyi's Horse-Guard," *Personal Recollection of the War of the Rebellion: Addresses Delivered Before the Commandery of the State of New York, MOLLUS*, 22:240, hereafter cited hereafter as Treichel; Foley, 5:519; *Report of the Joint Committee*, 186–187.

15. White's Battalion consisted of the "Prairie Scouts" and the "Irish Dragoons." The "Prairie Scouts" were a makeshift command consisting of Companies C and L, First Missouri Cavalry, commanded by Captains P. Kehoe and Charles Fairbanks, respectively; and the "Irish Dragoons" of the Twenty-third Illinois Infantry, which was commanded by Captain P. Naughton. The battalion was organized on October 4, 1861, and was commanded by Major Frank J. White, who was an Aid-de-Camp on Frémont's

lane, wheeled in line to the fence and emptied their revolvers into us. I cannot to this day help smiling when I remember the surprise and wonder expressed on the faces of many of our men, while they were fired on. Not one of us had ever been in a fight. We had no command given us. But every man grabbed his gun and poured shot and bullets into the lane. The yells and oaths could be heard above the rattle of firearms. Nothing between us but the rail fence. The Federals stayed until they had each emptied both revolvers; many drew their sabers and with oaths cut at us over the fence. Then they ran to the ravine and reloaded.[16] It seemed but a moment until they were again firing on us from the same position, many not over four feet from us. Each would raise his revolver to cock it and fire when bringing it down on us, which was the cause of their almost invariably firing over us.

Little Johnnie Wickersham,

had to this time never made use of a profane word. But, like all the rest of us, stood at the fence and swore like an old trooper.

Again they left us, this time running west.[17] Ten minutes passed, and we saw nothing of them. Lieut. Joe Craig[18] then ordered us to form line for the first time during the fight, parallel, but about fifty yards back from the fence, with positive orders for no one to fire until the command was given. Johnnie Wickersham was

---

staff. The unit had been on a scouting mission to Springfield when incorporated into Zagonyi's command for the attack on Springfield. Frank J. White, "Recapture of Lexington, Mo.," *Rebellion Record*, 3:DOC 202.

16. In the Federal description of the engagement, Zagonyi arrived at the battlefield on the west side of Springfield by first passing through a stand of timber. Emerging from the wood, at the top of a hill and on a country road, the Federal column was confined by fences on either side of the byway which constricted their movement. Almost immediately, according to some Federal accounts, they were met by fire from both sides of the fence lined lane. Zagonyi promptly ordered a charge down the lane to the bottom of the hill, where, being sheltered from the enemy's view, they broke down the fence to get at the rebel command. However, the commander of Company C, Frémont's Body Guard, recalled that over half the command had passed down the lane before the rebels opened fire, which seems to support what the writer of this article has presented—i.e., that the rebel command was not aligned to meet the charging Unionists. *O.R.*, 3:251; Treichel, 22:243; "St. Louis 'Democrat' Narrative," 238; Foley, 5:515.

17. After the initial engagement, Zagonyi's command became split; Frémont Body Guard moved down the lane to the east and the headwaters of Wilson's Creek, while White's men moved west where they circled around to take on the Confederate infantry (Schnabel's unit) from their left flank. Zagonyi would later imply in his report that White's command had left the battlefield, leaving Zagonyi to fend for himself. Captain Naughton, of White's command, would later ask for an inquiry on the matter, citing that a "gross injustice had been done to" his command by Zagonyi's report. A report was subsequently issued, though never released, and appears to have completely vindicated Naughton's position as to his command's participation in the engagement. Major White, for his part, reported the loss of 33 killed, wounded and missing, clearly indicating that his command was indeed seriously engaged in the battle. *O.R.*, 3:252–253; "St. Louis 'Democrat' Narrative," 238; "Major White's Report," 236–237.

18. Little is known of Craig save that he was a lieutenant in the MSG. Peterson has the name as James Craig, and Schnetzer has a Joel H. Craig as the second lieutenant of Company E, Third Infantry Regiment, Seventh Division, MSG. Joel Craig was also noted as having been at Zagonyi's Charge, which makes him the likely Craig in this case. Peterson, 205; Schnetzer, *More Forgotten Men*, 56.

on the extreme left of the line, where he could see down the lane toward the west. Immediately to his front was the gap in the lane before mentioned.[19]

Presently we heard him shout, "They are coming." An officer was in advance and we distinctively heard him give orders to charge the gap. He came with drawn saber at full gallop directly for it. Against our protests and commands, emphasized by many oaths, Johnnie Wickersham ran for the gap. Not being able to hold his gun "off hand," he knelt on one knee, placing elbow on the other, and awaited their coming. Every man cursed and yelled for him to come back; but he did not move. The officer came with sword up lifted to strike, when little Johnnie fired. The ball entered the officer's breast and he fell from his horse dead.[20] Ten feet behind him came the main body with drawn sabers.[21] They were crowded into the gap when their leader fell. They checked their horses, seemingly, for a moment, not knowing what to do. As soon as Johnnie had fired the fatal shot he threw down his gun, hat in the air and yelled and swore like a madman. Not hearing our command, couched in no bible language, to lie down. Craig finally ordered us to fire. Johnnie, although immediately between us, was unhurt, while five Federals fell dead in the gap and many wounded.[22] After our fire they again ran to the ravine, let down the fence, formed under the hill and came charging in solid line upon us. Johnnie had tied the officer's horse and secured the sword and two fine silver-plated pistols. In his excitement he did not notice that the charge had swept by him and driven us all back into the young oak timber. They tried to enter to enter after us, but brush and bullets were too thick. We gave a yell, and they scattered back over the field. Some sixteen or twenty started to escape through the gap. Johnnie Wickersham stood in it with saber almost as long as himself buckled around him

---

19. When the Confederates formed their line, the cavalry were on the left and perpendicular to the infantry on their right. The infantry in turn were perpendicular to both the advancing Federal column and their own cavalry. However, in the case of the Federal cavalry they had their backs to the Confederate Infantry, while they fronted the Confederate cavalry. This was hardly a formation to receive or surprise a cavalry column that was advancing on your position. After the first charge, Zagonyi's command reformed in the shelter of the creek bed (the headwaters of Wilson's Creek) and prepared to charge again—Company C, was on the left, B was in the center and Company A held the right. With this second charge, according to Federal accounts, the rebel cavalry "were scattered almost instantaneously; the infantry made a somewhat firmer stand, but it was for only a moment." In his testimony before Congress, Zagonyi stated that the rebels were broken and scattered in "less than five seconds." *Report of the Joint Committee*, 188; "St. Louis 'Democrat' Narrative," 238; Foley, 5:514, 516–517.

20. There was only one Federal officer killed or mortally wounded in Zagonyi's Charge—Patrick Connelly or Conolly of the Irish Dragoons. Additionally, there were three other Union officers wounded—Captain Patrick Naughton, Irish Dragoons, shot in arm near shoulder (slight); First Lieutenant N. Westerburg, Company B, Frémont Body Guard, shot in shoulder and lost one finger; Second Lieutenant J. W. Goff, Company C, Frémont Body Guard, shot in hip (slight). *O.R.*, 3:251–252; "St. Louis 'Democrat' Narrative," 238–239.

21. This was Major White's Battalion, which was led by the Irish Dragoons, which had circled around the rebel infantry line and came at them again in a fence gap that led to Springfield. "Major White's Report," 237; "St. Louis 'Democrat' Narrative," 238.

22. The Irish Dragoons lost 1 killed and 4 wounded by the time the engagement had ended—most would have been from this encounter described by Wickersham. "St. Louis 'Democrat' Narrative," 238–239.

with a revolver in each hand. When within twenty steps he opened fire on them, and for a moment they raised their horses to halt. We had then come from cover of the brush and were firing on them from the rear. They halted for only a moment and then charged the boy, one of them knocking him down with a revolver. This was the last act in the fight. After this we saw nothing more of them.[23] A detail was ordered to clear the lane of dead men and horses. Of the latter there were a great many. That night with our wagons and camp equipage we started north for Price's army.[24] On our arrival Gen. Price gave Johnnie Wickersham a commission as captain, and ordered all the boys of age of 15 in the army to report to him. On the return of the army to Springfield his eighty-odd boys were uniformed and armed, and afterwards did good service at Pea Ridge.

Almost every surviving soldier of Price's army of 1861 will remember the above incident.

One Of Them

* * * * * * *

---

23. The Federal forces made three charges during the engagement. The first was more of a running retreat as they sought to get out of the rebel "ambush" during the initial part of the engagement. The second occurred after Zagonyi had regrouped his command and charged the main rebel line sending them into the shelter of the woods. During this uncoordinated second charge White's Battalion struck the rebel left flank and rear, while Zagonyi engaged the Confederate front. The third charge occurred after the rebels fell back into the scrub oak forest, leaving Zagonyi's command to pursue the rebel cavalry into Springfield. After Zagonyi cleared Springfield, he reorganized what was left of his command of about 70 men, raised the Union flag in the courthouse square and quickly departed the city. According to Zagonyi, he left twenty horseless men to hold the city. However, a lieutenant in Zagonyi's command later recalled, that soon after Zagonyi's departure, "Corporal Sloan of the body-guard with sixteen men who had lost their horses in the attack, came into town, took possession of the courthouse, and held it" until the army arrived *O.R.*, 3:251–252; Treichel, 22:243–245; Foley, 5 515–518.

24. In the aftermath of the Springfield affair, Major White, who was a captive during the battle, escaped during the night and returned to Springfield. He later organized the dismounted men of Zagonyi's command to hold Springfield, and picket the roads into the city. The rebels, under Colonel Frazier, were not in Springfield to hold the city, but were on their way to join Price and so departed the area during the night. For his part Zagonyi reported the loss of 15 killed, 27 wounded, 10 missing, while White reported the loss 33 killed, wounded, and missing (extrapolating the figures in Dyer's *Compendium* would show 3 killed, 10 wounded and 20 missing in White's Battalion); total 85. Assorted Union accounts reported the Confederate loss as 23 to 107 killed, while the number of wounded were not known. Richard Musser, a captain in the MSG at the time, reported that the State Troops had lost six wounded—a far cry from what Zagonyi reported. *O.R.*, 3:251–252; "Major White's Report," 236–237; Musser, 5:104; Treichel, 22:245; Foley, 5:215–218; Dyer, 799; Britton, 155; Monaghan, 203.

Item: Criticism of General Grant's recent memoirs concerning his account of the Battle of Belmont, Missouri (November 7, 1861). Also gives an unknown Confederate participant's account of the battle, by "One of the Ten"; a member of the Fourth Tennessee Infantry.
Published: January 2, 1886.

Gen. Grant's Belmont.[25]

St. Louis, Dec. 16
Editor, *Republican*

The chapter of the great captain's memoirs[26] which treats of this small but severe battle, is not sufficiently ingenious to possess much historic value. It was obviously prepared, with some pain, to justify by afterthought a military movement which was conceived in indiscretion, executed with futility, and ended in disaster.

According to the general's narrative, in order to protect a Federal raiding column, which was seeking adventure in the backwoods of Southeast Missouri,[27] it became necessary to march one army from the Ohio River to a point between Mayfield, Ky., and Columbus, and push another army under the muzzles of the ordnance of a much larger hostile force in garrison at the latter place.[28] Hence the

---

25. The Battle of Belmont was fought on November 7, 1861, and was the only battle that Grant fought on the west side of the Mississippi River. General Frémont ordered Grant, in early November, to make a demonstration toward Charleston and Norfolk, Missouri, and Blandville, Kentucky, in support of operations against Columbus, Kentucky. Grant received word on the night of November 6–7, in the middle of the operation, that the Confederates were moving troops into Missouri to reinforce General Price, and reacted accordingly. The report would later prove to be false, but by then Grant had already changed his demonstration into an attack on Belmont. Boatner, 57–58; Nathaniel Cheairs Hughes, Jr., *The Battle of Belmont: Grant Strikes South* (Chapel Hill, NC, 1991), 2, 45, hereafter cited as Hughes.
26. *The Personal Memoirs of U. S. Grant*, a two volume set, was first published in 1885–1886, shortly after his death on July 23, 1885. The book, published by Mark Twain's company Charles L. Webster & Co., sold 300,000 copies and earned $450,000 for Grant's widow. The memoirs are "considered one of the greatest autobiographies in the English language." Boatner, 353; Warner, *Generals in Blue*, 186.
27. While Grant was making preparations to carry out his orders, he was informed on November 2 that Jeff Thompson's rebels were twenty-five miles below Greenville, Missouri, and an expedition was ordered to drive him back into Arkansas. However, Thompson was in Bloomfield, Missouri, and no where near Greenville as previously reported. Still, Grant was to support the move against Thompson, by sending troops from Cape Girardeau and Bird's Point. On November 3, the two columns left their bases in pursuit of Thompson. Two days later Grant received notice that the rebels were reinforcing General Price, and Grant was directed to begin his move against Columbus, as previously ordered. On November 6, Grant left Cairo to make his demonstration against Belmont. Lying up on the Kentucky side of the river, Grant received a message at 2:00 a.m. on November 7, that the Confederates had been crossing troops during the day for the purpose of cutting off his two columns that were supporting the operations against Thompson. To prevent the possible loss of his two columns Grant decided to attack Belmont. Grant's operations against Thompson and Belmont were based on faulty intelligence, which, in the end, led Grant to an unwise attack. *O.R.* 3:268–269; Hughes, 45–47.
28. On November 7, while Grant was moving on Belmont, he had a total of seven columns, comprising about 15,000 men in motion—three columns against Thompson commanded by Colonels R. J. Oglesby, J. B. Plummer and Colonel Lew Wallace; Grant's column against Belmont; and three

Movements Surrounding the Battle of Belmont
(November 3-7, 1861)

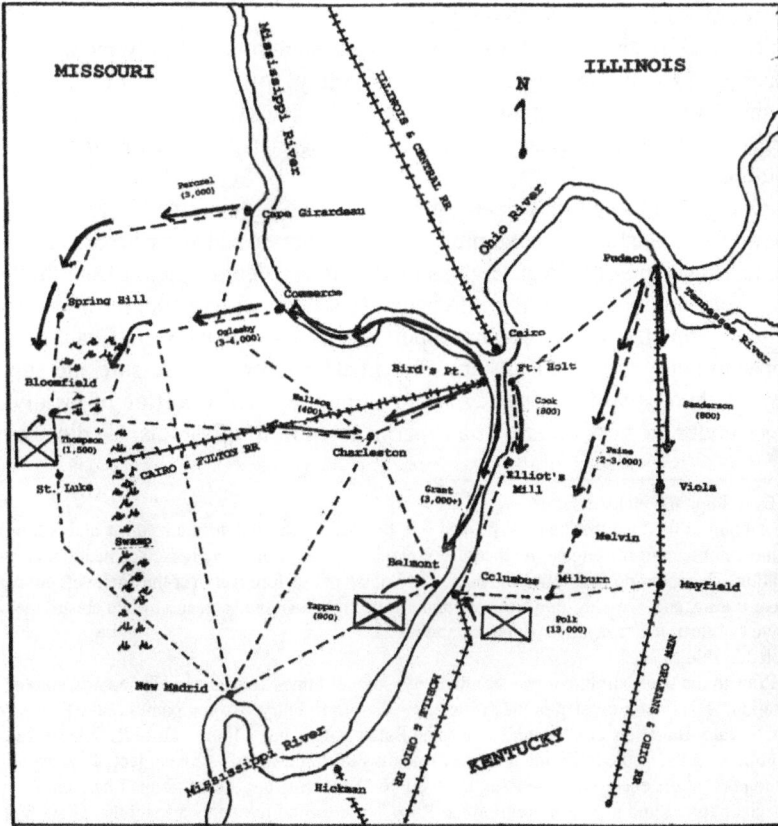

Battle of Belmont, in which four large side-wheel steamboat loads of national troops, after having engaged in detail and successively driven detachments of the enemy two miles during the greater part of a November day, forsook the engagement and hastened away from it four miles so precipitately that

Their General Escaped Capture

only by the unusual, not to say untriumphal, equestrian feat of sliding on horseback down a steep bank and trotting up the narrow gangplank of an unmoored and

---

columns against Columbus commanded by General E. A. Payne, Colonel W. L. Sanderson and Colonel John Cook. According to Nathaniel Hughes "these widespread simultaneous movements clouded Grant's objective" and confused the Confederates, who simply waited for the situation to develop. Hughes, 48, 55–56.

already departing transport.[29]

Without dwelling unduly on the humorous aspect of such a return from a so-called successful military expedition, let us turn to the alleged necessity of the campaign which ended so abruptly.

The path of the alleged necessity is the assumption that only by attacking a detachment (really one regiment and one battery)[30] in Missouri could a pressure be applied to a strictly defensive garrison in Kentucky, sufficient to prevent that garrison from detaching an offensive force dangerous to an adventurous raiding column.[31]

One general might have elected to recall or else reinforce the raiding party. Another strategist might have preferred, as a shorter and surer process to apply the necessary pressure by a single, straightforward demonstration from the Ohio River via Mayfield, upon the intrenched [entrenched] garrison.[32] Unfortunately for the symmetry of his eventual reputation as a strategist, Gen. Grant thought proper to apply a theoretically insufficient straightforward pressure and supplement its theoretical insufficiency by thrusting the smaller portion of his divided forces under the very muzzle of a superior force in fortifications. He did not per-

---

29. Describing the incident Grant wrote:
The captain of the boat that had just pushed out, but had not started, recognized me and ordered the engineer not to start the engine; he then had a plank run out for me. My horse seemed to take in the situation. There was no path down the bank...My horse put its fore feet over the bank without hesitation or urging, and, with his hind feet well under him, slid down the bank and trotted aboard the boat, twelve or fifteen feet away, over a single gang-plank.
Quoted in Ibid., 171.

30. Prior to the battle, Belmont was occupied by Colonel James Tappan and labeled a "Camp of Observation." His force consisted of the Thirteenth Arkansas Infantry, two companies of the First Mississippi Cavalry Battalion and Watson's Louisiana Battery of six guns. Ibid., 211; *O.R.*, 3:355, 782.

31. Following the Battle of Belmont Grant wrote his father and stated—"The object of the expedition was to prevent the enemy from sending a force into Missouri to cut off the troops I had sent there for a special purpose and to prevent reinforcing Price." There is no reason to suspect that Grant had any other reason for the engagement at Belmont—Why would Grant try to hoodwink his father? However, many writers, including the one who wrote this article, believed that Grant had other motives for his attack. John Harrell, of Arkansas, believed that Grant's attack was a "second thought" meant to "give diversion to his officers and men, and furnish evidence of activity to the expectant people who were demanding that the 'war be prosecuted.'" Hughes, in his work on Belmont, presents several opinions that have Grant seeking a battle. Hughes believed that, "Given Grant's personality, his itch to make something happen and to make a name for himself, it seems evident that he would attack—Belmont, probably; Columbus, perhaps." "Letter From Gen. Grant," *Rebellion Record*, 3:DOC 287; Hughes, 52–53; Harrell, *Arkansas, Confederate Military History*, 60.

32. As part of the overall plan for operations against Columbus, C. F. Smith, commanding Paducah, Kentucky, was directed by General Frémont to make a demonstration toward the Mississippi River town. Smith was directed to keep "columns moving to and fro on the road to Melvin and also to make minor demonstrations in the same manner on the roads to Lovelaceville and Mayfield." According to plan, on November 6, at 2:00 a.m., Smith dispatched General Paine with 2,000 men and four pieces of artillery to carry out the demonstration toward Columbus, via Melvin. An hour later another column of about 800 men, comprised of infantry, artillery and cavalry, started on the road to Mayfield. The purpose of this demonstration was the same as Grant's—"to occupy the enemy in the Mississippi Valley and prevent his throwing part of his forces into Northwestern Arkansas." *O.R.*, 3:299–301.

ceive that such strategy would afford his opponent the advantage of full opportunity to ascertain, by graduated resistance to the pressure, that the nearer and
smaller column

Was The Only Fighting One,

and then overwhelm it with sudden reinforcements. But although he did not fore-
see this probable and almost inevitable issue, it was precisely what happened.[33]

And approaching the question of strategy and success from another side—the
very one Gen. Grant, after twenty-five years reflection, elected to stand on and ask
the world to view it from, both the design and the outcome of the assault culmi-
nated in failure. For the alleged purpose was to protect the raiding column of Federals by holding the Confederate garrison within its entrenchments. But the result
of the attack was the very opposite to that. The attack drew over to Missouri, first,
[Gideon] Pillow's[34] demi-brigade,[35] and, second, the final and overwhelming rein-
forcement.[36] Only about one-third of the garrison of Columbus fired guns at Bel-

33. Federal participants at the time of the expedition put the failure not on General Grant, who "conducted [himself] gallantly," but on C. F. Smith, and the Paducah Garrison. One soldier wrote: "Where
was the force from Paducah, and the force from above which left several days ago? Fifteen thousand,
we thought, were there to engage the rebels at Columbus, while we were there to take them on at Belmont." Another wrote: "The plan was well laid, but poorly carried out. I do not think we should have
attacked Belmont at all, until we were sure the force from Paducah had begun their work or were ready
to do so." "Fight At Belmont," *Chicago Daily Tribune*, November 8, 1861; "Our Troops At Belmont,"
Chicago Daily Tribune, November 15, 1861; William, "Taylor's Battery of Chicago," *Chicago Daily
Tribune*, November 15, 1861.
34. Gideon J. Pillow, a resident of Tennessee, was a Mexican War veteran and a lawyer by profession. At the beginning of the Civil War, he fought at Belmont and Fort Donelson. After he passed the
command of Fort Donelson to General Simon B. Buckner, and fled, Pillow was later reprimanded for
his actions. He never commanded again in the Confederate Army. After the war he practiced law in
Memphis and died near Helena, Arkansas, on October 8, 1878. Boatner, 653–654; Warner, *Generals
in Gray*, 241.
35. Pillow's command was the First Division of the Western Department. It contained two brigades
commanded by Colonels J. K. Walker and R. M. Russell. For the Battle of Belmont, Pillow had three
Tennessee regiments from his Second Brigade and another from his First Brigade—they were the
Twelfth (633 men), Thirteenth, Twenty-first and Twenty-second Tennessee Infantries. Upon arrival
at the battle front, at about 9:15 a.m., Pillow assumed command of Tappan's force, which gave him a
total of 2,500–3,000 men, with 6 pieces of artillery; two 12-lb howitzers and four 6-lb smoothbores.
By 10:15 a.m., the Confederate skirmishers became engaged and the rest of the line stood ready to
receive Grant's force of roughly the same number. Hughes, 70, 211–212; *O.R.*, 3:325, 358, 723; *O.R.S.*,
pt 3, vol. 1:461.
36. The second group of reinforcements came over in spurts. The Second Tennessee Infantry, with
about 750 men from Memphis, arrived at about 10:30 a.m. They were quickly followed by the Fifteenth Tennessee and Eleventh Louisiana Infantries; the Fifteenth landed at about 11:00 a.m., while the
Eleventh arrived fifteen minutes later; these latter two regiments became engaged between noon and
1:00 p.m. Brigadier General Benjamin Cheatham and staff preceded the final group, arriving between
1:00–1:30 p.m. Between 1:30–2:00 p.m., Colonel Preston Smith arrived with the One Hundredth
Fifty-Fourth Senior Tennessee Infantry Regiment and the First Mississippi Battalion, adding another
1,000 men to the rebel force at Belmont. Two Tennessee cavalry companies also arrived at about 1:00
p.m., but accomplished little of note during the battle. Two batteries were also sent, but conditions on

mont. About two-thirds of that garrison remained fresh, and had been roused by many hours' inactive view of the unequal conflict to intense to eagerness to fight. At sunset the Federals were repulsed and fleeing in disorder from the field. What then hindered the Confederates from sending a column after the raiding Federals? If the gate to such an enterprise was ajar that morning, the results of the Federal strategy left it wide open that evening. The outcome of the attack was a strong temptation to the Confederates to assume the offensive; and the sound reason why they did not do so and never had any thought of doing so was the weighty fact that the entrenched garrison was the left flank of a long important and relatively weak defensive line, extending from the Mississippi River to the mountains of Kentucky. That garrison had already been entrenched and stripped of every man who could be spared to strengthen the center of that long, weak line. It was strictly a defensive garrison, entrenched to "hold the fort," and not

To Recklessly Experiment

on raiding Federals.

The simple truth is, Belmont was a Federal blunder due to inexperience, which, as long as the Confederate commander was shortening the fencing arm while feeling where to thrust, was an assailant's advance delusively resembling victory; and which, as soon as the real defensive skill and strength began to play, turned instantly into an assailant's retreat in utmost haste and much disorder. And this much truth, even if all other testimony should quickly perish, would be sifted from the following significant statements of the Federal commander:

p. 274. "I saw at the same time two steamers coming from the Columbus side towards the west shore above us, black—or gray—with soldiers from boiler deck to roof....They (his men) formed line rapidly and we started back to our boats. ... We could not stop, however, to pick them (stragglers) up, because the troops we had seen crossing the river had debarked by this time and were nearer our transports than we were. It would be prudent (just so) to get them behind us."[37]

The commander calmly admits all this, while coolly claiming that he was not defeated, then humorously (for he developed more by humor in his memoirs than he did sound strategy at Belmont) narrates how he rode out to bring in a regiment he had posted to guard the point of debarkation, and to his amazement found that

---

the field forced them back to the Kentucky shore. Latter, Marshal Polk's Battery landed, but performed no meaningful action in the battle. Additionally, two other regiments, including the writer's Fourth Tennessee Infantry, arrived in Belmont, but did not materially participate in the battle. *O.R.*, 3:307, 321, 331, 336, 345–346; United States War Department, *The War of the Rebellion: Official Records of the Union and Confederate Navies*, 31 vols. (Washington, D. C., 1894–1922), Series 1, 22:425–427 (hereafter cited as *O.R.N.*; all citations of *O.R.N.* refer to Series 1 unless indicated otherwise); Hughes, 2, 123, 168, 255; William K. Polk, "General Polk and the Battle of Belmont," *Battles and Leaders of the Civil War of the Civil War*, 1:355, hereafter cited as Polk.

37. Grant was referring to the arrival of the last group of reinforcements, at about 1:30 p.m., under Colonel Preston Smith. *O.R.*, 3:344, 346.

said regiment had decamped;[38] and how, while riding about to ponder on such indications as unsuccessful strategy, he soon perceived the enemy near at hand and saw and heard other of them firing close volleys of buck and ball into the transports, and how he then persuaded his steed to return with celerity to the only transport which had not hastily departed, a return effected by sliding on horseback down the

Steep River Bank,

and trotting up a narrow gang-plank, to the deck of a cut-loose and already moving steamboat.

To soften the outlines of his precipitate embarkation, the general registers his force as 2,500 men engaged, and the regiment in reserve at the landing.[39] But he inadvertently authenticates an official map, which allows his transports as the *Alex Scott,* the *[Belle] Memphis,* the *Chancellor* and the *Keystone*—four mammoth side-wheel steamers, selected, unquestionably, for their size or ferrying capacity.[40]

---

38. After Grant landed at Hunter's Farm, near Belmont, he detailed two companies of the Seventh Iowa and three companies of the Twenty-second Illinois Infantries to serve as his reserve. This make-shift battalion of 350 men was commanded by Captain John E. Detrich of Company I, Twenty-second Illinois. At 4:00 p.m. Detrich marched his battalion to the embarkation point, without orders, and loaded his command, even before the rest of Grant's command had made it to the landing. When Grant went looking for Detrich's Battalion, to cover his loading, they were nowhere to be found. Later Grant found them already at the landing and loaded aboard the *Belle Memphis.* Ibid., 3:294–295; Hughes, 79, 155, 170.

39. Grant's ground force, including his reserve, consisted of 3,138 men organized as follows: District of Southeast Missouri Expeditionary Command—Brigadier General U. S. Grant:

> McClernand's Brigade—Brigadier General John A. McClernand:
> 27th Ill. Inf. (724 men)—Col. Napoleon B. Buford
> 30th Ill. Inf. (522 men)—Col. Philip B. Fouke
> 31st Ill. Inf. (610 men)—Col. John A. Logan
> Dougherty's Brigade—Colonel Henry Dougherty:
> 7th Iowa Inf. (513 men)—Col. Jacob G. Lauman
> 22nd Ill. Inf. (529 men)—Lt. Col. Harrison E. Hart
> Unassigned:
> Dollin's Ill. Cav. Co. (70 men)—Captain Ezra Dollin
> Delano's Adams Cty., Ill. Co. (58 men)—Lt. James K. Catlin
> Battery B, 1st Ill. Lt. Art. (114 men)—Capt. Ezra Taylor

Note: In Grant's original report he puts his strength at 3,114. The difference in his number and mine are based on the number for the Twenty-seventh and Thirtieth Illinois Infantries. The numbers I used came from the *Chicago Daily Tribune,* which listed the strength as presented. In McClernand's report on the battle he has the Twenty-seventh at 722 men while the Thirtieth Illinois had 500 men that took part in the battle.

O.R., 3:277, 287, 290; Banasik, *Missouri In 1861,* 171, 243; "The Latest News," *Chicago Daily Tribune,* November 11, 1861; Hughes, 209.

40. In addition to the listed steamers, the Federals also used the *James Montgomery,* which carried the Twenty-seventh Illinois and Seventh Iowa Infantries. Of the other boats, the *Belle Memphis* carried the

The men who remember those boats will not believe that any skillful general ever ferried an army of 3,500 men twenty-five miles upon them. For, in those days, a small side-wheel steamer was ample ferrying for a large regiment. The little Yazoo packet *Charm*[41] on that day carried a load of 1,200 men to the field of Belmont, and the *Alex Scott* could have carried them on any one of her three capacious decks.[42]

Moreover, the Federal line was long enough to continuously overlap (outflank) the one opposing it.[43]

A View Of The Battle.

The yellow bluffs of Columbus [Kentucky] look down over a narrow south-

---

Twenty-second Illinois, a section of Taylor's Battery and Delano's cavalry. It also served as Grant's headquarters during the expedition. The *Alex Scott* carried the Thirtieth and Thirty-first Illinois Infantries, while the *Chancellor* carried Dollin's Cavalry and the *Keystone* carried most of the wagons of the expedition. The remaining units probably boarded the *Chancellor*. The *Rob Roy*, contrary to Hughes's portrayal, did not convey troops to Belmont, but would later convey prisoners and the wounded of the battle to Cairo following the engagement. Note: Hughes has the *Keystone State* as part of the expedition, however, the *Keystone State* was a sidewheel steamer purchased in Philadelphia in early 1861, and operated in the costal areas of the United States, not on the western waters. The Naval Records make clear that there were two vessels named the *Keystone*, one being the *Keystone State*, while the other was simply the *Keystone*. *O.R.*, 3:283, 291; *O.R.N.*., 22:401–403; *O.R.N.*., Series 2, 1:120–121; *O.R.N.*., Index:218; C., "The Battle of Belmont," *Chicago Daily Tribune*, November 11, 1861; B. R .K., "Another Account," *Rebellion Record*, 3:DOC 291; John Seaton, "The Battle of Belmont," *War Talks In Kansas: A Series of Papers Read Before the Military Order of the Loyal Legion of the United States, MOLLUS,* 15:308, hereafter cited as Seaton; Hughes, 49, 209.

41. The CSS *Charm* was a 223 ton, side-wheeled steamer built in 1860 in Cincinnati, Ohio. The vessel served as a transport and an ammunition carrier and was commanded by Captain W. L. Trask. It served with distinction during the Battle of Belmont, but did not survive the war. Scuttled by the Confederates on May 17, 1863 in the Big Black River, the *Charm* was burned to the waterline but was still visible a century after the war. Naval History Division, Navy Department, *Civil War Naval Chronology, 1861–1865* (Washington, DC, 1971), 6:208, hereafter cited as *Civil War Naval Chronology.*

42. The *Alex Scott* was the largest of Grant's steamers. As to the *Charm*—The vessel arrived at Columbus on the morning of November 7, and was directed to stand by for possible service. Shortly after 8:00 a.m. the *Charm* made its first of many trips conveying some commissary stores to Belmont. At 9:00 a.m. the *Charm* made another trip carrying medical personnel and about 150 troops. At 11:00 a.m. the *Charm* boarded the Eleventh Louisiana Infantry and conveyed them to Belmont, arriving there at noon. According to the captain of the *Charm*, he delivered Smith's Brigade of the 154th Tennessee and Blythe's Mississippi Battalion at 2:00 p.m. However, the commander of the 154th Tennessee stated that his command was carried by the *Kentucky*. The combined strength of Smith's Brigade was about 1,000 men. *O.R.*, 3:348; *O.R.N.*., 22:425–427; Hughes, 49, 184; Polk, 3:355.

43. When Pillow formed his line he failed to use the terrain to his advantage, placing his command largely in the open or in a cornfield, with its back to some timber. Only the Thirteenth Arkansas and Twelfth Tennessee were in a wooded area on the rebel right. The Federals for their part had woods for their protection and were about eighty yards from Pillow's line, making their position both stronger and partially concealed. "The Result," according to Nathaniel Hughes, "was a short, somewhat cramped line about 400 yards in length." This cramped line made it easy for the Federals to eventually outflank the Confederate position and had nothing to do with an imaginary larger force than Grant had. *O.R.S.*, pt. 3, vol. 1:462; Hughes, 74; Polk, 1:354.

Battle of Belmont
November 7, 1861

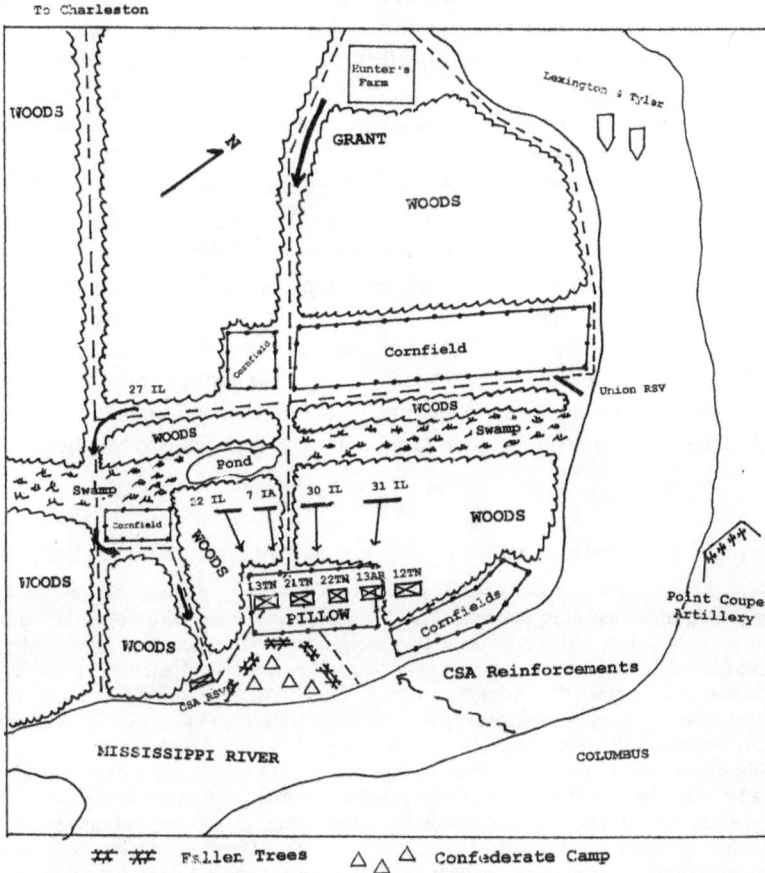

To Charleston

WOODS

Hunter's Farm

Lexington ; Tyler

GRANT

WOODS

Cornfield

27 IL

Union RSV

WOODS

WOODS

Swamp

Pond

Swamp

22 IL   7 IA   30 IL   31 IL

Cornfield

WOODS

WOODS

13TN 21TN 22TN 13AR 12TN

PILLOW

Cornfields

Point Coupe Artillery

WOODS

WOODS

CSA RSV

CSA Reinforcements

MISSISSIPPI RIVER

COLUMBUS

✗✗ ✗✗ Fallen Trees   △ △ △ Confederate Camp

west curve of the Mississippi River upon the hamlet of Belmont [Missouri][44] and the tall tree-tops of the Missouri bottom. In November, 1861, a luxuriant forest masked the Missouri shore from the spot of the Federal debarkation[45] down to a small camp of the Thirteenth Arkansas Infantry[46] and Beltzhoover's Louisiana

---

44. At the time, Belmont was little more than a ferry boat landing for the "Iron Banks Ferry." It was "'a name rather than a place.'" Consisting of some scattered log huts and numerous cornfields; the hamlet of Belmont does not exist today. Hughes, 82–83.

45. The Federal Army disembarked at Hunter's Farm, near Lucas Bend in the Mississippi River and about three miles from Belmont (Polk placed the distance at five to six miles). They began landing at 8:00 a.m., assembled and marched off to Belmont at 8:30 a.m. Ibid., 57, 84; *O.R.S.*, pt. 1, vol. 1:266, 269; Polk, 1:348; "The Battle of Belmont," *Chicago Daily Tribune*, November 12, 1861; , 15:312.

46. The Thirteenth Arkansas Infantry was organized in May 1861, at Harrisburg, Arkansas, by James C. Tappan and mustered into the Confederate service in July. The men came from southeastern Ar-

battery.[47] The camp was protected only by the few heavy guns then mounted on the heights of Columbus, opposite, and by some felled trees north and northwest of it, which filled the roads and encumbered the ground in those directions for perhaps 200 yards. South of the encampment, where the map authenticated by Gen. Grant, inaccurately shows uninterrupted forest, was an open area large enough for several regiments to drill, maneuver or fight in. This forest mask, and felled timber, and small encampment, and open area were all in near unobstructed view from the opposite heights.

The fortification of those heights had then been completed; but only a few heavy guns had yet been mounted. The garrison had been reduced to the proper compliment for manning the fortress, which constituted the left wing of the Confederate forces in Kentucky, and the surplus troops sent off to strengthen the center of that most important line.[48] A small force of infantry and artillery was encamped within the enclente. The bulk of the garrison was camped on those neighboring slopes which were most convenient to the glacis[49]. Just above or north of the fortifications the highway on the heights forked, one branch continuing northward, in the direction of Cairo, and the other turning eastward, en route to Mayfield.

In This Fork

of the highway lay the outpost camp of the Fourth Tennessee Infantry.[50] Both roads

---

kansas, principally from Phillips, Arkansas, and Monroe Counties. Tappan was a wealthy lawyer from Helena, who outfitted the regiment primarily from his own funds. He was commissioned on May 11, 1861, and served throughout the war, mainly in the Trans-Mississippi area. Harrell, *Arkansas, Confederate Military History,* 416–417; Hughes, 73; Crute, 50; 299; Sifakis, *Confederacy,* 275; Nash, 110.

47. Beltzhoover's Louisiana battery, better known as Watson's Battery, was organized in late summer 1861, by Augustus C. Watson in New Orleans. Watson paid $40,000–50,000 of his own money to equip the battery, which was recruited from the Creoles of New Orleans. In honor of Watson the men wore a "W" on their caps. Watson gave up the position of captain after Daniel Beltzhoover, a West Point graduate, Class of 1847, agreed to command the battery. Watson stayed on, enlisting as a private in the unit he organized. The battery contained two 12-lb howitzers and four 6-lb smoothbore cannon and carried 99 officers and men into the Battle of Belmont on November 7, 1861. After Belmont, the battery served its remaining time east of the Mississippi River. Beltzhoover went on to command the First Louisiana Artillery Regiment, survived the war and died on November 1, 1870. Heitman, 1:209; Crute, 160; Hughes, 69–70.

48. On October 31, 1861, seven days before the Battle of Belmont, the Columbus garrison, including the men at Belmont, contained 16,307 men "present for duty." This amount included John Bowen's command, which had moved to Camp Beauregard, near Felicana, Kentucky, during October to guard the Paducah Railroad. Located twenty-two miles (Porter has it at fifteen miles) southeast of Columbus, Bowen's Division was not available for the Battle of Belmont; deducting 3,165 men for Bowen's command, leaves 13,132 men in Polk's Columbus command at the time of the battle. *O.R.,* 3:730; *O.R.,* 4:557; *O.R.S.,* pt. 2, vol. 50:379–380; *Atlas to Accompany the Official Records,* plt. 153; *Confederate Military History,* vol. 8: *Tennessee,* by James T. Porter, 11, hereafter cited as Porter, *Tennessee, Confederate Military History.*

49. Glacis—"An embankment sloping gradually up to a fortification, so as to expose attackers to defending gunfire." Guralnik, 592.

50. The Fourth Tennessee Infantry was organized on May 15, 1861, at Germantown, Tennessee, and was transferred to the Confederate Service on August 25, 1861. The men comprising the regiment

were picketed out several miles, an arduous duty which devolved on the infantry, owing to a lack of organized, efficient cavalry.[51] To this deficiency in the scouting arm Gen. Grant unquestionably owed the head which he wore as president.

Just above the rampart, near the camp of the Fourth Tennessee, and nearer the bluff shore of the river, on wheels and without protection, stood the four light iron siege guns of the Memphis Southern Guards,[52] and the Federal gunboats, *Lexington,*[53] *Tyler,*[54] and *Conestoga*[55] were wont to come down as near as was deemed prudent and improve their gunnery by shelling the Southern Guards' Battery and the camp of the Fourth Tennessee. Thus the gunboats and that battery got range and practice, and the Fourth Tennessee an idea of what being shelled by heavy ordnance was like.[56] Every man in uniform, blue or gray, was jolly green

came from Coffee, DeKalb, Macon, Maury, Hickman, Rutherford, Summer, Williamson and Wilson Counties. The first colonel of the unit was Rufus P. Neely, who died in May 1864. During the Battle of Belmont the unit was not actively engaged, though it was transferred to Belmont in the latter stages of the battle. The regiment served their entire time east of the Mississippi River, being reorganized in April 1862, following the Battle of Shiloh. The regiment was consolidated with the Fifth Tennessee in December 1862, and was again consolidated in 1865. *O.R.S.*, pt. 2, vol. 78:507, 522; Crute, 279.

51. Polk did have cavalry available for picket duty out of Columbus, though it was limited. Miller's Mississippi Battalion had three companies available and indeed they were used to cover the road to Mayville. Polk also had a Tennessee Battalion, part of which was sent to Belmont during the battle. A total of nine companies were available, though some were at various stages of organization at the time of the battle and of limited value. *O.R.*, 3:308, 723; Hughes, 66, 213.

52. The Southern Guards Light Artillery or Memphis Southern Guards Artillery was raised in Memphis, Tennessee, on April 21, 1861, as a twelve month unit. The battery was also known as Johnston's Battery and was at first commanded by Captain James Hamilton; at Belmont the battery was commanded by Captain S. D. H. (or S. H. D.) Hamilton. The unit participated in the Battle of Belmont after which it was transferred to Island No. 10, where it was captured on April 8, 1862. Six days later the battery was mustered out of the service. *O.R.*, 3:307; *O.R.S.*, pt. 2, vol. 78:353–354; Crute, 318; *Encyclopedia of the Civil War*, 1050; Hughes, 66–67.

53. The *Lexington* was a wood side-wheel steamer. It was built in 1860 and purchased for government use in June 1861, for $20,666.66. It had three boilers, two engines, a draft of six feet, and was 177 feet by 36 feet, 10 inches. The vessel mounted six guns when first outfitted; "4 8-inch shell guns and 2 32-pounders." *O.R.N..*, Series 2, 1: 126–127; Henry Walke, "The Gunboats at Belmont and Fort Henry," *Battles and Leaders of the Civil War*, 1:358, hereafter cited as Walke.

54. The 180 foot, 575 ton *U.S.S. Tyler* was built in 1857, and purchased by the War Department in June 1861. It was a side-wheel steamer, mounting eight guns by the Battle of Belmont: "6 8-inch shell guns and 2 32-pounders." During the war, the *Tyler*, served on the western waters, fighting at Belmont, Missouri, Forts Henry and Donelson and engaged the rebel ram *Arkansas* on the Yazoo River. The *Tyler* was part of the Western Flotilla and played an important role in defeating the Confederate attack on Helena on July 4, 1863. *O.R.*, vol. 22, pt. 1:385–386; *O.R.N..*, Series 2, 1:227; Tony Gibbons, *Warships and Naval Battles of the Civil War* (New York, 1989), 73, hereafter cited as Gibbons; Walke, 1:359.

55. The 572 ton *U.S.S. Conestoga* was a side-wheel steamer and part of the Western Gunboat Flotilla. It was purchased in June 1861, and armed with four cannon. It was not at Belmont, but was at Forts Henry and Donelson in February 1862, and helped capture the unfinished Confederate ironclad *Eastport* on February 6. The *Conestoga* did not survive the war, being sunk after a collision with the U.S.S. *Sterling Price*, on the night of March 8, 1864, at Bondurant Point on the Mississippi River. *O.R.N..*, Series 2, 1:65; Gibbons, 73; *Civil War Naval Chronology*, 2:17–18.

56. After depositing Grant's land forces on the Missouri side of the Mississippi River, Commander Henry Walke led out the *Tyler* and *Lexington* to attack the defenses of Columbus at 8:30 a.m. The two Federal boats engaged the Columbus batteries three times between 8:30 a.m. and noon; The *Lexington*

in those days, and developments were regarded as matter-of-course which latter would have seemed exceedingly serious. One very young man, in particular, was under the impression that the first duty of a solider was to stand and take any amount of shelling and shooting, and the second to proceed up to the line of the enemy with more or less celerity, according to orders, and there conscientiously endeavor to insert his bayonet into the foe who happened to get in front of him.

One afternoon a special courier rode, in a foam, on the Mayfield road, and presently it was bruited that a large Federal force was advancing on Columbus via Mayfield. That night the garrison slept in the conviction that those breastworks would be gory on the morrow.[57]

At Daybreak

the cry was heard that Lucas Bend, above, was full of Federal warboats. This was, no doubt, a stirring cry to Col. [James] Tappan[58] of the Thirteenth Arkansas who, with his regiment and Beltzhoover's Battery of four [six] field guns, held the Missouri shore. At the first alarm the Fourth Tennessee turned out and thronged the bluff to see grim visaged war. What they saw was a mask of heavy forest, Tappan's camp cradled in its abatis, the open space lower down the river near the hamlet of Belmont and a fleet of steamers about four miles away, up stream. This spectacle, most of it familiar, soon grew monotonous. Federal gunboats and transports had been observed lower down in that bend, before, so the Fourth Tennessee presently adjourned to prepare for breakfast. It was not a protracted meal. About the time the coffee was being passed around by the high privates' body-servants, familiar sounds were heard. The first was a brisk "Look out!" and the others were a plaintive "Hoo! oo! oo!" and eager "where are you! where are you? Bang?" as numerous but uninvited guests, aptly yclept [called] "bums," began to drop

---

expended 18 shells and 1 solid shot, while the *Tyler* fired 3 solid shot, 25 grape shot and 106 shells. *O.R.N..*, 22:402–403, 772, 780.

57. Within days of the Battle of Belmont, Polk had been informed that the Federals were planning some type of operation against the city, but the scope was unclear. Between 2:00 and 3:00 a.m. on November 7, Polk was informed that the enemy were pressing Jeff Thompson's Missourians near Bloomfield, Missouri. At dawn, on the seventh, Polk was informed that the Federals were landing troops on the Missouri side just above Belmont—Polk put the distance at five to six miles above Belmont, though it was actually three miles from Belmont. *O.R.*, 3:306; Hughes, 65; Seaton, 15:312.

58. James Camp Tappan was born in Franklin, Tennessee, on September 9, 1825. He was educated in New Hampshire, then Yale, and studied law in Vicksburg, Mississippi. After passing the bar, Tappan relocated to Helena, Arkansas, where he resided at the beginning of the Civil War. Even though he possessed no military training, Tappan was elected colonel of the Thirteenth Arkansas Infantry. He fought at Belmont, moved his regiment east of the Mississippi and fought gallantly at Shiloh. After Bragg's Kentucky invasion, Tappan was promoted to brigadier general on November 5, 1862, and returned to the Trans-Mississippi Department. General T. H. Holmes assigned Tappan to command a brigade in Thomas C. Hindman's Division, on February 28, 1863. He fought at Pleasant Hill, Jenkins' Ferry, and was part of Price's 1864 Missouri Raid. After the war Tappan returned to Helena, practiced law, and died on March 19, 1906. *O.R.*, vol. 22, pt. 2:793; Warner, *Generals in Gray*, 298, 299; Harrell, *Arkansas, Confederate Military History*, 416, 417.

in sociably among the messes. Some finished their breakfast, between dodges. Others hastened to the brow of the bluff and ate a cold lunch later. By 8:30 a.m. the whole regiment were looking across the narrow curves, at the Missouri shore, with eyes well disciplined in picket vigilance. And at that time shells were coming like misfortunes. They were round and black and

Sailing On Curves

that meant business to the boys at the Southern Guards Battery. The gunboats seemed disposed to crowd the line the S.G. lads had often sharply drawn. The regular short fuses was getting too slow, when a large rifled gun in the parapet ruled it with emphasis and for six hours the jolly tars in blue respected it.[59] About 9 a.m. musketry began to pop and rattle in the woods some two miles above Tappan's camp. The unseen racket slowly moved down the stream, then paused, swelling in volumes as Pillow's last regiments and Beltzhoover's guns joined in the thrilling chorus. For perhaps half an hour the noise was something which men who have heard all still associate with the sounds of Shiloh,[60] Chickamauga[61] and Petersburg.[62] Nothing was seen but what has been suggested, except a hint of smoke that began to dim the tracery of the tree tops. Then came a culminating crash, a pulsing volley of artillery, and a sudden lull and the foreboding that the enemy had got Beltzhoover's battery.[63]

It was then between 11 a.m. and noon; four large transport loads of national

---

59. During the entire engagement with the Federal boats only one 24-lb shot penetrated either boat. The *Tyler* was hit sometime after noon in the starboard (right side) wheel, which passed into the ship decapitating one man and seriously injuring two others. *O.R.N..*, 22:403, 772.

60. The Battle of Shiloh (Union name) or Pittsburg Landing (Confederate name) took place on April 6–7, 1862, near the Mississippi and Tennessee border. General U. S. Grant commanded the Federals while Albert S. Johnston led the rebels. The initial, surprise attack, sent the Unionists reeling, but they rallied and stemmed the Confederate tide toward nightfall on the first day. Having received reinforcements during the latter part of April 6 and into the night, Grant counterattacked the following day and drove the rebels from the field. A total of 62,682 Union troops had engaged 40,335 rebels, losing in the process 13,047 men, while the Confederates suffered 10,694 killed, wounded or missing men. Boatner, 754–757.

61. The Battle of Chickamauga was fought in northern Georgia on September 19–20, 1863. Out of 58,222 effectives the Federals lost 16,170 troops (1,657 killed, 9,756 wounded, and 4,757 captured or missing), while the Confederates lost 18,454 (2,312 killed, 14,674 wounded, and 1,468 captured or missing) out of 66,326 men. Ibid., 150–153.

62. Petersburg, Virginia, underwent the longest siege in American history from June 15, 1864–April 3, 1865. Shortly after the city fell, General Robert E. Lee surrendered his army at Appomattox on April 9, 1865, effectively ending the Civil War. *Encyclopedia of the Civil War*, 1494–1504.

63. The main fighting during the Battle of Belmont began about 10:15 a.m., as Grant's forces moved toward the main rebel line and engaged Pillow's skirmishers. Grant, like Pillow, had no effective reserve as both commanders deployed their entire force on line. Pillow, for his part, had one company of the Thirteenth Tennessee Infantry which served as a flank guard and acted as a extremely small reserve. Grant had Detrich's makeshift battalion a mile to his left rear, which in the course of the battle, Grant seemed to have forgotten about until it was time to leave. By 11:00 a.m. the rebel skirmishers had been driven back to their commands and the battle proper began. *O.R.*, 3:307; Harrell, *Arkansas, Confederate Military History*, 62; Hughes, 85–86, 92.

troops were slowly and steadily outflanking and driving the Thirteenth Arkansas and a demi-brigade of Gen. Pillow. The commander of the garrison, unaided by cavalry, was waiting to hear from the column on the Mayfield road, in order to decide where was the feint and where the fight—in Kentucky or Missouri.[64] Noon came, but no news. A horse lay gasping in the road some miles out eastward; and a dust-grimmed soldier was earnestly begging at every clearing for a mount.[65] Suddenly—it was past noon—Pillow's hard-pressed, ever-flanked line was seen staggering out of the forest and dropping about in the felled timber, behind trunks and stumps. And then, with all due respect to the memory of those Arkansas and Tennessee and Mississippi and Louisiana soldiers, they clung to that felled timber for about an hour—until flanked again, on the west, they broke and ran, part through the tents

To The Water's Edge[66]

and part straight back south, into the open area, where this part of the broken line

---

64. While Polk watched the battle develop at Belmont, he awaited word as to the reported Federals coming from Paducah. Between noon and 1:00 p.m., Polk decided that any type of attack on Columbus had been delayed or would not take place and ordered Preston Smith's Brigade over to Belmont with two regiments from McGowan's Division to follow. The Fourth Tennessee Infantry was part of the latter group. *O.R.*, 3:308, 346, 353.

65. Between 11:00 a.m. and noon, the two opposing lines began to exchange fire in earnest. The Thirty-first Illinois occupied the Union left opposite the Thirteenth Arkansas and Twelfth Tennessee Infantries. After receiving fire into their left flank, Colonel John Logan, commanding the Thirty-first Illinois, adjusted his line to the left to better confront the Twelfth Tennessee, which actually overlapped the Unionist line and was charging the Federal left. Within a short time the Twelfth Tennessee halted its charge, began firing and was quickly out of ammunition, having only twenty rounds per man at the start of the contest. In the center, the Twenty-first and Twenty-second Tennessee Infantries were in a cornfield and exposed to concentrated fire from the Seventh Iowa, the Twenty-second and Thirtieth Illinois infantries. Toward 11:30, the center under Pillow's direction launched a bayonet charge that rippled down the line, but accomplished little. Union artillery, now planted in the center of their line, began pounding the two rebel units in the Confederate center. By twelve the line was still holding, though a "regiment and a battalion," were without ammunition. However, a dramatic change would take place over the next thirty minutes. Ibid., 3:326; *O.R.S.*. pt. 3, vol. 1:462; Hughes, 94–97, 100, 103. The writer may be referring to Grant as the "dust-grimmed soldier," as Grant notes in his *Memoirs* (1:223) that he had had his horse shot out from under him.

66. While the right and center of the rebel line was being punished by the unseen Yankees in the woods beyond the cornfield, the far left was also in a similar quandary. By noon the Thirteenth Tennessee faced the same problems—low ammunition and a constant flow of casualties against a largely unseen foe. While the men of the Thirteenth gamely held the left of the rebel line, they were startled to hear gunfire to their rear. Their one detached company, Pillow's sole reserve, became engaged by the Twenty-seventh Illinois which had approached the rebel rear via another road. Colonel John Wright, commander of the Thirteenth Tennessee, immediately communicated the information to General Pillow. "Finding it impossible longer to maintain" his position, Pillow "ordered the whole line to retreat to the river bank." With his line broken and troops "mingled together," back went the Thirteenth as did the rest of the line. On the right the Twelfth Tennessee was out of ammunition and retreated to the river bank to resupply. In the center the Twenty-first and Twenty-second Tennessee followed suit. Smelling blood the victorious Federals pressed the attack; panic set into the rebel lines as they rushed to the rear. *O.R.*, 3:326, 333–334; *O.R.S.*, pt. 3:462; Hughes, 109–113, 116–117.

lay down under the streaming battle-flags, and poured into the mass, which Gen. Grant describes as grouped demoralized among the tents, volleys as game as ever were fired in that war. Thousands of hearts thrilled with the impulse that goads swift succor, while watching those streaming flags and that straight, narrow, volleying line—and thrilled with mingled pain and rage and pride for fully half an hour. Meanwhile the other part of Pillow's line lay under the river bank, inactive, scattered but quiet, and visibly alert. It was Gen. Grant's opinion that they were waiting to surrender on demand. Possibly they may have been waiting to see how long Gen. Grant and his army would stand around, "demoralized," under those close, sweeping volleys of buck and ball. It is the opinion of an eye witness, based on some experience as to the effects of close, sweeping volleys on scattered, "demoralized" assailants, that if Columbus and its garrison had been eliminated from the contest, that firing would presently have routed the confessed demoralization, and swept it from the field. It was in this crisis, under that fire, that the tents were burned, exposing the Federal mass still more. The volleying line was not attacked. It lay in a cloud of smoke and fridge of flame; and visibly held the scattered assailants among the tents.[67]

While the last tents were blazing, the rifled gun on the bluff opened fire, and the call to arms resounded through the garrison. The dust-grimmed soldier had arrived, at last, and the commandant knew there were no fighting symptoms in the hostile column on the east.

Then a great shout was heard, as thousands ran and grasped their guns. The Fourth Tennessee fell in and went on the double to the wharf. There [R. A.] Stewart's Battery was rushing on board the *Kentucky No. 2*,[68] and the Fourth received plain orders to return from Belmont with a correct account of those brass guns.[69]

---

67. Pressing forward, Grant's men reached the rebel camp and prepared for the final assault. Firing several volleys they pressed into Camp Johnston, seized the Watson Battery and drove the rebel mob back to the safety of the levee, while others headed north, along the river to get away from the Federal attack; the time was 1:00 p.m. Meanwhile, the second group of rebel reinforcements had arrived and were organizing for a counterstroke. The Second Tennessee Infantry, under Colonel J. Knox Walker delivered the first blow halting the Federal pursuit in its tracks. In turn, the Second was devastated by Union artillery, including the recently captured Watson Battery, which stopped the Confederate counter thrust. However, Walker's attack did stymie the Union forces, allowing time for more troops to arrive from Columbus and more importantly, permitting the recently routed rebel units to reform. It also turned the Unionist's attention away from Pillow's troops which hugged the banks of the Mississippi River. By 1:30 p.m., Camp Johnston was burning, followed at about 2:00 p.m. by "an eerie lull" that settled over the battlefield and lasted for thirty minutes. *O.R.*, 3:308, 343; Hughes, 117–119, 121–124, 127. The author's repeated use of the word "demoralized" is apparently a reference to Grant's characterization of his own troops' failure to follow up his success: "At this point they became demoralized from their victory and failed to reap its full reward" (*The Personal Memoirs of U. S. Grant*, 1:223). Grant asserted that his assault faltered because his green troops stopped to ransack the rebel camp.

68. The *Kentucky No. 2* was a 500 ton side-wheel steamer also referred to as the *Kentucky* in the official reports surrounding the battle. At Belmont the boat was captained by a "Captain Lodwick." According to popular belief, the *Kentucky* also participated in the engagement at Island No. 10 and was probably captured at Memphis on June 6, 1862. *O.R.*, 3:409; *Civil War Naval Chronology*, 6:258–259.

69. Richard A. Stewart's Louisiana Battery was Company A, Pointe Coupee Artillery Battalion. The

The Fourth Tennessee was a 1,000-man regiment in those days, and the *Kentucky No. 2* was not a large steamboat; but the accommodations were ample, with the regiment on the boiler-deck and the battery below. As the boat glided out, the gunboats passed down and turned their

Great Guns

loose.[70] It was solid shot and shell, half and half, taken short and hot. Inspired by a commendable desire to get behind the enemy, the officer in command superintended navigation, which ran the flimsy passenger packet straight up into the broadsides of the gunboats. And by a miracle, so to speak, the hull was not riddled or the boilers rent. A long leg up stream plumped the adventurous side wheeler on the beach, almost abreast the United States flotilla and behind the boys in blue, who had been hunting a fight. But the felled timber covered the shore, and those brass guns were a trust to keep. While hastily forming the regiment under the bank, the colonel called for ten volunteers. And when ten men stepped forward, the promptest one was ordered to take the others up the beach and search for a spot where the cannon could be got up the bank into the open woods by hand. With a hostile army on the left-hand and a hostile navy on the right-hand, and such pressing duty of a critical search in process, the opportunity for general observation was limited. Why those gunboats did not blow that fragile steamboat out of the water and then transform the Fourth Tennessee into a legion of angels, this scribe knoweth not. Perhaps the fire of the rifled gun and the Southern Guards waxed warmer. Possibly the jolly tars deemed the steamer *Charm* and other midstream cruisers marks more tempting. At all events, The Fourth stood on the beach in double ranks, prepared to count those cannons against both bayonets and boats. "D____ [Damned] artillery anyhow!" remarked one of the ten volunteers, as he rose from a sudden obeisance to a "bum" and saw another of the reinforcing regiments[71] streaming away with glitter, over the bank and into the abatis. In another minute he espied a sloping place, climbed up it and judged it was too steep. A hundred yards or so above he tried another and shouted

---

battalion proper was stationed at Island No. 10, while Stewart's command was at Columbus, Kentucky. The battalion was recruited from Point Coupee, West Baton Rouge and Concordia Parishes. While stationed at Columbus, the battery was referred to as the Pointe Coupee Battery. The Battalion was captured at Island No. 10 in April 1862, exchanged and captured again at Vicksburg, Mississippi in July 1863. Again exchanged the battalion was consolidated into one company and fought during the Atlanta Campaign in 1864. It surrendered on April 25, 1865. *O.R.*, 3:307; *O.R.S.*, pt. 2, vol. 23:602; Crute, 159. At the beginning of the Battle of Belmont, Stewart's Battery engaged the Federal fleet, suffering the loss of two killed and one wounded, when one of its guns exploded. It appears that Stewart's Battery was subsequently ordered to Belmont, where it could better support the ground forces. Hughes, 67.

70. There is no indication in the *Official Records* that the Federal gunboats ever engaged the rebel transports as they crossed the Mississippi River to Belmont. However, Federal shore batteries did shell the transports, scoring some hits. *O.R.N.*. 22:426, passim.

71. The Fourth Tennessee and Twelfth Louisiana Infantries were the last of the rebel forces that arrived at Belmont. *O.R.*, 3:353.

"Here's The Place!"

Once on the bank, the smokey woods were open and obstructed only by Federal corpses—obviously the fighting ground of the national left, while the Confederates were clinging to the fallen timber and the Federal right swinging around upon Pillow's left flank.[72] A few moments' investigation revealed that, and the small detachment hurried back and reported the available route. The work of getting the artillery up then began. But it was arduous, and could not be hurried beyond an exasperating limit. All the other reinforcements, moving swiftly, were soon deep in the forest, their muskets crashing as they one by one discovered the circuitously fleeing foe. [Samuel] Marx's [Marks] Louisiana regiment[73] opened at close range on the running road full, within half a mile of the abatis, and followed, firing for four miles, or to the transports. The One Hundred and Fifty-fourth Tennessee,[74] a fairly fleet-footed regiment, could not "catch up" until the transports were cutting their cables, but they "got in" some close volleys then and there.[75]

---

72. During the thirty minute lull in the battle, the Federals celebrated, raising the stars and stripes upon Camp Johnston's flagpole. The band of the Twenty-second Illinois, which had accompanied the expedition as the "hospital corps," had their instruments and struck up a number of patriotic tunes. All was cheer before the storm as the jubilant Federals seemed to forget about their recently defeated foes and more so, the newly arriving Confederate reinforcements. Looting began. Meanwhile, General Frank Cheatham had arrived on the scene and buoyed Pillow's defeated men into assuming the offensive. The Eleventh Louisiana and Fifteenth Tennessee had also been active, moving around the flank of Grant's command, and setting the stage for a reverse of what had previously happened to the rebels at Belmont. Grant, being informed of the rebels landing in his rear, ordered a retreat at the double-quick. It was barely in time. Cheatham struck first, at about 2:30 p.m. with about 1,000–1,500 men of Pillow's previous forces. After fifteen minutes the Unionists buckled and headed for the safety of their boats; all semblance of order appeared lost. The Eleventh and Fifteenth, under Colonel Samuel Marks, to the right of Cheatham moved forward, serving as a blocking position for the Federals now trapped in Belmont. Grant ordered his command to cut its way through to the boats. Logan's Thirty-first Illinois led the way, pushing aside Marks's force, Grant's men hurried to the boats, leaving the road cluttered with their accouterments of war. Hughes, 127, 129–130, 138, 140, 142–145, 148–149, 153, 155; Harrell, *Arkansas, Confederate Military History,* 62; Seaton, 15:313.
73. The Eleventh Louisiana Infantry Regiment was organized in Baton Rouge, Louisiana in July 1861, and mustered into the Confederate Service on August 24, 1861. Samuel Marks was the unit's only commander. After Belmont the Eleventh was captured at Island Number No. 10 and exchanged. The regiment fought at Shiloh and was at the Siege of Corinth in May 1862. Colonel Marks, born about 1804, was a veteran of the Mexican War, a staunch Democrat and a resident of New Orleans at the beginning of the Civil War. Marks was later wounded at Shiloh on April 6, 1862, survived the war, but died in poverty in 1871. *O.R.,* vol. 10, pt. 1:421, 820; *O.R.S.,* pt. 2, vol. 36:235; Crute, 148; Hughes, 41, 217.
74. The 154th Senior Tennessee Infantry Regiment was first organized as a militia unit in 1842. The unit reorganized in May 14, 1861, to serve for one year, and was allowed to keep it original number. The unit fought at Belmont and other sites east of the Mississippi River. On May 3, 1862, the regiment was reorganized at Corinth, Mississippi, to serve for three years or the war. It was consolidated with the Thirteenth Tennessee Infantry in April 1863. The unit survived the war and was surrendered on April 26, 1865. Its commander at the beginning of the Civil War was Preston Smith. *O.R.S.,* pt. 2, vol. 67:188–189; Crute, 314.
75. The Federal troops began boarding transports at 2:40 p.m. and were finished by 4:00 p.m., except for the Twenty-seventh Illinois, which took a circuitous rout to the Mississippi River. By 4:00 p.m.

The Fourth Tennessee, tied to the battery, saw only the beginning of the foot-race, but they saw enough to eventually remember Belmont as the most effectually followed up victory and the most thoroughly cleaned-up battlefield they have ever seen or trod.

One of the Ten.

* * * * * * *

Item: The Battle of Salem, Missouri (December 3, 1861), by F. W. Fry, Tom Freeman's command.
Published: February 20, 1886.

Good Intentions, But Bad Luck.

Boulder, Colo., Feb. 11
Editor, *Republican*

Being a subscriber to the *Weekly Republican* I have read with pleasure the War Tales. Generally they are the first thing I read when I get the paper. Without commenting on what has been written, I will try to tell in a plain way something about the first fight I participated in, at least, the first in which anyone was killed.

The morning of December 2, 1861, Col. Tom Freeman,[76] with about 150 men,[77] started from in or near the south edge of Dent County, Missouri, to Salem,

---

Confederate units had arrived at the river and began shooting into the transports with but a small effect. To protect the embarkation, the *Lexington* and *Tyler* began shelling the shore, which eventually discouraged the Confederates. Meanwhile, the Twenty-seventh Illinois, under Colonel N. B. Burford, marched about three miles north of the regular embarkation point, flagged down the transport *Chancellor*, and arranged for the regiment's pickup even as the sun was setting. The Federals for their part lost 95 killed, 306 wounded and 205 missing; total 606 (total includes naval losses). The Confederates lost 120 killed, 431 wounded; total 551. Grant reported capturing 175 prisoners, while a period newspaper reported the number as 184. Polk reported his missing as 117, killed 105 and wounded as 419; total 641. The discrepancy in the reported losses is the difference between what regimental commanders reported and what the overall commanders reported. Most likely, some of the missing returned and the less wounded were discounted from the final casualty lists *O.R.*, 3:272, 281, 285; *O.R.N..*, 22:780; Hughes, 162–163, 184–185; "Our Troops At Belmont," *Chicago Daily Tribune*, November 15, 1861.

76. Thomas R. Freeman was born about 1828. He was from Phelps County, Missouri, and commanded the Sixth Infantry Regiment (mounted), Seventh Division, MSG. Captured on February 14, 1862, at Crane Creek, Missouri, with twenty-nine of his men, Freeman was imprisoned first at Myrtle Street Prison in St. Louis, then was transferred to Alton (Illinois) Prison on March 3, 1862, where he was locally paroled on June 18. On September 23, 1862, he was sent to Vicksburg for exchange. In 1863, Freeman operated as a guerrilla leader in southern Missouri. On January 26, 1864, he organized a regular cavalry regiment, which he led in Price's 1864 Missouri Raid. During the raid General Shelby gave Freeman the command of a brigade, which he led until his surrender to Federal authorities on May 11, 1865. He was paroled on June 5, 1865 and returned to Missouri. Peterson, 206; Schnetzer, *More Forgotten Men,* 85; Eakin, *Missouri Prisoners of War,* "Freeman, Thos. R." entry; *Branded As Rebels,* 152; National Archives, Record Group M322, Compiled Service Records, Freeman's Cavalry Regiment.

77. Federal reports put the rebels at 300 men under Colonels Tom Freeman and Lynch Turner, while the *St. Louis Democrat* reported that the rebels, commanded by Lynch Turner had 130 men. Peterson, 200; *Rebellion Record*, December 3, 1861, diary entry, 100–101.

the county seat, for the purpose of routing, killing and capturing some Federal soldiers that were there.[78]

About 3 o'clock a.m. on the 3d we were within half a mile of the town, where we dismounted, and tying our horses and leaving a few men with them, and marching towards town (if I remember correctly) from the west side. As we got near the outer edge of the village a few of our men turned north, where we could see a picket fire, and before the Federals were aware of the presence of an enemy our men

Had Fired on Them.[79]

Some of us had formed an irregular line, about fifty yards from a fence running north and south, and as soon as the pickets were fired on, one of them came darting down between us and the fence, and was fired on by our crowd, horse and rider both going down together, but getting up immediately. The horse starting back and the man turning the corner and running down the street. For our first battle this was exciting, and a volley was sent after him which brought him down. Whether he was killed or not I don't know, but as I passed him I could see he was stretched at the full length on his back, and some of our boys were going to pull his big boots off, something a good many of us needed badly.

A short distance further on was a small frame house in which were encamped Federal soldiers.[80] This we at once attacked by firing in at the windows, they in turn firing through the windows at us. This was kept up for some time, with what loss to those inside I can't say. We had two killed within fifteen feet of the house. I was standing near the back end of the house with Capt. Dodd, and just to my left was a man by the name of York. Right near his feet was a man lying on the ground dead, I think,

With His Brains Shot Out.

York was shot in the breast, was carried back and died in a few minutes, I was told. Just about this time two men—a lieutenant and sergeant—came out of the north door of the kitchen, apparently with the intention of charging on us, probably expecting others to follow them. But they had hardly got outside the door before Capt. Dodd and I had our guns leveled on them and ordered them to surrender which they did in much less time than I can tell about it. Very shortly after this we

---

78. On November 29, 1861, Major William D. Bowen left Rolla with a force of 120 men from Companies A, B, C and D, of the First Battalion Missouri Cavalry (Union)—30 men to a company. They arrived at Salem the same day and scouted the area on Sunday and Monday, securing eight prisoners. According to Major Bowen the attack occurred at 4:00 a.m. on December 3. *O.R.*, 8:33–34.

79. The Confederates had gotten inside the Federal picket line without being detected. According to Bowen's account, the rebels first fired on Company A, who were quartered in one of the houses of Salem. Bowen makes no mention, in his official report, that his picket was attacked. Ibid., 8:34; *Rebellion Record*, December 3, 1861, diary entry, 100–101.

80. This would be Company A, First Missouri Cavalry Battalion (Union). *O.R.*, 8:34.

heard the clatter of horses' feet coming up the street in front of the house. We had previously heard the bugle-call not very far away. When we heard cavalry coming it made quite a commotion in the crowd.[81] I moved to the south of the building and a few paces in front, and took as good aim as could in the dim light and fired at the moving body of horsemen in the street. As I turned to reload my squirrel rifle the ground about the house seemed to be almost deserted. The cavalry by this time were coming around the house on the north side, shooting and yelling at a fearful rate. I suppose our boys though it was not safe for them to stay there, and they had a great many of them skipped. I was probably scared as bad as any of them, but I tried to halt them, and as I could not do that I

Kept Pretty Close

to some of them that were trying to keep ahead of the bullets.

We ran about 300 yards and stopped for breath and could hear the occasional shot, but the fight was over and the Feds had driven us from the battlefield.[82] Just how many were killed and wounded on either side I never knew.[83] Besides the two I mentioned, George Brenner of St. Louis was killed, Capt. Dodd was wounded, left on the ground and died from the effects of his wound. Lieut. Dave Sigler was wounded in the knee. A man by the name of Pace was wounded in the thigh.

Lieut. Doley[84] captured a fine horse, saddled and bridled. About the close of the war I heard that he was captured in Franklin County by the militia, butchered like a hog and cut into pieces. Whether this is true or not I can't say. Some of the Home Guard so-called were none too good for such deeds. Doley was a brave and daring man.

I hope this is read by someone that can give more interesting account of the Salem fight.

---

81. After the fight began Bowen rallied the other three companies of his command, which were quartered about 500 yards (a local newspaper puts the distance at 100 yards) from Company A. Bowen led Companies B and C on foot to engage the rebels, while Captain Martin H. Williams led Company D in a cavalry charge down the street on the dismounted Confederates. Ibid.; *Rebellion Record*, December 3, 1861, diary entry, 100–101.
82. The combat between the dismounted foes took about twenty minutes followed by the cavalry charge, which quickly dispersed the rebel command. *O.R.*, 8:34.
83. Federal reports put their losses at 2 killed, 2 mortally wounded and 8 "slightly wounded," and the rebel losses at 6 killed, 10 mortally wounded and 20 slightly wounded. There was no indication of how the Federals came up with the rebel losses, though one period newspaper recorded: "Many of the rebels were killed and wounded, but the number was not ascertained." The *Chicago Daily Tribune* put the Confederate losses at "10 killed and 30 wounded, besides a great number of prisoners." Ibid., 8:34; *Rebellion Record*, December 3, 1861, diary entry, 100–101; "Fight Near Rolla," *Chicago Daily Tribune*, December 4, 1861.
84. Possibly August Dole, of Franklin County. Dole had killed two Missouri State Militia men in 1863, was caught in Dent County and sent to Rolla. On May 2, 1863, he was hanged at St. Clair, instead of being transferred to Franklin County for trial. Dole was "'a desperate individual' who had murdered, robbed and threatened Franklin County citizens." *Branded As Rebels*, 115.

F. W. Fry.[85]

* * * * * * *

Item: The Battle of Mt. Zion Church, Boone County, Missouri, December 28, 1861, by A. J. Coshow, late member of the St. Charles County Company (Captain Charles M. Johnson), Caleb Dorsey's Regiment, Second Division, Missouri State Guard.[86]
Published: October 9, 1886.

Battle Of Mt. Zion, MO.[87]

Dallas, Tex., Sept. 29
Editor, *Republican*
The undersigned was serving the third term as justice of the peace in Femme Osage Township, St. Charles County, Missouri, and because I would not take the Drake iron-clad oath,[88] it was talked around that I would be placed in prison for non-compliance, so on Sunday, the 16th of December, 1861, one Charles Kruger,[89] a German, raised by Willis B. Hays, now deceased, was at my home, and I asked him if he could find a chance for me getting to Gen. Price to let me know it. On the

---

85. Probably Francis W. Fry of Glenco, St. Louis County. After his service under Freeman, Fry enlisted in the "3 Battery Light Artillery," under William E. Dawson on December 24, 1861. Dawson commanded the "Saint Louis Light Artillery," while James C. Gorham commanded what would be known as the Third Missouri Light Artillery. In the MSG, Gorham's command was known as the Second Light Artillery, but later became the Third. Though not designated by a number, Dawson's command could have been the Third Battery in the MSG. Schnetzer, *More Forgotten Men*, 86; Peterson, 192, 293; Eakin, *Confederate Records*, 3:77–78.

86. Andrew J. Coshow, a descendent of Welsh immigrants who settled in St. Charles County in 1800, was born on February 21, 1815. He enlisted in the MSG in early December 1861—Charles M. Johnson's Company. The company was organized near Pauldingsville, St. Charles County, shortly thereafter. Johnson's Company was with Dorsey's regiment for only a few days and "voluntarily surrendered" in early January 1862. Peterson, 102; Eakin, *Confederate Records*, 2:106–107; Eakin, *Confederate Records*, 4:140; *History of St. Charles, Montgomery, and Warren Counties, Missouri, Written and Compiled From the Most Authentic Official and Private Sources, Including A History of Their Townships, Towns and Villages* (St. Louis, 1885), 183, 233, hereafter cited as *History of St. Charles County*.

87. The Battle of Mount Zion Church occurred on December 28, 1861, between forces commanded by General B. M. Prentiss and Colonel Caleb Dorsey. It took place nine miles northeast of Columbia, Missouri, near the intersection with modern-day Highways "OO" and "Z." The original church was destroyed in September 1862, by Federal soldiers, and rebuilt in 1903, and still stands today. Neal Fandek, "Battle at the Church," *Rural Missouri* (Jefferson City, MO), December, 2006, 32; hereafter cited as Fandek.

88. The writer is a bit confused about the chronology of events in Missouri during the war. The so-called "Drake Iron-Clad Oath" was proposed by St. Louis Radical Party member Charles D. Drake during the Missouri state convention of January 1865. "Community on Conflict: The Impact of the Civil War in the Ozarks: Postwar Politics," http://www.ozarkscivilwar.org/archives/458 (accessed November 28, 2009).

89. Charles Kruger or Krugar, like Coshow, was also a member of Johnson's Company, having enlisted in December 1861. Eakin, *Confederate Records*, 5:32; *History of St. Charles County*, 184.

19th C. K. came to my house and said a lot of men were to meet at Hay's Mill[90] to start. I met them that evening and went that night to Tuque Prairie. Next evening there was a general rendezvous from St. Charles and Warren Counties in the hills south of Hickory Grove.[91] We left there about 2 o'clock before day, eighty-four strong, with Dr. C. M. Johnson[92] as our captain. We traveled several days, until we got in sight of Col. Jeff Jones's farm,[93] when we met that one-handed man, [Alvin] Cobb,[94] and his fifteen men. After parlaying sometime, all turned back to Wil-

---

90. Hays Mill was one of the oldest mills in St. Charles County, being built on Femme Osage Creek. It was probably owned by a Daniel Hays a noted miller and Indian Fighter. *History of St. Charles County*, 116, 249; Daniel T. Brown, *Westering River, Westering Trail: A History of St. Charles County, Missouri to 1849* (St. Charles, MO, 2006), 125, 272, hereafter cited as Brown.

91. Hickory Grove was located about five miles southwest of Wright City, in eastern Warren County. *Atlas to Accompany the Official Records*, plt. 152.

92. Charles Montgomery Johnson was born on January 28, 1826, and his family moved to St. Charles County, Missouri, in 1835. He initially attended St. Charles College and began his study of medicine under Dr. John G. Tannor. Later he completed his medical education at the University of Pennsylvania, where he obtained his degree in 1850. Returning to Missouri, Johnson took up residence in Warrenton, then Troy, and in 1861, settled in the family homestead (the old Daniel Boone house). With the outbreak of the Civil War, Johnson organized a MSG infantry company, in December 1861, was captured at Mount Zion Church and was released on January 10, 1862, after taking the oath of allegiance. Johnson returned to his home and practiced medicine and in 1865, took up permanent residence in St. Charles City. Brown, 316; *History of St. Charles County*, 183–184, 230, 397–398; Eakin, *Confederate Records*, 4:140.

93. Colonel Jefferson F. Jones was born on November 6, 1817, in Montgomery County, Kentucky, and moved to Missouri at a young age. Educated in Fulton, Missouri, Jones lived in Callaway County at the beginning of the Civil War and appears to have never been regularly enrolled in either the MSG or the Confederate Army. Jones organized the "Callaway County Home Guard Defense Regiment" in September 1861; its sole purpose, "to suffer no invasion of [Callaway] County." Jones disbanded his regiment shortly after its formation and he was arrested in December 1861, for allegedly destroying the North Missouri Railroad. Acquitted, in the spring of 1862, Jones accepted parole, being confined in Callaway and Audrain Counties. During the remainder of the war Jones was arrested and released several times. In 1864, he was banished from Missouri, but was subsequently jailed in Gratiot Street Prison on May 29, 1864. Jones was still a prisoner, being held in the Myrtle Street Prison in St. Louis, on May 11, 1865, despite having taken the oath of allegiance on January 20, 1865. He returned to Callaway County after the war and died on January 24, 1879. Bartels, *Forgotten Men*, 190–191; Peterson, 103; Eakin, *Missouri Prisoners of War*, "Jones, Jeff F." entry; Griffin Frost, *Camp and Prison Journal* (Quincy, IL, 1867; reprint ed., Iowa City, IA, 1994), 288–292; Eakin, *Confederate Records*, 4:152.

94. Alvin Cobb was a resident of Montgomery County, having come to Missouri in 1847. At the beginning of the Civil War, he organized a small guerrilla band and later participated in the engagement at Mount Zion. He was a "mountaineer...forty-five years old—six feet tall, symmetrically formed, and weighing about one hundred and eighty...His hair hangs down to his shoulders, and his face...covered with beard,...reaching to the waist. His eyes are grey and piercing. He looks but little like a military man," particularly since his right hand was replaced by an awesome looking hook; he had accidentally shot off his arm. Cobb was an active guerrilla in 1861–1863, in Missouri. He survived the war, being "paroled out of the service." Later years found Cobb in the Indian Territory and in 1885 he was living in California. "The Rebel Col. Alvin Cobb," *Weekly California News* (California, MO), August 23, 1862; Joseph A. Mudd, *With Porter in North Missouri: A Chapter In the History of the War Between the States* (Washington, 1909), 159–160; *Branded As Rebels*, 82; Eakin, *Confederate Records*, 2:73; "Col. Cobb," *Columbia Missouri Statesman* (Columbia, MO), August 28, 1863.

liamsburg that night. Next night we went down to Danville.[95] There we got a scare and started west again, reaching Grand View at noon. After I partook of a small allowance of corn bread and beef (all cold), we were sworn in by a man who said he was a recruiting officer. We then elected our officers. I recollect only part of the officers' names; Caleb Dorsey,[96] Colonel; Thos. Brackenridge [Breckinridge][97] of St. Louis County, major; Dr. [C. M.] Pringle,[98] second lieutenant. The reason I have forgotten the names of the other officers is that after electing our officers we started for Mount Zion Church, in Boone County, to camp for the night with Isaac Chrisman[99] as pilot. We traveled southwest a mile or so, when forty-six Federals from Centralia

---

95. Johnson's Company was traveling west from St. Charles County, heading to Mount Zion Church. Williamsburg was located in eastern Callaway County, about seven miles west of Danville. Danville was located in Montgomery County, and about five miles from the North Missouri Railroad. Based upon Coshow's description, the company backtracked to Danville. *Atlas to Accompany the Official Records*, plt. 152.

96. Caleb Dorsey was born about 1833, and lived in Pike County at the beginning of the Civil War. He joined the MSG on June 27, 1861, being elected captain of a cavalry company from Pike County, in which position he served for six months. In December 1861, he organized an infantry regiment, in the Second Division, MSG, being elected colonel on December 27, 1861, at Greenville, Missouri, near Mount Zion Church. The following day his command was attacked and destroyed, though Dorsey escaped. He was captured on February 13, 1862, near the Osage River, while on recruiting service and was imprisoned at Alton Prison. Exchanged in August 1862, Dorsey returned to the Trans-Mississippi Department, where he enlisted in the regular Confederate Army, serving under Joseph Shelby. Dorsey rose to the rank of lieutenant colonel, was wounded twice under Shelby, and served until the end of the war. *O.R.*, 53:824; *O.R.*, Series 2, 1:441, 444; 4:437; 7:414; Bartels, *Forgotten Men*, 92; Eakin, *Missouri Prisoners of War*, "Dorsey, Caleb" entry; John Newman Edwards, *Shelby and His Men or the War in the West* (Cincinnati, OH, 1867; reprint ed., Waverly, MO, 1993), 502; Hale, 87; Peterson, 102; Schnetzer, *More Forgotten Men*, 67.

97. Thomas Breckinridge was wounded in right arm and the left breast and died a short time later. "Fight At Mount Zion," *Rebellion Record* 3:DOC 514.

98. Dr. Charles M. Pringle was born on March 14, 1824, in Hickory Grove, Missouri, educated by private tutors and received his formal medical training from the Missouri Medical College (McDowell's Medical College) in St. Louis. After medical school he returned to his farm, northeast of Foristell, Missouri, where he practiced medicine until the beginning of the Civil War. Pringle joined Johnson's MSG company in December 1861, in St. Charles, Missouri. In one source he was listed as the regimental surgeon of Dorsey's regiment, while another has Eugene W. Herndon as Dorsey's regimental surgeon. Pringle returned to his Hickory Grove farm after his short stint in the army and later relocated to Foristell in 1872. Married, Pringle and his wife had twelve children. Eakin, *Confederate Records*, 6:129; Peterson, 102; *History of St. Charles County*, 184, 521–522.

99. Isaac A. Chrisman or Chrismon was the eldest son of William and Margaret Chrismon. Upon marriage he lived his entire life in Maries County, Missouri. On August 10, 1862, he enlisted in the Tenth Missouri Infantry and was elected a lieutenant in Company K. Chrisman was promoted to first lieutenant on June 9, 1863, was captured at Helena, Arkansas, on July 4, and sent to Alton Prison. Wounded during a prison break in which he did not participate, Chrisman lost an arm and received the moniker "One-Armed Ike." He was sent to Johnson's Island in September 1863, survived the war, and returned to Missouri where he lived a fruitful life, raising eight children. Wayne H. Schnetzer, *Men of the Tenth: A Roster of the Tenth Missouri Infantry Confederate States of America* (Independence, MO, 1999.), 100; Eakin, *Missouri Prisoners of War*, "Chrisman, Isaac" entry; *History of Boone County, Missouri, Written and Compiled From the Most Authentic Official and Private Sources, Including a History of Its Townships, Towns and Villages* (St. Louis, 1882), 475–476, hereafter cited as *History of Boone County*.

Had A Fight

with our rear guard.[100] One of our rear guard came up with us in Parson Crisman's [Chrisman][101] lane in the evening, one mile before reaching the church. then Dr. [C. M.] Johnson ordered his men to follow him, so we went over one mile north, when we spied them going north on Hawsville [Hallsville] road. We gave them chase about three miles, when they threw down a stubble-field fence on the north and entered and commenced firing at us. As we were only one hundred and fifty yards distant, the balls passed over us. At this time it was getting dark, and I could see the blaze of their guns, and thence was the first time I ever heard a minnie ball whistle. None of us were wounded. We got three prisoners. One was a captain.[102] Capt. Johnson sent the prisoner to camp at the church. We started back some two miles and came to a place where we could lie in ambush on both sides of the road. We lay there for some time, like waiting for a deer to come to a deer lick. Then we went to the church, about 11 o'clock at night, as the ground had been covered with ice and snow for six days. I saw the men on brush piles for bedsteads. So after feeding our horses corn and hay, of which there was plenty, I crowded into the church with two stoves and was crowded, so I crawled in by a man that looked like he had more bed covering than one man needed. I asked him who he was; he replied, a prisoner. I was too sleepy and tried to think of the danger of getting

---

100. On December 23, 1861, General Benjamin Prentiss departed Palmyra, Missouri, heading to Sturgeon in the search for bridge burners, who were active on the North Missouri Railroad. His command consisted of six companies of the Third Missouri Cavalry, 240–300 men. They arrived at Sturgeon at 7:00 p.m., "having made a forced march, in the face of a bitter cold wind." Shortly after his arrival at Sturgeon, Prentiss was informed by Colonel John W. Birge, the commander of Sturgeon, that a sixty to eighty-man force of rebels was located at Mount Zion Church. On December 27, Prentiss dispatched Captain James T. Howland, with forty-six men of Company A (*Official Records Supplement* puts the strength at 67 men, while another source puts it at 46—the same as the author of the piece) to check out the information. Howland journeyed to Mount Zion, confirmed the report, and when returning to Sturgeon, encountered the rear guard of Colonel Dorsey's command two miles from Hallsville (about six miles southwest of Centralia). In the ensuing engagement on the twenty-seventh, which lasted about half an hour, Howland was wounded and captured with some of his men. The remainder of Howland's company made it back to Sturgeon and reported the information from their scout, thus setting the stage for the engagement at Mount Zion Church. "Account of the Battle By One Who Was Engaged In It," *Rebellion Record*, 3:DOC 516, hereafter cited as "Account of the Battle"; "Missouri 'Democrat' Account," *Rebellion Record*, 3:DOC 515, hereafter cited as "Missouri 'Democrat' Account"; *Atlas to Accompany the Official Records*, plt. 152; *O.R.*, 8:43–45, 439, 501, 694, 696–697, 702, 706; *O.R.S.*, pt. 2, vol. 50:684; Fandek.

101. This was probably Parson Elijah E. Chrisman a longtime resident of Boone County, Missouri. During his lifetime, Parson Chrisman founded several churches in the area. At the time of the Civil War he was the pastor of the Hickory Grove Christian Church, located on the eastern border of Warren County, near present day Foristell. These was no indication that Parson Chrisman had any children, but was probably a relative of Isaac and not his father as the writer will later indicate. *History of Boone County*, 1113–1114, 1116; Brown, 345.

102. This was Captain James T. Howland, commander of Company A, Third Missouri Cavalry. In addition to Howland, the *Official Records* stated that one man was taken, while another account has Captain Howland with three men being made prisoner. *O.R.*, 8:44; "Account of the Battle."

graybacks on me. Next morning, December 28th, I was up early and fed my horse. I knew the first ones to the feed pile would get plenty. While rubbing my horse I heard someone call out: "All that want to go out and see the battle ground get ready." So I saddled up, mounted and rode up in the crowd. It proved to be Capt. Johnson. He and I rode in front, as I was the oldest man in the command (over 46 years old), and near 100 followed. When passing Parson Crisman's house he invited us to stop on our return and feed our horses and

Take Breakfast,

so we proceeded near one mile north when we saw Gen. [Benjamin M.] Prentiss[103] with his 400 cavalry coming towards us about two miles distant.[104] We proceeded down into a flat and as we went up the hill in the lane the fence was thrown down on either side; all turned in either field about equal, but Dr. Johnson and my cousin

Van Zumwalt, rode in the lane to the top of the ridge. The ridge runs square across the lane. Also, there was a rail worm fence on either side with large peach trees in every corner. Dr. Johnson's orders were not to fire until he fired. The slope up to us was about 150 yards. They commenced firing as they started up the hill. When Prentiss's men got half way up Capt. Johnson fired his revolver, then we all fired, then mounted and started for the church. One of our men were killed and three wounded slightly and several taken prisoners.[105] The prisoners were

---

103. Benjamin M. Prentiss was born on November 23, 1819, in Bellville, Virginia (now West Virginia), moved to Missouri in 1836, and to Quincy, Illinois, in 1841. During the Mexican War, he commanded a company in the First Illinois Infantry, and thereafter studied law and ran an unsuccessful campaign for the U.S. Congress in 1860. At the beginning of the Civil War, Prentiss was elected colonel of the Tenth Illinois Infantry and on August 9, 1861, he was appointed brigadier general to rank from May 17. Prentiss served in Missouri for a short time until he was appointed commander of the Sixth Division, Army of the Tennessee on March 26, 1862. At the Battle of Shiloh, Prentiss commanded the division that held the "Hornet's Nest," which after heavy fighting, he was forced to surrender. Exchanged in October 1862, Prentiss served on the court martial of General Fitz-John Porter, and then was assigned to eastern Arkansas in February 1863. Prentiss won the Battle of Helena on July 4, 1863, but resigned from the army on October 28, 1863, citing health concerns. Returning to Quincy, he took up law and eventually moved to Bethany, Missouri, where he died on February 8, 1901. Warner, *Generals in Blue*, 385–386; Boatner, 667–668; Sifakis, *Union*, 322.

104. After Prentiss received word of the rebel location, he immediately organized an expedition to attack the Confederates at Mount Zion Church. At 2:00 a.m. on December 28, Prentiss's command of 470 men, marched for Mount Zion. In addition to the units of the Third Missouri Cavalry (Prentiss says he took only five companies, other sources, including the *Supplement to the Official Records* say he took all six), Prentiss also took five companies of John W. Birge's Missouri Sharpshooter Regiment (about 150 men; Companies A, B, D, G, and H). At 8:00 a.m., the Federals made contact with the 100-man scouting party led by Captain Johnson. *O.R.S.*, pt. 2, vol. 12:692, 697, 703, 714; "Account of the Battle"; "Missouri 'Democrat' Account."

105. In the initial contact, Prentiss ordered two companies of the sharpshooters to flank Johnson's command while Company B, Third Missouri Cavalry, under Lieutenant John W. Yates, dismounted and engaged them from the front with their Sharp's Carbines. Yates's command, which had been the advance guard of Prentiss's force, had been engaged but a few minutes when General Prentiss ordered Captain George D. Bradway, with Company E, Third Missouri Cavalry, to launch a mounted

exchanged that evening as we had been picking up some in our march up the country. When we got near the church about 200 formed in line. The balance of the rebs left, going west, taking with them wagons, teams and all the ammunition except what we had on our person. Well, when we formed in line the feds commenced firing at us when they were 200 yards distance. They aimed so high they shot off twigs far above our heads. Only one man so far as I know was hit. His right leg below the knee was shattered while he was near me. He was one of Capt. [Lycurgus] James' infantry of Warren County.[106] I was told the next day that the strap of his boot was struck by a spent ball. He hopped around and then sat down at a root of a tree and called for the surgeon. About this time someone in our rear ordered a charge, so we did charge down the hill and up the slope to the west and of the lane in front of Mr. Roberts' house, where lay

A Dozen Or More

dead and wounded men. Some prisoners were taken before they could unhitch and mount their horses.[107] By their retreating east half a mile, then north half a mile, they met Col. Birge's sharp-shooters.[108] Then we retraced our steps and formed

---

assault against the rebels on the hill. Bradway easily broke the Confederate line, killing 4–5, wounding 7 and capturing between 7–20 prisoners. Johnson's survivors fled the scene and warned the rest of the command, which had already formed near the church. Meanwhile, Prentiss had questioned his prisoners and obtained information on their numbers and camp location. Prentiss found that Dorsey's Confederates numbered between 350–900 men. *O.R.*, 8:44; *O.R.S.*, pt. 2, vol. 34:684, 706; "Account of the Battle"; Fandek; A. W. M. Petty, *A History of the Third Missouri Cavalry From Its Organization At Palmyra, Missouri, 1861 Up to November Sixth, 1864: With An Appendix and Recapitulation* (Little Rock, AR, 1865; reprint ed., Albany, MO, 1997), 98, hereafter cited as Petty.

106. Lycurgus James, according to Peterson, commanded the Montgomery County Company of Dorsey's Regiment; George Carter was listed as the commander of the Warren County Company. James enlisted in John Q. Burbridge's Infantry Regiment at the beginning of the Civil War as a private, having fought at Carthage, Wilson's Creek, Drywood Creek, and Lexington, before being mustered out of the service. He returned home to Boone County and later raised a 50-man company from Montgomery County. In December 1861, James's command was actively involved in tearing up the tracks of the North Missouri Railroad, before joining Dorsey's Regiment at Mount Zion Church. Peterson, 103; *Branded As Rebels*, 235; Schnetzer, *More Forgotten Men*, 124.

107. After a short delay, Prentiss's command moved forward to assault the main Confederate camp. Major Robert Carrick advanced to develop the enemy position with thirty dismounted men of Company C, Third Missouri Cavalry, hitting the enemy left in the woods. However, Prentiss failed to move the remainder of the command quickly enough to support Carrick, resulting in the loss of 3 killed, several wounded with the loss of 10 prisoners. *O.R.*, 8:44; "Account of the Battle"; "Missouri 'Democrat' Account."

108. The author was referring to John W. Birge's Missouri Sharpshooters, the Fourteenth Missouri Infantry. Originally a Home Guard unit, the regiment was mustered in on November 23, 1861, after which it served for a short time in Missouri, being engaged at Mount Zion Church. In early January 1862, the unit moved to Cairo, Illinois, and never returned to the Trans-Mississippi region. During its history, the regiment was claimed by both Missouri and Illinois, until on April 22, 1862, it was transferred to Illinois, where it was known as the Sixty-sixth Illinois Infantry. John W. Birge only served with the regiment until November 1861. *Union Army*, 4:262; Dyer, 1329; National Archives, Compiled Service Records, Missouri Home Guard, Record Group M405, roll no. 706.

on the other ridge near and east of the church.[109] Then the feds in force came for us. Then is when the rebs went dodging through the brush like wild turkeys. I was told afterwards that some of them, from 10 o'clock a.m. until daylight next morning, went over seventy miles on an empty stomach. Now to the second charge.[110] When I was wounded in the left hand, I started to run like an old turkey. As I was about to pass the church, with my hand bleeding, our second lieutenant (Dr. Pringle) was cutting around there on his roan bob-tailed pony. He called to me to go on into the church, as it was our hospital. I went in very quick and found several of our wounded men, and several doctors of the neighborhood; also the prisoners and their guards. At this time the feds surrounded the church and broke the glass in windows, but were prevented from shooting by the prisoners flocking to the windows. Then they came in and searched the most of us.[111] Presently Frank Henderson[112] and some other man entered with a flag of truce. After a conversation with Gen. Prentiss, it was agreed on for old Parson Crisman to haul in our killed and wounded, which was eight killed and twenty-eight wounded. The feds had Mr. Roberts' house as their hospital. I was told the next day they had thirty-two killed and fifty-seven wounded; some so badly that two died before they got back

---

109. While Carrick's small troop was engaged on the rebel left, Prentiss had organized the rest of his force for an assault on Dorsey's lines. The sharpshooters under Colonel Birge were to take the center through a still standing cornfield, while the cavalry under Colonel Glover moved to flank the enemy; one company of cavalry and one of the sharpshooters were kept in reserve. If executed correctly the maneuver was intended to surround Dorsey's command and capture the lot. However, the sharpshooters lost their way in the corn and became intermingled with the cavalry. Though the maneuver failed, it did stabilize the situation when the survivors of Carrick's assault came streaming back from the woods, where they had been overwhelmed. The moment lost, Glover dismounted his cavalry "as bushwhacking was the order of the day." "Account of the Battle"; "Missouri 'Democrat' Account."

110. For thirty minutes Glover's dismounted troopers and Birge's sharpshooters, with their long range rifles, poured round after round into the defending rebels. The Confederates, armed with a motley collection of shotguns and squirrel rifles answered as best they could and held their ground despite mounting casualties. Even though Dorsey's men had the advantage of cover, their short ranged weapons had only a limited effect on the Unionists they opposed. About 10:00 a.m., "Col. Glover gave the order to charge on the enemy. 'Come on men,' said he, 'let us fight them in their own way—let us bushwhack them. With a wild cheer" Glover's men, including the sharpshooters surged forward into the woods after Dorsey's overmatched men. The Confederates "were brave men, and fought well," according to one observer, but they were no match for the concerted Union effort. After ten minutes in the woods Dorsey's command broke and fled in every direction, with Unionists close on their tails. Birge's men stopped their pursuit after about a mile while the cavalry covered about two before they ended their romp. By 11:00 a.m. the battle was over. *O.R.*, 8:44; "Account of the Battle"; "Missouri 'Democrat' Account"; Fandek.

111. According to the *Missouri Republican*, Federal troops began firing into the church at first, but ceased firing when two Federal prisoners ran out shouting "There are no fighting men here! This is a hospital." Quoted in Fandek.

112. Frank or Francis C. Henderson was the Adjutant General of Dorsey's Regiment and arrived an hour after the battle to arrange for the burial of the dead and the caring for the wounded. After Zion Church, Henderson moved to Lincoln County, Missouri, where he was organizing a company when attacked at "Bob's Creek" near Troy. In the ensuing engagement Henderson was wounded and taken to Dr. Biscoe's near Warrenton, where he later died. *O.R.*, 8:330–331; "Account of the Battle"; Hale, 139.

to Centralia.[113] After leaving the church some of the Federal officers and privates stopped at old Parson Crisman's and called for dinner, and while eating one of the officers remarked to another officer that the dinner was very good one, and that it must have been cooked for them rebs. If you will recollect, Parson Crisman invited us in the morning to stop on our return and get breakfast; etc., but on our return we had no time to stop, as the cavalry were in hot pursuit. As I stated before that old Parson Chrisman was sent to collect

Our Killed And Wounded.

He called out that any of the wounded that wished, could get in his wagon and go to his house. His son Isaac, the two Bently brothers[114] from Montgomery County and your humble writer went in his wagon and while we were eating our dinners that old lady, Mrs. Chrisman, told us about the complaints passed on our breakfast that we failed to get, and that the feds had just finished up. I stayed under the hospital roof of Parson Crisman for fifteen days. Then James McKinney, a second cousin of mine, brought me a mare to go up about twenty miles west to cousin J. M. McKinney. I stayed there until the 12th day of March, when, I got on the steamer *Mill Boy,* commanded by Arch Bryan. There were a lot of Feds on the boat in charge of twelve rebs, bound for Gratiot Street Prison (McDowell's College).[115] Some of them asked why I was carrying my arm in a sling. The captain told them a young horse had thrown me and fractured my arm, so everything passed off quietly. I stayed the most of my time in the pilot house until I arrived at Missouriton landing, in Darst bottom, St. Charles County, where I was put ashore and walked home, one and a half mile distant. I got my parole before I left Boone County, signed by Col. Burge [Birge], etc. One thing occurred in our westward march worthy of mention in this sketch. On Sunday evening we got to Williamsburg, Callaway County; the snow was coming down fast and thick. I said to my

---

113. Like many battles of the Civil War, the reported losses varied based upon who provided the totals. Federal official reports put the Confederate losses at 25 killed, 150 wounded, with 30–35 prisoners, while reporting their own as 3–5 killed and 63 wounded. Several days after the battle Captain Johnson would surrender his entire company, another 60 men. Unofficial reports put Union dead at 6–9 with 15–25 wounded and as little as 2 killed and 5 wounded. *O.R.,* 8:44, 501; Dyer, 800; "Account of the Battle"; "Missouri 'Democrat' Account"; Petty, 10.

114. There are three known Bentlys from Montgomery County who served in Captain William Myer's Company, Dorsey's Regiment, MSG; John H., Joseph J. and William T. Of the three, John H. was captured at his home on January 1, 1862, sent to Alton Prison and was probably not one of the wounded Bentlys noted. Joseph J. and William T. would latter be taken into custody in 1862; William was sent East for exchange in 1863, while Joseph remained in Alton Prison until he took the oath and paid a bond in April 1865. Bartels, *Forgotten Men,* 20; Eakin, *Missouri Prisoners of War,* "Bently, John H., Joseph J., and Wm." entries; Schnetzer, *More Forgotten Men,* 20; Peterson, 102.

115. The McDowell Medical College Prison was renamed the Gratiot Street Military Prison on May 26, 1862. Gratiot served as the principle prison facility for prisoners of war and disloyal citizens in the St. Louis area. Its first prisoners were the men captured at Blackwater or Milford, Missouri, on December 19, 1861. Special Order No. 279, Provost Marshal General, Department of the Mississippi, May 26 1862, George E. Leighton Collection, box 1, folder 4, Missouri Historical Society; Winter, 79–80.

friend Charley Kruger that we would go up the hill and stay all night with Mr. [William R.] Kidwell,[116] as I had seen him before. When we got there fifteen had

Got There Before Us,

but the good lady took us in also, her husband being ten minutes off at his brother-in-law's store, and while we were eating our suppers, I remarked that my ears nearly froze that day, as my hair had been cut very short. A lady, a Miss McElhenny, a school-teacher boarding at Mr. Kidwell's, proposed to put covers on our hats for our ears from a muff she had, so I handed her my big white fur hat and I remarked that I was the oldest man in the crowd. There was near a dozen handed her. Next morning Miss McElhenny brought the hats in the parlor for us. We were very thankful for her kindness. Many were the favors we received from the heroic ladies on our nine day's march. After getting home I reported with a copy of my parole to the Provost Marshal, Arnold Krekel.[117] He and I were good friends. I was about the first young man he got acquainted with after landing in America. I was 71 years old the 14th of last February, and Judge Krekel is about my age. Now if any person I have named in this sketch wishes to correspond with me, they can direct to 1348 Elm Street, Dallas, Tex., I live seven and one half miles northeast from Dallas.

Yours truly,
A. J. Coshow.

* * * * * * *

116. William R. Kidwell was born in Fairfax County, Virginia, and later moved to Missouri, eventually settling in Williamsburg, where he raised ten children. When he first arrived in Missouri, he served as a local blacksmith and later ran a general merchandise store. In 1863, Kidwell was shot and killed while standing in his own doorway. *History of Callaway County, Missouri, Written and Compiled From the Most Authentic Official and Private Sources, Including a History of Its Townships, Towns and Villages* (St. Louis, 1883), 868, hereafter cited as *History of Callaway County*.

117. Arnold Krekel, arrived in Missouri in 1832, with his immigrant father and settled in St. Charles County. As a teeanger, Krekel attended St. Charles College for three years, then worked as a surveyor. In 1844 Krekel became a lawyer, and on January 1, 1852, he became the editor of the *St. Charles Democrat*. During the years preceding the Civil War, Krekel was active in politics, being elected to the Missouri Legislature in 1852 and subsequently nominated for Missouri Attorney General in both 1856 and 1860. A leader in the German community, Krekel helped organize the Union Home Guard of St. Charles County at the beginning of the Civil War and later became a colonel in the Missouri State Militia. His regiment, referred to as the "St. Charles County Regiment of Home Guards" or "Krekel's Dutch," was later reorganized as the First Battalion, Missouri State Militia. This unit disbanded in December 1862, and Krekel resigned from the army due to health concerns. However he remained active in Missouri politics after leaving the army, becoming a member of the Radical Union Party. He was president of the Missouri State Constitutional Convention in 1865 was and appointed a District Judge by President Lincoln, prior to the latter's death. He later moved to Jefferson City, then again relocated to Kansas City. Final disposition unknown. Anita M. Mallinckrodt, *A History of Augusta, Mo. and Its Area(I) 1850s–1860s As Reported In the St. Charles Demokrat* (Washington, MO, 1998), 5, 26, 55, 60, 83, 116; Ryle, 90, 93, 135; Gerteis, 75–76; *History of St. Charles County*, 107, 181–182, 199–200; Brown, 310.

Chapter 4

Missouri and the Confederacy

Item: The Confederate Government Support for Missouri, by General Daniel M. Frost.[1]
Published: February 20, 1886.

Gen. Frost's State Secret.

A remark concerning the failure of Gen. McCullough [McCulloch] to advance into Missouri to the support of Gen. Price in the latter part of 1861, made before the Southern Historical and Benevolent Society Friday night, led Gen. D. M. Frost to make a brief explanation of the situation in the West at the time, and why Gen. Price was not reinforced in Missouri, where, if he had remained, he might have soon collected about him a considerable army. The statement resulted in Gen. Frost's being requested to prepare a paper, to read before the society, on the failure of the Confederate government at Richmond to support any movements in Missouri and the effect that failure had upon the Confederacy. The brief statement, concerning the stand of the Richmond government, made by Gen. Frost was incorrectly reported by another paper yesterday, much to his annoyance. When questioned yesterday concerning the rebellion Gen. Frost said to a reporter of the Republican:

"After I had been a prisoner of war at Fort Jackson and released I started South, thinking that, for a time, it might be pleasant for me in that section. At Pitman's Ferry I met Gen. [William J.] Hardee,[2] whom I had met in the Mexican War

---

1. Daniel M. Frost was captured on May 10, 1861, when he surrendered Camp Jackson (St. Louis) to General Lyon. On October 26, 1861, Frost was exchanged with an effective date of November 2. Frost departed St. Louis on December 2, 1861, on aboard the steamer *Iatan* and stopped at Confederate-held Columbus, Kentucky, on December 3. Arriving at Memphis on December 9, Frost remained without a command until December 18, 1861, when he was assigned to command the Ninth Military District of Missouri. Frost then headed west to join Sterling Price, whom he met at Springfield, Missouri, in January 1862. *O.R.*, Series 2, 1:552–554, 558; Banasik, *Missouri Brothers in Gray*, 16, 91, 165; James E. McGhee, *Service With the Missouri State Guard: The Memoir of Brigadier General James Harding*. Springfield, MO: Oak Hills Publishing, 2000, 53, hereafter cited as McGhee, *Service With the Guard*; General Orders [no number] (December 18, 1861), Head Quarters Executive Department, Missouri, Mesker Papers, Box 1, Missouri Historical Society.
2. William J. Hardee was born in 1815, graduated from West Point in 1842 (number 26 of 45), fought in the Seminole War and the Mexican War, where he was captured and later exchanged. When Georgia seceded from the Union, Hardee resigned from the U.S. Army and was appointed a colonel in the Confederacy. Made a brigadier general in June 1861, Hardee was assigned to Arkansas for duty, where he organized his command at Pitman's Ferry in the summer of 1861. By the end of 1861, Hardee had transferred to the east side of the Mississippi River, where he completed his military service, rising to the rank of lieutenant general by the close of the war. He died in 1873. Boatner, 374. Pitman's

and with whom I was intimately acquainted. He was then in command of about 10,000 men at that point; but he was sorely dissatisfied with the organization in the West. In truth there was no organization, Missouri did not belong to the Confederacy, and the Missouri troops were only trying to defend themselves against the aggressions of the Federal troops. Gen. Price was then a major-general of the Missouri State Guard and commanded a few thousand men armed with shotguns and squirrel rifles. He was then going up to Lexington. Gen. McCullough had about 12,000 men in Northwest Arkansas, and he was entirely independent in his actions.[3] Gen. Hardee was also going it alone, and he suggested that I go on South, meet Gen. [Albert S.] Johnston[4] as soon as he appeared in the West,[5] lay the whole situation before him, and explain to him the necessity of concerted action in the state of Missouri. Gen. Price moved on toward Lexington, and at the insistence of Gen. Hardee I sought a

Conference With Gen. Albert Sidney Johnston,

whom I met at Columbus, [Kentucky] where Gen. Polk was in command of a small force. The conference was prolonged three days, beginning the day previous to and ending the day following our receiving the news of the taking of Lexington by Gen. Price.[6] Gen. Johnston had been given absolute control of the Confeder-

---

Ferry was located in northeast Arkansas, near the Missouri border on the Current River. From July–September, 1861, it served as the base of operations for William J. Hardee's command. On the surface, Frost could not have met Hardee at Pitman's Ferry before late December 1861, as Hardee had already departed the area and Frost was supposedly still on parole in St. Louis. By October 1861, Hardee was in Kentucky and nowhere near Pitman's Ferry. According to William Bull, Frost was in Jacksonport, Arkansas, in late December 1861, and nowhere near Hardee. However, there is evidence that Confederate soldiers captured at Camp Jackson, journeyed to the Confederate lines and later returned to St. Louis to "receive in person the certificate of exchange." There was no evidence that Frost ever did this, though, as will be seen in a later statement, Frost also says that he met with General Albert S. Johnston in late September 1861, at Columbus, Kentucky; again not feasible unless he left St. Louis and later returned to receive his exchange papers. Banasik, *Missouri Brothers in Gray*, 19–20; Banasik, *Embattled Arkansas*, 3; *O.R.*, 3:615, 702; *O.R.*, 4:444; *O.R.*, Series 2, 1:118.

3. Hardee's command in mid-September 1861, had 5,629 men present, just before he transferred his command to the east side of the Mississippi River. McCulloch's command had largely evaporated following the Battle of Wilson's Creek, leaving him with 5,743 men as an "Aggregate Present" on October 31, 1861, which included new acquisitions. Price, during this same time period reported between 10,000–12,000 men. *O.R.*, 3:702, 718, 730.

4. Albert Sydney Johnston was born in 1803, graduated from West Point (number 8 of 41) in 1826, served until 1834, when he resigned because of his wife's health. He fought in the Texas War for Independence, the Mexican War and was commissioned a colonel of the Second U.S. Cavalry in 1849. Johnston remained in the service until the beginning of the Civil War, resigning on April 10, 1861. Jefferson Davis gave Johnston the command of the Western Department, a position he held until his death at Shiloh, on April 6, 1862, while leading a charge. Boatner, 440.

5. Johnston was assigned to command Department No. 2 on September 10, 1861, and assumed his new post at Nashville five days later. *O.R.*, 4:405, 407.

6. Lexington fell on September 20, 1861, while Frost was a parolee. It appears that following his capture at Camp Jackson, Frost journeyed to the Confederate lines at Columbus, Kentucky, to confer with Johnston and Hardee, though there was no collaboration of the journey that I have found. Johnston was

ate forces west of the Allegheny Mountains, but he was a careful, considerate, conscientious man, and did not desire to take a step that he knew to be contrary to the desires of the Richmond government. I at once undertook to convince Gen. Johnston that the best interests of the Confederacy would be served by sending Gen. McCulloch and Gen. Hardee to the support of Price's rabble army, enabling a stand to be made on the Missouri River against Frémont's 40,000 men then stationed at St. Louis.[7] On the second day of the conference he could reply to the arguments I had advanced in favor of a campaign in Missouri by saying that it was contrary to the desire of Mr. Davis.[8] When the Confederate government, with Mr. Davis at its head, was established in Richmond one of the first things that received consideration was the fixing of a

Boundary Line

between the two sections in the event of the success of the rebellion. Mr. Davis did not believe that the North would consent on a boundary line extending north from the mouth of the Ohio River to embrace the state of Missouri in the Confederacy, and consequently it was not deemed expedient by him to get into any entangling alliance with that state. Another step that the Richmond government had counseled Gen. Johnston against when he set off for the West was interference with the

Neutrality Of The State Of Kentucky.

Mr. Davis had an exceedingly fine sense of honor, and I think he had made some promises of non-interference in Kentucky in case that state declared its neutrality, and he desired Gen. Johnston to consider there promises in his actions in the West.[9] Besides, Gen. Johnston no doubt, desired personally to keep the contest off his native heath as far as possible, and being a Kentucky man he would not favor a campaign in that state. Gen. Polk was the only auditor at the conference, and at its close he expressed himself as stoutly convinced of the expediency of some of my views in regard to action in the West. Gen. Johnston did not express an opinion of his own at any point, which was always his peculiarity."

---

in Columbus by September 19, 1861, which somewhat supports Frost's meeting in that time period. Ibid., 4:416; Dyer, 798.

7. On September 15, 1863, General John C. Frémont's Western Department had 55,693 men of which 38,581 were located on the west side of the Mississippi River. Frémont's command, west of the Mississippi River was scattered from St. Louis to Kansas. St. Louis at the time had 6,899 men. *O.R.*, 3:493.

8. This was Jefferson Davis, President of the Confederacy.

9. Following the firing on Fort Sumter, Kentucky declared its neutrality, and refused to supply troops to put down the rebellion. This neutrality held until early September 1861, when Federal troops landed on the Missouri shore opposite of Columbus. General Polk saw this as a threatening move and ordered the occupation of Columbus and Hickman on the evening of September 3. Kentucky was quickly occupied by both sides in the ensuing days, dragging it into the Civil War with the rest of the states. *O.R.*, 4:181, 188; Lowell H. Harrison, "Kentucky," *Encyclopedia of the Civil War*, 1116–1117.

"Did not the Confederate government send an agent to offer terms to Missouri at the time the state convention was called to determine whether or not the state should remain in the Union?"

"I believe Mr. [Daniel R.] Russell was sent to Missouri at that time,"[10] replied Gen. Frost, "but that was while the Confederate government was located in Montgomery, and before Mr. Davis had given the boundary line consideration. After the government was established at Richmond there was no attempt to embrace Missouri.[11] Gen. [John S.] Marmaduke[12] made a raid in the state after that time,[13] but there were no orders sent out from headquarters for a campaign in Missouri. As Gen. Price fell back from Lexington, an unsafe position for him, McCulloch was ordered to advance to his aid, and I thought for a time that there had been concert of action decided upon west of the river, but there was virtually nothing done. It was not the policy of the Richmond government to hamper itself with Missouri, and practically operations beyond the Mississippi were abandoned."

[Daniel M. Frost]

* * * * * * *

---

10. Daniel R. Russell was a commissioner from Mississippi sent to Missouri in January 1861, to convince Missouri to join with Mississippi in forming a southern Confederacy. On January 18, Russell addressed a joint secession of the Missouri Legislature and provided the reasons why Mississippi left the Union. Based on Russell's address, the Missouri Legislature passed an act that stated that Missouri would resist "at all hazards and to the last extremity" the coercion or the invasion of any Southern state. However, this was a moot point, as the people of Missouri were left to make the decision through a State Convention as to whether to support this type of action or not. Snead, 46–52; Ryle, 183–185.

11. The Confederate government had not given up on Missouri and continued to send representatives to the state. Luther J. Glenn, a Georgia commissioner, arrived on March 1, addressed the legislature the next day and on March 4 moved to St. Louis to address the State Secession Convention. Like Russell before him, little resulted from Glenn's visit. By October 1861, the question of Missouri's role in the Confederacy was settled, though little support was ever forthcoming. On October 29, a rump Missouri legislature meeting in Neosho passed an Ordnance of Secession, with but one dissenting vote. Ryle, 217–218; Eakin, *Diary,* 39.

12. John S. Marmaduke was born in 1833, graduated from West Point (number 30 of 38) in 1857, and served on the frontier until the beginning of the Civil War. Resigning from the army on April 17, 1861, he was appointed a colonel in the Missouri State Guard. Marmaduke commanded the MSG troops at Boonville and later entered the Confederate service. On November 15, 1862, Marmaduke was promoted to brigadier general and major general on March 15, 1865. Following the war he was elected governor of Missouri in 1884, and died while in office in 1887. For complete biography see Banasik, *Missouri Brothers in Gray,* 143; Boatner, 513.

13. Marmaduke was credited with two raids into Missouri—His first one began on December 31, 1862, and ended on January 25, 1863. This first raid centered on the western part of Missouri, with principle engagements at Springfield (January 8) and Hartville (January 11). The second raid occurred in eastern Missouri and began on April 17 and ended on May 2, 1863. The principle engagement of this raid occurred at Cape Girardeau on April 26, 1863. Other raids were also made into Missouri by Joseph Shelby in 1863 and Sterling Price in 1864. By far the most significant raid was Price's 1864 Missouri Raid which began in August and ended in October 1864. *O.R.*, vol. 22, pt. 1:178, 251, 621; Boatner, 669–671.

Item: Jefferson Davis's response to General Frost's article on the Confederate government's attitude toward Missouri, by R. J. Holcombe. **Published:** March 20, 1886.

That "State Secret."

Chillicothe, Mo., March 12

Editor, *Republican*

I noticed a controversy in the *Republican,* from day to day for a week or more, as to the truth of assertions made by certain prominent ex-Confederates, that in 1861 the Confederate government and especially Mr. Jefferson Davis, were opposed or reluctant to receive Missouri into the Confederacy. It was asserted that Mr. Davis did not believe that in the event of success of the Confederacy, the United States would ever consent that its Northern boundary should go north of the mouth of the Ohio River so as to include Missouri; that the success and early recognition of the Confederacy, therefore, would be more easily secured if Missouri were left out of the new government and that this "important state secret," as it was termed, accounted for the "failure" of the Confederate government to send large bodies of troops to the aid of Gen. Price and Gov. Jackson in the summer and fall of 1861.

Although not an ex-Confederate myself, I felt an interest in the sentiment and decision of this newly raised historical point and addressed a letter on the subject directly to Mr. Davis himself, enclosing slips cut from the *Republican,* and, containing the essentials of the controversy. Following is

Mr. Davis's Reply:

Beauvoir, Miss., March 8

Dear Sir: I have received your letter of the 2d inst., with the slip inclosed. ... Accustomed to much misrepresentation and misapprehension, I was not prepared for the existence of a report that I was opposed to receiving Missouri into the Confederacy. The story would be absurd, even if there was no evidence to disprove it; but my efforts to aid Missouri before she had entered the Confederacy and before her troops would agree to be mustered into the Confederate service, were so well known that I could not suppose anyone would, at this day, assert that I had anything else than the most friendly feelings for the people of the state.

While I desired both Missouri and Kentucky, to whom we had every bond of affinity, to join us in the organization of a separate government, I deemed that a matter entirely for their own decision and took no measures to influence their action. I then believed, and still believe, that if the people of those states had been left to the free exercise of their sovereign will, they would, with great unanimity, have placed Missouri and Kentucky by the side of their sisters of the South, and in that belief I did ardently desire the co-operation of both.[14]

When all my acts and utterances are on one side, it is hard to comprehend the circulation of a story so utterly opposed to what I did, said and thought. Very respectfully yours,

Jefferson Davis

R. J. Holcombe, Esq.

Mr. Davis' reply is itself a sufficient denial of the charge against him, but it may be well to supplement with the following

Corroborative Evidence:

In Col. Snead's recently published book, *The Fight for Missouri,* a work of intense interest and great value, it is made plain that from the first that Mr. Davis desired that Missouri should join the Confederacy and did what he could and perhaps did some things he should not have done to aid her in seceding. He furnished the secessionists of Missouri with cannon to attack the St. Louis Arsenal as early as in April and on April 23 he wrote a letter to Gov. Jackson informing him what had to be done, concurring with him in the propriety of capturing the arsenal, etc., and closing with the following:

"We look anxiously and hopefully for the day when the star of Missouri shall be added to the constitution of the Confederate States of America." (see *The Fight for Missouri,* page 168).

I presume the word "we" was intended to include the heads and leaders of the Confederate government.

I have not the time to examine the matter thoroughly, but July 8, 1861, Mr. Davis wrote to Col. E. C. Cabell:[15] "You have been heretofore advised of the

---

14. Missouri did have an election that decided the fate of the state. On February 18, 1861, a general election was held to elect delegates to a State Convention to consider the question of secession. The vote was a resounding defeat for the secessionists—140,000 votes were cast for Unionist candidates while the secessionist candidates received only 30,000 votes. Of the 99 members elected, not one declared for secession, even though 88 of the 99 delegates owned slaves. The Convention met on February 28 at Jefferson City, but later moved to St. Louis to complete their business beginning on March 4. On March 22 the Convention adjourned having passed several resolutions that put Missouri on the side of the Union. In the end, the Convention found that there was "'no adequate cause to impel Missouri to dissolve her relations with the Federal Union.'" Ryle, 210, 213–217, 232.

15. Edward Carrington Cabell was born in Richmond, Virginia, on February 5, 1816, educated at Washington College and the University of Virginia, and in 1837 moved to Florida. He was elected to the U.S. Congress in 1846, and served until 1853. Cabell married Anna Maria Wilcox of Columbia, Missouri, and moved to St. Louis after he left Congress to became a member of the St. Louis bar in 1860. With the beginning of the Civil War, Cabell was appointed a Commissioner from the State of Missouri to Richmond on September 26, 1861. While in Richmond, Cabell successfully sought military aid and recognition for Missouri from the Confederacy. Returning to the Trans-Mississippi region after two years in the Confederate capital, Cabell was appointed paymaster on Sterling Price's staff on April 1, 1863. He later served on E. Kirby Smith's staff. After the war Cabell returned to St. Louis, where he again practiced law and was elected to the Missouri Senate in 1878, for one term. He died in St. Louis on February 28, 1896. *O.R.,* 3:603–606, 639; *O.R.,* vol. 22, pt. 2:811; *O.R.,* vol. 34, pt. 4:79;

sympathy I feel for the cause of Missouri so graphically and feelingly described," etc. Other letters written to Confederate Missourians before the state seceded and of the same tenor may be quoted, showing Mr. Davis'desire for the secession of the state.

May 25, 1861, the Confederate Secretary of War, Hon. L. P. Walker[16] wrote to Gov. Jackson: "This department fully appreciates the sentiments of your heart, the embarrassments of your position and the judgement displayed in view of all the obstacles opposing your policy....I have only regretted that I have not, for the want of Confederate authority within your limits, been able to extend you that measure of relief called for by your necessities. I have nevertheless, set forward movements that I flatter myself will, before very long, contribute largely to disrupt the fetters that now shackle the freedom of your own and the popular action."

About the 1st of August the Confederate government at Richmond

Appropriated $1,000,000

for the defense and aid of Missouri, and Gen. Jas. Harding[17] was appointed by Gov. Jackson to receive the money.

It must be borne in mind that all these letters were written and all this action taken by the Confederate authorities long enough before Missouri pretended to secede (for the Neosho Ordinance of Secession was not adopted until October 28, 1861), and of course were designated to aid and influence the state in seceding. If Missouri's presence in the Confederacy was not desirable, why was it sought so persistently?

O.R., 53:750–752, 754; Winter, 117; Hale, 47.

16. Leroy Pope Walker, the first Confederate Secretary of War, was born 1817 in Huntsville, Alabama, and was educated at the University of Alabama and the University of Virginia. A lawyer by profession, Walker opened his first law office in Mississippi in 1837, but a short time later returned to Alabama, where he was active in the Democratic Party. He was elected to the Alabama Legislature (1840–1856) and headed the Alabama delegation to the Democratic Convention in 1860. Following the secession of his home state, Walker was appointed Confederate Secretary of War on February 16, 1861, a position he held without distinction, resigning on September 16, 1861. Appointed a brigadier general the following day, Walker served in unimportant positions, and resigned his commission on March 31, 1862. Walker completed his war years as a colonel and military judge. After the war he returned to Alabama, and resumed his law practice in Huntsville. He died at home in 1884. Boatner, 885; Heidler, "Walker, LeRoy Pope," *Civil War Encyclopedia*, 2049–2050.

17. James Harding was born in Boston, Massachusetts, on February 13, 1830, educated in Massachusetts schools until 1843, when he moved to St. Louis to live with a married sister. Spurning higher education, Harding worked as a seaman on a vessel heading for California and remained there for two years before returning to the east. Between 1851–1858, Harding worked on building railroads in Indiana and Missouri. He married in 1855, and made his home in Jefferson City, where he joined the local militia. At the beginning of the Civil War, Harding was appointed Quartermaster General of Missouri, a position he held for about a year, after which he joined the regular Confederate Army. Harding completed his Civil War service in various Confederate armories on the east side of the Mississippi River. After the war, he moved to Florida, but returned to Missouri in 1871, where he again involved himself in the railroad business. He died at his home, in Jefferson City, on April 4, 1902. McGhee, *Service With the Guard*, vi–x.

I think the "important state secret" must have been so "important" that nobody but a very few, and they not persons in authority, ever found it out. If the Confederacy had succeeded, Missouri would certainly have been a member thereof. The North would have as certainly consented to her departure from the Union as to that of South Carolina or Mississippi.

Some of the parties to the controversy under consideration incidentally mentioned that an "agent" of the Confederate government (a Mr. Russell) was sent to the Missouri State Convention "to offer terms to Missouri," etc. The confusion of memories on this point is so great as to be entertaining. The facts are that no "agent" of the Confederate government was ever sent to any legislative body of Missouri. January 18, 1861, Hon. D. R. Russell, a commissioner sent by the state of Mississippi, addressed our state legislature stating formally that his state had seceded and invited Missouri to do likewise. March 4 following Mr. Luther J. Glenn, a commissioner from the state of Georgia, addressed the State Convention in secession at St. Louis, informing that body of Georgia's secession, and urging and inviting Missouri co-operation in forming a Southern Confederacy. Both invitations were declined with thanks.

R. J. Holcombe

* * * * * * *

Item: The Confederate Government support for Missouri; based upon a conversation with Governor C. F. Jackson in the summer of 1861, by W. A. Adair.
Published: April 10, 1886.

Missouri And The Confederacy

W. A. Adair, editor of the Marshall (Tex.) *Messenger,* writes as follows regarding the attitude of the Confederacy towards Missouri:

Having read in the Missouri *Republican* the discussion by Gen. Frost and others, in regards to the attitude of the Confederate government towards Missouri, I think I can throw considerable light on the subject, especially as my authority is Gov. Jackson, whose knowledge was not only definite but official. In the summer of 1861, on my way to Missouri from Natchez, Miss., I met Gov. Jackson and staff returning to Missouri from Richmond, Va.[18] He appointed me on his staff, and

---

18. Governor Jackson began his journey to Richmond in July 1861, departing the state on the twelfth and proceeding to Fort Smith, Arkansas. He next stopped at Little Rock on July 19, addressing an assembled crowd. Pressing his way eastward, Jackson arrived at Memphis on July 22, parlayed with General Polk, and moved on to Richmond where he arrived on July 26. Jackson met with President Davis for two days, then departed Richmond on July 31, and headed back to Memphis. The meeting that Adair mentions took place in early August 1861, probably at Memphis. Christopher Phillips, *Missouri's Confederate: Claiborne Fox Jackson and the Creation of Southern Identity in the Border West* (Columbia, MO, 2000), 262–264.

from that time until near the time of his death I was with him almost constantly, and in various conversations with myself and others of the company, he stated very clearly and repeatedly the attitude of the Confederate government toward Missouri. He said that in several meetings with the cabinet the matter was discussed and options freely expressed. He said the policy determined upon was to regard no state, properly in the Confederacy without the action of the legislature passing the ordinance of secession, and that, as the convention of Missouri had

Failed To Pass

the ordinance Missouri could not be considered one of the Confederate states. Gov. Jackson said he laid before the cabinet the importance of Missouri as the proper battleground for the Trans-Mississippi Department, in view of the immense army supplies that could be procured for commissary and quartermaster departments. Gov. Jackson said he urged these considerations, and although they all regarded his views correct in the military point of view, and important as securing a strong ally in furnishing a large and brave body of troops, yet they could not consider Missouri in the Confederacy until the ordinance of secession was passed. Gov. Jackson then said he was going to Missouri and would call the legislature together and have them act and determine the position of Missouri. After the ordinance of secession was passed by the legislature assembled in southwest Missouri, and a large body of troops were organized under Gen. Price. [while] Gen. Frémont was massing an army, in southwest Missouri, and both Gen. Price and Gov. Jackson were very anxious to attack him before he could transport his whole force and prepare for battle. Gen. McCulloch, with his Arkansas and Texas troops, was camped about six miles from Gov. Jackson's headquarters in Arkansas. After consultation with Gen. Price, and having a report from scouts and citizens as to the condition of Gen. Frémont's army, Gov. Jackson determined to visit Gen. McCulloch's camp and get him to co-operate in the attack on Gen. Frémont. Col. [Richard] Gaines[19] and myself were requested to accompany him. After arriving at the camp

A Protracted Interview

was had with Gen. McCulloch, in which Gov. Jackson tendered him command

19. Richard Gains was born in Virginia in about 1826. After he moved to Missouri, he joined the Missouri State Guard on May 18, 1861, and was appointed an Aid-de-Camp to General Mosby M. Parsons and Assistant Adjutant General. On July 10, he was promoted to colonel and made an aide to Governor C. F. Jackson, to rank from July 4. Gains was at the Battle of Wilson's Creek and joined the Confederate Army on August 3, 1862, when he was assigned to duty on General Price's staff at the rank of captain. Commissioned a major of the Eighth Missouri Infantry Battalion on December 10, 1862, Gaines was transferred to the Ninth Missouri Infantry Regiment on February 3, 1863. He was in the Camden Expedition, bearing the rank of lieutenant colonel. Considered an "educated, intelligent and gallant officer," Gaines survived the war. *O.R.*. 3:102; *O.R.*, vol. 34, 1:810; Peterson, *Price's Lieutenants*, 33, 174; Schnetzer, *More Forgotten Men*, 87; McGhee, *Letter and Order Book Missouri State Guard*, unnumbered pages 2, 9 (entries page 1, 14); National Archives, Record Group M322, Compiled Service Records, Ninth Missouri Infantry.

of the State Guards. He declined, stating that his instructions were explicit, not to invade the territory of a state that had not passed the ordinance of secession. Gov. Jackson then stated to Gen. McCulloch that the legislature had been called together, and the ordinance of secession had been unanimously passed. Gen. McCulloch replied to me he would have to await further instructions. After the ordinance of secession was passed Gov. Jackson immediately sent official documents under the seal of the state to President Davis, setting forth the action of the legislature and a copy of the ordinance as passed. Not long afterwards a cordial response was received from President Davis, and Gov. Jackson repeatedly stated the fact to myself and others, and expressed himself fully satisfied with the attitude of the Confederate authorities toward Missouri, and said it was cordial and evinced the warmest sympathy, especially toward the noble and brave men who were not only in full accord with the Confederate cause in words, but in action as well.

There was never a lack of cordiality or sympathy toward Missouri by the Confederate authorities, but the line of policy adopted that dictated their action and caused Gov. Jackson to convene the legislature which passed the ordinance of secession. We might present other important facts bearing on this subject, but our article is sufficiently extended.

W. A. Adair

* * * * * *

Appendix A
Official Correspondence For 1861

Item: President Lincoln's Call For Troops and Response by Governor Claiborne F. Jackson.[1]

By The President Of The United States:
A Proclamation.

Whereas the laws of the United States have been for some time past and now are opposed and the execution thereof obstructed in the States of South Carolina, Georgia, Alabama, Florida, Mississippi, Louisiana and Texas by combinations too powerful to be suppressed by ordinary course of judicial proceedings or by the powers vested in the marshals by law:

Now, therefore, I, Abraham Lincoln, President of the United States in virtue of the power in me vested by the Constitution and the laws, have thought fit to call forth, and hereby do call forth, the militia of the several States of the Union, to the aggregate number of 75,000, in order to suppress said combinations and to cause the laws to be duly executed.

The details of this object will be immediately communicated to the State authorities through the War Department.

I appeal to all loyal citizens to favor, facilitate, and aid this effort to maintain the honor, the integrity, and existence of our National Union, and the perpetuity of popular government, and to redress wrongs already long enough endured.

I deem it proper to say that the first service assigned to the forces hereby called forth will probably be to repossess the forts, places, and property which have been seized from the Union, and in every event the utmost care will be observed, consistently with the objects aforesaid, to avoid any devastation, any destruction of or interference with property, or any disturbance of peaceful citizens in any part of the country.

And I hereby command the persons composing the combinations aforesaid to disperse and retire peaceably to their respective abodes within twenty days from date.

Deeming that the present condition of public affairs presents an extraordinary occasion, I do hereby, in virtue of the power in me vested by the Constitution, convene both houses of Congress.

Senators and Representatives are therefore summoned to assemble at their respective chambers at twelve o'clock noon on Thursday, the fourth day of July next, then, and there to consider and determine such measures as in their wisdom the public safety and interest may seem to demand.

In witness whereof I have hereunto set my hand and caused the seal of the

---

1. *O.R.*, Series 3, 1:67-68; 82-83.

United States to be affixed.

Done at the city of Washington this fifteenth day of April, in the year of our Lord one thousand eight hundred and sixty-one, and of the Independence of the United States the eighty-fifth.

Abraham Lincoln

By the President:

William H. Seward,
Secretary of State

* * * * * * *

Executive Department,
Jefferson City, Mo., April 17, 1861
Hon. Simon Cammeron,
Secretary of War:
Sir: Your dispatch of the 15th instant, making a call on Missouri for four regiments of men for immediate service, has been received. There can be, I apprehend, no doubt but the men are intended to form a part of the President's army to make war upon the people of the seceded States.

Your requisition, in my judgment, is illegal, unconstitutional, and revolutionary in its object, inhuman and diabolical, and cannot be complied with. Not one man will the State of Missouri furnish to carry on any such unholy crusade.

C. F. Jackson,
Governor of Missouri

* * * * * * *

Item: The Price-Harney Agreement.[2]

Saint Louis, May 21, 1861
The undersigned, officers of the United States Government and of the government of the State of Missouri, for the purpose of removing misapprehensions and allaying public excitement, deem it proper to declare publicly that they have this day had a personal interview in this city, in which it has been mutually understood, without the semblance of dissent on either part, that each of them has no other than a common object equally interesting and important to every citizen of Missouri—that of restoring peace and good order to the people of the State in subordination to the laws of the General and State Governments. It be thus understood, there seems no reason why every citizen should not confide in the proper officers of the General and State Governments to restore quiet, and, as among the best means of offering no counterinfluences, we mutually recommend to all

---

2. *O.R.,* 3:375.

persons to respect each other's rights throughout the State, making no attempt to exercise unauthorized powers, as it is the determination of the proper authorities to suppress all unlawful proceedings, which can only disturb the public peace.

General Price, having by commission full authority over the militia of the State of Missouri, undertakes, with the sanction of the governor of the State, already declared, to direct the whole power of the State officers to maintain order within the State among the people thereof, and General Harney publicly declares that, this object being thus assured, he can have no occasion, as he has no wish, to make military movements, which might otherwise create excitements and jealousies which he most earnestly desires to avoid.

We, the undersigned, do therefore mutually enjoin upon the people of the State to attend to their civil business of whatever sort it may be, and it is to be hoped that the unquiet elements which have threatened so seriously to disturb the public peace may soon subside and be remembered only to be deplored.

Sterling Price,
Major-General Missouri State Guard.
WM. S. Harney,
Brigadier-General, Commanding.

* * * * * *

Appendix B
Selected Biographies

Francis Preston Blair, Jr.

Francis P. Blair, Jr. was born on February 19, 1821, in Lexington, Kentucky. The youngest of six children, he was branded "Frank" by his family, friends and other acquaintances throughout his life. Probably educated in subscription schools in Kentucky until age nine, Frank attended private schools after the Blairs moved to the nation's capital in 1830. In 1835 Frank moved to Connecticut for a college prep school and entered Yale University in the fall of 1837. Dismissed from Yale in January 1838 for behavioral problems, Blair moved on to the University of North Carolina and was again asked to leave the institution in November 1838. However, upon agreement with the university that he would improve his behavior, Blair was allowed to stay. Growing tired of North Carolina, he moved on to Princeton University, where he finally obtained a delayed degree in 1842.

Known for his short temper, Blair was involved in several duels, all of which left his opponents wounded. Blair had actually graduated from Princeton in 1841, but was not given a degree until 1842. Writers on the subject believe that a barroom brawl involving another student, in which Blair shot the freshman just prior to graduation, caused the delay.

While waiting to obtain his degree from Princeton, Frank studied law at Transylvania University. He moved to St. Louis, in April 1842, where he joined his brother Montgomery in the practice of law. Growing bored with his profession, Blair moved west for a time, later joined in the Mexican War as a private and served under General Stephen Kearny. After the war, Blair became actively involved in politics: he founded the Free Soil Party in Missouri, was a member of the Missouri Legislature in 1852, and was elected to the U.S. Congress in 1856. A strong Unionist, Blair was credited with saving Missouri for the Union, by organizing the pro-German faction of St. Louis into a potent fighting force. Blair was appointed colonel of the First Missouri Infantry at the beginning of the Civil War and went on to serve throughout the conflict, attaining the rank of major general. Frank Blair enjoyed "the full confidence of his men," and was considered

General Francis P. Blair

"brave and capable"—"fear was unknown to him." To some of his troops he was known as the "Bejesus colonel." A fellow veteran called him a "man of rare powers, mental and physical, natural and acquired, and as bold and courageous as he was far seeing and able," but he was not loved by all. One junior officer recorded that Blair was a "supercilious Aristocrat, who will not even condescend to speak to 'Volunteer Officers'."

After the war, Blair returned to politics and was the Democratic Party vice-presidential nominee in 1868, but lost. He later served in the U.S. Senate from 1871–1873. Blair suffered a stroke in 1873 and never fully recovered. He died on July 9, 1875.[1]

* * * * * * *

James Jones Clarkson

James J. Clarkson was born in Kentucky about 1812, and moved to Missouri prior to the Mexican War. During the Mexican War Clarkson commanded Company F, Third Missouri Mounted Rifles, which he had raised in Dade County. After Mexico, Clarkson relocated to Leavenworth, Kansas, where he became the postmaster of the city and a supporter of pro-slavery rights in the Kansas Territory. As a "border ruffian" and leader of a band of "Regulators," during the mid-1850's, Clarkson participated in the sacking of Lawrence, Kansas, in 1856. In the fall of 1859, he returned to Greenfield, Dade County, Missouri.

At the beginning of the Civil War, Clarkson was elected colonel of the Fifth Infantry Regiment, Eighth Division, Missouri State Guard. Clarkson served in the MSG from July 12, 1861, to March 12,

Colonel James J. Clarkson

---

1. Banasik, *Missouri in 1861*, 86; Boatner, 67; Mortimer R. Flint, "The War On the Border," *Glimpses of the Nation's Struggle. Fifth Series. Papers Read Before the Minnesota Commandery of the Military Order of the Loyal Legion of the United States, 1897–1902, MOLLUS,* 30:402–403; Gilmore, 110; James F. How, "Frank P. Blair in 1861," *War Papers and Personal Reminiscences 1861–1865. Read Before the Commandery of the State of Missouri, Military Order of the Loyal Legion of the United States, MOLLUS,* 14:387, 394–395; Charles F. Larimer, ed., *Love and Valor: Intimate Civil War Letters Between Captain Jacob and Emeline Ritner* (Western Springs, IL, 2000), 100; Smith, "Blair, Francis Preston, Jr.," in *Encyclopedia of the Civil War,* 238–239.; Parrish, 1–4, 6–7, 9; Ware, 128, 154; Wherry, "General Nathaniel Lyon," 4:71.

1862, and then transferred to the Confederate service, with orders to raise a regiment to operate in the Indian Territory (modern-day Oklahoma). His new command was mustered into the Confederate Army on April 1, 1862, with nine companies of Missourians and one of Osage Indians.

Clarkson was captured at Locust Grove, Indian Territory, with fifty of his men, on July 2, 1862, following a short engagement, and sent to Leavenworth, where he was jailed "for conspiracy to overthrow the Government." Transferred to St. Louis in October 1862, and under the custody of the U.S. Marshals, Clarkson was held as a civilian until such time as the Confederate Government would acknowledge his position in the Confederate Army. On February 4, 1864, Clarkson was finally recognized as a prisoner of war and sent east to City Point, Virginia, for exchange.

Clarkson returned to the Trans-Mississippi Department in August 1864. While attempting to return to Missouri in early 1865, Clarkson was murdered by Mississippi River pirates.[2]

* * * * * * *

William Selby Harney

Born on August 27, 1800, near Hayboro, Tennessee on the Cumberland River, a short distance from Nashville, William Harney was educated locally and served in the military most of his life. He was commissioned a second lieutenant of infantry in the Regular Army, from Louisiana, on February 13, 1818. In his early career he fought in the Black Hawk War and against the Creeks and Seminole Indians in Florida; in the latter, Harney was cited for his gallantry and meritorious conduct. Harney was promoted successively in his early years, attaining the rank of lieutenant colonel of the Second Dragoons on August 15, 1836.

Just prior to the Mexican War, Harney was promoted to colonel of his regiment, which he led in the war. As senior cavalry commander under General Winfield Scott, Harney ran afoul of his commander, who relieved him of his command and court-martialed him for failing to obey an order. Although Harney was convicted, Scott "remitted the sentence" and returned Harney to duty. Shortly thereafter, President James Polk got wind of the affair, overruled Scott's decision, seeing it strictly as political, and reinstated Harney to command of the Second Dragoons. Harney subsequently led his regiment with distinction during the advance on Mexico City. For his "gallant and meritorious conduct in the Battle of Cerro Gordo," on April 18, 1847, Harney was breveted a brigadier general. His general officer rank was made permanent on June 14, 1858, making him one of

2. *O.R.*, Series 2, 4:335, 5:21–22; Bartels, *Forgotten Men*, 61; J. J. Clarkson Letter, February 29, 1864, J. J. Clarkson Collection, Missouri Historical Society; Eakin, *Missouri Prisoners of War*, "Clarkson, Jas. J." entry; Hale, 59; Heitman, 2:47; Peterson, 236; J. H. H., "From the Indian Expedition," *Wyandotte Commercial Gazette* (Wyandotte, KS), July 19, 1862; Observer, "From the Cherokee Nation," *White Cloud Chief* (White Cloud, KS), July 24, 1862.

General William S. Harney

only four general officers in the U.S. Army at the beginning of the Civil War.

Following the Mexican War, Harney served on the western plains and was appointed commander of the Department of Oregon in 1858, a position he held until relieved in 1860, "on account of border difficulties with England." On November 17, 1860, Harney was assigned as commander of the Department of the West, with his headquarters in St. Louis.

The Unionists of St. Louis, particularly Frank Blair, mistrusted Harney as a Southern sympathizer—in part because of his birth place, his marriage to a "wealthy woman from St. Louis [and that] he subscribed to the convictions of his slaveholding friends." Harney's position was exacerbated after he made an agreement with Sterling Price to cease hostilities in Missouri, after which Blair moved quickly to have the general removed from command. On May 31, 1861, after frequent clashes with Blair, Harney was relieved of command and returned to Washington for reassignment. Harney never commanded again, however; he left the army on August 1, 1863. Just before war's end Harney was promoted to major general for his "long and faithful service." After the war, Harney retired to Pass Christian, Mississippi.

Of the men who knew Harney, one veteran saw him as a "distinguished officer of long service and exceptional courage," but one who was easily manipulated and "hoodwinked" into non-action in the defense of the St. Louis Arsenal. Another veteran minced no words, simply calling Harney a "traitor." Overall, for the Unionists of St. Louis, "Harney's loyalty was also distrusted, though unjustly."

Harney was described as a man of "vigor," and "robust" despite his age of sixty when he assumed command in St. Louis. He was "very tall, broad-shouldered, and as straight as an arrow," but not considered particularly intelligent. As a slaveholder, Harney's had sympathies with the South, but he loved the Union more so and "was absolutely loyal to the flag." Harney was a man of honor and never betrayed his country. He died on May 9, 1889, in Orlando, Florida, and was buried in Arlington National Cemetery.[3]

---

3. Boatner, 376; Mortimer R. Flint, "The War On the Border," *Glimpses of the Nation's Struggle. Fifth Series. Papers Read Before the Minnesota Commandery of the Military Order of the Loyal Legion of the United States, 1897–1902, MOLLUS*, 30:404–405; Heitman, 1:502; Sifakis, *Union*, 178–179; Singletary, 121–121; Snead, 99–100; *Union Army*, 4:239, 8:118–119; Warner, *Generals in Blue*, 208–209; Wherry, "General Nathaniel Lyon," 4:71.

* * * * * *

Louis Hébert

He was born March 13, 1820, in Iberville Parish, Louisiana, and educated by private tutors until he entered Jefferson College in St James's Parish, where he graduated on December 10, 1840. Appointed to West Point in 1841, Hébert graduated number three in the Class of 1845 as a lieutenant of engineers. His first and only tour of duty was as an assistant engineer at Fort Livingston on Iberian Island, Louisiana. Hébert resigned from the army on February 15, 1846, because of illness in his family, and return to Iberville Parish, where he became a sugar planter.

Hébert was a militia major between 1847 and 1850, was elected to the Louisiana Senate in 1853 for a four year term, but only served for two. In 1855, he was

General Louis Hébert

appointed the State Engineer (1855-1859) and in 1860, was elected to the Board of Public Works. Hébert was commissioned a militia colonel (1855-1861) of East Baton Rouge, and served in that position until the beginning of the Civil War.

Hébert was elected colonel of the Third Louisiana Infantry on May 11, 1861, and led a brigade of troops at the Battles of Wilson's Creek and Pea Ridge. Captured on March 7, 1862, he was exchanged on March 20, 1862, and moved with his brigade to the east side of the Mississippi River in April 1862. Hébert was promoted to brigadier general on May 26, 1862, after which he led troops at Corinth and Iuka, Mississippi in late 1862. He was captured at Vicksburg on July 4, 1863, exchanged nine days later, and completed his Civil War service in North Carolina in the area of Fort Fisher, near Wilmington.

"As an officer, he was a strict disciplinarian, punctilious in enforcing a rigid adherence to all orders; as a man, he was genial and kind in manner and conversation." Hébert was a "great favorite" in the Third Louisiana Infantry; he was "cool, and exhibited his military training and education." At Wilson's Creek, Hébert was praised by General McCulloch for leading his troops "with the greatest of coolness and bravery."

Following the war, Hébert returned to Louisiana, resumed his life as a planter, became a teacher and editor of a newspaper. He never entered politics again. Hébert died in St. Mary's Parish on January 20, 1901 (Note: Warner has the date as

January 7, 1901.)[4]

* * * * * * *

General Walter P. Lane

Walter Paye Lane

Walter P. Lane was born in Ireland on February 18, 1817, and moved to the United States in 1821, where his parents settled in Fairview, Guernsey County, Ohio. At the age of 18, then living at Wheeling, Virginia (modern-day West Virginia), Lane headed to Texas. Stopping briefly at Louisville, Kentucky, to visit his brother, he met Stephen Austin of Texas. Lane moved on to New Orleans, then to Texas in March 1836, where on April 21, 1836, he participated in the Battle of San Jacinto as a member of Henry Karn's "spy company." Following the Texas War for Independence, Lane settled in Marshall, Texas, in 1836, after which he served on the privateer *Tom Tobby* in the Gulf of Mexico, taught school in San Augustine, Texas, clerked at a store (1840–41), and fought Indians.

During the Mexican War, Lane served in a company of scouts, making himself "efficient" and "indispensable" in the war effort. Lane fought in the Battles of Monterrey and Buena Vista in Hay's Texas Regiment. After a six month enlistment he was discharged and returned to Texas where he raised a company for Zachary Taylor's army. Elected major of his battalion, Lane completed his Mexican War service fighting guerrillas and Indians.

Lane returned to Marshall for a brief time, then journeyed to Wheeling to visit his parents. After six months in Virginia, Lane moved to California in search of gold. From 1849–1858, Lane continued his search for precious metals, spending time in Arizona and Peru.

At the beginning of the Civil War, Lane was elected lieutenant colonel of the South Kansas-Texas or Third Texas Cavalry Regiment on July 2, 1861. He fought at Wilson's Creek, where his horse was shot out from under him, at Chustenahlah, Indian Territory and Pea Ridge, where his command formed part of the rear guard for the retreating Confederate Army. Later, his regiment was dismounted in Arkansas, before taking passage to Memphis where the Third Texas completed its

---

4. *O.R.*, 3:106; Heitman, 1:519; Tunnard, 28–29; Boatner, 391; Dimitry, 305–307; Sifakis, *Confederacy*, 124; Warner, *Generals in Gray*, 130–131.

service.

Not wishing to stand again for colonel of the Third Texas Cavalry (Dismounted), Lane returned to Texas in mid-1862. He organized a new regiment, with many of the men coming from the San Augustine and Paris areas. Lane was elected colonel of this unit, known as the First Texas Partisan Cavalry Regiment, on August 8, 1862. General T. C. Hindman, who considered Lane a man with a "high reputation as a soldier and a gentleman," ordered his command to the Indian Territory in September 1862. While moving through the Indian Territory, Lane caught a fever, and R. Phillip Crump led the regiment for a time. Lane returned to Marshall to recover and did not rejoin his command until 1863.

The First Texas Partisans fought with distinction at Prairie Grove, under Lieutenant Colonel Crump, but was routed at Dripping Springs, Arkansas, on December 28, where the regiment lost all its baggage, and several members were taken as prisoners. In 1863, the regiment, with Lane back in command, participated in the West Louisiana Campaign, during which it captured Thibodaux, on June 30, 1863. In 1864, Lane was severely wounded at the Battle of Mansfield, where he led a brigade, which included his old command. Of Colonel Lane's performance at Mansfield, one officer recorded: "Col. W. P. Lane…was ever in the front rank encouraging his men by his voice and example. I know I express the feelings of the entire brigade when I say we wish for no braver or more experienced officer to command us."

Lane returned home to Marshall to recover from his wounds and eventually return to duty. He was recommended by E. Kirby Smith for promotion to general officer in October 1864. On March 17, 1865, Lane was confirmed as a brigadier general.

Following the war, Lane returned to Texas to spend his remaining years writing his memoirs and running a mercantile business. He died, an unmarried man, on January 28, 1892, and was buried in his hometown of Marshall.[5]

In summing up Walter P. Lane's life one biographer wrote:

The character of Walter P. Lane is without a blemish. His fearless bearing in the midst of danger was proverbial, and he had as cool a head to plan as a daring aim to execute. His modesty is insurmountable, and it is only to a confidential friend that he can be induced to recount his many hair-breadth escapes at all…The Marshal Ney of Texas.

* * * * * * *

---

5. *O.R.*, vol. 22, pt. 1:141–142, 156–157, 169, 171, 899; *O.R.*, vol. 26, pt. 1:218; *O.R.*, vol. 34, pt. 1:618; *O.R.S.*, pt. 2, vol. 67:702 (see Co. B, Cumby); Boatner, 471; Crute, 321; Lane, 7, 9, 20–26, 29, 31, 40, 42–43, 49, 52–53, 60–61, 74, 93, 95, 98, 105, 110, 115, 119, 121, 124, 135–136, 146; Warner, *Generals in Gray*, 173–174; Simpson, 85–86; Special Order No. 48 (August 8, 1862), Special Order Book No. 1; Letter, Newton to Lane (September 20, 1862), Copy Letter Book No. 1, 175.

James Spencer Rains

James S. Rains was born on October 2, 1817, in Tennessee. His family later moved to southwest Missouri, settling near Sarcoxie by 1840. Rains went into politics shortly after his arrival in Missouri and was elected a Newton County judge (1840-1842). In 1844, Rains was elected to the lower house of the Missouri legislature and a year latter was appointed as an Indian agent for the Neosho Agency. After three years in Neosho, Rains transferred to the Osage River Agency in 1848, then left for California in 1850 in search of gold. While in California Rains served as a brigadier general in the California Militia, but within a few years returned to Missouri where he was elected to the Missouri Senate (1854–1861) and also served in the Missouri Militia. In 1860, Rains ran for the U.S. Congress from the Sixth District, but lost in a close election to John S. Phelps.

With the coming of the Civil War, Governor Claiborne F. Jackson appointed Rains a brigadier general in the Missouri State Guard on May 18, 1861. Rains led the Second Division, MSG, at Carthage, Dug Springs, Wilson's Creek and Lexington. On December 4, 1861, Rains was elected brigadier general of the Eighth Division, MSG, and led the command at Pea Ridge, where he was wounded. An outspoken Rains severely criticized General Earl Van Dorn for his handling of the battle, stating to a soldier in Van Dorn's presence: "By God, nobody was whipped at Pea Ridge but Van Dorn!" Promptly arrested, Rains requested a court-martial, and was released on April 8, 1862, after being temporarily relieved of duty. Rains remained in the Trans-Mississippi after Van Dorn took the Confederate Army east of the Mississippi River in April 1862, probably more so for his dislike of Van Dorn, than his desire to remain in the Trans-Mississippi.

General James S. Rains

With the bulk of the Missouri State Guard serving on the east side of the Mississippi River, Rains, with the blessing of the new commander in Arkansas, General Thomas C. Hindman, began recruiting a brigade of 5,000 men for service in the Trans-Mississippi. Eventually Rains was given the command of a division composed of two cavalry brigades, but his performance was dogged by a drinking problem. His appointment as a Confederate brigadier general carried a caveat from General Hindman, who wrote to Rains on July 6, 1862:

"I am constrained to say to you upon the express condition that you immediately tender your resignation and forward the same to me with the understanding and upon the condition that the same shall take effect whenever you shall drink any intoxicating liquor after the date of its reception."

Hindman relieved Rains of command on October 22, 1862, for repeated episodes of drunkenness. As one soldier recalled: General Rains "preferred drinking to fighting—he got drunk, and resigned so that he might, I suppose, get drunk when he pleased." Having lost face in the army, Rains moved to Texas for a time to recover his health, but still remained in the Missouri State Guard. As an aid to the Governor of Missouri, Rains accompanied Price's army on his 1864 Missouri Raid.

After the war Rains settled in Wood County, Texas, for a couple of years, then relocated to Kaufman County, where he became a farmer, practiced law, promoted the railroad, and again became involved in politics. In 1878, Rains ran for lieutenant governor of Texas, under the Greenback Party, but lost. In his last political act, Rains was a delegate to the 1880 National Greenback Party Convention.

One colleague wrote that, as a military commander, Rains was a "brave,... gallant, [and] good officer," while John F. Snyder of Rains's staff recalled of him: "He was profoundly ignorant of everything pertaining to military affairs." Another shortcoming was that he "was so good natured that he could not say 'no' to any request, or enforce regulations that were distasteful to his men." When Rains was finally relieved of command, his men hated to see him leave, but they understood "that drunkenness was just cause for removal."

John S. Rains died at his home in Kaufman County, Texas on May 19, 1880.[6]

* * * * * * *

Index to Previous Biographies

Found in *Missouri Brothers in Gray* (vol. 1), *Serving With Honor* (vol. 2), *Reluctant Cannoneer* (vol. 3), *Missouri in 1861* (vol. 4), *Cavaliers of the Brush* (vol. 5) and *Duty, Honor and Country* (vol. 6).

---

6. *O.R.*, 3:20–22, 50, 127, 188–189; *O.R.*, 13:48; Allardice, 190–192; Banasik, *Embattled Arkansas*, 249; Bartels, *Forgotten Men*, 301; *History of Greene County*, 279; Letters, Hindman to Rains (July 6, 1862), Newton to Rains (October 22, 1862), Hindman to Anderson (November 17, 1862), Copy Letter Book No. 1, 60, 233, 364–365; Letter (December 15, 1913), John F. Snyder Papers, Missouri Historical Society; McGhee, *Letter and Order Book*, unnumbered page 48 (entry page 91); Norton, 64, 68–69, 137; Peterson, 11, 16, 209; Shea and Hess, 260, 377.

* * * * * * *

Appendix C
By Name Losses Of Parsons's Sixth Division
Missouri State Guard At
Wilson's Creek, August 10, 1861

Published: September 25, 1886.

[Note: The *Official Records* excluded the list of casualties when it published Parsons's report. See *O.R.,* 53:431–434, for the complete report.[1]

First Regiment of Infantry, Col. [Joseph M.] Kelly, commanding:

Capt. [Stephen O.] Coleman's company—Killed: Capt. S. O. Coleman (Mortally wounded, since dead), First Sergeant Stephen Lowry, Second Sergeant Bernard McMahon; Privates, Chas. Clark, Thomas Neinor, J. O'Hara, John Blake and John True—eight. Wounded: Corporal Kinsella; Privates, Peter C. Nugent, Thomas Skahan, S. G. Gibson,, James Conroy, Robert Lidwell, Wm. May, John Morrissey, James Kelly, James H. Kelly, Jas. Malloy, Orville J. Pomeroy, Jas. Fitzzimmon's, J. H. O'Hara and Lawrence Mooney—fifteen.

Capt. J. R. Champion's company—Killed: J. M. Larne—one. Wounded: N. B. Theobold, Thos. Sullivan, Dennis Casey, J. M. Martin, W. H. Robinson and David Powers—six.

Capt. [Samuel] Livingston's [or Livinstone's] company—[Killed: none.] Wounded: Second Sergt. Jas. K. Estes, Corporal S. C. Ward, Privates J. W. Lustre, Wm. Nevis and Jacob Weistaer—five.

Capt. McCarty's company—[Killed: None.] Wounded: Privates W. C. May and Jno. Clifford—two.

Lieut. [John] Still's company—Killed: Corporal S. R. Lynch—one. Wounded: First Lieut. Jno. Still, Corporal P. L. Blyze, Privates Joab Watson, J. N. Morrow, R. C. White and W. C. Wilson—six.

Capt. [D. M.] William's company—Killed: Sergt. Wm. Fry—one. Wounded: Lieut. P. W. Fisher, Privates Robert Davidson, Lewis Crandall and Peter Moran—four. Missing: Jas. Bain[—one.]

Artillery—Capt. H. Guibor commanding. Killed: Corporals J. Foley and W. H. Douglas; Privates W. N. Hicks—three. Wounded: First Sergt. J. J. Corkery,

---

1. First names of the various officers were found in Peterson, 174–178.

Privates R. J. Brown, N. Dayton, M. O'Neil, F. G. Studdard, J. G. Shockley, and C. D. Zumalt—seven.

First Regiment of Cavalry, Col. Wm. Brown commanding.
    Capt. [T. F.] Lockett's company—[Killed: None.] [Wounded: None.] Missing: Joseph J. Bolton and Mat Hall—two.

    Capt. [B. S.] Bond's company—Killed: Private Thos. Moran[—one.] Wounded: Private Wm. Wilson[—one.] Missing: George Berry[—one.]

    Capt. [George M.] Butler's company—Killed: J. F. Murray[—one.] Wounded: J. C. Wilson[—one.] Missing: John Berry[—one.]

    Capt. [C. M.] Southerlin's [or Sutherlin] company—[Killed: None.] Wounded: Privates Jas. Martin, Jno. Nowland and Geo. Potter—three.

    Capt. Crew's[2] company (attached to Col. Brown's regiment)—[Killed : None.] Wounded: Wm. Bishop—one.] Missing: Thos. Wheeler, David Lindsey, M. B. Cave, J. F. Priman and Fred Priman—[five.]

Total killed, wounded and missing, 78.

---

2. There were two Captains Crew or Crews in Parsons's Sixth Division, Missouri State Guard; Charles L. Crews commanded Company C, Second Cavalry Regiment and Captain T. W. B. Crews commanded Company D of the same regiment. Ibid.

Appendix D
Confederate Pieces Not Used, 1861
Not Trans-Mississippi Related

Item: A Woman's War Experience, by "A. K." A woman's story of how she saw the Civil War, from late 1860 through the Siege of Vicksburg. About half of the two part article deals with the siege of Vicksburg.
Published: July 24 and August 7, 1886.

Item: Clark's Battery, by Jo. A. Wilson, late member of the battery, and now a civil engineer in Lexington, Missouri. A history of Clark's Missouri Artillery, from its formation in 1861, at Lexington, to its surrender in April 1865, in Alabama. [Note: With few exceptions this pieces deals with the unit's service on the east side of the Mississippi River. A small portion that does apply to the Trans-Mississippi area will be covered in a latter volume of this series.]
Published: November 28, 1885.

Item: Unpublished Letters of Gen. Lee, by Robert E. Lee and Mary Curtis Lee. Letters of Robert E. Lee, sent to General E. G. W. Butler (oldest living West Point graduate in 1885). The letters date from June 1861, to February 1870 and deal mainly with post-war matters. Also includes two letters from Mary Curtis Lee, (the general's wife), concerning his death.
Published: October 3, 1885.

* * * * * * *

Previously Published

Item: Pre-war actions in Missouri; Extracts from a book entitled *The Fight For Missouri,* by Thomas L. Snead. Previously published in *The Fight For Missouri,* pages 101-110, 114-117.
Published: April 24, 1886.

Item: Samuel Clem's Civil War days in Missouri, May–June 1861, by Absolom Grimes. Previously published in Grimes's book, *Confederate Mail Runner,* 5–19.
Published: September 4, 1886.

Item: Guibor's Missouri State Guard Battery at Carthage, by William P. Barlow, Lieutenant, Guibor's Missouri State Guard Battery. Previously edited by Jeffery L. Patrick and published in *Civil War Regiments,* Volume

5, No. 4, 20–60.
Published: August 1, 1885

Item: Guibor's Battery at Oak Hills, by William P. Barlow. Previously edited by Jeffery L. Patrick and published in *Civil War Regiments,* Volume 5, No. 4, 20–60.
Published: August 1 and 22, 1885.

Item: Reminiscences of the Third Louisiana Infantry, by W. H. Tunnard, Second Sergeant, Company K, formerly of
Nachitoches, Louisiana. Previously published in Tunnard's book, *A Southern Record* (pages 49–54, 66–67).
Published: November 7, 1885.

Item: Missourians at the Battle of Oak Hill, by R. H. Musser. This small piece was extracted from Musser's article in the *Southern Bivouac* and was republished in 1993 by Broadfoot Publishing in North Carolina. Richard H. Musser, "The War in Missouri," *Southern Bivouac* (April, 1886; reprinted Wilmington, NC, 1993; 6 vols.), 4:679–680.
Published: March 20, 1886.

Item: General M. M. Parsons's official report and casualty list on the Battle of Wilson's Creek (August 10, 1861), for the Sixth Division, Missouri State Guard. The original report, minus the casualty list, which appears in Appendix C, was published in the *Official Records,* Series I, 53: 431–434.
Published: September 25, 1886.

Item: Guibor's Battery at Dry Wood (September 2, 1861) and Lexington (September 13–20, 1861), by William P. Barlow. Previously edited by Jeffery L. Patrick and published in *Civil War Regiments,* Volume 5, No. 4, 20–60.
Published: August 8, 1885.

* * * * * * *

Bibliography

Books/Pamphlets/Articles

Adamson, Hans Christian. *Rebellion in Missouri, 1861: Nathaniel Lyon and His Army of the West.* Rahway, NJ: Quinn & Boden Company, 1961.

Allardice, Bruce S. *More Generals in Gray.* Baton Rouge, LA: Louisiana State University Press, 1995.

Banasik, Michael E. *Cavaliers of the Brush: Quantrill and His Men.* Unwritten Chapters of the Civil War West of the River Volume V. Iowa City, IA: Camp Pope Bookshop, 2003.

_____. *Duty, Honor and Country: The Civil War Experiences of Captain William P. Black, Thirty-seventh Illinois Infantry.* Unwritten Chapters of the Civil War West of the River Volume VI. Iowa City, IA: Camp Pope Bookshop, 2006

_____. *Embattled Arkansas: The Prairie Grove Campaign of 1862.* Wilmington, NC: Broadfoot Publishing Company, 1996.

_____. *Missouri Brothers in Gray: The Reminiscences and Letters of William J. Bull and John P. Bull.* Unwritten Chapters of the Civil War West of the River Volume I. Iowa City, IA: Camp Pope Bookshop, 1998.

_____. *Missouri in 1861: The Civil War Letters of Franc B. Wilkie, Newspaper Correspondent.* Unwritten Chapters of the Civil War West of the River Volume IV. Iowa City, IA: Camp Pope Bookshop, 2001.

_____. *Serving With Honor: The Diary of Captain Eathan Allen Pinnell of the Eighth Missouri Infantry (Confederate).* Unwritten Chapters of the Civil War West of the River Volume III. Iowa City, IA: Camp Pope Bookshop, 1999.

_____. *Reluctant Cannoneer: The Diary of Robert T. McMahan of the Twenty-fifth Independent Ohio Light Artillery.* Unwritten Chapters of the Civil War West of the River Volume II. Iowa City, IA: Camp Pope Bookshop, 2000.

Bartels, Carolyn M. *The Forgotten Men: The Missouri State Guard.* Independence, MO: Two Trails Publishing, 1995.

_____. *Trans-Mississippi Men at War, Volume I: Missouri C.S.A.* Independence, MO: Two Trails Publishing, 1998.

Bearss, Edwin C. *The Battle of Wilson's Creek.* Bozman, MT: Wilson's Creek National Battlefield Foundation, 1988.

_____. "Fort Smith Serves General McCulloch As a Supply Depot." *Arkansas Historical Quarterly* 24 (Winter, 1965): 315–347.

Bently, Charles S., Edward D. Redington, and Jared W. Young, "Samuel Henry Melcher." *Memorial of Deceased Companions of the Commandery of the State of Illinois, Military Order of the Loyal Legion of the United States.* Chicago, 1923. Reprint. 70 vols. Wilmington, NC: Broadfoot Publishing Company, 1993. 13D:255–257.

Bevier, R. S. *History of the First and Second Missouri Confederate Brigades 1861–1865. And From Wakarusa to Appomattox, A Military Anagraph.* St. Louis: Bryan, Brand & Company, 1879.

Boatner III, Mark Mayo. *The Civil War Dictionary.* New York: David McKay Company, Inc., 1959.

Britton, Wiley. *The Civil War on the Border: A Narrative of Military Operations in Missouri, Kansas, Arkansas, and the Indian Territory.* 2 vols. New York: G. P. Putnam's Sons, 1899.

Broadfoot, Tom. *Civil War Books: A Priced Checklist With Advice.* Wilmington, NC: Broadfoot Publishing Company, 2000.

Brock, R. A., ed. *Southern Historical Society Papers.* 52 vols. Richmond, VA: Southern Historical Society, 1876–1959. Reprint. Wilmington, NC: Broadfoot Publishing Company, 1990–1992.

Brooksher, William Riley. *Bloody Hill: The Civil War Battle of Wilson's Creek.* Washington, DC: Brassy's, 1995.

Brown, Daniel T. *Westering River, Westering Trail: A History of St. Charles County, Missouri to 1849.* St. Charles, MO: St. Charles County Historical Society, 2006

Brugioni, Dino A. *The Civil War In Missouri As Seen From The Capital City.* Jefferson City, MO: Summers Publishing, 1997.

Burke, W. S. *Official Military History of Kansas Regiments During the War for the Suppression of the Great Rebellion.* Leavenworth, KS: W. S. Burke, 1870.

Busbey, Hamilton. *Recollections of Men and Horses.* New York: Dodd, Meade and Company, 1907.

"Community and Conflict: The Impact of the Civil War in the Ozarks: Postwar Politics," http://www.ozarkscivilwar.org/archives/458 (accessed November 28, 2009).

Crawford, Samuel J. *Kansas in the Sixties.* Chicago: A. C. McClurg & Co., 1911.

Crute, Joseph H. *Units of the Confederate States Army.* Midlothian, VA: Derwent Books, 1987.

Davis, Major George B., et al. *Atlas to Accompany the Official Records of the Union and Confederate Armies.* Washington, DC: Government Printing Office, 1891–1895. Reprint. New York: Fairfax Press, 1983.

Davis, William C. Ed. *The Confederate General.* 6 vols. Harrisburg, PA: National Historical Society, 1991.

Dougan, Michael B. *Confederate Arkansas: The People and Politics of a Frontier State in Wartime.* University, AL: University of Alabama Press, 1976.

_____, ed., *Confederate Women of Arkansas in the Civil War: Memorial Reminiscences.* Fayetteville, AR: University of Arkansas Press, 1993.

Dyer, F. H. *A Compendium of the War of the Rebellion.* Des Moines, 1908. Reprint. Dayton, OH: The Press of Morningside Bookshop, 1978.

Eakin, Joanne C. and Donald R. Hale. *Branded as Rebels: A List of Bushwhackers, Guerrillas, Partisan Rangers, Confederates and Southern Sympathizers from Missouri During the War Years.* Independence, MO: Wee Print, 1993.

Eakin, Joanne C. *Confederate Records From the United Daughters of the Confed-*

eracy Files. 8 vols. Independence, MO: Two Trails Publishing, 1995–2001.

_____. *Missouri State Guard Doctor Leaves A Diary in 1861.* Independence, MO: Two Trails Publishing, 1999.

_____. *Missouri Prisoners of War, From Gratiot Prison and Myrtle Prison, St. Louis, Missouri, and Alton Prison, Alton Illinois, Including Citizens, Confederates, Bushwhackers and Guerrillas.* Independence, MO: Joanne Eakin, 1995

Edwards, John Newman. *Shelby and His Men, or the War in the West.* Cincinnati, OH: Miami Printing and Publishing Co., 1867: Reprint. Waverly , MO: General Joseph Shelby Memorial Fund, 1993.

Edwards, William B. *Civil War Guns: The Complete Story of Federal and Confederate Small Arms: Design, Manufacture, Identification, Issue, Employment, Effectiveness, and Postwar Disposal.* Secaucus, NJ: Castle Books, 1962.

Etcheson, Nicole. *Bleeding Kansas: Contested Liberty in the Civil War Era.* Lawrence, KS: University Press of Kansas, 2004.

Evans, Clement A., ed. *Confederate Military History.* 13 vols. Atlanta: Confederate Publishing Co., 1899. Reprinted Secaucus, NJ: Blue & Gray Press, 1974.

Fandek, Neal. "Battle at the Church." *Rural Missouri* (December, 2006): 32.

Farthing, C. M. *Chronicles of the Civil War in Monroe County (Missouri).* Independence, MO: Two Trails Publishing, 1997.

Ferguson, John L., and J. H. Atkinson. *Historic Arkansas.* Little Rock, AR: Arkansas History Commission, 1966.

Flint, Mortimer R. "The War on the Border." *Glimpses of the Nation's Struggle. Fifth Series. Papers Read Before the Minnesota Commandery of the Military Order of the Loyal Legion of the United States, 1897–1902.* St. Paul, MN: Review Publishing Co., 1903. Reprint. 70 vols. Wilmington, NC: Broadfoot Publishing Company, 1992. 30:396–416.

Foley, James L. "With Frémont in Missouri." *Sketches of War History 1861–1865 Papers Prepared for the Commandery of the State of Ohio, Military Order of the Loyal Legion of the United States.* Cincinnati, OH: The Robert Clarke Company, 1903. Reprint. 70 vols. Wilmington, NC: Broadfoot Publishing Company, 1992. 5:508–521.

Frazer, Robert W. *Forts of the West: Military Forts and Presidios and Posts Commonly Called Forts West of the Mississippi River to 1898.* Norman, OK: University of Oklahoma Press, 1963.

Frazier, Donald S. *The United States and Mexico At War: Nineteenth-Century Expansionism and Conflict.* New York: Simon & Schuster Macmillan, 1998.

Frémont, Jesse Benton. *The Story of the Guard: A Chronicle of the War.* Boston: Ticknor & Fields, 1863.

Frost, Griffin. *Camp and Prison Journal.* Quincy, IL: Quincy Herald Book and Job Shop, 1867. Reprint. Iowa City, IA: Camp Pope Bookshop, 1994.

Fry, Alice L. *Kansas and Kansans in the Civil War: First Through Thirteenth Volunteer Regiments.* Kansas City, KS: Two Trails Publishing, 1996.

Fuenfhausen, Gary G. *A Guide to Historic Clay County Missouri: Architectural Resources and Other Historic Sites of the Civil War.* Kansas City, MO: Little Dixie Publications, 1996.

Gerteis, Louis S. *Civil War St. Louis.* Topeka, KS: University Press of Kansas, 2001.

Gibbons, Tony. *Warships and Naval Battles of the Civil War.* New York: W. H. Smith Publishers, Inc., 1989.

Gilmore, Donald L. *Civil War on the Missouri-Kansas Border.* Gretna, LA: Pelican Publishing Company, Inc., 2006.

Guralnik, David B., ed. *Second College Edition Webster's New World Dictionary of the American Language.* New York: The World Publishing Company, 1972.

Hale, Donald R. *Branded as Rebels, Volume 2.* Independence, MO: Blue & Grey Book Shoppe, 2003.

Heidler, David S., and Jeanne T. Heidler, eds. *Encyclopedia of the American Civil War: A Political, Social, and Military History.* New York: W. W. Norton & Company, 2000.

Heitman, Francis B. *Historical Register and Dictionary of the United States Army From Its Organization, September 29, 1789, to March 2, 1903.* 2 vols. Washington: Government Printing Office, 1903. Reprinted Gaitherburg, MD: Old Soldiers Books Inc., 1988.

Hewett, Janet, B., ed. *Supplement to the Official Records of the Union and Confederate Armies.* 100 vols. Wilmington, NC: Broadfoot Publishing Company, 1994–2001.

Hickey, Donald R. *The War of 1812.* Urbana, IL: University of Illinois Press, 1989.

Hinze, David C., and Karen Farnham. *The Battle of Carthage: Border War in Southwest Missouri, July 5, 1861.* Campbell, CA: Savas Pub. Co., 1997.

History of Audrain County, Missouri, Written and Compiled from the Most Authentic Official and Private Sources, Including a History of Its Townships, Towns and Villages. St. Louis: National Historical Company, 1884.

History of Boone County, Missouri, Written and Compiled From the Most Authentic Official and Private Sources, Including a History of Its Townships, Towns and Villages. St. Louis: Western Historical Company, 1882.

History of Callaway County, Missouri, Written and Compiled From the Most Authentic Official and Private Sources, Including a History of Its Townships, Towns and Villages. St. Louis: National Historical Company, 1884.

History of Greene County, Missouri, Written and Compiled From the Most Authentic Official and Private Sources, Including a History of Its Townships, Towns and Villages. St. Louis: Western Historical Company, 1883.

History of St. Charles, Montgomery and Warren Counties, Missouri, Written and Compiled From the Most Authentic Official and Private Sources, Including A History of Their Townships, Towns and Villages. St. Louis: National Historical Company, 1885.

Holcombe, R. I., and Adams. *An Account of the Battle of Wilson's Creek or Oak*

Hills. Springfield, MO: Independent Printing, Inc., 1961.

How, James F. "Frank P. Blair in 1861." *War Papers and Personal Reminiscences, 1861–1865. Read Before the Commandery of the State of Missouri, Military Order of the Loyal Legion of the United States.* St. Louis: Becktold & Co., 1892. 70 vols. Reprint. Wilmington, NC: Broadfoot Publishing Company. 14:382–395.

Hughes, Jr., Nathaniel Cheairs. *The Battle of Belmont: Grant Strikes South.* Chapel Hill, NC: The University of North Carolina Press, 1991.

Ingenthron, Elmo. *Borderland Rebellion: A History of the Civil War on the Missouri-Arkansas Border.* Branson, MO: Ozark Mountaineer, n.d.

Kirkpatrick, Arthur Roy. "Missouri in the Early Months of the Civil War." *Missouri Historical Review* 55 (Fall 1961): 235–266.

Lane, Walter P. *Adventures and Recollections of General Walter P. Lane, a San Jacinto Veteran, Containing Sketches of the Texian, Mexican and Late Wars, with Several Indian Fights Thrown In.* Marshall, TX: News Messenger Pub. Co., 1928.

Larimer, Charles F., ed. *Love and Valor: Intimate Civil War Letters Between Captain Jacob and Emeline Ritner.* Western Springs, IL: Sigourney Press, 2000.

Mallinckrodt, Anita M. *A History of Augusta, Mo. and Its Area (I) 1850s–1860s, As Reported in the St. Charles Demokrat.* Washington, MO: John Miller Publishing Company, 1998.

Martin, James Kirby, et al. *A Respectable Army: The Military Origins of the Republic, 1763–1789.* Arlington Heights, IL: Harlan Davidson, Inc. 1982.

McElroy, John. *The Struggle For Missouri.* Washington, DC: National Tribune Co., 1909.

McGhee, James E. *Letter and Order Book, Missouri State Guard 1861–1862.* Independence, MO: Two Trails Publishing, 2001.

_____. *Missouri Confederates: A Guide to Sources for Confederate Soldiers and Units 1861–1865.* Independence, MO: Two Trails Publishing, 2001.

_____. *Service With the Missouri State Guard: The Memoir of Brigadier General James Harding.* Springfield, MO: Oak Hills Publishing, 2000.

McKechnie, Jean L. *Webster's New Universal Unabridged Dictionary.* New York: Simon &Schuster, 1979.

Miles, Kathleen White. *Bitter Ground: The Civil War in Missouri's Golden Valley, Benton, Henry, and St. Clair Counties.* Warsaw, MO: The Printery, 1971.

Monaghan, Jay. *Civil War on the Western Border, 1854–1865.* New York: Bonanza Books, 1955.

Moore, Frank, ed. *The Rebellion Record A Diary of American Events.* 12 vols. Vols. 1–6, New York: Putnam, 1861–1863. Vols. 7–12, New York: Van Nostrand, 1864–1868. Reprint. New York: Arno Press, 1977.

Mudd, Joseph A. "What I Saw At Wilson's Creek." *Missouri Historical Review* 7 (January 1913): 89–105.

_____. *With Porter in North Missouri: A Chapter in the History of the War Between the States.* Washington: National Publishing Company, 1909.

Musser, Richard H. "The War in Missouri." In *Southern Bivouac.* 6 vols. Wilmington, NC: Broadfoot Publishing Company, 1993. 4:678–685, 745–752, 5:43–48, 102–107.

Nash, Charles Edward. *Biographical Sketches of Gen. Pat Cleburne and Gen. T. C. Hindman, Together With Humorous Anecdotes and Reminiscences of the Late Civil War.* Little Rock, AR: Tunnah & Pittard, Printers, 1895. Reprint. Dayton, OH: Morningside Bookshop, 1977.

Norton, Richard L. *Behind Enemy Lines: The Memoirs and Writings of Brigadier General Sidney Drake Jackman.* Springfield, MO: Oak Hills Publishing, 1997.

Parrish, William E. *Frank Blair: Lincoln's Conservative.* Columbia, MO: University of Missouri Press, 1998.

Patrick, Jeffery, ed. *Nine Months in the Infantry Service: The Civil War Journal of R. P. Matthews and Roster the Phelps Regiment Missouri Volunteers.* Springfield, MO: Greene County Historical Society, 1999.

_____. "Remembering the Missouri Campaign of 1861: The Memoirs of Lieutenant William P. Barlow, Guibor's Battery, Missouri State Guard." *Civil War Regiments: A Journal of the American Civil War* 5, no. 4 (1997): 20–66.

Pearce, N. B. "Arkansas Troops in the Battle of Wilson's Creek." *Battles and Leaders of the Civil War.* 4 vols. New York: Century Company, 1887–1888. 1:298–303.

Peckham, James. *Gen. Nathaniel Lyon, and Missouri in 1861: A Monograph of the Great Rebellion.* New York: American News Company, 1866.

Peterson, Richard C., et al. *Sterling Price's Lieutenants: A Guide to the Officers and Organization of the Missouri State Guard.* Jefferson City, MO: Two Trails Publishing, 1995.

Petty, A. W. M. *A History of the Third Missouri Cavalry From Its Organization At Palmyra, Missouri, 1861 Up to November Sixth, 1864: With An Appendix and Recapitulation.* Little Rock, AR: J. Wm. Demby, Publisher, 1865. Reprint. Albany, MO: Century Reprints, 1997.

Phillips, Christopher. *Damned Yankee: The Life of General Nathaniel Lyon.* Columbia, MO: University of Missouri Press, 1990.

_____. *Missouri's Confederate: Claiborne Fox Jackson and the Creation of Southern Identity in the Border West.* Columbia, MO: University of Missouri Press, 2000.

Phisterer, Frederick. *Statistical Record of the Armies of the United States.* New York: Charles Scribner's Sons, 1883.

Pictorial and Genealogical Record of Greene County, Missouri Together With Biographies of Prominent Men of Other Portions of the State, Both Living and Dead. Chicago: Goodspeed Brothers, Publishers, 1893.

Piston, William Garrett, and Richard W. Hatcher III. *Wilson's Creek: The Second Battle of the Civil War and the Men Who Fought It.* Chapel Hill, NC: University of North Carolina Press, 2000.

Polk, William K. "General Polk and the Battle of Belmont." *Battles and Leaders of the Civil War.* 4 vols. New York: Century Company, 1887–1888. 1:348–357.

Primm, James Neal. *Lion of the Valley: St. Louis, Missouri.* Boulder, CO: Pruitt Publishing, 1981.

Ross, Margaret. *Arkansas Gazette: The Early Years 1819–1866.* Little Rock, AR: Arkansas Gazette Foundation, 1969.

Ryle, Walter Harrington. *Missouri: Union or Secession.* Nashville, TN: The Journal Printing Company, 1931.

Scharf, J. Thomas. *History of Saint Louis City and County, From the Earliest Periods to the Present Day.* 2 vols. Philadelphia, 1883.

Schnetzer, Wayne H. *Men of the Eleventh: A Roster of the Eleventh Missouri Infantry, Confederate States of America.* Independence, MO; Two Trails Publishing, 1999.

_____. *Men of the Tenth: A Roster of the Tenth Missouri Infantry, Confederate States of America.* Independence, MO; Two Trails Publishing, 1999.

_____. *More Forgotten Men: The Missouri State Guard.* Independence, MO: Two Trails Publishing, 2003.

Schrantz, Ward L. *Jasper County, Missouri in the Civil War.* Carthage, MO: The Carthage Press, 1923. Reprint. Carthage, MO: The Carthage, Missouri Kiwanis Club, 1992.

Seaton, John. "The Battle of Belmont." *War Talks In Kansas: A Series of Papers Read Before the Kansas Commandery of the Military Order of the Loyal Legion of the United States.* Kansas City, MO: Press of the Franklin Hudson Publishing Company, 1906. Reprint. 70 vols. Wilmington, NC: Broadfoot Publishing Company, 1992. 15:305–319.

Shea, William L., and Earl J. Hess. *Pea Ridge: Civil War Campaign in the West.* Chapel Hill, NC: University of North Carolina Press, 1992.

Shalhope, Robert E. *Sterling Price: Portrait of a Southerner.* Columbia, MO: University of Missouri Press, 1971.

Sifakis, Stewart. *Who Was Who in the Confederacy: A Comprehensive, Illustrated Biographical Reference to More Than 1,000 of the Principal Confederacy Participants in the Civil War.* New York: Facts on File, 1988.

_____. *Who Was Who in the Union: A Comprehensive, Illustrated Biographical Reference to More Than 1,500 of the Principal Union Participants in the Civil War.* New York: Facts on File, 1988.

Sigel, Franz. "The Flanking Column at Wilson's Creek." *Battles and Leaders of the Civil War.* 4 vols. New York: Century Company, 1887–1888. 1:304–306.

Simpson, Harold B. *Texas in the War 1861–1865.* Hillsboro, TX: The Hill Junior College Press, 1965.

Singletary, Otis A. *The Mexican War.* Chicago: University of Chicago Press, 1960.

Smith, William Earnest. *The Francis Preston Blair Family in Politics.* 2 vols. New York: The Macmillan Company, 1933.

Snead, Thomas L. *The Fight For Missouri: From the Election of Lincoln to the Death of Lyon.* New York: Charles Scribner's Sons, 1886.

Stone, Norman, and Kenyon, J. P. *The Wordsworth Dictionary of British History.* Hertfordshire, England: Wordsworth Editions Ltd. 1994.

Switzler, William F., et al. *Switzler's Illustrated History of Missouri, From 1541 to 1877.* St. Louis: C. R. Barns, Editor and Publisher, 1879.

Treichel, Charles. "Major Zagonyi's Horse-Guard." *Personal Recollections of the War of the Rebellion: Addresses Delivered Before the Commandery of the State of New York, Military Order of the Loyal Legion of the United States.* New York: The Knickerbocker Press, 1907. Reprint. 70 vols. Wilmington, NC: Broadfoot Publishing Company, 1992. 22: 240–246.

Tunnard, W. H. *A Southern Record: The History of the Third Regiment Louisiana Infantry.* Baton Rouge, LA: W. H. Tunnard, 1866.

The Union Army A History of Military Affairs in the Loyal United States 1861–1865—Records of the Regiments in the Union Army—Cyclopedia of

Battles—Memoirs of Commanders and Soldiers. 8 vols. Madison, WI: Federal Publishing Company, 1908. Reprint. Wilmington, NC: Broadfoot Pub. Co., 1998.

Volo, James M., and Dorthy Denneen Volo. *Encyclopedia of the Antebellum South.* Westport, CT: Greenwood Press, 2000.

Walke, Henry. "The Gunboats at Belmont and Fort Henry." *Battles and Leaders of the Civil War.* 4 vols. New York: Century Company, 1887–1888. 1:358–367.

Ware, E. F. *The Lyon Campaign in Missouri: Being a History of the First Iowa Infantry.* Topeka, KS: Crane & Company, 1907. Reprint. Iowa City, IA: Camp Pope Bookshop, 1991.

Warner, Ezra J. *Generals in Blue: Lives of the Union Commanders.* Baton Rouge, LA: Louisiana State University Press, 1964.

_____. *Generals in Gray: Lives of the Confederate Commanders.* Baton Rouge, LA: Louisiana State University Press, 1959.

Webb, W. L. *Battles and Biographies of Missourians, or the Civil War Period of Our State.* Kansas City, MO: Hudson-Kimberly Pub. Co., 1900.

Wherry, William M. "General Nathaniel Lyon and His Campaign in Missouri in 1861." *Sketches of War History 1861–1865: Papers Prepared for the Commandery of the State of Ohio, Military Order of the Loyal Legion of the United States.* Cincinnati: The Robert Clarke Company, 1896. Reprint. 70 vols. Wilmington, NC: Broadfoot Publishing Company, 1991. 4:68–86.

_____. "Wilson's Creek and the Death of Lyon." *Battles and Leaders of the Civil War.* 4 vols. New York: Century Company, 1887–1888. 1: 289–297.

Wilson, James Grant, and John Fiske, eds. *Appleton's Cyclopædia of American Biography.* 6 vols. New York: D. Appleton and Company, 1889.

Winter, William C. *The Civil War in St. Louis: A Guided Tour.* St. Louis: Missouri Historical Society Press, 1994.

Woodward, Ashbel. *Life of General Nathaniel Lyon.* Hartford, CT: Case, Lockwood & Co., 1862.

Woodruff, W. E. *With the Light Guns in '61–'65: Reminiscences of Eleven Arkansas, Missouri and Texas Light Batteries, in the Civil War.* Little Rock, AR: Central Printing Company, 1903.

Wright, Marcus J. *General Officers of the Confederate Army.* New York: The Neale Publishing Company, 1911.

Wright, Willard E., ed. "An Unofficial Account of the Battle of Wilson Creek, August 10, 1861." *Arkansas Historical Quarterly* 15 (Winter, 1956): 360–364.

Young, R. E. *Pioneers of High, Water and Main: Reflections of Jefferson City.* Jefferson City, MO: Twelfth State, 1997.

Younger, Cole. *The Story of Cole Younger: An Autobiography of the Missouri Guerrilla, Confederate Cavalry Officer, and Western Outlaw.* Reprint. Springfield, MO: Oak Hills Publishing, 1996.

Government Sources

Davis, George B., Leslie J. Perry, and Joseph W. Kirkley. *Atlas to Accompany the Official Records of the Union and Confederate Armies.* Washington, DC: Government Printing Office, 1891–1895.

Library of Congress. *Newspapers in Microform, United States, 1948–1983, Volume I, A–O.* Washington, DC: Government Printing Office, 1984.

National Archives. Record Group 109. Chapter 7. Vol. 394. Parsons's Staff. Washington, DC.

_____. Record Group M322. Confederate Compiled Service Records. Assorted rolls and units. Washington, DC.

_____. Record Group M393. General Order Book (October 14, 1862–April 10, 1863). Army of the Frontier.

_____. Record Group M405. Union Compiled Service Records. Assorted rolls and units. Washington, DC.

_____. Record Group M861. Records of Confederate Movements and Activities. Assorted rolls and units. Washington, DC.

State of Missouri. *An Act to Provide For the Organization, Government, and Support of the Military Forces, State of Missouri: Passed at the Called Session of the Twenty-first General Assembly.* Jefferson City, MO, 1861. Reprint. Independence, MO, n.d.

Naval History Division. Navy Department. *Civil War Naval Chronology, 1861–1865.* 6 vols. Washington, DC: Government Printing Office, 1971.

United States Congress. *Report of the Joint Committee on the Conduct of the War: Part III—Department of the West.* Washington, DC: Government Printing Office, 1863.

United States War Department. *The War of the Rebellion: A Compilation of the Official Records of the Union and Confederate Armies.* 70 vols. comprising 128 books. Washington, DC: U.S. Government Printing Office, 1880–1901. Reprint. Harrisburg, PA: National Historical Society, 1985.

_____. *The War of the Rebellion: Official Record of the Union and Confederate Navies.* 31 vols. Washington, DC: U.S. Government Printing Office, 1894–1922.

Manuscripts/Special Collections

New York. Columbia University.
Peter W. Alexander Collection:
Copy letter book, June 1–Dec. 18, 1862. Hindman's command.
Copy letter book, June 11–Dec. 30, 1862. Hindman's command.
Miscellaneous correspondence.
Special Order letter book, June 1–Dec. 18, 1862. Hindman's command.
Telegrams.

St. Louis. Missouri Historical Society.
Camp Jackson Papers: Exchanged prisoner list.
Clarkson, J. J. Collection.
Leighton, George E. Collection.
Mesker Papers.
Missouri Militia Papers. Missouri Volunteer Militia scrapbook.
Snyder, John F. Papers.

Newspapers
Arkansas:
Van Buren Press

Illinois:
Chicago Daily Tribune
Rock Island Register

Kansas:
White Cloud Chief
Wyandotte Commercial Gazette

Missouri:
Columbia Missouri Statesman
St. Louis Missouri Republican
Jefferson City Rural Missouri
Weekly California News

Unpublished Works
Westover, John G. "The Evolution of the Missouri Militia, 1804–1919." PdD
 diss., University of Missouri, Columbia, 1948.

Credits

Photographs and Illustrations

Batesville, AR. Independence County Historical Society: Colonel John A. Schnable.

Baton Rouge, LA. Hill Memorial Library, LSU: General Daniel Frost.

Britton, Wiley, *The Union Indian Brigade in the Civil War* (Kansas City: Franklin Hudson Publishing, 1922): General Ben McCulloch, following page 32.

McElroy, John. *The Struggle for Missouri*: Claiborne F. Jackson, following page 32; General Nathaniel Lyon, following page 16.

Roberts, Oran M. *Confederate Military History: Texas*: General Walter P. Lane, page 232.

St. Louis, MO. Missouri History Museum, St. Louis: Clarkson, James J., Colonel, Confederate Army (IM 001-006977).

St. Louis Missouri Republican, April 17, 1886: "Exchanging Civilities" nameplate.

Washington, DC. Library of Congress, Prints & Photographs Division, Civil War Photographs: Maj. Gen. Frank P. Blair (LC-B813-1704 A[P&P]); C.S.A. Veterans, Gettysburg, Pa., 1913 (cover) (LC-F81-44565[P&P]); Maj. Gen. W. S. Harney (LC-B8155-7928 A[P&P]); Sterling Price, C.S.A. (LC-B813-6765 A[P&P]; James S. Rains (misidentified as Gabriel J. Rains) C.S.A. (LC-DIG-cwpb-07529).

Washington, DC. National Park Service: General Louis Hébert.

Maps

Michael E. Banasik: Area Battle Map, 1861 (adapted from *Battles and Leaders of the Civil War,* Map of Operations in Missouri, 1861, 1:263); Zagonyi's Charge; Movements Surrounding the Battle of Belmont; Battle of Belmont.

Battles and Leaders of the Civil War: Battle of Wilson's Creek or Oak Hills, 1:290.

Index

www.ingramcontent.com/pod-product-compliance
Lightning Source LLC
Chambersburg PA
CBHW022017090426
42739CB00006BA/167